## Why you should use this book

- **It is up-to-date.** Excel 2016 is the first Excel version that is continually updated (by regular automatic updates). This book is also continually updated to match the latest semi-annual release of Excel 2016. This means that the screen grabs will exactly match what you see on your screen and the instructions will be easy to follow. It can be very frustrating to try to learn Excel 2016 using an out-of-date book.

- **Learning success is guaranteed.** For over fifteen years, Smart Method® classroom courses have been used by large corporations, government departments and the armed forces to train their employees. This book has been constantly refined (during hundreds of classroom courses) by observing which skills students find difficult to understand and then developing simpler ways of explaining them. This has made the book effective for students of all ages and abilities. We have never had a student who has failed to learn Excel after taking one of our courses.

- **It is the book of choice for teachers.** As well as catering for those wishing to learn Excel by self-study, Smart Method® books have long been the preferred choice for Excel teachers as they are designed to teach Excel and not as reference books. Books follow best-practice adult teaching methodology with clearly defined objectives for each learning session and an exercise to confirm skills transfer. With single, self-contained lessons, the books cater for any teaching or self-learning period (from minutes to hours).

- **Smart Method® books are #1 best sellers.** Every paper printed Smart Method® Excel book (and there have been ten of them starting with Excel 2007) has been an Amazon #1 best seller in its category. This provides you with the confidence that you are using a best-of-breed resource to learn Excel.

- **No previous exposure to Excel is assumed.** You will repeatedly hear the same criticism of most Excel books: "you have to already know Excel to understand the book". This book is different. If you've never seen Excel before, and your only computer skill is using a web browser, you'll have absolutely no problems working through the lessons. No previous exposure to Excel is assumed and everything is explained clearly and in a simple way that absolutely any student, of any age or ability, can easily understand.

- **It focuses upon the everyday Excel skills used in the workplace.** This *Essential Skills* book will equip you with excellent Excel 2016 skills, good enough to impress any employer, but it doesn't confuse by attempting to teach skills that are not common in the workplace. Only users who have advanced requirements need progress to the *Expert Skills* book.

- **It covers both versions of Excel.** There are now two Windows versions of Excel 2016: **Excel 2016** (the pay-once version) and **Excel 2016 for Office 365 Subscribers** (the subscription version). Great care has been taken to avoid confusion caused by the differences between the two versions. Where there are differences, you'll always find them clearly documented within the text of this book.

## Learn Excel in just a few minutes each day (or in as little as one full day)

Excel is a huge and daunting application and you'll need to invest some time in learning the skills presented in this book. This will be time well spent as you'll have a hugely marketable skill for life. With 1.2 billion users worldwide, it is hard to imagine any non-manual occupation today that doesn't require Excel skills.

This book makes it easy to learn at your own pace because of its unique presentational style. The book contains short self-contained lessons and each lesson only takes a few minutes to complete.

You can complete as many, or as few, lessons as you have the time and energy for each day. Many learners have developed Excel skills by setting aside just a few minutes each day to complete a single lesson. Others have worked through the entire book in a single day.

## Every lesson is presented on two facing pages

> Pray this day, on one side of one sheet of paper, explain how the Royal Navy is prepared to meet the coming conflict.
>
> *Winston Churchill, Letter to the Admiralty, Sep 1, 1939*

Winston Churchill was aware of the power of brevity. The discipline of condensing thoughts into one side of a single sheet of A4 paper resulted in the efficient transfer of information.

A tenet of our teaching system is that every lesson is presented on *two* facing sheets of A4. We've had to double Churchill's rule as they didn't have to contend with screen grabs in 1939! If we can't teach an essential concept in two pages of A4 we know that the subject matter needs to be broken into two smaller lessons.

## How this book avoids wasting your time.

Over the years I have read many hundreds of computer text books and most of my time was wasted. The big problem with most books is that I must wade through thousands of words just to learn one important technique. If I don't read everything I might miss that one essential insight.

Many presentational methods have been used in this book to help you to avoid reading about things you already know how to do, or things that are of little interest to you.

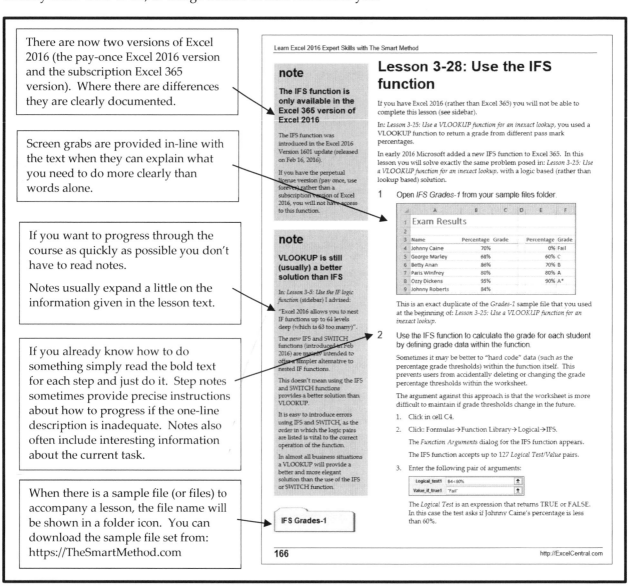

There are now two versions of Excel 2016 (the pay-once Excel 2016 version and the subscription Excel 365 version). Where there are differences they are clearly documented.

Screen grabs are provided in-line with the text when they can explain what you need to do more clearly than words alone.

If you want to progress through the course as quickly as possible you don't have to read notes.

Notes usually expand a little on the information given in the lesson text.

If you already know how to do something simply read the bold text for each step and just do it. Step notes sometimes provide precise instructions about how to progress if the one-line description is inadequate. Notes also often include interesting information about the current task.

When there is a sample file (or files) to accompany a lesson, the file name will be shown in a folder icon. You can download the sample file set from: https://TheSmartMethod.com

# Learning by participation

Tell me, and I will forget. Show me, and I may remember. Involve me, and I will understand.

*Confucius, Chinese teacher, editor, politician and philosopher (551-479 BC)*

Confucius would probably have agreed that the best way to teach IT skills is hands-on (actively) and not hands-off (passively). This is another of the principal tenets of The Smart Method® teaching method.

Research has backed up the assertion that you will learn more material, learn more quickly, and understand more of what you learn if you learn using active, rather than passive methods.

For this reason, pure theory pages are kept to an absolute minimum with most theory woven into the hands-on lessons, either within the text or in sidebars.

This echoes the teaching method used in Smart Method classroom courses where snippets of pertinent theory are woven into the lessons themselves so that interest and attention is maintained by hands-on involvement, but all necessary theory is still covered.

Whenever something can easily go wrong, or when the subject text is particularly important, you will see the *important* sidebar. You should always read important sidebars.

Each lesson models a real-world business problem. You'll immediately appreciate the value and relevance of each skill you learn.

A goal of this book is not to waste your time by explaining any skill twice. Sometimes you may forget something that has already been covered earlier in the course.

Cross-references are extensively used pointing you back to the lesson in which the relevant skills were learned. The cross-references also help when you use this course as a reference book but have forgotten the more basic skills needed to complete each step.

## Hardly anybody understands how to use <u>every</u> Excel feature

It is important to realize that Excel is probably the largest and most complex software application ever created. Hardly anybody understands how to use *every* Excel feature and for almost all business users, large parts of Excel's functionality wouldn't even be useful.

Many learners make the fundamental error of trying to learn from an Excel reference book that attempts to document (though not teach) *everything* that Excel can do. Of course, no single book could ever actually do this. (There are some advanced Excel features that easily justify an entire book of their own).

By the end of this *Essential Skills* book you will have excellent Excel skills, good enough to impress any employer, and your Excel skills will be better than most office workers (even those with many years of experience). You'll be able to create beautifully laid-out worksheets that will really impress. You'll also have mastered many advanced features that few Excel users understand such as absolute and relative cell references, visualizations, advanced charts, conditional formatting, date serial numbers, themes and cloud computing.

## We also have a follow-on book that will teach you expert-level skills

The *Expert Skills* book teaches Excel to an extremely high level of competence that is very rarely found in the workplace (even amongst top professionals). At *Expert* level your skills will be greater and broader than almost all other Excel users and you will understand (and be able to use) absolutely every Excel feature. You'll have a complete mastery of skills that are often even a mystery to Excel power users.

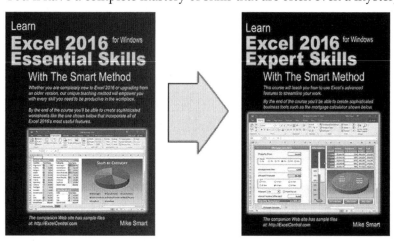

The full course outlines for the *Expert Skills* book can be viewed on the https://thesmartmethod.com web site.

# Who Is This Book For?

If you need good Excel skills for your work or want to add Excel skills to your resume or CV, you've found the right book.

If you've never used *Excel 2016 for Windows* before, this book will give you all of the skills you need to be thoroughly competent. By the end of the book, your Excel skills will be better than most office workers with many years of experience.

This book is for *Excel 2016 for Windows* users who:

- Need to acquire essential Excel skills quickly.

- Have never used Excel before, or who have only basic Excel skills.

- Want to learn Excel skills from first principles.

- Are moving to *Excel 2016 for Windows* from an earlier version.

## Use of this book as courseware

This book is also the official courseware for The Smart Method's *Excel 2016 for Windows Essential Skills* course.

Smart Method courses have been taken by a varied cross-section of the world's leading companies. We've had fantastic feedback from the vast number of professionals we've empowered with Excel skills.

This book is also suitable for use by other training organizations, teachers, schools, colleges and universities to provide structured, objective-led, and highly effective classroom courses.

## This book is not suitable for learning *Excel 2016 for Mac*

You could be forgiven for thinking that the (confusingly named) *Excel 2016 for Mac* (suitable only for Apple desktop and laptop computers) was "just the same" as *Excel 2016 for Windows*. Unfortunately, this is not the case. The *Excel 2016 for Mac* version has a reduced feature set and a radically different user interface to the *Excel 2016 for Windows* version.

We've produced a special version of this book suitable for Apple Mac users:

**Learn Excel 2016 Essential Skills for Mac with The Smart Method®**
**ISBN: 978-1-909253-11-7**

# Learn Excel 2016 Essential Skills with The Smart Method

Mike Smart

**Learn Excel 2016 Essential Skills with The Smart Method®**

**Published by:**

The Smart Method® Ltd
Burleigh Manor
Peel Road
Douglas, IOM
Great Britain
IM1 5EP

Tel: +44 (0)845 458 3282 Fax: +44 (0)845 458 3281

E-mail:  Use the contact page at https://thesmartmethod.com/contact
Web:     https://thesmartmethod.com

International Standard Book Number (ISBN13):  978-1-909253-08-7

The Smart Method® and ExcelCentral.com® are registered trademarks of The Smart Method Ltd.

6 8 10 9 7

# Contents

## Session Three: Taking Your Skills to the Next Level    119

## Session Four: Making Your Worksheets Look Professional     167

## Session Five: Charts and Graphics     221

## Session Six: Working with Multiple Worksheets and Workbooks · 287

# Introduction

Welcome to *Learn Excel 2016 Essential Skills with The Smart Method®*. This book has been designed to enable students to master Excel 2016 by self-study. The book is equally useful as courseware in order to deliver courses using The Smart Method® teaching system.

Smart Method publications are continually evolving as we discover better ways of explaining or teaching the concepts presented.

## Feedback

At The Smart Method® we love feedback – both positive and negative. If you have any suggestions for improvements to future versions of this book, or if you find content or typographical errors, the author would always love to hear from you.

You can make suggestions for improvements to this book using the online form at:

https://thesmartmethod.com/contact

Future editions of this book will always incorporate your feedback so that there are never any known errors at time of publication.

If you have any difficulty understanding or completing a lesson, or if you feel that anything could have been more clearly explained, we'd also love to hear from you. We've made hundreds of detail improvements to our books based upon reader's feedback and continue to chase the impossible goal of 100% perfection.

## Downloading the sample files

In order to use this book it is sometimes necessary to download free sample files from the Internet.

The process of downloading the free sample files will be explained later, in: *Lesson 1-5: Download the sample files and open/navigate a workbook.*

## Problem resolution

If you encounter any problem using any aspect of the course you can contact us using the online form at:

https://thesmartmethod.com/contact

We'll do everything possible to quickly resolve the problem.

## The Excel versions that were used to write this book

This edition was written using both the *Excel 2016* perpetual license (the one-time payment version) and *Excel 2016 for Office 365 subscribers* (semi-annual version 1803, released on Jul 10 2018). You'll discover which version your computer is running in: *Lesson 1-2: Check that your Excel version is up to date.* In this book, the perpetual license version of Excel is referred to as: *Excel 2016* and the subscription version as *Excel 365*.

This book is written purely for Excel 2016.

If you are using Excel 2007, Excel 2010 or Excel 2013, you should either upgrade to Excel 2016 or purchase one of the earlier versions of this book: *Learn Excel 2007 Essential Skills with The Smart Method, Learn Excel 2010 Essential Skills with The Smart Method or Learn Excel 2013 Essential Skills with The Smart Method.* You'll find the relevant ISBN numbers at the end of this book.

# Typographical Conventions Used in This Book

This guide consistently uses typographical conventions to differentiate parts of the text.

| When you see this | Here's what it means |
|---|---|
| Click *Line Color* on the left-hand bar and then click *No line*. | Italics are used to refer to text that appears in a worksheet cell, an Excel dialog, on the Ribbon, or elsewhere within the Excel application. Italics may sometimes also be used for emphasis or distinction. |
| Click: Home→Font→Underline. | Click on the Ribbon's *Home* tab and then look for the *Font* group. Click the *Underline* button within this group (that's the left-hand side of the button, not the drop-down arrow next to it). <br><br> Don't worry if this doesn't make sense yet. We cover the Ribbon in depth in session one. |
| Click: Home→Font→ Underline Drop Down→Double Underline. | Click on the Ribbon's *Home* tab and then look for the *Font* group. Click the drop-down arrow next to the Underline button (that's the right-hand side of the button) within this group and then choose *Double Underline* from the drop-down list. |
| Click:<br><br>File→Options→<br>Advanced→General→<br>Edit Custom Lists→Import | This is a more involved example.<br><br>1. Click the *File* tab on the Ribbon, and then click the *Options* button towards the bottom of the left-hand pane.<br><br>The *Excel Options* dialog appears.<br><br>2. Choose the *Advanced* list item in the left-hand pane and scroll down to the *General* group in the right-hand pane.<br><br>3. Click the *Edit Custom Lists...* button.<br><br>Yet another dialog pops up.<br><br>4. Click the *Import* button. |
| Type: **European Sales** into the cell. | Whenever you are supposed to actually type something on the keyboard it is shown in bold faced text. |
| Press <Ctrl> + <Z>. | You should hold down the **Ctrl** key and then press the **Z** key. |

| ∑ AutoSum ▾ | When a lesson tells you to click a button, an image of the relevant button will often be shown either in the page margin or within the text itself. |

## note

In Excel 2007/2010/2013/2016 there are a possible 16,585 columns and 1,048,476 rows. This is a great improvement on earlier versions.

If you want to read through the book as quickly as possible, you don't have to read notes.

Notes usually expand a little on the information given in the lesson text.

## important

Do not click the *Delete* button at this point as to do so would erase the entire table.

Whenever something can easily go wrong, or when the subject text is particularly important, you will see the *important* sidebar.

You should always read important sidebars.

## tip

### Moving between tabs using the keyboard

You can also use the **<Ctrl>+<PgUp>** and **<Ctrl>+<PgDn>** keyboard shortcuts to cycle through all of the tabs in your workbook.

Tips add to the lesson text by showing you shortcuts or time-saving techniques relevant to the lesson.

The bold text at the top of the tip box enables you to establish whether the tip is appropriate to your needs without reading all of the text.

In this example you may not be interested in keyboard shortcuts so do not need to read further.

## anecdote

I ran an Excel course for a small company in London a couple of years ago...

Sometimes I add an anecdote gathered over the years from my Excel classes or from other areas of life.

If you simply want to learn Excel as quickly as possible you can ignore my anecdotes.

## trivia

The feature that Excel uses to help you out with function calls first made an appearance in Visual Basic 5 back in 1996 …

Sometimes I indulge myself by adding a little piece of trivia in the context of the skill being taught.

Just like my anecdotes you can ignore these if you want to. They won't help you to learn Excel any better!

**The World's Fastest Cars**

When there is a sample file (or files) to accompany a lesson, the file name will be shown in a folder icon. You can download the sample file from: *https://thesmartmethod.com*. Detailed instructions are given in: *Lesson 1-5: Download the sample files and open/navigate a workbook.*

# How to use this course

This course utilizes some of the tried and tested techniques developed after teaching vast numbers of people to learn Excel during many years teaching Smart Method classroom courses.

In order to master Excel as quickly and efficiently as possible you should use the recommended learning method described below. If you do this there is absolutely no doubt that you will master the advanced Excel skills taught in this book.

## Three important rules

### #1 - Complete the course from beginning to end

It is always tempting to jump around the course completing lessons in a haphazard way.

We strongly suggest that you start at the beginning and complete lessons sequentially.

That's because each lesson builds upon skills learned in the previous lessons and one of our goals is not to waste your time by teaching the same skill twice. If you miss a skill by skipping a lesson you'll find the later lessons more difficult, or even impossible to follow. This, in turn, may demoralize you and make you abandon the course.

### #2 If possible, complete a session in one sitting

The book is arranged into *sessions* and *lessons*.

You can complete as many, or as few, lessons as you have the time and energy for each day. Many learners have developed Excel skills by setting aside just a few minutes each day to complete a single lesson.

If it is possible, the most effective way to learn is to lock yourself away, switch off your telephone, and complete a full session, without interruption, except for a 15-minute break each hour. The memory process is associative, and we've ensured that the lessons in each session are very closely coupled (contextually) with the others. By learning the whole session in one sitting, you'll store all that information in the same part of your memory and will find it easier to recall later.

The experience of being able to remember all of the words of a song as soon as somebody has got you "started" with the first line is an example of the memory's associative system of data storage.

### #3 Rest at least every hour

In our classroom courses we have often observed a phenomenon that we call "running into a wall". This happens when a student becomes overloaded with new information to the point that they can no longer follow the simplest instruction. If you find this happening to you, you've studied for too long without a rest.

You should take a 15-minute break every hour (or more often if you begin to feel overwhelmed) and spend it relaxing rather than catching up with your e-mails. Ideally you should relax by lying down and closing your eyes. This allows your brain to use all of its processing power to efficiently store and index the skills you've learned. We've found that this hugely improves retention of skills learned.

# How to work through the lessons

## At the end of each session, complete the session exercise

Keep attempting the exercise at the end of each session until you can complete it without having to refer to lessons in the session. Don't start the next session until you can complete the exercise from memory.

## At the end of each session, review the objectives

The session objectives are stated at the beginning of each session.

Read each objective and ask yourself if you have truly mastered each skill. If you are not sure about any of the skills listed, revise the relevant lesson(s) before moving on to the next session.

You will find it very frustrating if you move to a new session before you have truly mastered the skills covered in the previous session. This may demoralize you and make you abandon the course.

# How to best use the incremental sample files

Many lessons in this course use a sample file that is incrementally improved during each lesson. At the end of each lesson an interim version is always saved. For example, a sample file called Sales-1 may provide the starting point to a sequence of three lessons. After each lesson, interim versions called Sales-2, Sales-3 and Sales-4 are saved by the student.

A complete set of sample files (including all incremental versions) are provided in the sample file set. This provides three important benefits:

- If you have difficulty with a lesson it is useful to be able to study the completed workbook (at the end of the lesson) by opening the finished version of the lesson's workbook.

- When you have completed the book, you will want to use it as a reference. The sample files allow you to work through any single lesson in isolation, as the workbook's state at the beginning of each lesson is always available.

- When teaching a class one student may corrupt their workbook by a series of errors (or by their computer crashing). It is possible to quickly and easily move the class on to the next lesson by instructing the student to open the next sample file in the set (instead of progressing with their own corrupted file or copying a file from another student).

# The time you spend learning Excel is hugely worthwhile

Excel is a huge and daunting application and you'll need to invest some time in learning the skills presented in this course. This will be time well spent as you'll have a hugely marketable skill for life. With 1.2 billion users worldwide, it is hard to imagine any organization of any size that does not value Excel skills.

If you persevere with this course there is no doubt that you will master Excel. A little time and effort is needed but the skills you'll acquire will be hugely valuable for the rest of your life.

Enjoy the course.

# Session One: Basic Skills

> A bad beginning makes a bad ending.
>
> *Euripides, Aegeus (484 BC - 406 BC).*

Even if you are a seasoned Excel user, I urge you to take Euripides' advice and complete this session. You'll fly through it if you already know most of the skills covered.

In my classes I often teach professionals who have used Excel for over ten years and they *always* get some nugget of fantastically useful information from this session.

In this session, I teach you the absolute basics you need before you can start to do useful work with Excel 2016.

I don't assume that you have any previous exposure to Excel (in any version) so I have to include some very basic skills.

## Session Objectives

By the end of this session you will be able to:

- Start Excel and open a new blank workbook
- Check that your Excel version is up to date
- Change the Office Theme
- Maximize, minimize, re-size, move and close the Excel window
- Download the sample files and open/navigate a workbook
- Save a workbook to a local file
- Understand common file formats
- Pin a workbook and understand file organization
- View, move, add, rename, delete and navigate worksheet tabs
- Use the Versions feature to recover an unsaved Draft file
- Use the Versions feature to recover an earlier version of a workbook
- Use the Ribbon
- Understand Ribbon components
- Customize the Quick Access Toolbar and preview the printout
- Use the Mini Toolbar, Key Tips and keyboard shortcuts
- Understand views
- Hide and show the Formula Bar and Ribbon
- Use the Tell Me help system
- Use other help features

## note

### Windows 8.1 Users

When Windows 10 was released in July 2015, Microsoft recommended that any Windows 8.1 users update free to the new version (the free update offer ended in July 2016).

Mainstream support for Windows 8.1 officially ended on January 9, 2018.

For these reasons, by the time that you read this book it is unlikely that there will be many Windows 8 users left in the world.

*Windows 7 start menu*

# Lesson 1-1: Start Excel and open a new blank workbook

If you are using Windows 8 see sidebar.

## Startup in Windows 7

1   Click the *Windows Start Button* at the bottom left of your screen.

2   Click the *All Programs* item at the bottom of the pop-up menu.

3   Scroll down the list and click on the *Microsoft Office 2016* item.

4   Pin *Microsoft Excel 2016* to the start menu.

You'll be using Excel a lot, so it makes sense to pin it to the start menu. This will make it appear at the top of the list in future, so you'll be able to start Excel with just two clicks.

To pin to the start menu, point to *Microsoft Excel 2016* in the list, right-click your mouse and then choose *Pin to Start Menu* from the shortcut menu.

5   Left-click *Microsoft Excel 2016* to start Excel.

Excel starts and is displayed on the screen.

## Startup in Windows 10

1   Click the Start Button ⊞ in the bottom left corner of the Windows 10 screen.

2   Drag the *Excel* icon to the top of the start menu.

If you can't find the Excel icon, see the sidebar for instructions on how to locate it.

You'll be using Excel a lot, so it makes sense to move the icon to the top of the Windows 10 start menu. You'll then be able to start Excel without having to search for the icon.

1.   Point to the Excel icon.

2.   Click and hold down the left mouse button.

3.   With the left button held down, move your mouse towards the top of the start menu. The icon will move with the mouse cursor.

## note

### If you can't find the Excel icon in Windows 10

When you install Excel 2016 on a Windows 10 computer an icon is automatically added to the Start Menu. If you can't find the icon proceed as follows:

1. When the Windows 10 start menu is displayed, type: **excel** on the keyboard. You will then see the Excel application icon on the screen. If you don't, Excel is not installed on this computer.

2. Right-click the Excel application icon and click: *Pin to Start* from the shortcut menu:

You will now be able to locate the Excel icon on the start menu (though you may have to scroll down to the bottom of the icon list to find it).

## note

### Potential problems when using templates

Many of Microsoft's templates have been created using some very advanced Excel skills and techniques. If you make use of them there's a danger that you may depend upon a workbook you don't understand and are unable to maintain.

In: *Lesson 3-15: Create a template,* you'll learn how to create your own custom templates.

Templates you create yourself are far more useful. Because you understand how they are built, you will be able to maintain them, and any workbook created from them.

4. When you reach the top of the start menu, release the left mouse button.

The Excel 2016 icon is now permanently positioned at the top of the Windows 10 start menu.

3   Left-click *Excel 2016* to start Excel.

## After you've started Excel

Now that Excel has started, Excel needs to know whether you want to create a new workbook, or whether you want to open a workbook that was created earlier.

When creating a new workbook, Excel also offers to give you a "flying start" by using a template. Templates are sample workbooks that you can adapt and modify for your own needs. The idea is very good but, in reality, templates are not usually a good choice as it can take longer to adapt them to your true needs than to design from scratch (see sidebar).

In this lesson you'll create a blank workbook.

1   Create a new blank workbook.

Left-click the mouse button on the *Blank workbook* template.

Note that, from now onwards, I will simply use the term "click" when I mean left-click (the mouse button you will use most of the time) and "right-click" only when you need to click the (less-used) right mouse button.

The Excel 2016 screen is displayed showing a blank workbook:

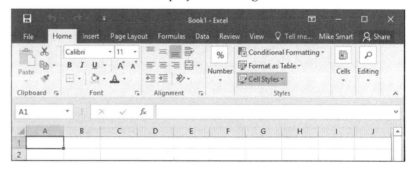

2   Leave the workbook open for the next lesson.

## important

### Update Channels

Update channels determine *when* users will receive the latest Excel version.

### Excel 2016 perpetual users

If you have a perpetual license (the pay-once version of Excel 2016) you will not receive any feature updates, so you do not have an update channel.

### Excel 365 home users

If you have a subscription version of Excel 2016 (this is referred to as *Excel 365* in this book) that is targeted at home users, you are required to receive monthly updates

This is called the *Monthly Channel*.

You will potentially receive new or improved features every month.

### Excel 365 business users

New features added in the *Monthly Channel* may have bugs, as they will not yet have been extensively tested by real-world use.

If you have an Excel 365 version that is targeted at business users (usually called *Excel Pro Plus*), you will (by default) have a different update channel (the *Semi-annual Channel*).

*The Semi-annual Channel* allows new features to be thoroughly tested before use. It is possible (though difficult) for Excel Pro-Plus users to change their update channel to the *Monthly Channel*.

The *Semi-annual Channel* only updates Excel twice each year (in January and July).

This book was written using the *July 2018March 2018 Semi-Annual Version 1803*.

# Lesson 1-2: Check that your Excel version is up to date

## Automatic Updates

Normally Excel will look after updates without you having to do anything. By default, automatic updates are enabled. This means that updates are downloaded from the Internet and installed automatically.

It is possible that automatic updates have been switched off on your computer. In this case there is a danger that you may have an old, buggy, unsupported and out of date version of Excel installed.

This lesson will show you how to make sure that you are using the latest (most complete, and most reliable) version of Excel.

**1** Start Excel and open a new blank workbook (if you have not already done this).

You learned how to do this in: *Lesson 1-1: Start Excel and open a new blank workbook.*

**2** Make sure that automatic updates are enabled.

1. Click the *File* button ▇File▇ at the top-left of the screen.

   This takes you to *Backstage View*. Backstage View allows you to complete an enormous range of common tasks from a single window.

2. Click: *Account* ▇Account▇ in the left-hand list.

   Your account details are displayed on screen. Notice the *Office Updates* button displayed in the right-hand pane.

   If all is well, and automatic updates are switched on, you will see a button similar to this:

   If *automatic updates* have been switched off, you will see a similar button to this.

   In this case you will need to switch *automatic updates* on (see next step).

**3** Switch on *automatic updates* if necessary.

Click: Update Options→Enable Updates.

## note

### Version number and Build

A new Excel version is usually released to the monthly update channel every month.

Each new version may add new features to Excel 365.

If bugs or security issues are found in a new version, Microsoft will fix them and publish a new *build* of the same version.

It is quite normal for there to be several new builds of each new version during the month that it is released.

4 If there are updates waiting to install, apply them.

Sometimes Excel will download updates but will not install them automatically.

In this case you will see an update button similar to the following:

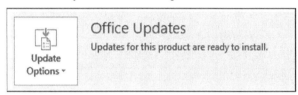

If you see this type of button you should apply the update.

Click: Update Options→Apply Updates.

You may be asked to confirm that you want to apply the update, and to close any open programs to apply the update.

5 Notice your version number and update channel.

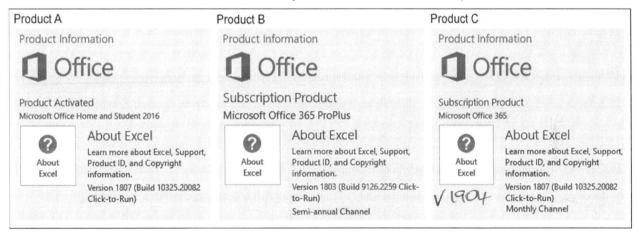

## note

### Perpetual license versions have different features

Perpetual license holders still receive monthly updates but these only include security updates and bug fixes (not new features).

A perpetual license holder running Version 1803 will thus see less features than a subscription license holder running the same Excel version.

You will see product information section displayed. If you see the number *365* or the words *Subscription Product,* you will know that you are using the subscription version of Excel 2016 (this is the case for products B and C above). Otherwise you are using the *perpetual license* version (this is the case for product A above). In this book, the perpetual license version will be referred to as *Excel 2016* and the subscription version as *Excel 365.*

Notice also the *update channel* and *version numbers* (see sidebars).

6 Click the *Back* button to leave *Backstage View* and return to the worksheet.

7 Click the *Close* button in the top-right corner of the Excel screen to close Excel.

## note

### The new Excel 365 Black theme

The new *Black* theme was introduced as part of the Feb 2016 version 1601 update.

The *Black* theme provides even higher contrast than the *Dark Gray* theme.

## note

### Themes and Backgrounds affect every Office application on all of your devices

When you set a theme or background in Excel you are actually changing the theme and background for the entire Office suite.

This means that you will have a consistent experience when using other Office applications such as *Word* and *PowerPoint*.

In: *Session Eight: Cloud Computing,* you'll discover that Excel 2016 now includes features that are useful to users with multiple devices (such as a work computer, home computer, laptop, tablet and smartphone).

If you are logged into a *Microsoft Account,* the theme you select will also magically change on all your devices.

Cloud computing is a challenging concept that is still quite new, so don't worry if all of this sounds rather confusing at the moment. All will be clear by the end of this book.

# Lesson 1-3: Change the Office Theme

Excel allows you to change the colors of screen elements (such as the menu bar and ribbon) by selecting a *theme*. Excel 2016 users have three themes available: *White, Dark Gray* and *Colorful*, while Excel 365 users have an additional *Black* theme also available (see sidebar).

## Colorful

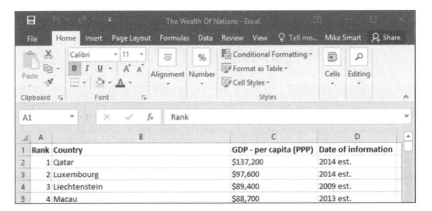

Excel 2016 uses the *Colorful* theme as the default. The previous version of Excel (Excel 2013) used the *White* theme as the default. The colorful theme makes it clear which of the Office applications you are using as Word, Excel, PowerPoint, Outlook and other Office applications each have their own unique color.

## White

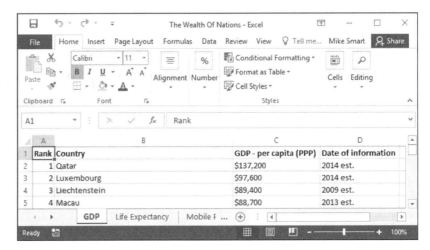

The *White* theme has very low contrast and shading. Some designers feel that this gives Excel a modern and "minimalist" appearance but it was widely criticized by some users of Excel 2013 for causing eye strain and being difficult to work with.

https://TheSmartMethod.com

## note

### You can also personalize Excel by changing the background

Background customization can only be done if you are connected to the Internet and logged into a Microsoft Account. You'll learn more about Microsoft Accounts later, in: *Session Eight: Cloud Computing*.

If you are logged into your Microsoft Account, you will see an *Office Background drop-down* list (above the *Office Theme* setting) that enables backgrounds to be set:

When you choose a background a "tattoo" is added to the area above the Ribbon with your chosen design:

## note

### Audio cues

Audio Cues were introduced in the *July 27, 2017 Version 1707* update.

If you enable *Audio Cues* a different sound will be played whenever you complete common Excel actions (such as cut and paste).

The idea is that you will subconsciously link sounds with actions so that when you make a mistake it will "sound wrong".

To enable Audio cues:

1. Click: File→Options→ Ease of Access→ Feedback options→ Provide Feedback with sound.

You are also able to choose between two different *Sound Schemes*.

## Dark Gray

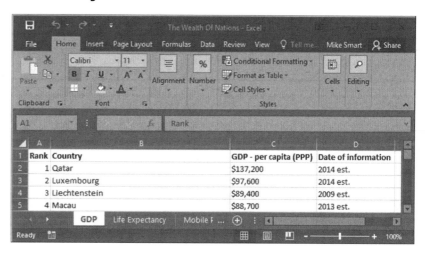

The *Dark Gray* theme provides high contrast between different screen elements. It has been suggested that this theme would be particularly useful for users with impaired vision.

1  Open Excel and open a new blank Excel workbook.

2  Change the *Office Theme*.

1.  Click the *File* button [File] at the top-left of the screen.

2.  Click the *Options* button [Options] near the bottom of the left-hand menu bar.

    The *Excel Options* dialog box appears.

    In the *Personalize your copy of Microsoft Office* section, you'll see an *Office Theme* drop-down list. Click the drop-down arrow to see the different themes available.

3.  Click the *Dark Gray* theme.

4.  Click *OK* to return to the Excel screen.

    Experiment with each theme until you discover the one you prefer. All of the screen grabs in this book were done using the *Colorful* theme. If you choose a different theme the screen grabs in the book may look slightly different to what you see on your computer screen.

3  Close Excel.

# Lesson 1-4: Maximize, minimize, re-size, move and close the Excel window

The main Excel window has a dazzling array of buttons, switches and other artifacts. By the end of this book they will all make sense to you and you'll really feel really comfortable with Excel.

For now, you'll explore the big picture by looking at how the Excel window can be sized and moved. The details will come later.

1 Open Excel.

2 Use the *Blank workbook* template to open a new blank workbook.

> You learned how to do this in*: Lesson 1-1: Start Excel and open a new blank workbook.*

3 Understand the *Maximize, Minimize, Close* and *Restore Down* buttons

> At the top right corner of the Excel window you'll see three buttons.

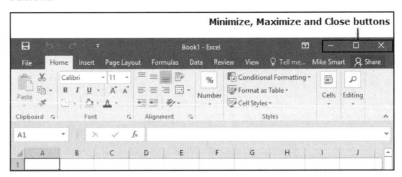

> The buttons that you see will depend upon how the Excel window was left last time the application closed down. Normally the Excel screen is maximized to fill the screen and you'll see:

> But if you had reduced the size of the Excel window so that it didn't fill the screen you'd see this instead:

> Try clicking the *Maximize, Minimize* and *Restore Down* buttons.

> ■ *Maximize* makes the Excel window completely fill the screen.

■ *Minimize* reduces Excel to a button on the bottom task bar.

Click this button again to restore the window to its previous size.

■ *Restore Down* makes the Excel window smaller, allowing you to re-size the window.

4   Re-size the Excel window.

After clicking the *Restore Down* button you are able to re-size the Excel window. Hover over either the side of the window, or a corner of the window, with your mouse cursor. The cursor shape will change to a double-headed arrow.

When you see either cursor shape, hold down the left mouse button and move the mouse (this is called *click and drag*) to re-size the window.

Clicking and dragging a corner allows you to change both the height and width of the window.

Clicking an edge allows you to change only one dimension.

**note**

**Other ways to close down Excel**

There are two other ways of closing Excel.

1. Click *File* on the Ribbon and then *Close* on the left-hand menu bar.

2. Press the <Alt>+<F4> keys on your keyboard.

5   Move the Excel window.

Click and drag the *Title Bar* (the bar at the very top of the window) to move the Excel window around the screen.

6   Close Excel.

Click on the *Close* button ☒ at the top right of the Excel window.

This is the most common way to close down Excel

There are also two lesser known (and lesser used) methods of closing Excel (see sidebar).

Excel often provides many different ways to do exactly the same thing.

## important

### Organizing your sample files folder

When you complete a lesson that involves a sample file that is changed, you will be instructed to save the file with a suffix.

By the time you've completed the course you'll have sample files such as:

Sales-1
Sales-2
Sales-3
Sales-4 ... etc

The first file is the sample file that you downloaded and the others (with the number suffix) are interim versions as you complete each lesson.

The sample file set includes the starting sample file and all interim versions.

The interim versions are provided for three reasons:

1. If your work-in-progress becomes unusable (for example after a system crash) you can continue without starting at the beginning again.

2. If a lesson doesn't seem to give the results described, you can view the example to get some clues about what has gone wrong.

3. When you have completed the course you will use this book as a reference. The interim versions allow you to work through any of the lessons in isolation if you need to remind yourself how to use a specific Excel feature.

It is a good idea to place the sample files in a different folder to your saved work. If you don't do this you'll be over-writing the sample interim files (such as Sales-1, Sales-2 etc) with your own finished work.

**The Wealth of Nations**

# Lesson 1-5: Download the sample files and open/navigate a workbook

Excel uses the analogy of a book that has many pages. In Excel terminology, the term: *Workbook* is used for the entire book and *Worksheet* for each of the pages. You'll be learning more about worksheets later in this session in: *Lesson 1-9: View, move, add, rename, delete and navigate worksheet tabs.*

1   Download the sample files (if you haven't already done so).

   1.   Open your web browser and type in the URL:

        **https://thesmartmethod.com**

   2.   Click the *Sample Files* link on the top right of the home page.

   3.   Download the sample files for *Excel 2016 Essential Skills*.

        If you have any difficulty downloading the sample files there is a FAQ section at the bottom of the page detailing the solution to common problems.

2   Open the sample workbook: *The Wealth of Nations*.

   1.   Open Excel.

   2.   Click *Open Other Workbooks* on at the bottom of the left-hand menu bar.

   3.   Click: *Browse* in the list beneath *Open*.

   4.   Navigate to your sample files. If you downloaded using the recommended option and didn't change the normal file location, you will find these in the *C:/Practice* folder.

   5.   Open the *Excel 2016 Essential Skills* folder.

   6.   Open the *Session 1* folder.

   7.   Double click *The Wealth of Nations* to open the sample workbook.

3   Go to Cell ZZ3 using the Name Box.

## Potential problem when downloading sample files

*Protected View* is a security feature that was first introduced in Excel 2010. It is designed to protect you from potential viruses by treating all files downloaded from the Internet as being suspicious.

Any workbooks that are downloaded from the Internet, or are sent by e-mail attachment, will open in *Protected View* by default.

PROTECTED VIEW  Be careful— to edit, it's s

The user then has to click an *Enable Editing* button to use the file as normal:

Enable Editing

While some users may find it useful to be reminded about the origin of their files, others may find this feature annoying.

To avoid seeing this message whenever you open a sample file, we provide the sample files as a digitally-signed self-extracting download. This means that the sample files will open.

We also offer an alternative zip file method to download (the link to this page is in the FAQ section at the bottom of the web page).

The alternative zip file has been provided because some companies (or anti-virus products) block the download of executable files.

If you download using the zip file option, you'll have to click the *Enable Editing* button every time you open a sample file.

Excel uses the letter of the column and the number of the row to identify cells. This is called the *cell address*. In the above example, the cell address of the active cell is B3.

In Excel 2016 there are a little over a million rows and a little over sixteen thousand columns. You may wonder how it is possible to name these columns with only 26 letters in the alphabet.

When Excel runs out of letters it starts using two: X, Y, Z and then AA, AB, AC etc. But even two letters are not enough. When Excel reaches column ZZ it starts using three letters: ZX, ZY, ZZ and then AAA, AAB, AAC etc.

The currently selected cell is called the *Active Cell* and has a green line around it. The Active Cell's address is always displayed in the *Name Box* and its contents are displayed in the *Formula Bar*.

You can also use the *Name Box* to move to a specific cell.

To see this in action, type **ZZ3** into the *Name Box* and then press the **<Enter>** key. You are teleported to cell ZZ3:

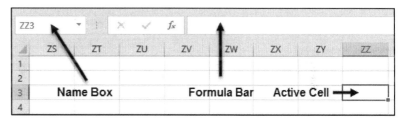

4   Return to Cell A1 by pressing <Ctrl>+<Home>.

5   Go to the end of the worksheet by pressing <Ctrl>+<End>.

6   Use the scroll bars.

There are two scroll bars for the Excel window.

The vertical scroll bar runs from top to bottom of the window and allows you to quickly move up and down the worksheet.

The horizontal scroll bar is at the bottom right hand side of the window and allows you to move to the left and right in wide worksheets. Here's how the scroll bars work:

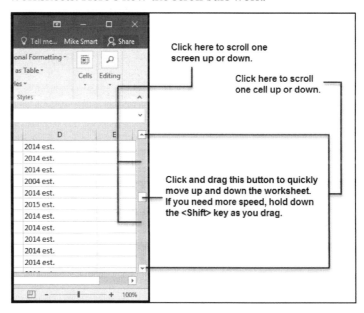

# Lesson 1-6: Save a workbook to a local file

1 Open *The Wealth of Nations* from your sample files folder (if it isn't already open).

2 Save the workbook.

**note**

You can also use the **<Ctrl>+<S>** keyboard shortcut to save your work.

When you are editing a workbook, the changes you make are only held in the computer's memory. If there is a power cut or your computer crashes, you will lose any work that has been done since the last save.

For this reason, you should get into the habit of regularly saving your work.

Even though you haven't changed this workbook, save it by clicking the *Save* button on the *Quick Access Toolbar* at the top left of the screen.

**note**

You can also use the **<F12>** key to instantly display the *Save As* dialog.

3 Save the workbook with a different name.

1. Click the *File* button. File at the top-left of the screen.

2. Click: *Save As* Save As in the left-hand list.

3. Click *Browse* Browse in the *Save As* menu.

The following dialog will appear if you are using Windows 10. The dialog may be slightly different for Windows 7 or 8 users but you should easily be able to figure out the differences:

**The Wealth of Nations**

# note

## OneDrive and Cloud Computing

You may have noticed that the *Save As* dialog also has an option to save your workbook to a OneDrive:

A OneDrive can be thought of as a "disk drive in the sky".

It is just like the C:\ drive on your computer but exists on a Microsoft server many miles away, accessed via the Internet.

The OneDrive can be very useful when you need to access your files from several different computers.

A OneDrive also provides an easier way to share files with others.

The OneDrive is part of a completely new way of working called *Cloud Computing*.

Support for Cloud Computing was first added in the Excel 2013 release.

Because Cloud Computing is such an involved (and complex) subject I have devoted an entire session to it in: *Session Eight: Cloud Computing*.

I advise you not to jump ahead to the last session at this stage in your learning, as this session will be difficult to understand until you have completed the earlier sessions.

1. Click the drop-down arrow to the right of the *Save as type* drop-down list.

2. A list appears showing a large number of different file types:

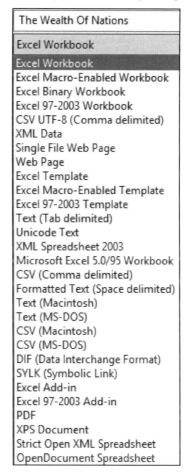

Most of the time you'll want to use the default format: *Excel Workbook* but there may be times when you'll need to save in one of the other formats. You'll learn all about the most important formats (and when you should use them) in the next lesson: *Lesson 1-7: Understand common file formats.* For now, you'll stay with the default: *Excel Workbook* format.

3. Click inside the *File name* box.

4. Type: **The Wealth of Nations Copy**

5. Click the *Save* button.

Notice that the name of the workbook in the title bar (at the top of the window) has now changed indicating that you are now viewing the new workbook that you have just saved.

# Lesson 1-7: Understand common file formats

**1** Open a new blank workbook.

You learned how to do this in: *Lesson 1-1: Start Excel and open a new blank workbook.*

**2** View the file formats supported by Excel.

1. Click the *File* button at the top-left of the screen.

2. Click: *Save As* in the left-hand list.

3. Click *Browse* in the *Save As* menu.

The *Save As* dialog appears.

4. Click the drop-down arrow to the right of the *Save as type* list.

A list appears showing all of the different file formats supported by Excel (see sidebar).

**3** Understand the most important file formats.

## Excel Workbook (the Open XML format)

Before Office 2007 was released, every program stored its information on the hard disk in a completely different way. These incompatible formats are called *binary formats*. This made it very difficult to write applications that could be used together.

All of this changed with a new format that was first introduced in Office 2007: *Office Open XML* .

## Excel Macro-Enabled Workbook

An Excel Macro-Enabled Workbook is simply a workbook that has program code (called VBA code) embedded within it. Macros are beyond the scope of this book but are covered in the *Excel Expert Skills* book in this series.

While macro code is very powerful it can also be destructive as it is extremely simple to write damaging viruses within Excel macro code.

Macro programming (also called VBA programming) is a vast subject of its own and is not useful to the vast majority of Excel users. The Smart Method® run comprehensive classroom Excel VBA courses but they are usually only taken by scientists and engineers who need to add very advanced functionality to Excel.

Versions of Excel before Excel 2007 could potentially allow a workbook to infect your machine with a macro virus because all Excel files were capable of carrying macros. Because the formats are now separate, it is easier to avoid opening potentially infected files.

---

The Wealth Of Nations

Excel Workbook

Excel Workbook
Excel Macro-Enabled Workbook
Excel Binary Workbook
Excel 97-2003 Workbook
CSV UTF-8 (Comma delimited)
XML Data
Single File Web Page
Web Page
Excel Template
Excel Macro-Enabled Template
Excel 97-2003 Template
Text (Tab delimited)
Unicode Text
XML Spreadsheet 2003
Microsoft Excel 5.0/95 Workbook
CSV (Comma delimited)
Formatted Text (Space delimited)
Text (Macintosh)
Text (MS-DOS)
CSV (Macintosh)
CSV (MS-DOS)
DIF (Data Interchange Format)
SYLK (Symbolic Link)
Excel Add-in
Excel 97-2003 Add-in
PDF
XPS Document
Strict Open XML Spreadsheet
OpenDocument Spreadsheet

---

## Excel 97-2003 Workbook

This is the old binary format that allows users with earlier versions of Excel to open your workbooks. Some features won't work in earlier versions and if you've used those in your workbook, Excel will display a warning when you save telling you which features will be lost.

## Excel Binary Workbook

An oddity in Excel is a binary format called: *Excel Binary Workbook*. This is a binary alternative to Open XML but it can't be read by earlier versions of Excel. The advantages of this format are that it generally results in smaller file sizes and loads and saves more quickly than Open XML. You will only notice a speed difference when working with very large worksheets.

The *Excel Binary Workbook* format may also present a security threat as (just like the *Excel Macro-Enabled Workbook* format) it can contain macros that could infect your machine with a macro virus.

## PDF

If you need to send a worksheet to a user who does not own a copy of Excel, you can save it in PDF (Portable Document Format). This format was invented by Adobe and is also sometimes called *Adobe Acrobat* or simply *Acrobat*.

All major web browsers can open and display PDF files. In Windows 10 PDF files will, by default, open using the new Edge browser. If you send a user a PDF file you can be confident that they will be able to read and print (but not change) the worksheet.

If you are reading this book as an e-book you are using a PDF file right now as all Smart Method e-books are published using the PDF file format.

## Other formats

As you can see, there are several other less commonly used formats supported by Excel 2016 but the above formats are the only ones you'll normally encounter. The most important thing to remember is that, unless there's a good reason to use a different format, you should always save documents in the default *Excel Workbook* format.

note

### Sharing files using Cloud Computing features

You should be aware that Excel 2016 provides another way to share files with users that do not have Excel 2016 (or, indeed, any version of Excel) installed upon their computer. This is done using Excel 2016's built in *Cloud Computing* features.

Cloud Computing also allows users to open (and even edit) Excel workbooks using devices such as iPads, Android pads, Apple Macs and Smartphones.

Support for Cloud Computing was originally introduced in the Excel 2013 release.

Because Cloud Computing is such an involved (and complex) subject I have devoted an entire session to it in: *Session Eight: Cloud Computing*.

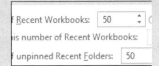
**The Wealth of Nations**

# Lesson 1-8: Pin a workbook and understand file organization

1  Close down and restart Excel.

2  Pin a workbook to the *Recent Workbooks* list.

Notice that there is a list of recently opened documents at the top of the left-hand menu bar.

The list begins with the most recently opened workbook (probably the *Wealth of Nations Copy* workbook saved in: *Lesson 1-6: Save a workbook*).

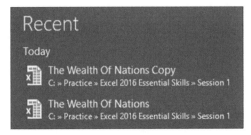

1. Hover the mouse cursor over one of the files in the *Recent* list:

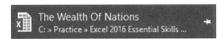

Note that a pin icon ⊡ has appeared next to the workbook name.

When you hover the mouse cursor over the pin a tooltip is displayed saying: *Pin this item to the list*.

This can be a great time saver as it enables any workbook that you use a lot to always be at the top of the *Recent* list. You won't have to waste time looking for it on the hard drive.

2. Click the pin icon. The item moves to the top of the list and the pin icon changes from unpinned ⊡ to pinned. ⊡

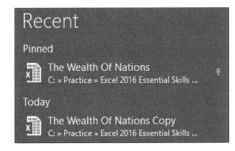

3. Click on *The Wealth of Nations* to open the workbook.

3  Understand file organization.

By default, Excel saves all workbooks into your *Documents* folder along with other Office documents (such as Word and PowerPoint files). This clearly is going to cause problems when you have a few hundred files.

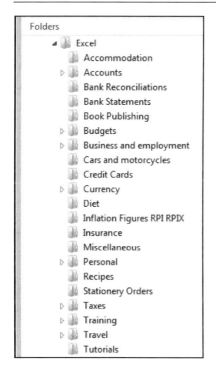

**Folders**
- ⌄ 📁 Excel
  - 📁 Accommodation
  - ▷ 📁 Accounts
  - 📁 Bank Reconciliations
  - 📁 Bank Statements
  - 📁 Book Publishing
  - ▷ 📁 Budgets
  - ▷ 📁 Business and employment
  - 📁 Cars and motorcycles
  - 📁 Credit Cards
  - ▷ 📁 Currency
  - 📁 Diet
  - 📁 Inflation Figures RPI RPIX
  - 📁 Insurance
  - 📁 Miscellaneous
  - ▷ 📁 Personal
  - 📁 Recipes
  - 📁 Stationery Orders
  - ▷ 📁 Taxes
  - ▷ 📁 Training
  - ▷ 📁 Travel
  - 📁 Tutorials

## note

### How do I create a subfolder?

The concept of folders, subfolders and files is a very fundamental Windows skill rather than an Excel skill.

If you do not have basic Windows skills (an understanding of how Windows organizes files) you would get good value from a Windows book to give you the foundation skills you need to use any Windows program.

Here's how you create a new subfolder:

1. Right-click on the *Documents* folder.

2. Click: New→Folder, from the shortcut menu.

A new folder will appear called *New Folder*.

3. You will now be able to type: **Excel** in order to name the folder.

If this doesn't work for you, right-click the new folder and select *Rename* from the shortcut menu. You'll then be able to type: **Excel** to rename the folder.

It is better to organize yourself from the start by setting up an orderly filing system.

**4** Create an *Excel* subfolder beneath your *Documents* folder.

I create a folder called *Excel* beneath the *Documents* folder. In this folder, I create subfolders to store my work. You can see a screen grab of my Excel folder in the sidebar (of course, your needs will be different to mine).

See sidebar if you don't know how to create a subfolder.

**5** Set the default file location to point to the new *Excel* folder.

If you take my advice and create an Excel folder, you will waste a mouse click every time you open a file because Excel will take you to the *Documents* folder by default.

Here's how to reset the default file location to your new Excel folder:

1. Open Excel and click the *Blank Workbook* template to open a new blank workbook.

2. Click the *File* button at the top left of the screen.

3. Click the *Options* button towards the bottom of the left-hand list.

   The *Excel Options* dialog appears.

4. Choose the *Save* category from the left-hand side of the dialog.

   During the remainder of the book I'll explain the above three steps like this:

   Click: File→Options→Save.

   This will save a lot of time and forests!

5. Change the *Default local file location*.

   Type: **\Excel** after the end of the current *Default local file location*.

   You have to actually type this manually. Microsoft seem to have forgotten to add a browse button!

When you click File→Open→Browse in future you'll automatically be taken to your Excel folder ready to choose a category.

## note

### Changing the default number of worksheets created in new workbooks

When you open a new blank workbook in Excel 2016, one new worksheet is automatically created called *Sheet1*.

In older versions of Excel (Excel 2010 and earlier), three worksheets were created called *Sheet1, Sheet2* and *Sheet3*.

This is a change for the better as it keeps things neater. Most of my workbooks only need one worksheet.

But if you long for the "good old days" here's how you can make Excel 2016 mimic Excel 2010 (and earlier versions) at start-up:

1. Click:

File→Options→General→ When creating new workbooks →Include this many sheets:

2. Enter the number of sheets required:

# Lesson 1-9: View, move, add, rename, delete and navigate worksheet tabs

When you save an Excel file onto your hard disk, you are saving a single workbook containing one or more worksheets. You can add as many worksheets as you need to a workbook.

There are two types of worksheet. *Regular* worksheets contain cells. *Chart* sheets, as you would expect, each contain a single chart. You'll be exploring charts in depth in: *Session Five: Charts and Graphics*.

1   Open *The Wealth of Nations* from your sample files folder (if it isn't already open).

2   Move between worksheets.

Look at the tabs in the bottom left corner of your screen. Notice that this sample workbook contains three worksheets. Click on each tab in turn to view each worksheet.

3   Add a new worksheet and name it: **Population**

1.   Click the *New Sheet* button (the circle with a plus sign inside it next to *Mobile Phones*). ⊕ A new tab appears named *Sheet1*.

2.   Double-click the *Sheet1* tab.

3.   Type the word **Population** followed by the **<Enter>** key.

4   Move a worksheet's tab.

1.   Click on the *Population* tab (you may have to do this twice).

2.   Hold the mouse button down and drag to the left or right. As you drag you'll notice an icon of a page and a black arrow showing you where the tab will be placed.

3.   Release the mouse button to move the tab to the location of your choice.

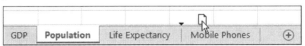

5   Understand the tab scroll buttons.

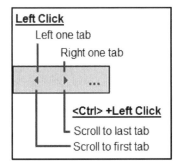

### The Wealth of Nations

Because this workbook only has four tabs, there's no need to use the tab scroll buttons (in fact, they don't do anything and are grayed out when all tabs are visible).

When there are more tabs than will fit on the screen the *tab scroll buttons* are used to move between tabs.

6   Move between worksheets using the keyboard.

You can move between worksheets using only the keyboard by pressing the **<Ctrl>+<PgUp>** and **<Ctrl>+<PgDn>** keyboard shortcuts to cycle through all the tabs in your workbook.

7   Change tab colors.

1.   Right-click on any of the tabs and choose *Tab Color* from the shortcut menu.

2.   Choose any color.

It is best practice to choose a color from the top block of *Theme Colors* rather than one of the *Standard Colors*.

You'll discover why later, in: *Lesson 4-9: Understand themes* and in: *Lesson 4-11: Add color and gradient effects to cells (sidebar).*

3.   Repeat for the other tabs on the worksheet.

8   Delete a worksheet.

Right click on the *Population* tab and click *Delete* from the shortcut menu.

9   Delete several worksheets at the same time.

1.   Hold down the **<Ctrl>** key.

2.   Click each tab that you want to delete in turn. Don't select them all as it isn't possible to delete every worksheet in a workbook.

3.   Right click any of the selected tabs and select *Delete* from the shortcut menu.

Don't worry about the missing tabs. You're going to close the workbook without saving it so you won't overwrite the original workbook.

10   Close the workbook without saving it.

1.   Click: File→Close.

A dialog is displayed:

2.   Click *Don't Save* so that you don't over-write the workbook.

Because you haven't saved the workbook it will remain in its original state when you next open it.

## note

### The versions feature will not protect you from a hard drive failure

Carnegie Melon University conducted a study of 100,000 hard drives in 2007. They found that there's a probability of between 1 in 50 and 1 in 25 of your hard drive failing each year.

In an office of 100 workers that means that between two and four unlucky workers will suffer a hard drive failure every year.

To insure against drive failure, you need to back up your data to a different hard drive (or other media).

If your computer is part of an office network, the normal solution is to save your files to a shared network drive. The IT department are then responsible for backing this up every night.

For home users (or small companies that only have one computer) you should back up all of your data to an external hard drive (or a memory stick if your files are not very large).

Cloud computing offers an even better solution to prevent potential file loss after hard drive failure. In: *Session Eight: Cloud Computing*, you'll learn how to use a OneDrive to store a workbook in the cloud.

# Lesson 1-10: Use the Versions feature to recover an unsaved Draft file

Excel 2010 introduced a major new feature called *Versions*. The Versions feature is fantastically useful as it finally solves two common problems that are as old as computing itself:

1. Your computer crashes, there's a power cut, or you close your work without saving, and then discover that you've lost all of your work since the last save.

2. You delete parts of your workbook and then save, only to realize that you deleted something important before saving. Because saving over-writes the old version of the file, you find that you've lost the deleted work forever.

Microsoft has finally figured out how to solve both problems. The Versions feature works like this:

1. Every so often Excel saves a backup of your workbook (called a *Version*) for you. The default time interval for these automatic backups is every 10 minutes (but you can change this to any interval). You'll see the Versions feature at work in the next lesson: *Lesson 1-11: Use the Versions feature to recover an earlier version of a workbook.*

2. If you create a new workbook and then close it without saving, Excel will still keep the last automatic backup it made. Excel calls this a *Draft* version. Draft versions are automatically deleted after four days. The Draft feature is the subject of this lesson.

You'll need a watch or clock with a second hand for this lesson.

**1** Open a new blank workbook.

You learned how to do this in: *Lesson 1-1: Start Excel and open a new blank workbook.*

**2** Set the AutoSave interval to one minute and check that AutoSave features are enabled

1. Click: File→Options→Save.

2. Change the *Save AutoRecover information every* box to 1 minute.

3. Make sure that the other options are set in the same way as in this screen grab (the two check boxes will already be checked unless another user has changed them):

4. Click: *OK* and check the time on your clock or watch. The first AutoSave will happen one minute from now!

# note

## RAID arrays are a special super-reliable type of disk drive

Many years ago, I implemented an EDM (electronic document management system) for the world's largest car manufacturer.

It would have been a disaster for them to lose even one hours' work, so I specified a special drive called a RAID Array (Redundant Array of Independent Disks) to store the documents.

The simplest RAID array consists of two hard drives and automatically writes all data to both drives (this is called mirroring). If one drive fails, the other will still have the data meaning that any data loss is very unlikely.

RAID arrays don't stop workflow for even a moment. If a disk fails, the users don't even notice as data continues to be available from the other disk (or disks).

When the faulty disk drive is replaced, the files automatically restore themselves from the good disk (or disks) restoring the reliability of the array.

# note

## The Versions feature isn't just for Excel

Microsoft has also included the Versions feature in Word and PowerPoint.

Now that you've learned how to use it in Excel, you should be able to figure out the small differences in the way it is implemented in the other Office applications.

5. Type the following into cells A1 and A2 , pressing the **<Enter>** key after each line:

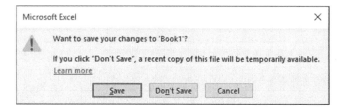

6. Wait for at least one minute. (After one minute Excel will automatically save your workbook).

    After a little over a minute try to close the workbook. The following dialog should appear:

    Excel is telling you that it has already saved a draft copy of the workbook.

7. Click the *Don't Save* button.

    Even though you told Excel not to save, a draft copy has been secretly saved just in case you made a mistake and may need the file later.

3    Recover the draft document.

1. Open Excel.

2. Click: *Open Other Workbooks* at the bottom of the menu bar.

3. Click: *Recover Unsaved Workbooks.*

    You'll find this at the bottom center of the screen (you may need to scroll down).

4. A dialog appears showing the unsaved document that you were working on:

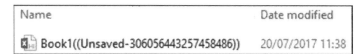

5. Double-click the document to open it.

    The document is now shown on screen (even though you have never saved it).

6. Recover the unsaved file.

    Click the *Save As* button in the top information bar.

7. Save the file in your sample files folder with the name: **Mary.**

# Lesson 1-11: Use the Versions feature to recover an earlier version of a workbook

Excel's ability to automatically backup your document at a chosen time interval was explored in the previous lesson: *Lesson 1-10: Use the Versions feature to recover an unsaved Draft file.*

This lesson will show you how to view the automatic backups and to revert to an earlier version if you've messed up the current version.

You can even cut-and-paste sections from older versions of a workbook and paste them into the current version.

You'll need a watch or clock with a second hand for this lesson.

1    Open *Mary* from your sample files folder (if it isn't already open).

2    Cause Excel to automatically save a different version of the workbook.

In the last lesson: *Lesson 1-10: Use the Versions feature to recover an unsaved Draft file*, you set the time interval for automatic backups to 1 minute. If you are not completing this course sequentially, you will need to go back to this lesson and make sure that this setting is set to 1 minute.

Add the following text to cells A4 and A5, pressing the **<Enter>** key after each line:

|  | A | B | C | D |
|---|---|---|---|---|
| 1 | Mary had a little lamb | | | |
| 2 | Its fleece was white as snow | | | |
| 3 | | | | |
| 4 | and everywhere that Mary went | | | |
| 5 | The lamb was sure to go | | | |
| 6 | | | | |

Look at your watch or clock and wait for a little over one minute. Excel should have automatically saved a new version of the workbook.

3    Make sure that Excel AutoSaved the new version.

Some users have reported that Excel sometimes takes as long as ten minutes to AutoSave a file (even when the AutoSave interval is set to one minute). Here's how to check that it performed as it should:

1. Click the *File* button.   `File`

   You should see an AutoSave file version alongside the *Manage Workbook* button.

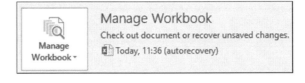

**Mary**

If you don't see the AutoSave version, click the *Back* button  wait another minute and then click the *File* tab again. Don't move on to the next step until it has appeared.

**4**    Further modify the file and then save it.

1.  Add the following text to cells A7 and A8 pressing the **<Enter>** key after each line:

| | A | B | C |
|---|---|---|---|
| 7 | It followed her to school one day | | |
| 8 | It was against the rules | | |

2.  Save the workbook.

**5**    View the earlier version that Excel automatically saved.

1.  Click the *File* button.    File

2.  Click the earlier AutoSaved version.

Today, 11:36 (autorecovery)

The earlier version opens in Excel.

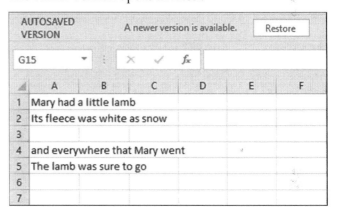

Notice that Excel advises that there is a later version of your workbook available should you need to go back to the version that you have just replaced.

Notice also that it would be possible to copy and paste sections from the older version into the newer version if you needed to do that.

**6**    Replace the current version of the workbook with the earlier AutoSaved version.

1.  Click the *Restore* button on the top information bar.

2.  Click the OK button to confirm.

**7**    Reset the AutoSave interval to 10 minutes.

You learned how to do this in: *Lesson 1-10: Use the Versions feature to recover an unsaved Draft file.*

# Lesson 1-12: Use the Ribbon

The Ribbon provides fast access to hundreds of Excel features.

The sheer breadth of Excel features can seem overwhelming. This book will gently introduce all of the most important features, one at a time.

By the end of the book you'll be really comfortable and productive with the Ribbon.

1 Start Excel and open a new blank workbook.

You learned how to do this in: *Lesson 1-1: Start Excel and open a new blank workbook.*

2 Use Ribbon tabs.

Each Ribbon tab has its own toolkit available to you. By far the most important tab is the *Home* tab which has buttons for all of the most common and useful features.

Click each tab in turn and view the buttons. The screen grab below has the *Insert* tab selected. Don't worry if the buttons seem cryptic at the moment. Most of them will make complete sense by the end of this book. (And if you later go on to complete the *Expert Skills* course, Excel will have no mysteries left at all)!

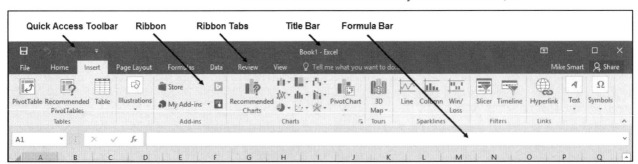

## note

### Contextual Tabs

Sometimes Excel will show you even more tabs.

For example, in: *Session Five: Charts and Graphics,* you'll learn how to create charts.

When you click on a chart a new tab called *Chart Tools* appears.

The new tab provides access to a range of features relating to Charts.

3 Type the word **Test** into any blank cell and then press the **<Enter>** key on the keyboard once.

Notice how the active cell moves to the cell beneath.

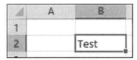

4 Make the cell with the word *Test* into the active cell.

Click once on the word *Test* or use the arrow keys on the keyboard to navigate back to the cell. Be very careful not to double-click, otherwise Excel will think that you want to edit the cell.

5 Click the *Home* tab on the Ribbon and focus upon the Font command group (it's the second panel from the left). Try clicking each of the buttons and you will see the word *Test* change to reflect your choices.

This drop-down allows you to change the font to something different to the default Calibri.

This drop-down allows you to change the size of the font (measured in points).

These buttons allow you to change the cell's background and text color.

Click here once to make the text Bold, Italic or Underlined (or all three). Click again to restore it to Normal.

This drop-down arrow allows you to add a double underline.

Clicking here puts a single underline along the entire length of the bottom of the cell. Try the drop-down arrow too for more border options.

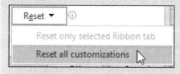
6   Minimize the Ribbon.

1.  Double-click any of the Ribbon tabs except the *File* tab (for example the *Home* tab or the *Insert* tab).

    Notice how the Ribbon is now minimized in order to save screen space (though the *Formula Bar* is still visible).

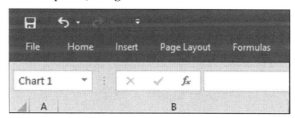

2.  Click once on any tab, except the *File* tab, to temporarily bring the Ribbon back to full size.

    Notice that as soon as you click back onto the worksheet the Ribbon is minimized again.

7   Bring back the Ribbon.

Double-click on any tab except the *File* tab to permanently bring back the Ribbon.

8   Close Excel without saving changes.

1.  Click: File→Close or click the cross ⊠ in the top right corner.

2.  When asked if you want to save your changes, click the *Don't Save* button.

# Lesson 1-13: Understand Ribbon components

*The whole is more than the sum of its parts.*
*Aristotle, Greek critic, philosopher, physicist & zoologist*
*(384 BC – 322 BC)*

The Ribbon is made up of several different controls.

## Command group

Similar actions are grouped into a cluster. For example, every control relating to numbers is clustered into the *Number* group.

## Normal button

Simply executes a command when clicked. The *Bold* button on the *Home* tab is a good example.

## Menu button

This type of button has a little down-arrow on it. It will display a *list*, *menu* or *rich menu* drop-down when clicked.

## Split button

This is the hardest button to understand because these buttons look almost the same as the *Menu* button. When you hover the mouse cursor over a split button, the icon and drop-down arrow highlight separately as different "buttons within a button".

A good example is the *underline* button on the Home toolbar.

Clicking the icon part of a split button (the <u>U</u>) will perform the default action of the button (in this case a single underline). Clicking the arrow part of the button will display a drop-down list of further choices (in this case the choice between a single and double underline).

## Drop-down list

I often shorten this to simply "Drop-Down" in this book. A drop-down is a simple menu listing several choices.

If you see an ellipsis (…) after a drop-down list item, this means that a dialog will be displayed after you click, offering further choices.

## Rich menu

The rich menu is a drop-down list with added help text explaining what each item will do.

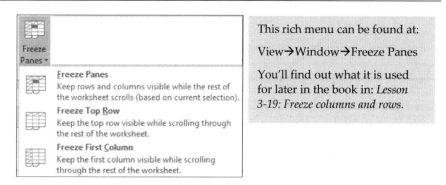

This rich menu can be found at:

View→Window→Freeze Panes

You'll find out what it is used for later in the book in: *Lesson 3-19: Freeze columns and rows.*

## Drop-down gallery

This is a little like a drop-down list but has graphics to visually demonstrate the effect of each choice.

## Check box

A little square box that you can click to switch an option on or off.

In this example (from the *Page Layout* Ribbon tab) you are able to switch the gridlines on and off for the screen display and/or the printout.

## Dialog launcher

Dialog launchers appear on the bottom right-hand corner of some command groups. Dialogs offer more choices than it is possible for the Ribbon to express graphically.

**Dialog Launcher**

## note

### There are many more commands available in Excel 365 than there are in Excel 2016

In this lesson, I have shown screen grabs from the Excel 2016 Quick Access Toolbar but Excel 365 users will notice an extra button (included on the quick access toolbar by default):

The Touch/Mouse Mode button

The new button adds more space between commands to make Excel easier to use with a touch screen.

With the increasing availability of touch screen computers running Windows 10, this is a very useful new Excel 365 feature if you use this type of device.

If you are using Excel 2016 (the pay once, use forever version of Excel) you will not be able to use this feature.

# Lesson 1-14: Customize the Quick Access Toolbar and preview the printout

You can customize the *Quick Access Toolbar* to suit your own special requirements. In this lesson, you'll add some useful buttons to the *Quick Access Toolbar* to save a few clicks when accessing common commands.

The *Quick Access Toolbar* is one of the keys to being really productive with Excel. This lesson will introduce you to the main features.

1 Open *The Wealth of Nations* from your sample files folder.

2 Preview how the *Life Expectancy* worksheet will look when printed.

   1. Click the *Life Expectancy* tab at the bottom of the worksheet.

   2. Click: File→Print.

      *Backstage View* is displayed.

      Backstage view displays a huge number of print-related features. A preview of how the page will look when it is printed is displayed on the right-hand side of the screen.

   3. Click the *Next Page* and *Previous Page* buttons to move through the print preview.

      Notice there's a button to the bottom-left of the preview pane that allows you to cycle through each page:

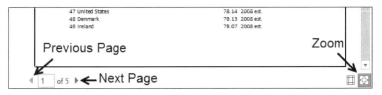

   4. Use the *Zoom* button to magnify the page for a clearer view. (You may not notice much of a zoom if you have a large screen).

   5. Click the *Back* button ⬅ at the top left of *Backstage View* to return to the workbook.

Customize Quick Access Toolbar Button

The Wealth of Nations

3 Add a *Print Preview* button to the Quick Access Toolbar.

   The quick *Print Preview* offered by the *Backstage View* is a very useful feature and you'll probably use it a lot. Every time you use it, however, it is going to take two clicks of the mouse. Wouldn't it be better if you could show a print preview with just one click?

   1. Click the *Customize Quick Access Toolbar* button (see sidebar).

   2. Click the *Print Preview and Print* item in the drop-down list.

      A new button now appears on the Quick Access Toolbar. You are now able to *Print Preview* your work with a single click of the mouse.

## note

**Some amazing "hidden" Excel features cannot be used at all without customizing the Quick Access Toolbar or the Ribbon**

One of my favourite "hidden" features in Excel 2016 is its ability to read the workbook to me via its *Text to Voice* facility.

When I need to input lots of numbers from a sheet of paper and want to check them, I get Excel to read them to me as I tick each off my list. This is much faster and nicer than continuously looking first at the screen, then at the paper, for each entry.

This feature is covered in depth in the *Expert Skills* book in this series.

You can't use this feature at all unless you either add some custom buttons to the Quick Access Toolbar or customize the Ribbon.

## tip

The Quick Access Toolbar is one of the keys to being really productive with Excel 2016.

Always try to minimize the number of mouse clicks needed to do common tasks.

If you find yourself forever changing tabs to use a button, change two clicks into one by adding the button to the Quick Access Toolbar.

All of those extra clicks add up to a lot of time over the weeks and years.

**4** Add a *Font Color* button to the Quick Access Toolbar.

A *More Commands...* option is available when you click the *Customize Quick Access Toolbar* button. This enables you to add any of Excel's commands to the toolbar. But there's an easier way!

1. Click the *Home* tab on the Ribbon (if it isn't already selected).

2. Right-click on the *Font Color* button in the *Font* group.

3. Click *Add to Quick Access Toolbar* from the shortcut menu.

   A *Font Color* button is added to the Quick Access Toolbar.

**5** Remove a button from the Quick Access Toolbar.

1. Right-click on the *Font Color* button that you've just added to the Quick Access Toolbar.

2. Click *Remove from Quick Access Toolbar* from the shortcut menu.

**6** Add separators to make a heavily customized Quick Access Toolbar more readable.

When you add many items to the Quick Access Toolbar it is a good idea to use separators to split icons into logical groups.

1. Click the *Customize Quick Access Toolbar* button.

2. Click *More Commands...* from the shortcut menu.

3. Click the `<Separator>` item at the top of the *Commands* list.

4. Click the `Add >>` button.

5. Use the up and down buttons to move the separator to the required location.

6. Click the OK button.

Here's a screen grab of my own Quick Access Toolbar. I've added buttons for all of the features I use most often. This means that I can always access these features with a single click of the mouse:

**Separators**

---

# Lesson 1-15: Use the Mini Toolbar, Key Tips and keyboard shortcuts

1   Open the *Wealth of Nations* sample worksheet (if it isn't already open).

2   Select cell B2 (Qatar) on the GDP worksheet.

   1.   Click on the *GDP* tab.

   2.   Click on cell B2 (Qatar).

   Make sure that you only click once, otherwise Excel will think that you are trying to edit the cell.

| | A | B | C |
|---|---|---|---|
| 1 | Rank | Country | GDP - per capita (PPP) |
| 2 | 1 | Qatar | $137,200 |

3   Make cell B2 (Qatar) bold, italicized and underlined.

   1.   Click: Home→Font→Bold.

   2.   Click: Home→Font→Italic.

   3.   Click: Home→Font→Underline.

| | A | B | C |
|---|---|---|---|
| 1 | Rank | Country | GDP - per capita (PPP) |
| 2 | 1 | *Qatar* | $137,200 |

4   Display *Key Tips*.

Hold down the **<Alt>** key on the keyboard.

Notice how *Key Tips* are now displayed on the Ribbon and the Quick Access Toolbar:

5   Use the *Key Tips* to show a print preview using only the keyboard.

The key tips reveal the key you need to press to simulate clicking any of the Ribbon and Quick Access Toolbar icons.

Hold down the **<Alt>** key and press the relevant number to show a print preview (in the above example this is 4).

NB: Your toolbar, and the number you need to press, may look different to the screen grab above. Note that the print preview button will not be on the Quick Access Toolbar unless you added it during: *Lesson 1-14: Customize the Quick Access Toolbar and preview the printout.*

## note

### Keyboard shortcuts are one of the secrets of maximizing productivity with Excel

Many years ago, I took my mouse and stuck it to the back of my monitor with sticky tape.

For a whole day, I struggled to work without it.

The first few hours weren't much fun, but after that my work became faster and faster. It became a challenge to figure out how to do things without the mouse.

You will be far more productive if you can get into the same habit.

These days, there are some things that you simply need the mouse for, and some things that are genuinely faster (or easier) with the mouse.

For many common tasks, however, you'll find it faster and more efficient to work with the keyboard.

The Wealth of Nations

**note**

**The shortcut menu**

If you right-click on a cell, a shortcut menu is displayed.

The shortcut menu doesn't display *everything* that you can do to a cell but Excel's best guesses at the *most likely* things you might want to do.

Because Excel is guessing at the actions you might want to take in the context of what you are doing, the *shortcut menu* is also sometimes referred to as the *contextual menu.*

6 Click the *Back* button  to leave *Backstage View* and return to the worksheet.

7 Use the mouse to select the text *Qatar* in cell B2.

1. Double-click the cell containing the text.

    You'll see the cursor flashing in the cell. This means that you have entered *Edit Mode,* enabling you to change the contents of the cell

2. Position the cursor just after the word *Qatar* and hold down the left mouse button.

3. Drag the mouse across the complete word until it is highlighted like this:

4. Release the mouse button but do not move it away from the text.

8 Observe the *Mini Toolbar.*

Provided you didn't move the mouse cursor away from cell B2 you will now see the mini toolbar above the cell:

9 Use the *Mini Toolbar* to restore the text to non-bold and non-italic.

Click on the Bold **B** and Italic *I* buttons to remove the bold and italic attributes from the text.

Qatar

10 Show a bigger Mini Toolbar with a right-click.

Right-click on *Bermuda* (Cell B6). Notice that, as well as the shortcut menu (see sidebar), you now get an even better Mini Toolbar with a few extra buttons.

11 Remove the underline from Qatar using a shortcut key.

1. Click once on Qatar (cell B2).

2. Press the **<Ctrl>+<U>** keys on the keyboard to remove the underline.

But how can you remember cryptic keyboard shortcuts like **<Ctrl>+<U>**? Fortunately, you don't have to. Hover the mouse over the underline button **U** (on the Home tab of the Ribbon) and you'll see the keyboard shortcut listed in the tooltip.

# Lesson 1-16: Understand views

Views provide different ways to look at your worksheet.

Excel 2016 has three main views. They are:

| View | Icon | What it is used for |
|------|------|---------------------|
| Normal | | This is the view you've been using until now. It's the view most users use all of the time when they are working with Excel. |
| Page Layout | | This view allows you to see (almost) exactly what the printout will look like.<br><br>Unlike running a *Print Preview*, you are able to edit cells just as you can in *Normal* view. |
| Page Break Preview | | A page break indicates when the printer should advance onto a new sheet of paper.<br><br>We'll use this view in: *Lesson 7-5: Insert, delete and preview page breaks* to make sure that the page breaks in the right place. |

1   Open the *Wealth of Nations* sample workbook (if it isn't already open).

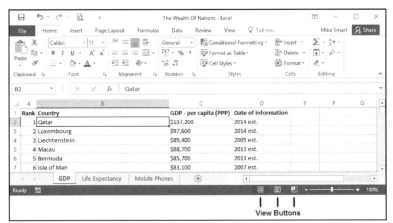

You can change views in two ways:

1.  By clicking one of the View buttons at the bottom of the window (see above).

2.  By clicking one of the buttons in the *Workbook Views* group on the Ribbon's *View* tab (see below).

**The Wealth of Nations**

2   View the GDP worksheet in *Page Layout* view.

1.  Click on the *GDP* tab to select it.

Normal   Page Break   Page   Custom
         Preview      Layout  Views

Workbook Views

2.  Click: View→Workbook Views→Page Layout.

The worksheet is displayed in *Page Layout* view. You are able to see (almost) exactly what will be printed. Headers, footers and margins are all shown.

You are also able to edit the worksheet.

You may wonder why Excel users don't use *Page Layout* view all of the time when editing worksheets. While some users may prefer to do this, most will want to see the maximum amount of data possible on screen and so will prefer the *Normal* view.

3  Select Page Break Preview view.

Click: View→Workbook Views→Page Break Preview.

The worksheet is displayed in *Page Break Preview* view (you may also see a help dialog first).

This view shows each page with a watermark to indicate which sheet of paper it will be printed on:

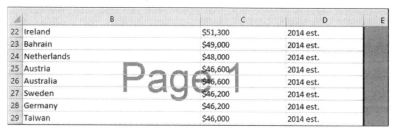

This view also shows the break between each page as a dotted line:

| | A | B | C | D | E |
|---|---|---|---|---|---|
| 49 | | 48 Korea, South | $35,400 | 2014 est. | |
| 50 | | 49 New Zealand | $35,300 | 2014 est. | |
| 51 | | 50 Italy | $35,100 | 2014 est. | |
| 52 | | 51 Saint Pierre and Miquelon | $34,900 | 2006 est. | |
| 53 | | 52 Spain | $33,800 | 2014 est. | |
| 54 | | 53 Malta | $33,200 | 2014 est. | |
| 55 | | 54 Israel | $33,100 | 2014 est. | |
| 56 | | 55 Trinidad and Tobago | $32,200 | 2014 est. | |

It is possible to click and drag the dotted line to change the place where the page breaks.

Adjusting page breaks using click and drag will be covered in depth later in: *Lesson 7-6: Adjust page breaks using Page Break Preview.*

4  Select *Normal* view.

Click: View→Workbook Views→Normal.

# Lesson 1-17: Hide and Show the Formula Bar and Ribbon

Most desktop computers have large display screens. The space taken by the Ribbon and Formula Bar isn't usually a problem.

As you'll discover in: *Session Eight: Cloud Computing,* it is now possible to run Excel 2016 on tablet computers (and even on Smartphones). These devices often have a very small display screen, meaning that the Ribbon and Formula Bar take up too much valuable screen space.

When screen space is limited, you may wish to hide the Formula Bar, Ribbon, or even both, to maximize the number of cells visible on the screen.

1   Open *The Wealth of Nations* from your sample files folder (if it isn't already open) and click the *Life Expectancy* tab.

   Notice that the *Ribbon* and *Formula Bar* are taking up space that could be used to display the contents of the worksheet.

   Consider the screen below:

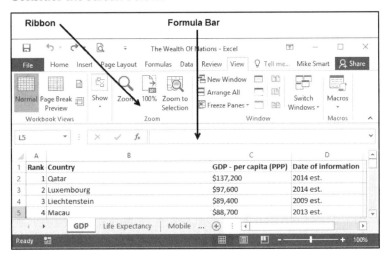

   This is the type of smaller screen you might see on a small tablet device or Smartphone.

   Only five rows are visible, making the worksheet difficult to work with. Hiding the Ribbon, Formula Bar, or both, will free up some valuable screen space.

1   Hide the Formula Bar.

   Click: View→Show→Formula Bar.

   The Formula Bar vanishes:

**The Wealth of Nations**

**2** Use the *Ribbon Display Options* to reduce the Ribbon display to only show tabs.

In: *Lesson 1-12: Use the Ribbon,* you learned how to hide the Ribbon by double-clicking any of the Ribbon tabs (except the *File* tab).

In this lesson, you'll do the same thing in a different way by using the *Ribbon Display Options* button.

1. Click the *Ribbon Display Options* button  at the top right of the Excel window.

   A *Rich Menu* is displayed showing three different ways to hide the Ribbon.

2. Click *Show Tabs* to reduce the Ribbon to a row of tabs.

   The Ribbon now reduces in size to only show tabs. You can still access the Ribbon. It now pops up when you click on any tab and disappears when you click back onto the worksheet.

**3** Completely hide both the Ribbon and Ribbon tabs.

1. Click the *Ribbon Display Options* button  at the top right of the Excel window.

2. Click *Auto-hide Ribbon* on the rich menu.

   This time both the Ribbon, and Ribbon tabs disappear. The worksheet also fills the entire screen. This is called *Full Screen View.*

When you are in *Full Screen View* you can temporarily bring back the Ribbon by clicking at the very top of the screen. The Ribbon then re-appears but vanishes once again when you click back into the body of the worksheet.

**4** Restore the Ribbon and the Formula Bar.

1. Click the *Ribbon Display Options* button  at the top right of the Excel window.

2. Click: *Show Tabs and Commands* on the rich menu.

   The Ribbon is restored.

3. Click: View→Show→Formula Bar.

   The Formula Bar is restored.

## note

### You need an Internet connection to use Excel 2016's help features

In previous versions of Excel, it was possible to access offline help when no Internet connection was available.

Support for offline help has been dropped from Excel 2016. If you have no Internet connection, you will not be able to access Excel's help features.

## note

You can also use the <Alt>+<Q> shortcut keys to instantly move the cursor into the *Tell Me* help box.

## note

### The screen grabs shown in this lesson may differ from those you see on your screen

The Excel 2016 help system is delivered online. This means that Microsoft are able to constantly correct and update help topics.

For this reason, the information you see on your screen may differ from the screen grabs shown in this lesson.

The Wealth of Nations

# Lesson 1-18: Use the Tell Me help system

Microsoft have completely redesigned the help system for Excel 2016 and they really have done a wonderful job. Help is now delivered in a far more sophisticated way than in any previous Excel version. Microsoft call this new feature: *Tell Me* help.

*Tell Me* help is novel because it not only provides information about Excel features but also enables you to execute Ribbon commands directly from inside the help system. This can be a huge time saver.

1  Open the *Wealth of Nations* from your sample files folder (if it isn't already open).

2  Click inside the *Tell Me* help box located on the right-hand side of the Ribbon tabs.

When you click inside the *Tell Me* help box, a flashing cursor appears and you can type a question.

3  Ask Excel how you can save a file.

You learned how to save a file in: *Lesson 1-6: Save a workbook to a local file.* In that lesson, you clicked the *Save* button on the *Quick Access Toolbar.*

Imagine that you have forgotten how to save a file.

Type your question into the *Tell Me* help box.

You could ask Excel the question in several ways. You could use a plain English sentence such as:

Or you could just ask using a single word:

No matter which way you ask the question the result will, in this case, be the same. Excel simply latches on to the *Save* keyword and displays a menu of choices.

Notice that the list is delineated into three sections. The first section contains commands. The second has the type of regular help topic that you are used to reading in traditional help systems, and the third allows you to research the topic using a wider Internet search.

Note that the help features will only work if you are connected to the Internet (see facing page sidebar).

4   Execute the Save command directly from *Tell Me* help.

Click the *Save* command at the top of the menu:

In a traditional help system, you would have expected to see some text explaining how the *Save* command works. Instead *Tell Me* help executes the command. The workbook is saved in the same way it would have been if you had clicked the *Save* button on the *Quick Access Toolbar*.

You can see how useful *Tell Me* help is when you can't remember where a command is situated on the Ribbon and want to execute the command as quickly as possible.

You can also see that it could be dangerous to execute commands that you don't understand.

5   Understand the other *Tell Me* help options.

*Tell Me* help also allows you to execute two other commands and to access regular help that you can read as a reference:

*   *Save As.* You learned how to use the *Save As* command in: *Lesson 1-6: Save a workbook to a local file.*

*   *Save As Other Format.* You learned about different file formats in: *Lesson 1-7: Understand common file formats.*

*   *Save Custom View.* Custom Views is an expert-level skill that isn't used by most Excel users but is covered in depth in the *Expert Skills* book in this series.

*   *Themes.* You're going to learn about *Themes* later, in: *Lesson 4-9: Understand themes.*

6   Read the Excel help topic relating to the Save command.

Click: *Get Help on "Save".*

Links to several topics from the Excel 2016 reference manual are shown. You can click on any of these links to read any of Microsoft's help topics about *Save* related features.

## note

### The screen grabs shown in this lesson may differ from those you see on your screen

The Excel 2016 help system is delivered online. This means that Microsoft can constantly correct and update help topics.

For this reason, the information you see on your screen may differ from the screen grabs shown in this lesson

# Lesson 1-19: Use other help features

*Tell Me* help (discussed in: *Lesson 1-18: Use the Tell Me help* system) is a fantastic brand-new feature for Excel 2016. You'll probably use this most of the time as your help system of first choice.

You can also access the same help topics that are available in *Tell Me Help* directly from their associated Ribbon commands. This can be useful when exploring new and unfamiliar features you may discover on Excel's many Ribbon tabs.

Later, in: *Lesson 2-13: Create functions using Formula AutoComplete*, you'll learn how to access and use Excel's vast function library (that contains over 300 functions such as SUM and AVERAGE). You'll also learn how to access a special Excel help feature that documents the use of each function.

1   Access help using the *Help task pane*.

   1.   Press the **<F1>** key. A *Help task pane* appears at the right of the screen. You'll learn more about task panes later, in: *Lesson 3-7: Use the Multiple Item Clipboard*.

   2.   Type: **Save** into the text box at the top of the page:

   3.   Click the magnifying glass icon or press the **<Enter>** key.

        A list of help topics relating to *Save* topics appears (see sidebar). Note that this list is served from the Internet and is constantly updated.

   4.   Click on any of the help topics displayed to read a detailed description.

2   Get help directly from the Ribbon.

   1.   Close the *Help task pane* by clicking the close button ⊠ in the top right corner of the help pane.

   2.   Click the *Home* tab on the Ribbon and hover the mouse cursor over the drop down arrow to the right of the word *General* in the *Number* group.

   3.   If you keep the mouse still, after a short delay a screen tip pops up providing a short description of what the drop-down list is for:

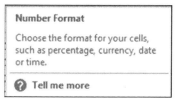

## note

### Why can't you learn Excel using the Help system?

Excel's Help system is designed as a reference work and not as a structured tutorial.

Try reading the detailed help about any of the topics. You'll usually find that to make sense of the help topic you will already need to have learned to use Excel. This is because the writer assumes that you already know how to use Excel.

Many Excel books are also written in this way (as reference books).

This book is a carefully structured *tutorial*. The book is carefully structured to teach Excel by building new skills upon existing skills so that each lesson is easy to understand.

Once you have learned Excel (using Smart Method tutorials) you will find Excel's reference topics easy to understand.

A *Tell me more* hyperlink is also provided offering more detailed help. This will only work if you are connected to the Internet.

4.  Click the *Tell me more* hyperlink.

The *Help task pane* will re-appear displaying a list of help topics relating to *Number Format* topics

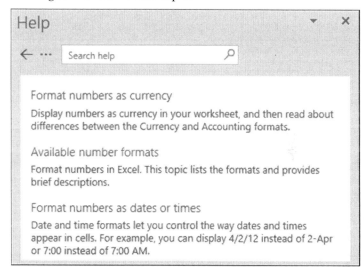

5.  Click on any of the help topics displayed to read a detailed description.

# Session 1: Exercise

In this exercise you'll try to remember the name of each of the Excel screen elements. The answers are on the next page so you might want to recap by turning the page for a little revision before you start.

Keep trying until you are able to name each of the screen elements from memory. You'll be seeing this terminology during the remainder of the book, so it's important that you can correctly identify each element.

A. Ribbon
B. File Button (Backstage)
C. Name bar
D. Quick Access Toolbar
E. Active Cell
F. Formula Bar
G. Column Header
H. Title Bar
I. Tell me help
J. Ribbon Display Options
K. minimise maximise Restore down Close
L. Sheet navigator Tab Scroll
M. Row
N. new sheet tab
O. Add sheet
P. Status Bar
Q. scroll bars
R. Page view

If you need help slide the page to the left

## Session 1: Exercise answers

Ribbon

File button (this opens the Backstage View)

Minimize, Maximize and Close buttons ―

Name Box

Formula Bar

Ribbon Display Options button

Quick Access Toolbar

Column Header

Title bar

Active Cell

Tell Me Help

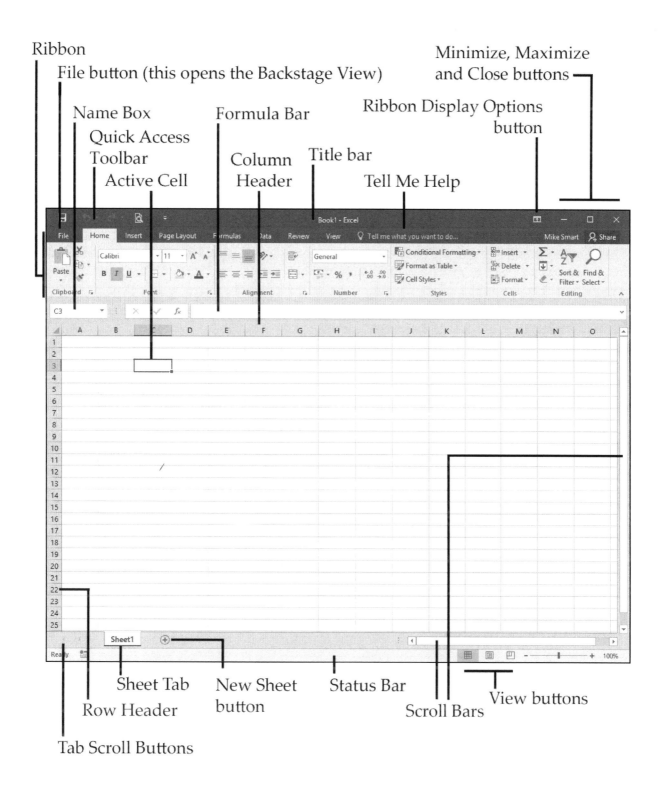

Sheet Tab

New Sheet button

Status Bar

View buttons

Row Header

Scroll Bars

Tab Scroll Buttons

# Session Two: Doing Useful Work with Excel

*Only those who have the patience to do simple things perfectly ever acquire the skill to do difficult things easily.*

***Unknown author***

Now that you've mastered the basics, you are ready to do really useful work with this amazing tool. In this session, you will learn to use all of Excel's basic features properly. This will put you far ahead of anybody that hasn't been formally trained in Excel best practice. You'll be doing simple things, but you'll be doing them perfectly!

Even after years of daily use, many users are unable to properly use Excel's fundamental features. They often reach their goal, but get there in a very inefficient way, simply because they were never taught how to do things correctly. By the end of this session you'll be astonished with how well you are working with Excel.

## Session Objectives

By the end of this session you will be able to:

- Enter text and numbers into a worksheet
- Create a new workbook and view two workbooks at the same time
- Use AutoSum to quickly calculate totals
- Select a range of cells and understand Smart Tags
- Enter data into a range and copy data across a range
- Select adjacent and non-adjacent rows and columns
- Select non-contiguous cell ranges and view summary information
- AutoSelect a range of cells
- Re-size rows and columns
- Use AutoSum to sum a non-contiguous range
- Use AutoSum to calculate average and maximum values
- Create your own formulas
- Create functions using Formula AutoComplete
- Use AutoFill for text and numeric series
- Use AutoFill to adjust formulas and use AutoFill options
- Speed up your AutoFills and create a custom fill series
- Understand linear and exponential series
- Use Flash Fill to split and concatenate text
- Use the zoom control
- Print out a worksheet

# Lesson 2-1: Enter text and numbers into a worksheet

Excel beginners tend to reach for the mouse far too often. One of the keys to productivity with Excel is to avoid using the mouse when entering data. In this lesson, you'll quickly populate a worksheet without using the mouse at all.

1    Open *First Quarter Sales and Profit* from your sample files folder.

| | A | B | C | D |
|---|---|---|---|---|
| 1 | Sales and Profit Report - First Quarter 2016 | | | |
| 2 | | | | |
| 3 | | Jan | Feb | Mar |
| 4 | New York | 22,000 | 29,000 | 19,000 |
| 5 | Los Angeles | | | |
| 6 | London | | | |
| 7 | Paris | | | |
| 8 | Munich | | | |

2    Notice the difference between values and text.

Cells can contain values or text. Values can be numbers, dates or formulas (more on formulas later).

Excel usually does a great job of recognizing when there are values in a cell and when there is text. The giveaway is that text is always (by default) left aligned in the cell and values are right aligned.

Look at the numbers on this worksheet. Notice how they are all right aligned. This lets you know that Excel has correctly recognized them as values and will happily perform mathematical operations using them.

3    Save a value into a cell.

1.   Type the value 42000 into cell B5. Notice that the mouse cursor is still flashing in the cell.

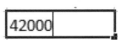

At this stage, the value has not been saved into the cell.

If you change your mind, you can still undo the value by pressing the **<ESC>** key at the top left of your keyboard or by clicking the *Cancel* button ⌧ on the left-hand side of the Formula Bar.

2.   Decide that you want to keep this value in the cell by either pressing the **<Enter>, <Tab>** or an **<Arrow>** key on the keyboard, or by clicking the *Enter* button ☑ on the left-hand side of the Formula Bar.

4    Enter a column of data without using the mouse.

When you enter data into a column, there's no need to use the mouse. Press the **<Enter>** key after each entry and the active cell

First Quarter Sales and Profit

### The many ways of entering numbers

#### Negative numbers

-123.56
(123.56)

#### Currency prefixes

Excel is quite happy for you to prefix a number with a currency symbol. The currency symbol it will accept depends upon how you defined the regional options in your operating system.

$123.56 (works in USA)
£123.56 (works in UK)

In: *Lesson 4-3: Format numbers using built-in number formats* you'll learn an easy method of setting $, £ and € currency prefixes whatever your locale.

#### Commas

12,234,567.78

#### Fractions

You must leave a space between a number and a fraction for this to work.

**6 1/4**
(six, space, one, /, four)

The above will appear on the worksheet as 6.25 after you enter it in this way.

**0 1/4**
(zero, space, one,/,four)

The above will appear on the worksheet as 0.25. The leading zero is needed to prevent Excel from assuming that you are entering a date.

### Formula Bar

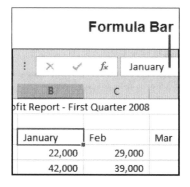

moves to the cell beneath. Try this now with the following January sales data:

1. Type **18,000** into cell B6.

2. Press the **<Enter>** key to move to cell B7.

3. Do the same to enter the following values into the next two cells.

| | A | B | C | D |
|---|---|---|---|---|
| 3 | | Jan | Feb | Mar |
| 4 | New York | 22,000 | 29,000 | 19,000 |
| 5 | Los Angeles | 42,000 | | |
| 6 | London | 18,000 | | |
| 7 | Paris | 35,000 | | |
| 8 | Munich | 12,000 | | |

**5** Enter a row of data without using the mouse.

You can also enter a row of data without using the mouse.

1. Click in cell C5.

2. Type **39,000** and then press the **<Tab>** key on your keyboard.

   The <Tab> key is on the left-hand side of the keyboard above the <Caps Lock> key. Notice how pressing the <Tab> key saves the value into the cell and then moves one cell to the right.

3. Type **43,000** into cell D5 and press the **<Enter>** key.

   You magically move to cell C6, as Excel guesses that you probably want to begin entering data into the next row.

**6** Complete the table without using the mouse.

By using the **<Tab>** or **<Enter>** key in the right places you should be able to complete the table now without using the mouse:

| | A | B | C | D |
|---|---|---|---|---|
| 3 | | Jan | Feb | Mar |
| 4 | New York | 22,000 | 29,000 | 19,000 |
| 5 | Los Angeles | 42,000 | 39,000 | 43,000 |
| 6 | London | 18,000 | 20,000 | 22,000 |
| 7 | Paris | 35,000 | 26,000 | 31,000 |
| 8 | Munich | 12,000 | 15,000 | 13,000 |

**7** Change the text in cell B3 to January.

1. Double-click cell B3. Notice that there is now a flashing cursor in the cell.

2. Type: **uary** on the keyboard to change Jan to January.

3. Press the **<Enter>** key.

**8** Change the text in cell B3 back to **Jan** using the formula bar.

Click once in cell B3 and then change the text in the formula bar back to **Jan** (see sidebar).

**9** Save your work as *First Quarter Sales and Profit-2*.

# Lesson 2-2: Create a new workbook and view two workbooks at the same time

1   Create a new workbook by opening Excel.

    1.   Open Excel.

    2.   Click the *Blank workbook* template to create a new workbook.

        Excel helpfully creates a workbook, unimaginatively named *Book1*. If you already have a workbook open called *Book1*, the new workbook will be called *Book2...* and so on.

        Notice that *Book1 – Excel* is displayed on the *Title Bar.*

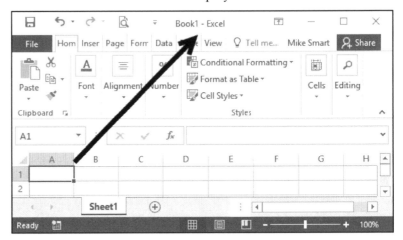

2   Create another new workbook.

    1.   Click the *File* button 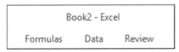 at the top left of the screen and click the *New* button in the left-hand menu.

        You are presented with the same familiar dialog that you see when you start up Excel.

    2.   Click the *Blank workbook* template. A new blank workbook called *Book2* is displayed in the workbook window.

        You could be forgiven for thinking that nothing has happened but you can see that the *Title Bar* now says: *Book2 – Excel,* showing that you are now looking at a different workbook.

<table>
<tr><td colspan="3">Book2 - Excel</td></tr>
<tr><td>Formulas</td><td>Data</td><td>Review</td></tr>
</table>

3   Use the taskbar to move between workbooks.

    You'll see an Excel icon with two right-hand borders at the very bottom-left of the screen (this area is called the Windows taskbar). Hover over this icon with your mouse.  A gallery will pop up showing two workbooks: *Book1* and *Book2.*

# note

## Finding a workbook when many are open

An alternative way to quickly find a workbook when many are open is to click:

View→Window→
Switch Windows

This presents you with a list of all open workbooks.

You can also use the **<Ctrl>+<Tab>** keyboard shortcut to cycle through all open workbooks.

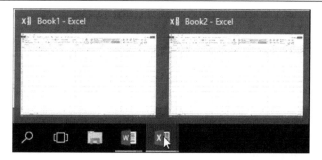

Hover over each item in the pop-up gallery to display each workbook. The only difference you will see is the *Title Bar* changing from *Book1* to *Book2* because both workbooks are empty.

See sidebar for other methods of switching windows.

4  Display both *Book1* and *Book2* at the same time.

1.  Click: View→Window→Arrange All.

The *Arrange Windows* dialog is displayed.

2.  Choose the *Horizontal* arrangement and click the OK button.

Both workbooks are now shown, one above the other. Each window occupies exactly half of your screen:

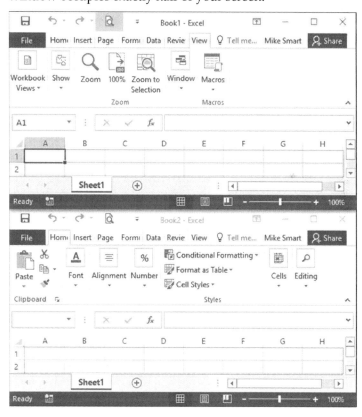

Notice that as you click each workbook window the *Title Bar* and the *Close/Minimize/Restore Down* buttons light up, to show that this is the active window.

5  Close *Book2* and maximize *Book1* to restore the display to a single workbook.

If you've forgotten how to do this, refer back to: *Lesson 1-4: Maximize, minimize, re-size, move and close the Excel window.*

---

# Lesson 2-3: Use AutoSum to quickly calculate totals

Excel's *AutoSum* feature is a really useful and fast way to add the values in a range of cells together.

1    Open *First Quarter Sales and Profit-2* from your sample files folder.

2    In cell A9 type the word **Total** followed by the **<Tab>** key.

The active cell moves to the right and is now in cell B9:

| | A | B | C | D |
|---|---|---|---|---|
| 7 | Paris | 35,000 | 26,000 | 31,000 |
| 8 | Munich | 12,000 | 15,000 | 13,000 |
| 9 | Total | | | |

3    Click: Home→Editing→ Σ (this is the AutoSum button).

Something interesting has happened to the worksheet:

| | A | B | C | D |
|---|---|---|---|---|
| 3 | | Jan | Feb | Mar |
| 4 | New York | 22,000 | 29,000 | 19,000 |
| 5 | Los Angeles | 42,000 | 39,000 | 43,000 |
| 6 | London | 18,000 | 20,000 | 22,000 |
| 7 | Paris | 35,000 | 26,000 | 31,000 |
| 8 | Munich | 12,000 | 15,000 | 13,000 |
| 9 | Total | =SUM(B4:B8) | | |
| 10 | | SUM(**number1**, [number2], ...) | | |

Excel has placed a *marquee* around the number range that AutoSum has guessed you want to work with. The pattern of dots that marks the boundary of the marquee are called the *marching ants.*

The marching ants surround all the numbers in the column above, up to the first blank cell or text cell (in this case, up to the word: Jan).

**=SUM(B4:B8)** is your first glimpse of an Excel *Formula*. Formulas always begin with an equal sign. This formula is using the SUM *function* to compute the Sum (or total) of the values in cells B4 to B8. You'll learn more about functions later, in: *Lesson 2-13: Create functions using Formula AutoComplete.*

4    Press the **<Enter>** key or click the AutoSum button Σ once more to display the total January sales:

| | A | B | C | D |
|---|---|---|---|---|
| 3 | | Jan | Feb | Mar |
| 4 | New York | 22,000 | 29,000 | 19,000 |
| 5 | Los Angeles | 42,000 | 39,000 | 43,000 |
| 6 | London | 18,000 | 20,000 | 22,000 |
| 7 | Paris | 35,000 | 26,000 | 31,000 |
| 8 | Munich | 12,000 | 15,000 | 13,000 |
| 9 | Total | 129,000 | | |

## tip

### Entering an AutoSum using only the keyboard

You can also execute an AutoSum using the keyboard shortcut:

**<Alt>+<=>**

5   Type the word **Total** into cell E3 and press the **<Enter>** key once.

The active cell moves down one row and is now in cell E4.

| | A | B | C | D | E |
|---|---|---|---|---|---|
| 3 | | Jan | Feb | Mar | Total |
| 4 | New York | 22,000 | 29,000 | 19,000 | |
| 5 | Los Angeles | 42,000 | 39,000 | 43,000 | |

6   Use AutoSum to calculate the total sales for New York.

1.   Click: Home→Editing→AutoSum. Σ

This time AutoSum correctly guesses that you want to sum the values to the left of cell E4:

| | B | C | D | E | F |
|---|---|---|---|---|---|
| 3 | Jan | Feb | Mar | Total | |
| 4 | 22,000 | 29,000 | 19,000 | =SUM(B4:D4) | |
| 5 | 42,000 | 39,000 | 43,000 | SUM(number1, [number2], …) | |

## note

### You can also add an AutoSum formula using the Quick Analysis button

Later, in: *Lesson 2-4: Select a range of cells and understand Smart Tags,* you'll learn how to select a range of cells.

Whenever you select a range of cells, a *Quick Analysis* button appears just outside the bottom-right corner of the selected range.

| Jan | Feb |
|---|---|
| 22,000 | |
| 42,000 | |
| 18,000 | |
| 35,000 | |
| 12,000 | |

When you click the *Quick Analysis* button, the *Quick Analysis* dialog appears.

One of the menu options on this dialog is *Totals.*

The *Totals* dialog allows you to add an AutoSum beneath a selected range (in a similar way to the AutoSum button method described in this lesson).

Sum

2.   Press the **<Enter>** key, or click the AutoSum button once more.

| | A | B | C | D | E |
|---|---|---|---|---|---|
| 1 | Sales and Profit Report - First Quarter 2016 | | | | |
| 2 | | | | | |
| 3 | | Jan | Feb | Mar | Total |
| 4 | New York | 22,000 | 29,000 | 19,000 | 70,000 |
| 5 | Los Angeles | 42,000 | 39,000 | 43,000 | |
| 6 | London | 18,000 | 20,000 | 22,000 | |
| 7 | Paris | 35,000 | 26,000 | 31,000 | |
| 8 | Munich | 12,000 | 15,000 | 13,000 | |
| 9 | Total | 129,000 | | | |
| 10 | | | | | |

7   Save your work as *First Quarter Sales and Profit-3.*

# Lesson 2-4: Select a range of cells and understand Smart Tags

1   Open *First Quarter Sales and Profit-3* from your sample files folder (if it isn't already open).

2   Observe the formula behind the value in cell B9.

Click once on cell B9 or move to it with the arrow keys on your keyboard.

Look at the *formula bar* at the top of the screen. Notice that the cell displays the *value* of a calculation and the formula bar shows the *formula* used to calculate the value:

## note

### You can also delete cell contents using the mouse

Pressing the **<Delete>** key is the fastest way to delete cell contents.

You can also delete the contents of a cell using the mouse. To do this:

1.   Right-click the cell.

2.   Click *Clear Contents* from the shortcut menu.

| B9 | ▼ | ⋮ | ✕ | ✓ | *fx* | =SUM(B4:B8) |
|----|---|---|---|---|------|-------------|

| | A | B | C | D |
|---|---|---|---|---|
| 8 | Munich | 12,000 | 15,000 | 13,000 |
| 9 | Total | 129,000 | | |
| 10 | | | | |
| 11 | | Value | | Formula |

3   Delete the contents of cell B9.

Press the **<Delete>** key on your keyboard.

4   Change the word *Total* in cell A9 to *USA Sales* and press the **<Tab>** key once.

The cursor moves to cell B9.

| 8 | Munich | 12,000 |
|---|--------|--------|
| 9 | USA Sales | |

5   Select cells B4:B5 with your mouse.

When the mouse cursor is hovered over a selected cell there are three possible cursor shapes:

| Cursor | What it does |
|--------|--------------|
| ⊹1.6 | The white cross (Select) cursor appears when you hover over the center of the active cell. You can then click and drag to select a range of cells. |
| 1.6 + | The black cross (AutoFill) cursor appears when you hover over the bottom right-hand corner of the active cell. You'll be covering AutoFill later in this session. |
| 1.6 ✛ | The four-headed arrow (Move) cursor appears when you hover over one of the edges of the active cell (but not the bottom right corner). |

**First Quarter Sales and Profit-3**

## note

### Selecting cells with the keyboard

To select cells with the keyboard hold down the **<Shift>** key and then use the **<Arrow>** keys to select the range needed.

## note

### Selecting a large range of cells with the <Shift>-click technique

If you need to select a very large range of cells it is sometimes useful to use this technique:

1. Click the cell in the top left corner of the required range.

2. If necessary, use the scroll bars to make the bottom right corner of the required range visible.

3. Hold down the **<Shift>** key.

4. Click in the bottom right corner of the required range.

Beginners often have difficulty selecting cells and end up moving them or AutoFilling them by mistake.

Carefully position the mouse at the center of cell B4 so that you see the white cross (Select) cursor. When you see the white cross, hold down the left mouse button and drag down to cell B5. You have now selected cells B4 and B5 (in Excel terminology you'd say that you have selected the *range* B4:B5).

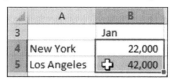

6   Display total USA sales in cell B9.

Because you have selected only the cells containing USA sales, (cells B4:B5), AutoSum can be used to show the value of the selected cells.

Click the AutoSum button $\Sigma$ to display the total value of the selected cells.

USA sales are shown in cell B9.

Notice the small green triangle at the top left of cell B9. This is Excel's way of saying: "I think you may have made a mistake".

7   Inspect a potential error using a Smart Tag.

1.   Click once on cell B9 to make it the active cell.

An *Exclamation Mark* icon appears ◈. This is called a *Smart Tag*.

2.   Hover the mouse cursor over the Smart Tag.

A tip box pops up telling you what Excel thinks you may have done wrong (see below). Of course, in this case, everything is fine.

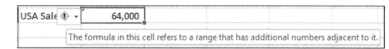

The Smart Tag thinks that perhaps you didn't want to total just the USA sales – but, in this case, the Smart Tag is wrong.

8   Examine the remedial actions suggested by the Smart Tag.

1.   Hover the mouse cursor over the Smart Tag icon ◈.

2.   Click the drop-down arrow that appears.

A list of possible remedial actions is displayed. In this case you can choose *Ignore Error* to remove the green triangle from the corner of the cell.

9   Save your work as *First Quarter Sales and Profit-4.*

# Lesson 2-5: Enter data into a range and copy data across a range

Now that you have mastered the technique of selecting cells, you can use it to speed up data entry.

When you select a range of cells prior to entering data, Excel knows that all data entered belongs in that range. Several key combinations are then available to greatly speed up data entry.

1   Open a new workbook and save it as *Data Range Test*.

2   Select cells B2:D4.

> You learned how to do this in: *Lesson 2-4: Select a range of cells and understand Smart Tags.*

3   Type: **London**

> The text appears in cell B2, the top left cell in the range selected.

4   Press the **<Enter>** Key.

> The cursor moves to cell B3 as it normally would.

5   Type: **Paris** followed by the **<Enter>** key.

> The cursor moves to cell B4 as it normally would.

6   Type: **New York** followed by the **<Enter>** key.

> This time something new happens. The cursor doesn't move to cell B5 as you might expect but jumps to cell C2 instead.

7   Type: **150,000** followed by the **<Enter>** key.

> The value appears in C2 and Excel moves down the column again to cell C3.

8  Press the **<Enter>** key without entering a value to leave C3 blank.

Excel moves down the column to cell C4.

9  Type **225,000** followed by the **<Enter>** key.

The cursor jumps to cell D2.

10  Press **<Shift>+<Enter>** twice to change your mind about leaving the value for Paris blank.

   1. Press **<Shift>+<Enter>** to move backwards to the value for New York.

   2. Press **<Shift>+<Enter>** a second time and you are back to the Paris cell.

| | A | B | C | D | E |
|---|---|---|---|---|---|
| 1 | | | | | |
| 2 | | London | 150,000 | | |
| 3 | | Paris | | | |
| 4 | | New York | 225,000 | | |
| 5 | | | | | |

11  Type **180,000** followed by the **<Tab>** key.

<Tab> moves you across the range, to cell D3.

| | A | B | C | D | E |
|---|---|---|---|---|---|
| 1 | | | | | |
| 2 | | London | 150,000 | | |
| 3 | | Paris | 180,000 | | |
| 4 | | New York | 225,000 | | |
| 5 | | | | | |

You can now appreciate how to use the technique of <Enter>, <Tab>, <Shift>+<Tab> and <Shift>+<Enter> to save a lot of time when entering a whole table of data.

12  Select cells D2:D4.

13  Type **50%** but don't press the <Enter> or <Tab> keys.

The challenge this time is to place the same value into cells D3 and D4 without having to type the value two more times.

14  Press **<Ctrl>+<Enter>**.

The value is replicated into all of the other cells in the selected range.

| | A | B | C | D | E |
|---|---|---|---|---|---|
| 1 | | | | | |
| 2 | | London | 150,000 | 50% | |
| 3 | | Paris | 180,000 | 50% | |
| 4 | | New York | 225,000 | 50% | |
| 5 | | | | | |

15  Click the Save button to save the *Data Range Test* workbook.

The *Save* button is at the left of the *Quick Access Toolbar* at the top left of your screen.

# Lesson 2-6: Select adjacent and non-adjacent rows and columns

1 Open *First Quarter Sales and Profit-4* from your sample files folder (if it isn't already open).

2 Select all of column A.

    1. Hover the mouse cursor over the letter **A** at the top of the column. The column header lights up and the mouse cursor changes to a black down arrow:

    2. Click to select the entire column. The column becomes slightly shaded and a green line surrounds all of the cells.

| | A | B | C | D |
|---|---|---|---|---|
| 1 | Sales and Profit Report - First Quarter 2016 | | | |
| 2 | | | | |
| 3 | | Jan | Feb | Mar |
| 4 | New York | 22,000 | 29,000 | 19,000 |

3 Bold face all of the contents of column A.

Click: Home→Font→Bold **B**

Because the whole column was selected, all of the values become bold faced.

| | A | B | C | D |
|---|---|---|---|---|
| 1 | **Sales and Profit Report - First Quarter 2016** | | | |
| 2 | | | | |
| 3 | | Jan | Feb | Mar |
| 4 | **New York** | 22,000 | 29,000 | 19,000 |
| 5 | **Los Angeles** | 42,000 | 39,000 | 43,000 |
| 6 | **London** | 18,000 | 20,000 | 22,000 |

4 Click: Home→Font→Bold **B** once more to change the type in column A back to normal.

5 Select all of row 4.

    1. Hover the mouse cursor over the number on the left-hand side of row 4. The number button lights up and the mouse cursor changes to a black arrow pointing across the row:

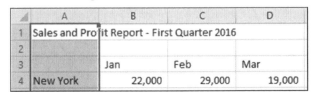

    2. Click to select the row.

6 Select columns B and C.

First Quarter Sales and Profit-4

Hover the mouse cursor over the letter at the top of column B until you see the black down arrow. When you see the arrow, click and drag to the right to select columns B and C.

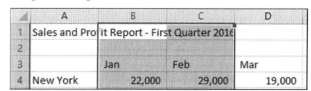

7   Select rows 6 and 7.

1.   Hover over the number at the left of row 6 until you see the black arrow pointing across the row.

2.   When you see the arrow, click and drag down to row 7 to select both rows.

| 5 | Los Angeles | 42,000 | 39,000 |
| 6 | London | 18,000 | 20,000 |
| 7 | Paris | 35,000 | 26,000 |

8   Select columns A, B, C, D and E without dragging the mouse.

Sometimes you will need to select a large number of adjacent columns or rows. You could drag across them, but it is often easier to use the following technique:

1.   Select column A.

2.   Hold down the **<Shift>** key.

3.   Select column E.

Columns A to E are selected.

| | A | B | C | D | E |
|---|---|---|---|---|---|
| 1 | Sales and Profit Report - First Quarter 2016 | | | | |
| 2 | | | | | |
| 3 | | Jan | Feb | Mar | Total |
| 4 | New York | 22,000 | 29,000 | 19,000 | 70,000 |

9   Select rows 4 and 6.

Perhaps you need to perform an operation on two non-adjacent rows. To select rows 4 and 6 you need to:

1.   Select row 4.

2.   Hold down the **<Ctrl>** key on the keyboard.

3.   Select row 6.

| 3 | | Jan | Feb | Mar |
|---|---|---|---|---|
| 4 | New York | 22,000 | 29,000 | 19,000 |
| 5 | Los Angeles | 42,000 | 39,000 | 43,000 |
| 6 | London | 18,000 | 20,000 | 22,000 |
| 7 | Paris | 35,000 | 26,000 | 31,000 |

## important

### You can also Deselect cells using Ctrl-Click

Excel 365 Version 1801 (released in February 2018) added the ability add or remove cells from a selection using **<Ctrl>+<Click>**.

Here's an example of how you can use this (fantastically useful) new feature:

1. Select cells B4:B5

| | A | B |
|---|---|---|
| 3 | | Jan |
| 4 | New York | 22,000 |
| 5 | Los Angeles | 42,000 |
| 6 | London | 18,000 |

2. Hold down the **<Ctrl>** key and then select cells B6:B7.

The selected cells are added to the selection:

| | A | B |
|---|---|---|
| 3 | | Jan |
| 4 | New York | 22,000 |
| 5 | Los Angeles | 42,000 |
| 6 | London | 18,000 |
| 7 | Paris | 35,000 |
| 8 | Munich | 12,000 |

3. Hold down the **<Ctrl>** key and then click on cell B4.

Cell B4 is removed from the selection:

| | A | B |
|---|---|---|
| 3 | | Jan |
| 4 | New York | 22,000 |
| 5 | Los Angeles | 42,000 |
| 6 | London | 18,000 |
| 7 | Paris | 35,000 |
| 8 | Munich | 12,000 |

**First Quarter Sales and Profit-4**

# Lesson 2-7: Select non-contiguous cell ranges and view summary information

Non-contiguous is a very impressive word! It simply means a range of cells that is split across two or more blocks of cells in different parts of the worksheet.

Non-contiguous ranges can be selected using both the mouse and keyboard. The keyboard method may seem a little involved at first but some users prefer it.

1 Open *First Quarter Sales and Profit-4* from your sample files folder (if it isn't already open).

2 Select the contiguous range B4:D8 with the keyboard.

When you need to select a contiguous range with the keyboard here's how it's done:

1. Use the arrow keys on the keyboard to navigate to cell B4.

2. Hold down the **<Shift>** key on the keyboard

3. Still holding the **<Shift>** key down, use the arrow keys on the keyboard to navigate to cell D8

The contiguous range B4:D8 is selected.

| | A | B | C | D | E |
|---|---|---|---|---|---|
| 1 | Sales and Profit Report - First Quarter 2016 | | | | |
| 2 | | | | | |
| 3 | | Jan | Feb | Mar | Total |
| 4 | New York | 22,000 | 29,000 | 19,000 | 70,000 |
| 5 | Los Angeles | 42,000 | 39,000 | 43,000 | |
| 6 | London | 18,000 | 20,000 | 22,000 | |
| 7 | Paris | 35,000 | 26,000 | 31,000 | |
| 8 | Munich | 12,000 | 15,000 | 13,000 | |
| 9 | USA Sales | 64,000 | | | |

3 Select the non-contiguous range B4:B8,D4:D8 using the mouse.

1. Select the range B4:B8 using the mouse.

2. Hold down the **<Ctrl>** key and select the range D4:D8 using the mouse.

The non-contiguous range B4:B8,D4:D8 is selected:

| | A | B | C | D | E |
|---|---|---|---|---|---|
| 3 | | Jan | Feb | Mar | Total |
| 4 | New York | 22,000 | 29,000 | 19,000 | 70,000 |
| 5 | Los Angeles | 42,000 | 39,000 | 43,000 | |
| 6 | London | 18,000 | 20,000 | 22,000 | |
| 7 | Paris | 35,000 | 26,000 | 31,000 | |
| 8 | Munich | 12,000 | 15,000 | 13,000 | |
| 9 | USA Sales | 64,000 | | | |

# note

## "Extend Selection" mode and "Add to Selection" mode

In this lesson, you use Excel's *Add to Selection* mode.

There's also an *Extend Selection* mode that can be used instead of the <Shift> key (in this lesson) but it is not recommended as it is less efficient.

**Extend Selection Mode**

The <F8> key switches *Extend Selection Mode* on and off.

Try pressing the <F8> key once. You'll see the words *Extend Selection* appear at the bottom left of the screen:

When you press the <F8> key once again, the words: *Extend Selection* disappear showing that you have switched this mode off.

In this lesson, you could have selected cells B4:B8 using *Extend Selection* mode like this:

1. Navigate to cell B4.

2. Press the <F8> key to enter *Extend Selection* mode.

3. Use the <Down Arrow> key to move down the column to cell B8.

4. Press the <F8> key to switch *Extend Selection* mode off.

**Add to Selection mode**

This mode is far more useful and is switched on and off by pressing the <Shift>+<F8> key combination.

*Add to Selection* mode keeps any selected cells selected as you navigate to a new position on the worksheet using the keyboard.

You don't need to explicitly turn this mode off as Excel will do this for you.

4  Select the same non-contiguous range with the keyboard.

This is a little more involved than using the simple <Shift>+<Arrow keys> method used earlier.

Here's how it's done:

1. Use the arrow keys on the keyboard to navigate to cell B4

2. Hold down the <Shift> key and then use the <Down Arrow> key to move down the column to cell B8.

3. Press: <Shift>+<F8> to enter *Add to Selection* mode (see sidebar).

4. Use the arrow keys to navigate to cell D4.

5. Hold down the <Shift> key and then use the <Down Arrow> key to move down the column to cell D8.

The non-contiguous range B4:B8,D4:D8 is selected:

| | A | B | C | D | E |
|---|---|---|---|---|---|
| 3 | | Jan | Feb | Mar | Total |
| 4 | New York | 22,000 | 29,000 | 19,000 | 70,000 |
| 5 | Los Angeles | 42,000 | 39,000 | 43,000 | |
| 6 | London | 18,000 | 20,000 | 22,000 | |
| 7 | Paris | 35,000 | 26,000 | 31,000 | |
| 8 | Munich | 12,000 | 15,000 | 13,000 | |
| 9 | USA Sales | 64,000 | | | |

5  Obtain a total sales figures for January and March using the status bar.

The status bar contains summary information for the currently selected range.

Look at the bottom right of your screen. You can see the average sales and total sales (sum of sales) for January and March:

Average: 25,700   Count: 10   Sum: 257,000

6  View the maximum and minimum sales for January and March using the status bar.

Right-click the status bar and click *Maximum* and *Minimum* on the shortcut menu.

| | | |
|---|---|---|
| ✓ | A̲verage | 25,700 |
| ✓ | C̲ount | 10 |
| | Numerical Coun̲t | |
| ✓ | Mi̲nimum | 12,000 |
| ✓ | Ma̲ximum | 43,000 |
| ✓ | S̲um | 257,000 |

The status bar now also displays maximum and minimum values.

Average: 25,700   Count: 10   Min: 12,000   Max: 43,000   Sum: 257,000

7  Close the workbook without saving.

# Lesson 2-8: AutoSelect a range of cells

1 Open *Sales Report* from your sample files folder.

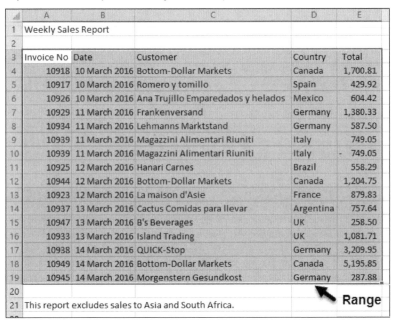

This report contains a single block of cells in the range A3 to E19.

When data is arranged in this way it is referred to as a *Range*.

You will often want to select a row or column of cells within a range, or even the entire range.

You can select ranges by using any of the techniques covered so far but this could be very time consuming if the range encompassed hundreds, or even thousands, of rows and columns.

In this lesson, you'll learn how to select range rows, range columns and entire ranges with a few clicks of the mouse.

2 Select all cells within the range to the right of cell A7.

1. Click in cell A7 to make it the active cell.

2. Hover over the right-hand border of cell A7 until you see the four-headed arrow cursor shape.

3. When you see this cursor shape, hold down the **<Shift>** key and double-click.

All cells to the right of A7, but within the range, are selected.

3 Select all cells within the range except the header row.

1. Click in cell A4 to make it the active cell.

2. Hover over the right-hand border of cell A4 until you see the four-headed arrow cursor shape.

**Sales Report**

https://TheSmartMethod.com

# note

## Other ways to AutoSelect a range

### Using the keyboard

Here's how you would select the entire range in the *Weekly Sales Report* (excluding the header row) using the keyboard method.

Make cell A4 the active cell by navigating to it with the **<Arrow>** keys.

1.  Press: **<Ctrl>+<Shift>+ <DownArrow>**

    Cells A4:A19 are selected.

2.  Press: **<Ctrl>+<Shift>+ <RightArrow>**

    The entire range (excluding the header row) is selected.

### Using shortcut keys

The shortcut keys method is the fastest way to select the entire range *including* the header row.

1.  Click anywhere inside the range.

2.  Press: **<Ctrl>+<A>**

    The entire range (including the header row) is selected.

### From the Ribbon

You can select the entire range including the header row (described as the *Current Region* in the dialog) using the Ribbon. This method is the least efficient way to select an entire range.

Make sure that the active cell is within the range.

1.  Click:

    **Home→Editing→ Find & Select→ Go To Special...**

    The *Go To Special* dialog is displayed.

2.  Click the *Current Region* option button and then click the OK button.

The entire range (including the header row) is selected.

3.  When you see this cursor shape, hold down the **<Shift>** key and double-click.

    All cells to the right of cell A4, but within the range, are selected.

4.  Hover over the bottom border of the selected cells until you see the four-headed arrow cursor shape.

5.  When you see this cursor shape, hold down the **<Shift>** key and double-click.

The entire range (except the header row) is selected.

You can also use this technique to select cells to the left of the active cell or above the active cell.

4   Close the workbook without saving.

**First Quarter Sales and Profit-4**

# Lesson 2-9: Re-size rows and columns

1 Open *First Quarter Sales and Profit-4* from your sample files folder.

Notice that columns B, C, D and E are far too wide for their contents. It would be useful to make them narrower to keep the worksheet compact.

2 Re-size column B so that it is just wide enough to contain the January sales figures.

1. Hover the mouse cursor over the line separating the letters B and C until you see the *re-size* cursor shape:

2. When you see the *re-size* cursor shape, keep the mouse still and then click and drag to the left. Column B will re-size as you drag. Make it narrower so that the values just fit in the column. Notice that the column width is displayed in characters and pixels (see sidebar) as you drag.

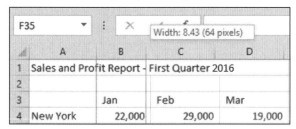

3 Re-size column B so that it is too narrow to contain the January sales figures.

Notice that when the column isn't wide enough to contain the contents, hash signs are shown instead of values (if you're used to hashes being called **pound signs** or **number signs** see the sidebar).

| | A | B | C | D | E |
|---|---|---|---|---|---|
| 1 | Sales and Profit Report - First Quarter 2016 | | | | |
| 2 | | | | | |
| 3 | | Jan | Feb | Mar | Total |
| 4 | New York | ### | 29,000 | 19,000 | 70,000 |

4 Automatically re-size column B so that it is a perfect fit for the widest cell in the column.

1. Hover over the line separating the letters B and C until you see the re-size cursor shape:

2. When you see this shape, double-click to automatically re-size column B.

5 Automatically re-size every column in the worksheet in one operation.

## note

### Other ways to re-size rows and columns

You can also re-size rows and columns using the Ribbon.

Click: Home→Cells→Format.

A drop-down menu appears.

You can use the *Row Height* and *Column Width* options to set the row or column to a specific number of characters (for column widths) or points (for row height).

You can also use the *AutoFit Row Height* and *AutoFit Column Width* options to automatically re-size the row or column (you achieved this more efficiently with a double-click in the lesson).

*Default Width…* allows you to set a new width for all columns but will not affect columns that have already been manually resized.

## note

### Making several columns or rows the same size

Select the columns that you want to resize and then click and drag the intersection of any of the selected columns.

When the mouse button is released, this will make each of the selected columns exactly the same width.

1. Select every cell in the worksheet by clicking the *Select All* button in the top left corner of the worksheet (you can also do this by clicking in any blank cell and then pressing **<Ctrl>+<A>**).

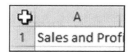

2. Hover over the intersection of any two columns until you see the re-size cursor shape and then double-click.

Every column is now perfectly sized.

Notice that AutoFit has done its job rather too well. Column A is now wide enough to accommodate all of the text in cell A1.

|   | A | B |
|---|---|---|
| 1 | Sales and Profit Report - First Quarter 2016 | |

6 Automatically re-size column A so that it is only wide enough to contain the longest city name (Los Angeles).

1. Select cells A4:A9.

2. Click: Home→Cells→Format→AutoFit Column Width.

This time the column is automatically sized so that it is wide enough to contain all of the text in the selected cells.

|   | A | B | C | D | E |
|---|---|---|---|---|---|
| 1 | Sales and Profit Report - First Quarter 2016 | | | | |
| 2 | | | | | |
| 3 | | Jan | Feb | Mar | Total |
| 4 | New York | 22,000 | 29,000 | 19,000 | 70,000 |
| 5 | Los Angeles | 42,000 | 39,000 | 43,000 | |

Notice that the text has spilled over from cell A1 into the adjoining columns B, C, D and E. This always happens when a cell contains text and the adjacent cells are empty.

7 Manually re-size row 3 so that it is about twice as tall as the other rows.

Do this in the same way you re-sized the column but, this time, hover between the intersection of rows 3 and 4 until you see the re-size cursor shape, and then click and drag downwards.

8 Auto-resize row 3 so that it is the same size as the other rows again.

1. Hover over the line separating the numbers 3 and 4 until you see the re-size cursor shape.

2. When you see this shape, double-click to automatically re-size row 3.

9 Close Excel without saving.

# Lesson 2-10: Use AutoSum to sum a non-contiguous range

In: *Lesson 2-7: Select non-contiguous cell ranges and view summary information*, you learned how to view the sum of January and March sales using the status bar. But how can you put that value onto the worksheet?

Now that you have the hang of selecting non-contiguous ranges, you can use this skill in conjunction with your AutoSum skills to create a formula that will calculate the total of a non-contiguous range.

1   Open *First Quarter Sales and Profit*-4 from your sample files folder.

2   Enter the text: **Jan/Mar Sales** in cell A10 and press the <Tab> key.

The active cell moves to cell B10.

3   Re-size column A so that it is wide enough to contain the text.

1.   Hover over the line separating the letters A and B until you see the re-size cursor shape:

2.   When you see this shape, keep the mouse still and then click and drag to the right. Column A will re-size as you drag. Make it wider so that the words *Jan/Mar Sales* comfortably fit in the column:

| | A | B | C | D |
|---|---|---|---|---|
| 1 | Sales and Profit Report - First Quarter 2016 | | | |
| 2 | | | | |
| 3 | | Jan | Feb | Mar |
| 4 | New York | 22,000 | 29,000 | 19,000 |
| 5 | Los Angeles | 42,000 | 39,000 | 43,000 |
| 6 | London | 18,000 | 20,000 | 22,000 |
| 7 | Paris | 35,000 | 26,000 | 31,000 |
| 8 | Munich | 12,000 | 15,000 | 13,000 |
| 9 | USA Sales | 64,000 | | |
| 10 | Jan/Mar Sales | | | |

4   Use AutoSum to calculate the total sales for January and March in cell B10.

1.   Click Home→Editing→  (the AutoSum button).

An AutoSum appears in cell B10 but it isn't the formula you need. AutoSum guesses that you simply want to repeat the value in the USA Sales cell.

| 8 | Munich | 12,000 | 15,000 | 13,000 |
|---|---|---|---|---|
| 9 | USA Sales | 64,000 | | |
| 10 | Jan/Mar Sales | =SUM(B9) | | |
| 11 | | SUM(**number1**, [number2], ...) | | |

2.   Select the range B4:B8 with the mouse.

**First Quarter Sales and Profit-4**

3. Hold down the **<Ctrl>** key and select the range D4:D8 with the mouse.

Notice that the non-contiguous range **B4:B8,D4:D8** is shown in the AutoSum's formula:

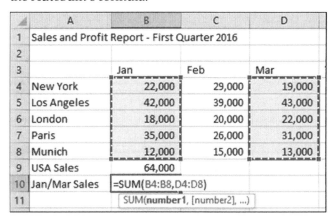

4. Press the **<Enter>** key or click the AutoSum button $\Sigma$ again to show the sales for January and March in cell B10.

5 Save your work as *First Quarter Sales and Profit-5*.

# Lesson 2-11: Use AutoSum to calculate average and maximum values

1 Open *First Quarter Sales and Profit-5* from your sample files folder (if it isn't already open).

2 Delete cells E3:E4.

Select cells E3 and E4 and press the **<Delete>** key on your keyboard.

3 Type the word *Average* in cell E3 and press the **<Enter>** key.

The cursor moves to cell E4:

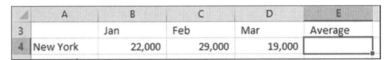

| | A | B | C | D | E |
|---|---|---|---|---|---|
| 3 | | Jan | Feb | Mar | Average |
| 4 | New York | 22,000 | 29,000 | 19,000 | |

4 Use AutoSum to create a formula that will show the average New York sales in cell E4.

1. Click: Home→Editing→AutoSum→Drop-down arrow (see sidebar).

   A drop-down menu is displayed showing different ways in which AutoSum can operate upon a range of cells:

2. Click *Average*.

   Excel generates an AVERAGE function and inserts the cell range B4:D4. This is exactly what you want:

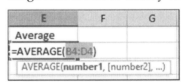

| E | F | G |
|---|---|---|
| Average | | |
| =AVERAGE(B4:D4) | | |
| AVERAGE(**number1**, [number2], ...) | | |

3. Press the **<Enter>** key or click the AutoSum button $\Sigma$ again to see the average sales for New York:

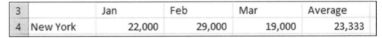

| 3 | | Jan | Feb | Mar | Average |
|---|---|---|---|---|---|
| 4 | New York | 22,000 | 29,000 | 19,000 | 23,333 |

5 Type the word: **Maximum** into cell F3 and then press the **<Enter>** key.

6 Use AutoSum to create a formula in cell F4 that will show the Maximum New York Sales for this period.

1. Place an AutoSum in cell F4 but this time, choose *Max* from the drop-down menu.

   This time you have a small problem. AutoSum is including the average value (23,333) in the calculation.

**First Quarter Sales and Profit-5**

| | B | C | D | E | F |
|---|---|---|---|---|---|
| | Jan | Feb | Mar | Average | Maximum |
| | 22,000 | 29,000 | 19,000 | 23,333 | =MAX(B4:E4) |

2. Select cells B4:D4 with the mouse

The marquee now covers the correct cells.

| 3 | | Jan | Feb | Mar | Average | Maximum |
|---|---|---|---|---|---|---|
| 4 | New York | 22,000 | 29,000 | 19,000 | 23,333 | =MAX(B4:D4) |

Notice that the MAX function is now working with the (correct) range B4:D4.

3. Press the **<Enter>** key or click the AutoSum button $\Sigma$ once more to see the maximum sales the New York office managed during the first quarter of the year:

| 3 | | Jan | Feb | Mar | Average | Maximum |
|---|---|---|---|---|---|---|
| 4 | New York | 22,000 | 29,000 | 19,000 | 23,333 | 29,000 |

**7** Change the words *USA Sales* in cell A9 back to *Sales* and press the **<Tab>** key.

**8** Press the **<F2>** key on the keyboard (or double-click cell B9) to bring back the marquee (shown as a blue box).

**9** Adjust the marquee using click and drag so that all offices are included in the Sales total.

Notice that there is a small blue spot on each corner of the range. These are called *sizing handles*.

1. Hover the mouse cursor over the bottom right (or bottom left) sizing handle until the cursor shape changes to a double-headed arrow. It is really important that you see the double-headed arrow and not the four-headed arrow or white cross.

| 4 | New York | 22,000 |
|---|---|---|
| 5 | Los Angeles | 42,000 |

2. When you see the double headed arrow click and drag with the mouse down to cell B8.

3. Release the mouse button.

4. Press the **<Enter>** key or click the AutoSum button $\Sigma$ again.

| | A | B |
|---|---|---|
| 3 | | Jan |
| 4 | New York | 22,000 |
| 5 | Los Angeles | 42,000 |
| 6 | London | 18,000 |
| 7 | Paris | 35,000 |
| 8 | Munich | 12,000 |
| 9 | Sales | 129,000 |
| 10 | Jan/Mar Sales | 257,000 |

**10** Save your work as *First Quarter Sales and Profit-6*.

# Lesson 2-12: Create your own formulas

The AutoSum tool is very useful for quickly inserting SUM(), AVERAGE(), COUNT(), MAX() and MIN() formulas into cells. Many Excel users never get any further with their formulas than this.

In this session, you'll create your own formulas without the use of AutoSum. You'll be amazed at how easy it is.

1 Open *First Quarter Sales and Profit*-6 from your sample files folder (if it isn't already open).

2 Select cells A10:B10 and press the **<Delete>** key once.

The previous contents of cells A10:B10 are removed.

3 Type the word **Costs** into cell A11 and **Profit** into cell A12.

4 Type the value **83,000** into cell B11 and press the **<Enter>** key to move down to cell B12.

| 11 | Costs | 83,000 |
|----|-------|--------|
| 12 | Profit | |

5 Enter a formula into cell B12 to compute the profit made in January.

   1. Type: **=B9-B11** into cell B12.

   2. Press the **<Enter>** key.

The profit for January is displayed:

| 9 | Sales | 129,000 |
|----|-------|---------|
| 10 | | |
| 11 | Costs | 83,000 |
| 12 | Profit | 46,000 |

## important

Formulas automatically recalculate whenever any of the cells in the formula change.

For example: If you were to change the *Paris* sales to 45,000 this would cause cell B9 to re-calculate to 139,000.

Because B9 has changed this would, in turn, cause the profit to recalculate to 56,000.

6 Enter the formula again using the mouse to select cell references.

The method that you have just used to enter the formula works just fine but it isn't the best method. Eventually you will make a mistake. For example, you could easily type **=B8-B11** resulting in an incorrect answer.

To eliminate such errors, you should always select cell references visually rather than simply typing them in. You can visually select cells using either the mouse or the keyboard. First, you'll use the mouse method.

   1. Click in cell B12 and press the **<Delete>** key on the keyboard to clear the old formula.

   2. Press the equals <=> key on the keyboard.

   3. Click once on the value 129,000 in cell B9.

   4. Press the minus <-> key on the keyboard.

**First Quarter Sales and Profit-6**

5. Click once on the value 83,000 in cell B11.

6. Press the <Enter> key on the keyboard.

If you followed the above steps carefully you will see that you have created the same formula but with a much lower possibility of making a mistake.

7  Enter the formula again using the visual keyboard technique.

The very best Excel experts hardly use the mouse. You waste valuable seconds every time you reach for the mouse.

Here's the expert technique of visual selection via keyboard:

1. Use the arrow keys to navigate to cell B12 and then press the <Delete> key on the keyboard to clear the old formula.

2. Press the <=> key on the keyboard.

3. Press the <Up Arrow> key three times to move to cell B9.

4. Press the <-> key on the keyboard.

5. Press the <Up Arrow> key once to move to cell B11.

6. Press the <Enter> key on the keyboard.

8  Enter a formula that uses the multiplication operator to calculate a 10% bonus paid upon profits.

This employer is very generous and pays the staff ten percent of all profits as an incentive bonus.

In cell A13 type the words: **10% Bonus** and then press the <Tab> key on the keyboard to move to cell B13.

The multiplication operator is not an X as you might expect but an asterisk (*). The other Excel operators are shown in the sidebar.

You need to press <Shift>+<8> to enter an asterisk. If you are using a full size keyboard with a numeric keypad at the right-hand side you can also use the numeric keypad's <*> key.

Whichever key you use you'll still see an asterisk in the formula.

Use either the *mouse selection* technique or the *visual keyboard* technique to enter the formula shown below into cell B13 and then press the <Enter> key to see how much bonus was earned:

| | A | B |
|---|---|---|
| 11 | Costs | 83,000 |
| 12 | Profit | 46,000 |
| 13 | 10% Bonus | =B12*0.1 |

Note that multiplying a value by 0.1 calculates ten percent of the value. You'll learn more about calculating percentages later, in: *Lesson 4-3: Format numbers using built-in number formats.*

| | | |
|---|---|---|
| 11 | Costs | 83,000 |
| 12 | Profit | 46,000 |
| 13 | 10% Bonus | 4,600 |

9  Save your work as *First Quarter Sales and Profit-7.*

**important**

**The Excel Operators**

| | Name | Example |
|---|---|---|
| + | Addition | 1+2 |
| - | Subtraction | 7-5 |
| * | Multiplication | 6*3 |
| / | Division | 15/5 |
| % | Percent | 25% |
| ^ | Exponentiation | 4^2 |

## note

### Excel automatically adds closing brackets to functions

If you type:

**=SUM(B4:B5**

... and then press the **<Enter>** key, Excel will automatically add the closing bracket for you resulting in:

**=SUM(B4:B5)**

First Quarter Sales and Profit-7

# Lesson 2-13: Create functions using Formula AutoComplete

1    Open *First Quarter Sales and Profit-7* from your sample files folder (if it isn't already open).

2    Type the words **USA Sales** into cell A15 and **European Sales** into cell A16.

3    If necessary, re-size column A so that it is wide enough for the words *European Sales* to fit within the column.

You learned how to do this in: *Lesson 2-9: Re-size rows and columns.*

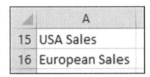

4    Click into cell B15 and type **=S** into the cell.

Something amazing happens:

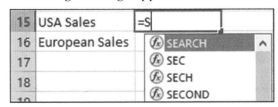

A list appears showing every function in the Excel function library beginning with S. This feature is called *Formula AutoComplete* (if AutoComplete didn't display as expected see the facing-page sidebar).

You've already encountered the SUM(), AVERAGE() and MAX() functions courtesy of AutoSum.

You may be pleased (or dismayed) to know that there are over 300 functions in the Excel function library. The good news is that most untrained Excel users only ever get to understand SUM() and AVERAGE().

When you typed =S Excel listed all functions beginning with S.

5    Continue typing: **=SU**

Notice that the list now only shows functions beginning with SU and look... there's the *SUM()* function you need three down in the list.

You could simply click on the Sum() function with the mouse but let's work like an Excel pro and use the keyboard.

6    Press the **<Down Arrow>** key twice to move the cursor over the SUM function.

The SUM function now has a tip telling you what the function does:

# note

### Enabling and disabling AutoComplete

As with so many other features, Microsoft allows you to turn this very useful feature off.

You'd never want to do this but you may work on a machine that has had Formula AutoComplete switched off and you need to turn it on again.

Click: File→Options→Formulas and make sure that the *Formula AutoComplete* box is checked.

# note

### The syntax box

The Syntax box tells you which arguments (sometimes called parameters) the function needs.

SUM(**number1**, [number2], ...)

The first argument has no square brackets meaning that you can't leave it out.

The second argument (shown in square brackets) is optional.

The third argument is an ellipsis (a row of three dots). This means that you could continue with more arguments such as [number3], [number4] etc.

For such a simple function as SUM() the syntax box is hardly needed but later you'll encounter functions that require several arguments and then the syntax box will be invaluable.

| 15 | USA Sales | 64,000 |
| 16 | European Sales | 65,000 |

7   Display Excel's help topic for the SUM() function.

The tip tells you a little about the SUM() function but to get the full story press the **<F1>** key while SUM is still highlighted in the dropdown list.

The Excel help system opens showing detailed help for the SUM() function.

Read the help text if you are interested and then close the help window.

Notice that Excel has now left you with only *=SU* in the cell.

8   Complete the formula by typing: **M(**

Notice that a little box has appeared beneath the function. This box displays the *Syntax* of the SUM function (see sidebar for more information).

9   Select the cells that you need to sum (cells B4:B5) with the mouse or keyboard.

If you want to be a real pro you should select them with the keyboard. To do this:

1.  Press the **<Up Arrow>** key repeatedly until you reach cell B4.

2.  Hold down the **<Shift>** key and press the **<Down Arrow>** key once to select cells B4:B5.

10   Type a closing bracket to complete the formula and then press the <Enter> key.

The total USA sales are displayed in cell B15.

11   Use the same technique to create a SUM() function in cell B16 to show the total European sales (cells B6:B8).

1.  Click in cell B16.

2.  Type **=SU**

3.  Press the **<Down Arrow>** key twice to move the cursor over the SUM function.

4.  Press the **<Tab>** key to automatically enter the SUM function into cell B16.

5.  Select the range B6:B8.

6.  Type the closing bracket (this isn't actually necessary – see sidebar facing page).

7.  Press the **<Enter>** key.

The formula should now be: **=SUM(B6:B8)**

12   Save your work as *First Quarter Sales and Profit-8*.

# Lesson 2-14: Use AutoFill for text and numeric series

1    Open *First Quarter Sales and Profit-8* from your sample files folder (if it isn't already open).

2    Delete the text **Feb** and **Mar** from cells C3:D3.

Select cells C3:D3 and then press the **<Delete>** key on your keyboard.

3    Make B3 the active cell

Click once inside cell B3. Notice that there is a green border around the cell and a spot on the bottom right-hand corner. This is the AutoFill handle. If you don't see it, refer to the sidebar.

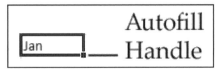

4    Hover over the AutoFill handle with your mouse until the cursor shape changes to a black cross.

Many of my students have great difficulty with this when they try it for the first time.

- You don't want the four-headed arrow: ✥ – that would move the cell.

- You don't want the white cross: ⇧ – that would select the cell.

- You want the black cross: ✚ – the AutoFill cursor.

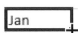

5    When the black cross cursor is visible, hold down the mouse button and drag your mouse to the right to AutoFill the other months: **Feb** and **Mar**.

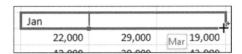

Notice the tip that appears as you drag, previewing the month that will appear in each cell.

When you release the mouse button, the name of each month appears in cells C3 and D3.

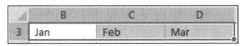

6    Type: **Monday** into cell A18 and AutoFill down to cell A24 to show the days of the week.

(If you are not using an English language version of Excel you will need to type **Monday** in your own language).

**First Quarter Sales and Profit-8**

7  In cell B18 type the number **1** and in cell B19 type the number **2**.

8  Select cells B18 and B19.

9  AutoFill down to B24 to create sequential numbers:

| | A | B |
|---|---|---|
| 18 | Monday | 1 |
| 19 | Tuesday | 2 |
| 20 | Wednesday | 3 |

10  In cell C18 type **9** and in cell C19 type **18**.

11  Select cells C18 and C19.

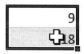

12  AutoFill down to cell B24 to create the nine times table.

| | A | B | C |
|---|---|---|---|
| 18 | Monday | 1 | 9 |
| 19 | Tuesday | 2 | 18 |
| 20 | Wednesday | 3 | 27 |

These are both examples of linear series. You'll learn more about linear series later, in: *Lesson 2-18: Understand linear and exponential* .

13  Use AutoFill to create sequential dates.

1.  Type: **01-Jan-16** into cell D18.

2.  Type: **02-Jan-16** into cell D19.

3.  Select cells D18:D19.

4.  AutoFill down to D24 to create sequential dates.

14  Use AutoFill to quickly copy text.

Sometimes you will want to duplicate the value from one cell into many others to the right of, left of, beneath, or above the active cell.

When a cell containing text is the active cell and it isn't defined as a *fill series* (the built-in fill series are days of the week and months of the year), AutoFill will simply duplicate the contents of the cell.

Type the text **Adjusted** into cell E18 and then AutoFill it down as far as cell E24. The same text is now shown in each of the cells:

| | A | B | C | D | E |
|---|---|---|---|---|---|
| 18 | Monday | 1 | 9 | 01-Jan-16 | Adjusted |
| 19 | Tuesday | 2 | 18 | 02-Jan-16 | Adjusted |
| 20 | Wednesday | 3 | 27 | 03-Jan-16 | Adjusted |
| 21 | Thursday | 4 | 36 | 04-Jan-16 | Adjusted |
| 22 | Friday | 5 | 45 | 05-Jan-16 | Adjusted |
| 23 | Saturday | 6 | 54 | 06-Jan-16 | Adjusted |
| 24 | Sunday | 7 | 63 | 07-Jan-16 | Adjusted |

15  Save your work as *First Quarter Sales and Profit-9*.

# Lesson 2-15: Use AutoFill to adjust formulas

AutoFill can save you a lot of time when extending or copying text and number sequences. But the story's not over yet.

AutoFill's ability to copy and adjust formulas is one of the most powerful tools in Excel's impressive armory.

1   Open *First Quarter Sales and Profit-9* from your sample files folder (If it isn't already open).

2   Consider the formula in cell B9.

Click onto cell B9 and view the formula displayed in the formula bar (the formula bar is at the top right of the screen grab below).

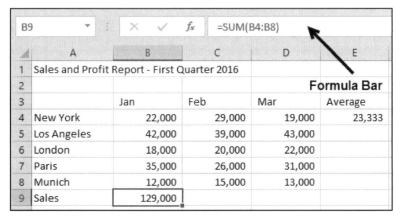

The formula is **=SUM(B4:B8).** AutoSum created it for you in: *Lesson 2-3: Use AutoSum to quickly calculate totals.* The formula uses the SUM() function to add together the values in the range B4:B8.

Think about the formula that would work in cell C9 (the total sales for February). It would be: **=SUM(C4:C8)**. Similarly the formula that would work in cell D9 (the total sales for March) would be **=SUM(D4:D8).**

As you move to the right, all that is needed is to increment the letter for each cell reference in the formula and you'll get the right answer every time.

AutoFill is very clever and realizes this. When you AutoFill a cell containing a formula to the right, AutoFill increments the letters in each cell reference.

*Most of the time* that is exactly what we want.

Later, in *Lesson 3-12: Understand absolute and relative cell references,* and *Lesson 3-13: Understand mixed cell references* you'll learn how to fine-tune the way in which AutoFill adjusts cell references. This will allow you to implement some more advanced AutoFill techniques.

3   AutoFill cell B9 to the right as far as cell D9.

You learned how to do this in: *Lesson 2-14: Use AutoFill for text and numeric series.*

**First Quarter Sales and Profit-9**

You may see a row of hashes in cell C9 and/or D9. This is because the value may be too wide to fit in the cell. If this is the case, AutoFit the column using the skills learned in: *Lesson 2-9: Re-size rows and columns.*

The correct answers for *Feb* and *Mar* sales are shown on the worksheet. Click on the *Feb* total cell (C9) and look at the formula in the formula bar.

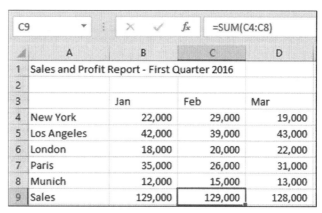

You can see that AutoFill has done its job perfectly, creating the sum of the values in cells C4:C8. Our five branches have sold exactly the same amount in both January and February, but a little less in March.

4    Consider the formula in cell E4.

Click onto cell E4 and view the formula displayed in the formula bar.

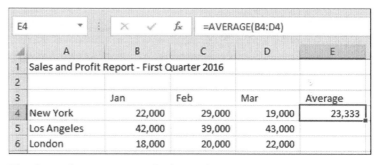

The formula is **=AVERAGE(B4:D4).** AutoSum created it for you in:

*Lesson 2-11: Use AutoSum to calculate average and maximum values.*

Think about the formula that would work in cell E5 (the average sales for Los Angeles). It would be: **=AVERAGE(B5:D5)**. Similarly the formula that would work in cell E6 (the average sales for London) would be **=AVERAGE(B6:D6)**.

As you move downward, all that is needed is to increment the number for each cell reference in the formula. This is exactly what AutoFill will do.

| E | F |
| --- | --- |
| Average | Maximum |
| 23,333 | 29,000 |
| 41,333 | 43,000 |
| 20,000 | 22,000 |
| 30,667 | 35,000 |
| 13,333 | 15,000 |

5    AutoFill cell E4 down to E8 to see the Average sales for each branch.

6    AutoFill cell F4 down to F8 to view the maximum sales for each branch.

7    Save your work as *First Quarter Sales and Profit-10.*

# Lesson 2-16: Use AutoFill options

Sometimes AutoFill begins to misbehave and actually gets in the way of efficient work by wrongly anticipating what you need.

1 Open *First Quarter Sales and Profit-10* from your sample files folder (If it isn't already open).

2 Populate cells F18 to F24 with sequential dates beginning with 1-Jan-16 using AutoFill.

    1. In cell F18 type the date: **1-Jan-16**

    2. AutoFill cell F18 down as far as cell F24.

       The cells are populated with sequential dates:

| | A | B | C | D | E | F |
|---|---|---|---|---|---|---|
| 18 | Monday | 1 | 9 | 01-Jan-16 | Adjusted | 01-Jan-16 |
| 19 | Tuesday | 2 | 18 | 02-Jan-16 | Adjusted | 02-Jan-16 |
| 20 | Wednesday | 3 | 27 | 03-Jan-16 | Adjusted | 03-Jan-16 |
| 21 | Thursday | 4 | 36 | 04-Jan-16 | Adjusted | 04-Jan-16 |
| 22 | Friday | 5 | 45 | 05-Jan-16 | Adjusted | 05-Jan-16 |
| 23 | Saturday | 6 | 54 | 06-Jan-16 | Adjusted | 06-Jan-16 |
| 24 | Sunday | 7 | 63 | 07-Jan-16 | Adjusted | 07-Jan-16 |

3 Populate cells G18 to G24 with the date *31-Mar-16* using the AutoFill Smart Tag.

    1. In cell G18 type the date: **31-Mar-16.**

    2. AutoFill down as far as cell G24.

       At some time, you'll need to add transaction dates to a worksheet and will have four or five entries with the same date.

       AutoFill is perfect for eliminating the need to re-type the date for each transaction, but its insistence upon incrementing the date every time could be very frustrating.

       Fortunately, you can change the default behavior.

    3. Click the Auto Fill Options Smart Tag at the bottom right corner of the filled cells.

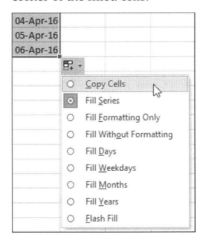

**First Quarter Sales and Profit-10**

4. Click *Copy Cells* to tell AutoFill not to increment the date.

4  Understand AutoFill options.

The *Fill Formatting* options will be covered later in: *Session Four: Making Your Worksheets Look Professional.*

*Flash Fill* will be introduced later in: *Lesson 2-19: Use automatic Flash Fill to split delimited text.* Here's what the other options will do:

| Copy Cells | Fill Series | Fill Days | Fill Weekdays | Fill Months | Fill Years |
|---|---|---|---|---|---|
| This is what we just did.<br><br>The first cell is copied to the other cells. | The default for dates that include the day.<br><br>The date increments by one day at a time. | The date increments by one day at a time. | Because 1st April 2016 is a Friday the weekend days are omitted and the series jumps from 1st April to 4th April. | Normally this would show the same day number for each month. In this example, there are only 30 days in three of the months so 30th is shown instead of 31st. | The same calendar day is shown for each subsequent year. |
| 31-Mar-16 | 31-Mar-16 | 31-Mar-16 | 31-Mar-16 | 31-Mar-16 | 31-Mar-16 |
| 31-Mar-16 | 01-Apr-16 | 01-Apr-16 | 01-Apr-16 | 30-Apr-16 | 31-Mar-17 |
| 31-Mar-16 | 02-Apr-16 | 02-Apr-16 | 04-Apr-16 | 31-May-16 | 31-Mar-18 |
| 31-Mar-16 | 03-Apr-16 | 03-Apr-16 | 05-Apr-16 | 30-Jun-16 | 31-Mar-19 |
| 31-Mar-16 | 04-Apr-16 | 04-Apr-16 | 06-Apr-16 | 31-Jul-16 | 31-Mar-20 |
| 31-Mar-16 | 05-Apr-16 | 05-Apr-16 | 07-Apr-16 | 31-Aug-16 | 31-Mar-21 |
| 31-Mar-16 | 06-Apr-16 | 06-Apr-16 | 08-Apr-16 | 30-Sep-16 | 31-Mar-22 |

5  Populate cells F18 to F24 with sequential dates using a right-click AutoFill.

1. Click on cell F18 to make it the active cell.

2. AutoFill down to cell F24, but this time hold down the right mouse button.

When you release the mouse button you are instantly presented with the AutoFill options (see sidebar).

There are two new options here: *Linear Trend* and *Growth Trend.*

You'll learn how these can be used later, in: *Lesson 2-18: Understand linear and exponential series.*

This method is preferred to the Smart Tag method because it is faster (one click instead of two).

3. Click: *Fill Series* or *Fill Days.*

In this example *Fill Series* and *Fill Days* produce exactly the same result.

6  Save your work as *First Quarter Sales and Profit-11.*

Copy Cells

Fill Series

Fill Formatting Only

Fill Without Formatting

Fill Days

Fill Weekdays

Fill Months

Fill Years

Linear Trend

Growth Trend

Flash Fill

Series...

# Lesson 2-17: Speed up your AutoFills and create a custom fill series

In this lesson, you're going to learn some advanced AutoFill techniques that will massively speed up your efficient use of the AutoFill feature.

1 Open *First Quarter Sales and Profit*-11 (if it isn't already open).

2 Use an AutoFill double-click to populate cells G19:G24 with sequential dates.

1. Delete the contents of cells G18:G24.

2. Type: **31-Mar-16** into cell G18.

| | A | B | C | D | E | F | G |
|---|---|---|---|---|---|---|---|
| 17 | | | | | | | |
| 18 | Monday | 1 | 9 | 01-Jan-16 | Adjusted | 01-Jan-16 | 31-Mar-16 |
| 19 | Tuesday | 2 | 18 | 02-Jan-16 | Adjusted | 02-Jan-16 | |
| 20 | Wednesday | 3 | 27 | 03-Jan-16 | Adjusted | 03-Jan-16 | |
| 21 | Thursday | 4 | 36 | 04-Jan-16 | Adjusted | 04-Jan-16 | |
| 22 | Friday | 5 | 45 | 05-Jan-16 | Adjusted | 05-Jan-16 | |
| 23 | Saturday | 6 | 54 | 06-Jan-16 | Adjusted | 06-Jan-16 | |
| 24 | Sunday | 7 | 63 | 07-Jan-16 | Adjusted | 07-Jan-16 | |

3. Double click the AutoFill handle to automatically fill cells G19:G24.

   Hover over the AutoFill handle (the black spot at the bottom right hand corner of cell G18). When you are sure that you have the correct black cross cursor shape, double click to automatically fill down to the end of the range.

3 Use an *AutoFill <Ctrl>-Drag* to copy the value in cell G18 to cells G19:G24.

1. Delete all of the dates from cells G19:G24 leaving only the date *31-Mar-16* in cell G18.

2. Click in cell G18 to make it the active cell.

3. Hold down the **<Ctrl>** key and AutoFill cell G18 down as far as cell G24 by dragging the AutoFill handle down with the mouse.

4. Release the mouse button.

   Because you held the <Ctrl> key down, AutoFill simply copied the cell instead of creating a series of values.

| | A | B | C | D | E | F | G |
|---|---|---|---|---|---|---|---|
| 17 | | | | | | | |
| 18 | Monday | 1 | 9 | 01-Jan-16 | Adjusted | 01-Jan-16 | 31-Mar-16 |
| 19 | Tuesday | 2 | 18 | 02-Jan-16 | Adjusted | 02-Jan-16 | 31-Mar-16 |
| 20 | Wednesday | 3 | 27 | 03-Jan-16 | Adjusted | 03-Jan-16 | 31-Mar-16 |
| 21 | Thursday | 4 | 36 | 04-Jan-16 | Adjusted | 04-Jan-16 | 31-Mar-16 |
| 22 | Friday | 5 | 45 | 05-Jan-16 | Adjusted | 05-Jan-16 | 31-Mar-16 |
| 23 | Saturday | 6 | 54 | 06-Jan-16 | Adjusted | 06-Jan-16 | 31-Mar-16 |
| 24 | Sunday | 7 | 63 | 07-Jan-16 | Adjusted | 07-Jan-16 | 31-Mar-16 |

**First Quarter Sales and Profit-11**

This is even faster than using the right-click method when you want to prevent the date (or a number) from incrementing.

4   Create a custom list containing the values: *North, South, East* and *West.*

1.   Click: File→Options→Advanced.

2.   Scroll down the *General* category and click the *Edit Custom Lists...* button.

The *Custom Lists* dialog appears.

3.   Click in the *List entries* window and add four custom list entries: **North, South, East** and **West** (pressing the **<Enter>** key after each entry).

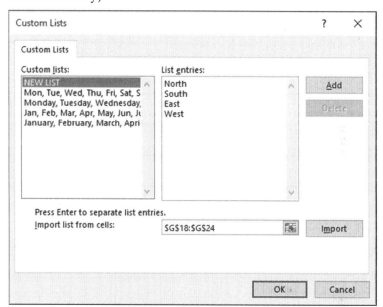

4.   Click the OK button and OK again to close the dialogs.

5   Use the newly created custom list.

Type **North** in any cell and AutoFill down.

As you AutoFill, the custom list entries appear in the worksheet (see sidebar).

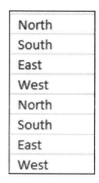

6   Delete the North, South, East, West... cells from the worksheet.

7   Save your work as *First Quarter Sales and Profit-12.*

Excel uses different terminology in various menus, dialog boxes and task panes that mean the same thing (in the context of this lesson):

*Series*, *Forecast* and *Trend* mean the same thing.

*Growth* and *Exponential* also mean the same thing.

In this lesson I'll consistently use the terminology *Series* and *Exponential*.

## note

### Excel can calculate a linear series when the step values of cells are not equal

Excel calculates a linear series (Autofill also calls this a *fill series*) using this formula:

Start Value + Step Value

Sometimes you may need to produce linear series values from a series of numbers that have different step values. For example, consider this range:

In this case Excel will use a more complex mathematical operation (called the *least-squares algorithm*) to determine the correct step value to use. In the above example, Excel would calculate a step value of 1.01.

**Rabbit Population**

# Lesson 2-18: Understand linear and exponential series

## Linear series

In: *Lesson 2-14: Use AutoFill for text and numeric series*, you used AutoFill's *Fill Series* method to automatically create these numeric series:

| | A | B | C |
|---|---|---|---|
| 18 | Monday | 1 | 9 |
| 19 | Tuesday | 2 | 18 |
| 20 | Wednesday | 3 | 27 |

These are both examples of *Linear* series.

Imagine that you had originally selected cells B1:B2 before auto filling column B:

| | B |
|---|---|
| 1 | 9 |
| 2 | 18 |
| 3 | |

To calculate a linear series Excel first identifies the *step value*. The linear series in column B has a *step value* of nine (18-9=9).

When you use AutoFill to *Fill Series*, Excel adds the *step value* to the *start value* (the number shown in the previous cell).

After you have AutoFilled down to cell B3, the value shown in cell B3 will thus be twenty-seven (18 (the start value) +9 (the step value) = 27)

This is an example of a very simple linear series. Excel is also able to calculate a linear series even when the step values of the selected cells are not equal (see sidebar).

## Exponential (or Growth) series

An exponential series is calculated by *multiplying* (rather than adding) the *start value* by the *step value*. This type of series is usually referred to as an *exponential* (rather than linear) series. Excel also uses the term *growth series* as a synonym for *exponential series* (see sidebar).

Here's an example:

- A truly excellent restaurant opens in town. On the first day they only have one customer but the customer is so delighted by the food, service and value that the customer tells two friends.

- The next day the two friends eat there and the restaurant has two diners.

- The two friends are also so pleased with their experience that they each also tell two friends. On the third day the restaurant has four diners.

You can see that the restaurant owner might expect that this trend will continue and that each day the number of diners will double (in Excel's

# note

Here's how you could have used the Ribbon to complete this lesson:

1. Enter the value **200** into cell B4.

2. Select cells B4:B51.

3. Click: Home→Editing→ Fill→Series...

The *Series* dialog appears.

4. Enter the following values into the *Series* dialog:

Note that the value: **1.2** is used because an exponential (growth) series multiplies each *start value* by the *step value*.

# trivia

According to an old legend, the inventor of the game of Chess presented his new game to a powerful king. The king was so pleased with the game that he offered the inventor any reasonable reward.

The inventor asked for one grain of rice for the first square on the chessboard, two for the second, four for the third... and so on for each square on the chessboard.

The king thought the inventor was foolish to ask for such a simple gift. Much later he found that there was not enough rice in the entire world to fulfil the inventor's request.

With the Excel skills you have learned in this lesson, you should easily be able to model the King's dilemma and discover exactly how many grains of rice would have been needed (about 18.5 Quintillion).

terminology, the *step value* is 2). Eventually, of course, the restaurant will become full and the trend will have to end (in Excel's terminology the number of seats in the restaurant is the *stop value*).

In this lesson you will model this type of exponential series.

1 Open *Rabbit Population* from your sample files folder.

2 If the rabbit population of an island increases at the rate of 20% per month, use an exponential progression to calculate how a newly introduced community of 200 rabbits will grow in four years.

1. Type the value: **200** into cell B4 to set the rabbit population at the beginning of the period.

2. Type the value: **240** into cell B5 to set the rabbit population after one month.

3. Select the range B4:B5.

4. Hold down the right-click mouse button on the AutoFill handle at the bottom-right of the selected range and drag down to Autofill to cell B51.

5. Click *Growth Trend* on the shortcut menu. Note that this is the shortcut menu's synonym for: *Exponential Series*.

| | A | B |
|---|---|---|
| 37 | | Copy Cells |
| 38 | | Fill Series |
| 39 | | Fill Formatting Only |
| 40 | | Fill Without Formatting |
| 41 | | |
| 42 | | Fill Days |
| 43 | | Fill Weekdays |
| 44 | | Fill Months |
| 45 | | Fill Years |
| 46 | | |
| 47 | | Linear Trend |
| 48 | | Growth Trend |
| 49 | | |
| 50 | | Flash Fill |
| 51 | | Series... |

After four years (48 months) the 200 rabbits will have grown to a population of a little over a million.

| | A | B |
|---|---|---|
| 49 | 46 | 731,452 |
| 50 | 47 | 877,743 |
| 51 | 48 | 1,053,291 |

3 Save your work as *Rabbit Population-1.*

## note

### If Flash Fill doesn't work for you, somebody has switched it off

It's almost certain that Flash Fill will be enabled on any computer that you work on. It is such a useful feature that you wouldn't want to disable it.

If Flash Fill doesn't work, there are two possible explanations:

1. You are using an earlier version of Excel. Flash Fill is a relatively new feature introduced in Excel 2013.

2. Somebody has switched Flash Fill off.

To switch it back on click:

File→Options→Advanced

In the first section (*Editing Options*) make sure that the *Automatically Flash Fill* check box is checked.

## note

### Help Flash Fill to work correctly by formatting header rows differently

You will notice that, in this lesson's sample file, I have bold-faced the header row:

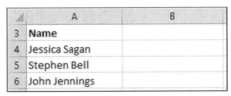

When Flash Fill sees different formatting in the first row, it will treat this row (correctly) as a header row. Flash Fill then excludes the value in this row from its logic, providing more reliable results.

**Employee Names-1**

# Lesson 2-19: Use automatic Flash Fill to split delimited text

When you place data in cells it is useful to observe an important rule:

**"Keep data atomic"**

If you strictly observe this rule you'll avoid an enormous number of potential problems.

The rule means that, in the same way that the atom is the smallest basic unit you can divide matter into, each worksheet cell should contain the smallest possible amount of data.

Here's a simple example to illustrate the concept:

|   | A | B |
|---|---|---|
| 3 | Name | |
| 4 | Jessica Sagan | |
| 5 | Stephen Bell | |
| 6 | John Jennings | |

Imagine that you want to use the worksheet above to create a mail merge in Word. In this case you'd need the first names in a cell of their own. This would enable you to personalize the mail merge with an introduction such as: *Dear Jessica.*

If you had observed the *keep data atomic* rule, you would have split your data into multiple columns like this:

|   | B | C |
|---|---|---|
| 3 | First Name | Last Name |
| 4 | Jessica | Sagan |
| 5 | Stephen | Bell |
| 6 | John | Jennings |

Excel 2013 added a wonderful new feature called *Flash Fill*. This feature enables you quickly and simply split delimited text (such as the above) into separate cells. The term *delimited text* means text that is split using a separator. In this case the separator is a space (see facing page sidebar).

*Automatic Flash Fill* will only work for very simple text splitting tasks such as the one described above. In the lessons that follow you'll learn more complex Flash Fill techniques that will enable you to perform some very advanced text splitting tasks.

1  Open *Employee Names-1* from your sample files folder.

2  Add column headings for *First Name* and *Last Name* in cells B3 and C3.

   1.  Click in cell B3.

   2.  Type: **First Name**

   3.  Press the **<Tab>** key to move to cell C3.

   4.  Type: **Last Name**

   5.  Press the **<Tab>** key to save the value into the cell and move to cell D3.

3  Bold face the text in cells B3 and C3.

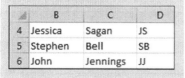
You learned how to do this in: *Lesson 1-15: Use the Mini Toolbar, Key Tips and keyboard shortcuts.*

4   Use *Flash Fill* to extract the *First Name* values from column A into column B.

1. Type: **Jessica** into cell B4. Be careful to type it exactly as it is spelled in cell A4. Be careful not to leave any leading or trailing spaces.

2. Press the **<Enter>** key to move to cell B5.

3. Type: **S** (the first letter of *Stephen*) into cell B5.

   Notice that something interesting has happened. *Flash Fill* has figured out that you possibly want to extract all the first names from column A and has displayed them all as grayed out names in the cells below:

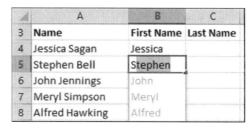

4. Press the **<Enter>** key to instruct Flash Fill to enter all the remaining *First Name* values.

   All the first names appear in column B.

| | A | B | C |
|---|---|---|---|
| 3 | Name | First Name | Last Name |
| 4 | Jessica Sagan | Jessica | |
| 5 | Stephen Bell | Stephen | |
| 6 | John Jennings | John | |
| 7 | Meryl Simpson | Meryl | |
| 8 | Alfred Hawking | Alfred | |

The status bar (at the bottom left of the screen) also confirms how many cells were changed:

| |
|---|
| Ready    Flash Fill Changed Cells: 23 |

5   Use *Flash Fill* to extract the *Last Name* values from column A into Column C.

Follow the same procedure you used to extract the first names:

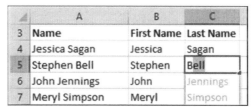

6   Save your work as *Employee Names-2.*

## note

### You can also Flash Fill more quickly by using the AutoFill handle

The *AutoFill handle* is the small black dot on the bottom-right corner of the active cell (or range of cells).

In: *Lesson 2-16: Use AutoFill options,* you learned that if you right-click and drag the AutoFill handle you are presented with *AutoFill options*:

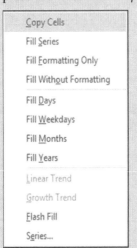

You can use the *Flash Fill* item on the *AutoFill options* list to request a Flash Fill.

This will do the same as clicking:

Home→Editing→Fill→Flash Fill

You'll find that this method is faster than using the Ribbon.

This method is also the preferred way to provide Flash Fill with more than one example result for more complex problems (you'll do this in: *Lesson 2-21: Use multiple example Flash Fill to concatenate*

**Phone Book-1**

# Lesson 2-20: Use manual Flash Fill to split text

Here are two examples of international telephone numbers.

+44 (0)113-4960227 (a UK telephone number)
+356 (0)2138-3393 (a Maltese telephone number)

The *country code* (or international dialing code) is shown as a + symbol followed by one or more numbers. The *NDD* (National Direct Dialing prefix) is shown in brackets. This is the access code used to make a call within the relevant country but is omitted when calling from outside the country. The *Area Code* consists of the numbers after the closing bracket but before the hyphen.

In this lesson, you'll use *Manual Flash Fill* to split telephone numbers into the *Country Code, Area Code* and *Phone Number* like this:

| | A | B | C | D | E |
|---|---|---|---|---|---|
| 3 | Company | Telephone | Country Code | Area Code | Phone Number |
| 4 | Books A Million | +44 (0)113-4960227 | +44 | 113 | 4960227 |
| 5 | Maltese Books | +356 (0)2138-3393 | +356 | 2138 | 3393 |
| 6 | Bargain Bookstore | +44 (0)115-4960498 | +44 | 115 | 4960498 |

In Excel versions prior to Excel 2013 you had to use some very complex formulas to split this type of text. With the new *Flash Fill* feature, you can achieve the same result in seconds.

1. Open *Phone Book-1* from your sample files folder.

2. Extract the *Country Code* from the telephone number in column B and place it into column C.

    If you were to type **+44** into cell C4, Excel would interpret it as a positive number and display the result as 44 (without the plus sign).

    In order to signal to Excel that you want the plus sign to be displayed, you will need to indicate that +44 should be regarded as text rather than as a number.

    You discovered the technique for doing this in: *Lesson 2-1: Enter text and numbers into a worksheet.*

    If an apostrophe is placed before a number, Excel will regard it as text.

    1. Type: **'+44** into cell C4 (an apostrophe followed by **+44**).

    2. Press: **<Enter>**

    3. Making sure that the active cell is in one of the cells that will be Flash Filled (ie anywhere in the range C3:C18), click:

        Home→Editing→Fill→Flash Fill

        (Alternatively, you could also use the shortcut keys: **<Ctrl>+<E>** to flash fill).

    The country code is extracted into the remaining cells in column C.

| | A | B | C |
|---|---|---|---|
| 3 | Company | Telephone | Country Code |
| 4 | Books A Million | +44 (0)113-4960227 | +44 |
| 5 | Maltese Books | +356 (0)2138-3393 | +356 |
| 6 | Bargain Bookstore | +44 (0)115-4960498 | +44 |

Notice that Excel has placed a green triangle in the top-left corner of each cell. Excel thinks you may have made an error but, of course, the value is fine. If you want to remove the green triangles, use the method you learned in: *Lesson 2-4: Select a range of cells and understand Smart Tags.*

3   Extract the *Area Code* from the telephone number in column B and place it into column D.

Use the same method as you did for the country code. The first area code you need to type is: '**113**

Even though there is no plus sign, it is still useful to include the apostrophe as it will prevent Excel from re-formatting numbers (see next step for more on this).

4   Extract the *Phone Number* from the telephone number in column B and place it into column E.

Use the same method as you did for the country code. The first telephone number is: '**4960227**

In this case you must use a leading apostrophe to prevent Excel from re-formatting large numbers. For example, the telephone number: *20180948* would be displayed as *2E+07* if you didn't include the apostrophe.

The *Country Code, Area Code* and *Phone Number* are now extracted for every international telephone number:

| | A | B | C | D | E |
|---|---|---|---|---|---|
| 3 | Company | Telephone | Country Code | Area Code | Phone Number |
| 4 | Books A Million | +44 (0)113-4960227 | +44 | 113 | 4960227 |
| 5 | Maltese Books | +356 (0)2138-3393 | +356 | 2138 | 3393 |
| 6 | Bargain Bookstore | +44 (0)115-4960498 | +44 | 115 | 4960498 |

5   Save your work as *Phone Book-2.*

**note**

**Flash Fill doesn't understand mathematics**

Consider this problem:

|  | A | B |
|---|---|---|
| 1 | 100 | 101 |
| 2 | 1120 | 1121 |
| 3 | 180 |  |
| 4 | 149 |  |

You could be forgiven for thinking that Flash Fill could populate cells B3 and B4 with the numbers 181 and 150. In order to produce this result Flash Fill would have to detect a mathematical relationship between the numbers in columns A and B.

Because Flash Fill doesn't understand mathematics, it will always see the problem as a textual one and will produce this result:

|  | A | B |
|---|---|---|
| 1 | 100 | 101 |
| 2 | 1120 | 1121 |
| 3 | 180 | 181 |
| 4 | 149 | 141 |

Flash Fill has used the logic "replace the last character displayed in column A with 1" and not "Add one to the value displayed in column A".

# Lesson 2-21: Use multiple example Flash Fill to concatenate text

## Understand concatenation

In: *Lesson 2-19: Use automatic Flash Fill to split delimited text,* you learned how to split text with this example:

|  | A | B | C |
|---|---|---|---|
| 3 | **Name** | **First Name** | **Last Name** |
| 4 | Jessica Sagan | Jessica | Sagan |
| 5 | Stephen Bell | Stephen | Bell |

In the above example, the text: *Jessica Sagan* was split into two separate words: *Jessica* and *Sagan.*

Concatenation is exactly the opposite of splitting. The two separate words *Jessica* and *Sagan* can be concatenated to produce the single word: *Jessica Sagan.* This is an example of very simple concatenation.

In this lesson, you'll perform some very advanced concatenation using *Flash Fill.*

1 Open *Client Names-1* from your sample files folder.

This workbook contains a list of very inconsistently formatted client names:

|  | A | B | C | D |
|---|---|---|---|---|
| 3 | **Last** | **Middle** | **First** |  |
| 4 | Sagan | Elizabeth | Jessica |  |
| 5 | Bell | p | Stephen |  |
| 6 | Jennings |  | John |  |

You want to clean up this data so that client names are consistently formatted like this:

|  | A | B | C | D |
|---|---|---|---|---|
| 3 | **Last** | **Middle** | **First** | **Formatted Name** |
| 4 | Sagan | Elizabeth | Jessica | Sagan, Jessica E. |
| 5 | Bell | p | Stephen | Bell, Stephen P. |
| 6 | jennings |  | John | Jennings, John |
| 7 | Simpson | Jane | Meryl | Simpson, Meryl J. |
| 8 | hawking |  | Alfred | Hawking, Alfred |
| 9 | Ashe | m | Lucille | Ashe, Lucille M. |

For Flash Fill to automate this task you will need to tell Flash Fill what is needed by providing more than one example.

2 Type: **Formatted Name** into cell D3 and bold face the text.

(Excel will probably bold-face the text automatically).

It is important that the header text in row 3 is bold faced.

**Client Names-1**

When Flash Fill sees different formatting in the first row the row is assumed to be a header row. Flash Fill then excludes the value in the header row from its logic, providing more reliable results.

**3** Provide a single example result in cell D4.

Type: **Sagan, Jessica E.** into cell D4.

**4** Flash fill cells D5:D9 based upon the example result in cell D4.

You learned how to do this in: *Lesson 2-20: Use manual Flash Fill to split text.*

Excel completes the task but the results are not what you wanted (see sidebar).

With only one example, Flash Fill has completely misunderstood the requirement.

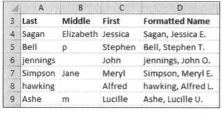

| | A | B | C | D |
|---|---|---|---|---|
| 3 | Last | Middle | First | Formatted Name |
| 4 | Sagan | Elizabeth | Jessica | Sagan, Jessica E. |
| 5 | Bell | p | Stephen | Bell, Stephen T. |
| 6 | jennings | | John | jennings, John O. |
| 7 | Simpson | Jane | Meryl | Simpson, Meryl E. |
| 8 | hawking | | Alfred | hawking, Alfred L. |
| 9 | Ashe | m | Lucille | Ashe, Lucille U. |

**5** Provide two example results in cells D4 and D5.

1. Delete the names in cells D5:D9.

2. Provide another example of the correct result (in cell D5).

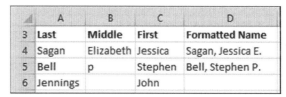

| | A | B | C | D |
|---|---|---|---|---|
| 3 | Last | Middle | First | Formatted Name |
| 4 | Sagan | Elizabeth | Jessica | Sagan, Jessica E. |
| 5 | Bell | p | Stephen | Bell, Stephen P. |
| 6 | Jennings | | John | |

**6** Flash fill cells D6:D9 based upon the example results in cells D4 and D5.

1. Select cells D4:D9.

2. Click: Home→Editing→Fill→Flash Fill.

This time Flash Fill has done a better job (see sidebar).

Notice the two blank results (for *John Jennings* and *Alfred Hawking*).

Flash Fill doesn't yet understand how to treat clients without a middle name. The blank spaces are Flash Fill's way of asking you for yet another example.

| | A | B | C | D |
|---|---|---|---|---|
| 3 | Last | Middle | First | Formatted Name |
| 4 | Sagan | Elizabeth | Jessica | Sagan, Jessica E. |
| 5 | Bell | p | Stephen | Bell, Stephen P. |
| 6 | jennings | | John | |
| 7 | Simpson | Jane | Meryl | Simpson, Meryl J. |
| 8 | hawking | | Alfred | |
| 9 | Ashe | m | Lucille | Ashe, Lucille M. |

**7** Provide another example result in cell D6.

1. Type: **Jennings, John** into cell D6.

2. Press the **<Enter>** key.

Usually Flash Fill will instantly replace the value in cell D8. If it doesn't, you'll have to manually Flash Fill the entire list based upon the three examples provided. Do this by completing the following steps:

3. Select cells D4:D9.

4. Click: Home→Editing→Fill→Flash Fill.

This time Flash Fill has completed the task successfully (see sidebar).

| | A | B | C | D |
|---|---|---|---|---|
| 3 | Last | Middle | First | Formatted Name |
| 4 | Sagan | Elizabeth | Jessica | Sagan, Jessica E. |
| 5 | Bell | p | Stephen | Bell, Stephen P. |
| 6 | jennings | | John | Jennings, John |
| 7 | Simpson | Jane | Meryl | Simpson, Meryl J. |
| 8 | hawking | | Alfred | Hawking, Alfred |
| 9 | Ashe | m | Lucille | Ashe, Lucille M. |

**8** Save your work as *Client Names-2*.

# Lesson 2-22: Use Flash Fill to solve common problems

Flash Fill (introduced in Excel 2013) is one of Excel's most useful features. It isn't possible to over-state how useful this tool is. I find myself using Flash Fill almost every day to solve a huge number of different problems.

This lesson gives examples of many everyday tasks that I have found can be quickly and simply completed using Flash Fill. I've also included all of the examples in the sample file: *Flash Fill Examples.*

In the following examples, Flash Fill filled the shaded cells.

### Split text

| Full Name | First Name | Last Name |
|---|---|---|
| Jessica Elizabeth Sagan | Jessica | Sagan |
| Stephen Bell | Stephen | Bell |
| John Paul Jennings | John | Jennings |

### Extract initials from names

| Name | Initials |
|---|---|
| Jessica Elizabeth Sagan | JES |
| Stephen Bell | SB |
| John Paul Jennings | JPJ |

### Remove title from names

| Full Name | Short Name |
|---|---|
| Miss Jessica Elizabeth Sagan | Jessica Sagan |
| Mr Stephen Bell | Stephen Bell |
| Mr John Paul Jennings | John Jennings |

### Add commas
### (a useful name format for alphabetical sorting)

| Name | Sort Name |
|---|---|
| Jessica Elizabeth Sagan | Sagan, Jessica |
| Stephen Bell | Bell, Stephen |
| John Paul Jennings | Jennings, John |

### Concatenate text

| First Name | Middle Name | Last Name | Full Name |
|---|---|---|---|
| Jessica | Elizabeth | Sagan | Jessica Elizabeth Sagan |
| Stephen | | Bell | Stephen Bell |
| John | Paul | Jennings | John Paul Jennings |

Flash Fill Examples

## Concatenate text and insert extra text

| First Name | Middle Name | Last Name | Full Name |
|---|---|---|---|
| Jessica | Elizabeth | Sagan | First Name: Jessica, Last Name: Sagan |
| Stephen | | Bell | First Name: Stephen, Last Name: Bell |
| John | Paul | Jennings | First Name: John, Last Name: Jennings |

## Change capitalization

| Mixed Case | Title Case |
|---|---|
| jessica elizabeth sagan | Jessica Elizabeth Sagan |
| stephen Bell | Stephen Bell |
| john Paul jennings | John Paul Jennings |

## Extract the day, month or year from a date

In all the date-based examples note that the *Date* column is formatted as a date. You will learn how to format cells as dates later in: *Lesson 4-1: Format dates.*

| Date | Day | Date | Month | Date | Year |
|---|---|---|---|---|---|
| 19th January 2013 | 19 | 19th January 2013 | January | 19th January 2013 | 2013 |
| 5th August 1967 | 5 | 5th August 1967 | August | 5th August 1967 | 1967 |
| 20th September 1999 | 20 | 20th September 1999 | September | 20th September 1999 | 1999 |

## Extract the day/month from a date

| Date | Day/Month |
|---|---|
| 19th January 2013 | 19th January |
| 5th August 1967 | 5th August |
| 20th September 1999 | 20th September |

## Extract domain names from e-mail addresses

| E-mail address | Domain |
|---|---|
| Mary@QuiteContrary.com | QuiteContrary.com |
| Humpty@Dumpty.com | Dumpty.com |
| Jack@Nimble.com | Nimble.com |

## Format telephone numbers

| Name | Tel (unformatted) | Tel (formatted) |
|---|---|---|
| Books A Million | 1134960227 | (113) 496-0227 |
| Bargain Bookstore | 1154960498 | (115) 496-0498 |
| Books for Less | 1164960593 | (116) 496-0593 |

# Lesson 2-23: Use the zoom control

Zooming is used to magnify or reduce the worksheet. If you have a lot of rows in a worksheet and have good eyes, you might want to zoom out sometimes to see more of the worksheet on one screen.

1    Open *First Quarter Sales and Profit-12* from your sample files folder.

2    Zoom in and out of the worksheet using the mouse wheel.

The fastest way to zoom a worksheet is by using the mouse.

Most mice these days have a wheel in the middle of the buttons. To zoom using this wheel hold down the **<Ctrl>** key on the keyboard and roll the wheel to zoom in and out.

3    Zoom in and out of a worksheet using the zoom control.

The zoom control is at the bottom right of your screen.

Click and drag on the zoom control slider to zoom in and out of your worksheet. You can also zoom by clicking the plus and minus buttons on either side of the Zoom control.

4    Use the Zoom dialog to make cells A3:D9 fill the screen.

    1.    Select cells A3:D9.

| | A | B | C | D | E |
|---|---|---|---|---|---|
| 2 | | | | | |
| 3 | | Jan | Feb | Mar | Average |
| 4 | New York | 22,000 | 29,000 | 19,000 | 23,333 |
| 5 | Los Angeles | 42,000 | 39,000 | 43,000 | 41,333 |
| 6 | London | 18,000 | 20,000 | 22,000 | 20,000 |
| 7 | Paris | 35,000 | 26,000 | 31,000 | 30,667 |
| 8 | Munich | 12,000 | 15,000 | 13,000 | 13,333 |
| 9 | Sales | 129,000 | 129,000 | 128,000 | |

    2.    Click on the right-hand side of the zoom bar.

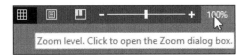

Zoom level. Click to open the Zoom dialog box.

The *Zoom* dialog is displayed.

**First Quarter Sales and Profit-12**

https://TheSmartMethod.com

3.  Select the *Fit Selection* option button.

4.  Click the OK button.

The worksheet is zoomed so that the selected cells completely fill the screen.

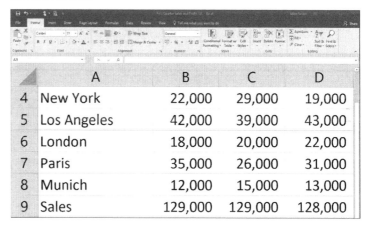

| | A | B | C | D |
|---|---|---|---|---|
| 4 | New York | 22,000 | 29,000 | 19,000 |
| 5 | Los Angeles | 42,000 | 39,000 | 43,000 |
| 6 | London | 18,000 | 20,000 | 22,000 |
| 7 | Paris | 35,000 | 26,000 | 31,000 |
| 8 | Munich | 12,000 | 15,000 | 13,000 |
| 9 | Sales | 129,000 | 129,000 | 128,000 |

5  Zoom back to 100% using the Ribbon.

You'll probably find the zoom bar to be the quickest and most convenient way to zoom, but you can also zoom using the Ribbon.

Click: View→Zoom→100%.

The screen is restored to normal size.

# Lesson 2-24: Print out a worksheet

You aren't going to explore every option for preparing and printing a worksheet in this lesson. Printing is such a huge subject that this course devotes a whole session to it later, in: *Session Seven: Printing Your Work.*

This lesson only aims to teach you the bare minimum skills you need to put your work onto paper.

1    Open *First Quarter Sales and Profit-12* from your sample files folder (if it isn't already open).

| | A | B | C | D | E | F | G |
|---|---|---|---|---|---|---|---|
| 1 | Sales and Profit Report - First Quarter 2016 | | | | | | |
| 2 | | | | | | | |
| 3 | | Jan | Feb | Mar | Average | Maximum | |
| 4 | New York | 22,000 | 29,000 | 19,000 | 23,333 | 29,000 | |
| 5 | Los Angeles | 42,000 | 39,000 | 43,000 | 41,333 | 43,000 | |
| 6 | London | 18,000 | 20,000 | 22,000 | 20,000 | 22,000 | |
| 7 | Paris | 35,000 | 26,000 | 31,000 | 30,667 | 35,000 | |
| 8 | Munich | 12,000 | 15,000 | 13,000 | 13,333 | 15,000 | |
| 9 | Sales | 129,000 | 129,000 | 128,000 | | | |
| 10 | | | | | | | |
| 11 | Costs | 83,000 | | | | | |
| 12 | Profit | 46,000 | | | | | |
| 13 | 10% Bonus | 4,600 | | | | | |
| 14 | | | | | | | |
| 15 | USA Sales | 64,000 | | | | | |
| 16 | European Sales | 65,000 | | | | | |
| 17 | | | | | | | |
| 18 | Monday | 1 | 9 | 01-Jan-16 | Adjusted | 01-Jan-16 | 31-Mar-16 |
| 19 | Tuesday | 2 | 18 | 02-Jan-16 | Adjusted | 02-Jan-16 | 31-Mar-16 |
| 20 | Wednesday | 3 | 27 | 03-Jan-16 | Adjusted | 03-Jan-16 | 31-Mar-16 |
| 21 | Thursday | 4 | 36 | 04-Jan-16 | Adjusted | 04-Jan-16 | 31-Mar-16 |
| 22 | Friday | 5 | 45 | 05-Jan-16 | Adjusted | 05-Jan-16 | 31-Mar-16 |
| 23 | Saturday | 6 | 54 | 06-Jan-16 | Adjusted | 06-Jan-16 | 31-Mar-16 |
| 24 | Sunday | 7 | 63 | 07-Jan-16 | Adjusted | 07-Jan-16 | 31-Mar-16 |

2    Click File→Print.

*Backstage View* appears offering many preview and print options:

**First Quarter Sales and Profit-12**

3   Click on the zoom button  to see the zoom feature working.

Each time you click on the button the page zooms in and out.

If you have a large screen you may not see a lot of difference when you zoom.

4   Print the worksheet.

Click the *Print* button:

The page is printed on the selected printer.

## Session 2: Exercise

**1**     Open a new blank workbook.

**2**     Use AutoFill to put the three months Jan, Feb, and Mar into cells A4:A6.

**3**     Using only the keyboard, add the following data:

| | A | B | C | D | E |
|---|---|---|---|---|---|
| 1 | Profit Analysis | | | | |
| 2 | | | | | |
| 3 | | London | Paris | New York | Average |
| 4 | Jan | 2,500 | 3,100 | 2,300 | |
| 5 | Feb | 2,200 | 2,700 | 2,600 | |
| 6 | Mar | 2,100 | 2,600 | 2,800 | |
| 7 | Total | | | | |

**4**     Use AutoSum to compute London's total profit for Jan/Feb/Mar in cell B7.

**5**     Use AutoSum to compute the average January profit in cell E4.

**6**     Use AutoFill to extend the London total in cell B7 to the Paris and New York totals in cells C7 and D7.

**7**     Use AutoFill to extend the January average profit in cell E4 to the February and March average profits in cells E5 and E6.

**8**     Select all of Column A and all of Column E (at the same time) and bold face the values in them.

**9**     Select row 3 and row 7 (at the same time) and bold face the values in them.

| | A | B | C | D | E |
|---|---|---|---|---|---|
| 1 | **Profit Analysis** | | | | |
| 2 | | | | | |
| 3 | | **London** | **Paris** | **New York** | **Average** |
| 4 | **Jan** | 2,500 | 3,100 | 2,300 | **2,633** |
| 5 | **Feb** | 2,200 | 2,700 | 2,600 | **2,500** |
| 6 | **Mar** | 2,100 | 2,600 | 2,800 | **2,500** |
| 7 | **Total** | **6,800** | **8,400** | **7,700** | |

**10**    Select cells B4:B6 and cells D4:D6 at the same time and then read the total London and New York sales figure for Jan, Feb and March from the summary information displayed on the status bar.

**11**    Select cells B4:D6 and zoom the selection so that these cells fill the screen.

**12**    Save your work as *Exercise2-End*.

If you need help slide the page to the left

## Session 2: Exercise answers

These are the questions that students find the most difficult to answer:

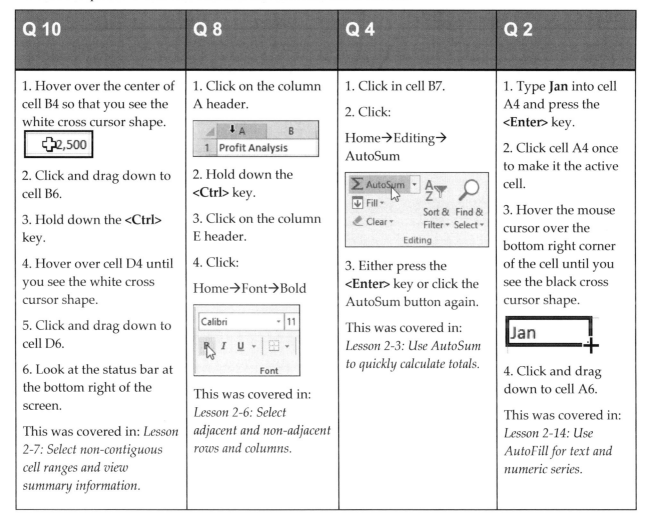

| Q 10 | Q 8 | Q 4 | Q 2 |
|---|---|---|---|
| 1. Hover over the center of cell B4 so that you see the white cross cursor shape. | 1. Click on the column A header. | 1. Click in cell B7. | 1. Type **Jan** into cell A4 and press the **<Enter>** key. |
| 2. Click and drag down to cell B6. | 2. Hold down the **<Ctrl>** key. | 2. Click: | 2. Click cell A4 once to make it the active cell. |
| 3. Hold down the **<Ctrl>** key. | 3. Click on the column E header. | Home→Editing→ AutoSum | 3. Hover the mouse cursor over the bottom right corner of the cell until you see the black cross cursor shape. |
| 4. Hover over cell D4 until you see the white cross cursor shape. | 4. Click: | 3. Either press the **<Enter>** key or click the AutoSum button again. | |
| 5. Click and drag down to cell D6. | Home→Font→Bold | This was covered in: *Lesson 2-3: Use AutoSum to quickly calculate totals.* | 4. Click and drag down to cell A6. |
| 6. Look at the status bar at the bottom right of the screen. | | | This was covered in: *Lesson 2-14: Use AutoFill for text and numeric series.* |
| This was covered in: *Lesson 2-7: Select non-contiguous cell ranges and view summary information.* | This was covered in: *Lesson 2-6: Select adjacent and non-adjacent rows and columns.* | | |

If you have difficulty with the other questions, here are the lessons that cover the relevant skills:

**1**  Refer to: **Lesson 1-1: Start Excel and open a new blank workbook.**

**3**  Refer to: **Lesson 2-1: Enter text and numbers into a worksheet.**

**5**  Refer to: **Lesson 2-3: Use AutoSum to quickly calculate totals.**

**6**  Refer to: **Lesson 2-15: Use AutoFill to adjust formulas.**

**7**  Refer to: **Lesson 2-15: Use AutoFill to adjust formulas.**

**9**  Refer to: **Lesson 2-6: Select adjacent and non-adjacent rows and columns.**

**11**  Refer to: **Lesson 2-23: Use the zoom control.**

**12**  Refer to: **Lesson 1-6: Save a workbook to a local file.**

# Session Three: Taking Your Skills to the Next Level

> One only gets to the top rung of the ladder by steadily climbing up one at a time, and suddenly all sorts of powers, all sorts of abilities which you thought never belonged to you – suddenly become within your own possibility.
>
> *Margaret Thatcher,*
> *Prime Minister of the United Kingdom from 1979-1990*

After mastering all the techniques covered in session two, you're already able to do useful work with the world's most powerful business tool, but of course, you're only on the first rung of a very long ladder.

While you are now able to do the simple things well, there are a few more insights you need to really get Excel working.

Most of the skills covered in this session will take your powers beyond those of casual Excel users.

## Session Objectives

By the end of this session you will be able to:

- Insert and delete rows and columns
- Use AutoComplete and fill data from adjacent cells
- Cut, copy and paste
- Cut, copy and paste using drag and drop
- Use Paste Values
- Increase/decrease decimal places displayed
- Transpose a range
- Use the multiple item clipboard
- Use Undo and Redo
- Insert, View and Print cell comments
- Understand absolute, relative and mixed cell references
- Understand templates and set the default custom template folder
- Create a template
- Use a template
- Add an Office Add-In to a workbook
- Freeze columns and rows
- Split the window into multiple panes
- Check spelling

# Lesson 3-1: Insert and delete rows and columns

1    Open *The World's Fastest Cars* from your sample files folder.

| | A | B | C | D | E | F | G |
|---|---|---|---|---|---|---|---|
| 1 | The World's Fastest Cars | | | | | | |
| 2 | | | | | | | |
| 3 | Make | Model | Top Speed (MPH) | 0-60 | BHP | Price (USD) | Country |
| 4 | Ferrari | F12 Berlinetta | 227 | 3.1 | 730 | 330,000 | Italy |
| 5 | Lamborghini | Aventador Super Veloce | 217 | 2.8 | 690 | 493,095 | Italy |
| 6 | Aston Martin | V12 Vantage S | 205 | 3.7 | 565 | 123,695 | UK |
| 7 | Ferrari | 488 GTB | 205 | 2.9 | 661 | 242,737 | Italy |
| 8 | Lamborghini | Huracán | 202 | 2.5 | 602 | 237,250 | Italy |
| 9 | Porsche | 911 Turbo S Sport+ | 197 | 3.1 | 560 | 241,105 | Germany |
| 10 | Aston Martin | Vanquish Volante | 197 | 3.8 | 568 | 299,000 | UK |
| 11 | Mercedes | SLS AMG Black Series | 196 | 3.5 | 622 | 275,000 | Germany |
| 12 | Lotus | Evora 400 | 186 | 4.1 | 400 | 89,900 | UK |
| 13 | Tesla | Model S P90D | 155 | 2.6 | 762 | 130,700 | USA |

A worksheet opens showing some of the fastest cars in the world.

The list does not, however, show the true fastest production car in the world (in August 2018 this was the *Bugatti Veyron Super Sport* but there may be an even faster car by the time you read this book).

You need to insert a row above row 4 to add the Bugatti to the list.

2    Insert a blank row above row 4.

Right-click the row header button `4` and click *Insert* from the shortcut menu.

3    Add the following data to the new row:

| | | | | | | | |
|---|---|---|---|---|---|---|---|
| 3 | Make | Model | Top Speed (MPH) | 0-60 | BHP | Price (USD) | Country |
| 4 | Bugatti | Veyron Super Sport | 268 | 2.4 | 1,184 | 1,700,000 | Germany |
| 5 | Ferrari | F12 Berlinetta | 227 | 3.1 | 730 | 330,000 | Italy |

4    If the text is bold faced restore it to normal.

You learned how to do this in: *Lesson 1-15: Use the Mini Toolbar, Key Tips and keyboard shortcuts.*

5    Add a column to the left of column A.

Adding columns is just like adding rows. Right-click on the column header `A` and then click *Insert* from the shortcut menu.

A blank column appears on the left-hand side of the worksheet:

| | A | B | C | D | E |
|---|---|---|---|---|---|
| 1 | | The World's Fastest Cars | | | |
| 2 | | | | | |
| 3 | | Make | Model | Top Speed (MPH) | 0-60 |
| 4 | | Bugatti | Veyron Super Sport | 268 | 2.4 |
| 5 | | Ferrari | F12 Berlinetta | 227 | 3.1 |
| 6 | | Lamborghini | Aventador Super Veloce | 217 | 2.8 |

## note

### Other ways of inserting and deleting rows and columns

The right-click method, described in this lesson, is the fastest and most intuitive way to insert rows and columns, but there are two additional methods.

### To insert rows or columns:

1. Click: Home→Cells→Insert (drop down list)

2. Select: *Insert Sheet Rows* or *Insert Sheet Columns.*

**OR**

1. Press **<Ctrl>+<Shift>+<+>**

2. Select: *Entire Row* or *Entire Column.*

### To delete rows or columns:

Click: Home→Cells→Delete (drop down list)

**OR**

Press **<Ctrl>+<->**

(and then select *Entire row* or *Entire column*).

The World's Fastest Cars

6   Delete the newly-inserted column A.

Deleting is just like adding. Right-click on the column header

> A

but, this time, select *Delete* from the shortcut menu.

7   Insert four rows above row 3.

Nearly every Excel user does this by inserting a single row four times until they learn the correct technique.

1. Select the four rows 3:6 by clicking and dragging across the row header buttons.

2. Right-click anywhere in the selected area.

3. Click *Insert* from the shortcut menu.

Four blank rows are inserted.

| | A | B | C | D | E | F |
|---|---|---|---|---|---|---|
| 1 | The World's Fastest Cars | | | | | |
| 2 | | | | | | |
| 3 | | | | | | |
| 4 | | | | | | |
| 5 | | | | | | |
| 6 | | | | | | |
| 7 | Make | Model | Top Speed (MPH) | 0-60 | BHP | Price (USD) |
| 8 | Bugatti | Veyron Super Sport | 268 | 2.4 | 1,184 | 1,700,000 |
| 9 | Ferrari | F12 Berlinetta | 227 | 3.1 | 730 | 330,000 |

8   Delete the four newly-inserted rows.

1. Select the four rows you want to delete (by dragging the mouse cursor over row headers 3,4,5 and 6).

2. Right-click anywhere in the selected area.

3. Click *Delete* from the shortcut menu.

9   Save your work as: *The World's Fastest Cars-2.*

# Lesson 3-2: Use AutoComplete and fill data from adjacent cells

1    Open *The World's Fastest Cars-2* from your sample files folder (if it isn't already open).

| | A | B | C | D | E | F | G |
|---|---|---|---|---|---|---|---|
| 1 | The World's Fastest Cars | | | | | | |
| 2 | | | | | | | |
| 3 | Make | Model | Top Speed (MPH) | 0-60 | BHP | Price (USD) | Country |
| 4 | Bugatti | Veyron Super Sport | 268 | 2.4 | 1,184 | 1,700,000 | Germany |
| 5 | Ferrari | F12 Berlinetta | 227 | 3.1 | 730 | 330,000 | Italy |
| 6 | Lamborghini | Aventador Super Veloce | 217 | 2.8 | 690 | 493,095 | Italy |
| 7 | Aston Martin | V12 Vantage S | 205 | 3.7 | 565 | 123,695 | UK |
| 8 | Ferrari | 488 GTB | 205 | 2.9 | 661 | 242,737 | Italy |
| 9 | Lamborghini | Huracán | 202 | 2.5 | 602 | 237,250 | Italy |
| 10 | Porsche | 911 Turbo S Sport+ | 197 | 3.1 | 560 | 241,105 | Germany |
| 11 | Aston Martin | Vanquish Volante | 197 | 3.8 | 568 | 299,000 | UK |
| 12 | Mercedes | SLS AMG Black Series | 196 | 3.5 | 622 | 275,000 | Germany |
| 13 | Lotus | Evora 400 | 186 | 4.1 | 400 | 89,900 | UK |
| 14 | Tesla | Model S P90D | 155 | 2.6 | 762 | 130,700 | USA |
| 15 | | | | | | | |

2    Type the letter **F** into cell A15.

Notice that Excel guesses that you want to type *Ferrari* into the cell. This is because the word Ferrari appears above it in the column.

If this doesn't happen, somebody has switched AutoComplete off. See the sidebar to find out how to switch it back on.

| 13 | Lotus | Evora 400 | 186 | 4.1 | 400 | 89,900 | UK |
|---|---|---|---|---|---|---|---|
| 14 | Tesla | Model S P90D | 155 | 2.6 | 762 | 130,700 | USA |
| 15 | Ferrari | | | | | | |

3    Press the **<Tab>** key to accept the guess.

4    Enter **LaFerrari** for the model and **217** for the top speed.

| 14 | Tesla | Model S P90D | 155 | 2.6 | 762 | 130,700 | USA |
|---|---|---|---|---|---|---|---|
| 15 | Ferrari | LaFerrari | 217 | 2.6 | 950 | 1,690,000 | Italy |

5    Use the *Fill* command to enter **2.6** into cell D15.

The Ferrari has the same 0-60 time as the Tesla P90D. Instead of typing **2.6** into the cell we can use the *Fill* command.

1. Click in cell D15.

2. Click: Home→Editing→Fill→Down.

The World's Fastest Cars-2

Notice that there are also *Right, Up* and *Left* options. These can be used to copy values from adjacent cells in any direction.

The *Across Worksheets…* option can only be used in conjunction with worksheet groups. You'll learn about worksheet groups later, in: *Lesson 6-7: Understand worksheet groups.*

6    Enter **950** for the BHP value and **1,690,000** for the price.

7    Right-click in G15 and choose *Pick from Drop down list...* from the shortcut menu.

A unique list of all countries that currently exist in column G are displayed as a list.

| | A | B | C | D | E | F | G |
|---|---|---|---|---|---|---|---|
| 1 | The World's Fastest Cars | | | | | | |
| 2 | | | | | | | |
| 3 | Make | Model | Top Speed (MPH) | 0-60 | BHP | Price (USD) | Country |
| 4 | Bugatti | Veyron Super Sport | 268 | 2.4 | 1,184 | 1,700,000 | Germany |
| 5 | Ferrari | F12 Berlinetta | 227 | 3.1 | 730 | 330,000 | Italy |
| 6 | Lamborghini | Aventador Super Veloce | 217 | 2.8 | 690 | 493,095 | Italy |
| 7 | Aston Martin | V12 Vantage S | 205 | 3.7 | 565 | 123,695 | UK |
| 8 | Ferrari | 488 GTB | 205 | 2.9 | 661 | 242,737 | Italy |
| 9 | Lamborghini | Huracán | 202 | 2.5 | 602 | 237,250 | Italy |
| 10 | Porsche | 911 Turbo S Sport+ | 197 | 3.1 | 560 | 241,105 | Germany |
| 11 | Aston Martin | Vanquish Volante | 197 | 3.8 | 568 | 299,000 | UK |
| 12 | Mercedes | SLS AMG Black Series | 196 | 3.5 | 622 | 275,000 | Germany |
| 13 | Lotus | Evora 400 | 186 | 4.1 | 400 | 89,900 | UK |
| 14 | Tesla | Model S P90D | 155 | 2.6 | 762 | 130,700 | USA |
| 15 | Ferrari | LaFerrari | 217 | 2.6 | 950 | 1,690,000 | |
| 16 | | | | | | | Germany |
| 17 | | | | | | | Italy |
| 18 | | | | | | | UK |
| | | | | | | | USA |

8    Click *Italy* to automatically enter the country.

9    Save your work as *The World's Fastest Cars-3.*

The World's Fastest Cars-3

# Lesson 3-3: Cut, copy and paste

1 Open *The World's Fastest Cars-3* from your sample files folder (if it isn't already open).

2 Click cell A1 to make it the active cell.

3 Copy the text from cell A1 to the clipboard.

The clipboard is a container for copied text and is common to all of Microsoft Office. When you ask Excel to copy, Excel takes the value in cell A1 (in this case text) and places a copy of it onto the clipboard. The existing contents of cell A1 remain unaltered.

The clipboard is useful because you can later paste the clipboard's contents back into the worksheet (or into any other Office document such as a PowerPoint presentation, Word document or Outlook Email).

There are three ways to copy but these two are the quickest:

**EITHER**

Right click and select *Copy* from the shortcut menu.

**OR**

Press **<Ctrl>+<C>** on the keyboard.

The third (and slowest) method is to click:

Home→Clipboard→Copy

4 Click cell A17 to make it the active cell.

5 Paste the copied text into cell A17.

There are also three ways to paste but these two are the quickest:

**EITHER**

Right click cell A17 and then select: Paste Options→Paste from the shortcut menu (see sidebar). The other paste options will be covered later in this lesson.

**OR**

Click cell A17 and then press **<Ctrl>+<V>** on the keyboard.

The third (and slowest) method is to click:

Home→Clipboard→Paste

The text appears in cell A17.

| 14 | Tesla | Model S P90D | | 155 |
|----|-------|--------------|---|-----|
| 15 | Ferrari | LaFerrari | | 217 |
| 16 | | | | |
| 17 | The World's Fastest Cars | | | |

6 Edit the text in cell A17 to read: **The World's Fastest Italian Cars.**

You learned how to do this in: *Lesson 2-1: Enter text and numbers into a worksheet.*

**7** Select all of row 5 and copy it to the clipboard.

Selecting an entire row was covered in: *Lesson 2-6: Select adjacent and non-adjacent rows and columns.*

**8** Select all of row 19 and paste into it.

The contents of row 5 are copied to row 19.

| 17 | The World's Fastest Italian Cars | | | | |
|----|----------------------------------|--|--|-----|-----|
| 18 | | | | | |
| 19 | Ferrari | F12 Berlinetta | | 227 | 3.1 |

**9** Use the same technique to paste row 6 into row 20.

**10** Cut the text from the range A8:G9 to place it onto the clipboard.

When you cut text, the text is copied from the source cell(s) to the clipboard. If you then paste the text to a new location, the text is then automatically deleted from the source cells(s).

1. Select the range A8 to G9.

2. Cut the range to place it onto the clipboard.

   There are three ways to cut but these two are the quickest:

   **EITHER**

   Right click and select *Cut* from the shortcut menu.

   **OR**

   Press **<Ctrl>+<X>**.

   The third (and slowest) method is to click:

   Home→Clipboard→Cut.

**11** Click in cell A21 to make it the active cell.

**12** Paste the cut range into the range beginning in cell A21.

The cut text appears with the top left-hand corner in cell A21.

| 7  | Aston Martin | V12 Vantage S          | 205 | 3.7 | 565 | 123,695   | UK      |
|----|--------------|------------------------|-----|-----|-----|-----------|---------|
| 8  |              |                        |     |     |     |           |         |
| 9  |              |                        |     |     |     |           |         |
| 10 | Porsche      | 911 Turbo S Sport+     | 197 | 3.1 | 560 | 241,105   | Germany |
| 11 | Aston Martin | Vanquish Volante       | 197 | 3.8 | 568 | 299,000   | UK      |
| 12 | Mercedes     | SLS AMG Black Series   | 196 | 3.5 | 622 | 275,000   | Germany |
| 13 | Lotus        | Evora 400              | 186 | 4.1 | 400 | 89,900    | UK      |
| 14 | Tesla        | Model S P90D           | 155 | 2.6 | 762 | 130,700   | USA     |
| 15 | Ferrari      | LaFerrari              | 217 | 2.6 | 950 | 1,690,000 | Italy   |
| 16 |              |                        |     |     |     |           |         |
| 17 | The World's Fastest Italian Cars | |  |     |     |           |         |
| 18 |              |                        |     |     |     |           |         |
| 19 | Ferrari      | F12 Berlinetta         | 227 | 3.1 | 730 | 330,000   | Italy   |
| 20 | Lamborghini  | Aventador Super Veloce | 217 | 2.8 | 690 | 493,095   | Italy   |
| 21 | Ferrari      | 488 GTB                | 205 | 2.9 | 661 | 242,737   | Italy   |
| 22 | Lamborghini  | Huracán                | 202 | 2.5 | 602 | 237,250   | Italy   |
| 23 |              |                        |     |     |     |           |         |

**13** Save your work as *The World's Fastest Cars-4.*

# Lesson 3-4: Cut, copy and paste using drag and drop

1   Open *The World's Fastest Cars-4* from your sample files folder (if it isn't already open).

2   Move cells A21:G22 to cells A8:G9 using drag and drop.

The World's Fastest Cars-4

1.   Select cells A21:G22.

2.   Hover the mouse cursor over the black border surrounding the range until you see the four-headed arrow cursor shape.

| 20 | Lamborghini | Aventador Sup | 217 | 2.8 | 690 | 493,095 | Italy |
| 21 | Ferrari | 488 GTB | 205 | 2.9 | 661 | 242,737 | Italy |
| 22 | Lamborghini | Huracán | 202 | 2.5 | 602 | 237,250 | Italy |
| 23 | | | | | | | |

It is very important that you see the four-headed arrow and not the white cross or AutoFill cursor shape.

If you do not see a four-headed arrow somebody may have switched the drag and drop facility off. See sidebar for how to bring it back.

3.   Click and drag the selected cells, dropping them to their previous location (beginning at cell A8).

You'll see a green outline showing where the cells will be dropped. Move them to the location shown in the screen grab below.

| 7 | Aston Martin | V12 Vantage S | 205 | 3.7 | 565 | 123,695 | UK |
| 8 | | | | | | | |
| 9 | | | | | | | |
| 10 | Porsche | 911 Turbo S Sport+ | A8:G9 | 7 | 3.1 | 560 | 241,105 | Germany |

4.   Release the mouse button.

The contents of the cells are moved back to A8:G9.

| 7 | Aston Martin | V12 Vantage S | 205 | 3.7 | 565 | 123,695 | UK |
| 8 | Ferrari | 488 GTB | 205 | 2.9 | 661 | 242,737 | Italy |
| 9 | Lamborghini | Huracán | 202 | 2.5 | 602 | 237,250 | Italy |
| 10 | Porsche | 911 Turbo S Sport+ | 197 | 3.1 | 560 | 241,105 | Germany |

3   Copy cells A8:G9 to cells A22:G23 using right-click drag and drop.

1.   Select cells A8:G9.

2.   Hover the mouse cursor over the green border surrounding the range until you see the four-headed arrow cursor shape.

3.   Right-click and drag the rectangle to rows 21 and 22.

4.   Release the mouse button.

Several options are presented (see sidebar).

5.   Click *Copy Here* from the shortcut menu.

This time the contents of the cells are copied rather than moved.

## note

**Another way to copy cells via drag and drop**

Hover over the border of the selected cells with the **<Ctrl>** key held down. You will see the mouse cursor shape change to a plus sign.

You can now drag and drop (holding the left mouse button down) to copy the cells to a new location.

| 17 | The World's Fastest Italian Cars | | | | | | |
|----|------|-------|-----|-----|-----|---------|-------|
| 18 | | | | | | | |
| 19 | Ferrari | F12 Berlinetta | 227 | 3.1 | 730 | 330,000 | Italy |
| 20 | Lamborghini | Aventador Super Veloce | 217 | 2.8 | 690 | 493,095 | Italy |
| 21 | Ferrari | 488 GTB | 205 | 2.9 | 661 | 242,737 | Italy |
| 22 | Lamborghini | Huracán | 202 | 2.5 | 602 | 237,250 | Italy |

**4** Copy the contents of row 15 to row 23 using right-click drag and drop.

| 17 | The World's Fastest Italian Cars | | | | | | |
|----|------|-------|-----|-----|-----|---------|-------|
| 18 | | | | | | | |
| 19 | Ferrari | F12 Berlinetta | 227 | 3.1 | 730 | 330,000 | Italy |
| 20 | Lamborghini | Aventador Super Veloce | 217 | 2.8 | 690 | 493,095 | Italy |
| 21 | Ferrari | 488 GTB | 205 | 2.9 | 661 | 242,737 | Italy |
| 22 | Lamborghini | Huracán | 202 | 2.5 | 602 | 237,250 | Italy |
| 23 | Ferrari | LaFerrari | 217 | 2.6 | 950 | 1,690,000 | Italy |

**5** Rename Sheet1 to *World Cars*.

You learned how to rename worksheet tabs in: *Lesson 1-9: View, move, add, rename, delete and navigate worksheet tabs.*

**6** Add a new worksheet and name it: *Italian Cars*.

You learned how to add new worksheets in: *Lesson 1-9: View, move, add, rename, delete and navigate worksheet tabs.*

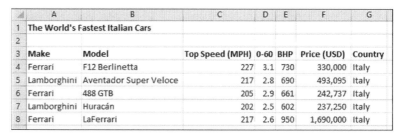

**7** Move cells A17:G23 on the *World Cars* worksheet to cells A1:G7 on the *Italian Cars* worksheet.

1. Select cells A17:G23 on the *World Cars* worksheet.

2. Cut the cells and paste them into cell A1 of the *Italian Cars* worksheet.

**8** Insert one blank row above row 3 on the *Italian Cars* worksheet.

You learned how to do this in: *Lesson 3-1: Insert and delete rows and columns.*

**9** Copy the titles from row 3 of the *World Cars* worksheet to row 3 of the *Italian Cars* worksheet.

| | A | B | C | D | E | F | G |
|---|------|-------|-----------------|-----|-----|-----------|---------|
| 1 | The World's Fastest Italian Cars | | | | | | |
| 2 | | | | | | | |
| 3 | Make | Model | Top Speed (MPH) | 0-60 | BHP | Price (USD) | Country |
| 4 | Ferrari | F12 Berlinetta | 227 | 3.1 | 730 | 330,000 | Italy |
| 5 | Lamborghini | Aventador Super Veloce | 217 | 2.8 | 690 | 493,095 | Italy |
| 6 | Ferrari | 488 GTB | 205 | 2.9 | 661 | 242,737 | Italy |
| 7 | Lamborghini | Huracán | 202 | 2.5 | 602 | 237,250 | Italy |
| 8 | Ferrari | LaFerrari | 217 | 2.6 | 950 | 1,690,000 | Italy |

**10** Resize all columns on the *Italian Cars* worksheet so that they are wide enough to display their contents.

You learned how to do this in: *Lesson 2-9: Re-size rows and columns.*

**11** Save your work as *The World's Fastest Cars-5*.

# Lesson 3-5: Use Paste Values and increase/decrease decimal places displayed

1    Open *The World's Fastest Cars-5* from your sample files folder (if it isn't already open).

2    Select the *World Cars* worksheet and add a new column to the left of column D.

Right click on the column D header and click *Insert* from the shortcut menu.

3    Rename cell C3 from *Top Speed (MPH)* to *MPH*.

4    Type **KM/H** into cell D3.

5    Re-size column C so that it is just wide enough for the contents.

This skill was covered in: *Lesson 2-9: Re-size rows and columns.*

6    Given that one mile=1.609344 Km, enter a formula into cell D4 to convert MPH into KM/H.

This skill was covered in: *Lesson 2-12: Create your own formulas.*

The correct formula is: **=C4\*1.609344.**

The Bugatti's top speed is now displayed in Kilometers per hour.

| | A | B | C | D | E | F |
|---|---|---|---|---|---|---|
| 3 | Make | Model | MPH | KM/H | 0-60 | BHP |
| 4 | Bugatti | Veyron Super Sport | 268 | 431.304192 | 2.4 | 1,184 |

7    AutoFill the formula in cell D4 down to the bottom of the list (cell D15).

This skill was covered in: *Lesson 2-15: Use AutoFill to adjust formulas.*

| | A | B | C | D | E | F |
|---|---|---|---|---|---|---|
| 3 | Make | Model | MPH | KM/H | 0-60 | BHP |
| 4 | Bugatti | Veyron Super Sport | 268 | 431.304192 | 2.4 | 1,184 |
| 5 | Ferrari | F12 Berlinetta | 227 | 365.321088 | 3.1 | 730 |

The worksheet is giving the right answers, but you're not really interested in seeing speeds to six decimal places. It would be nice to simply show whole numbers (also called integers) in the same way that values are shown for MPH.

8    Use the *Decrease Decimal* button to format the values in column D to display as whole numbers.

    1.  Select cells D4:D15.

    2.  Click the Home→Number→Decrease Decimal button six times.

9    Make column D narrower to make things neater.

This skill was covered in: *Lesson 2-9: Re-size rows and columns.*

The World's Fastest Cars-5

| | B | C | D |
|---|---|---|---|
| | Model | MPH | KM/H |
| | Veyron Super Sport | 268 | 431 |
| | F12 Berlinetta | 227 | 365 |

## note

### Other ways to paste values

### Using the Smart Tag

If you perform a regular *paste* and then suddenly realize that you really wanted to *paste values* you don't need to start again.

Notice that a Smart Tag is displayed at the bottom right corner of the pasted cells.

You can click the Smart Tag to change the paste to *Values*.

### Using the Ribbon

If you click:

Home→Clipboard→Paste (drop-down arrow)

... you'll be presented with the same set of icons. You've only learned about the *Paste* and *Paste Values* options so far but you'll encounter some of the others later in this course:

**10** Copy cells D4:D15 to cells D17:D28 using copy and paste.

1. Select cells D4:D15.

2. Right-click anywhere in the selected range and then click *Copy* from the shortcut menu.

3. Right-click cell D17 and click: Paste Options→Paste from the shortcut menu.

Unexpectedly, all of the values are pasted as zeros.

| ⊿ | A | B | C | D | E |
|---|---|---|---|---|---|
| 16 | | | | | |
| 17 | | | | 0 | |
| 18 | | | | 0 | |

**11** Inspect the formula in cell D17.

Click in cell D17 and look at the formula displayed in the Formula Bar at the top of the screen:

=C17*1.609344

It is now clear why the value was correctly calculated as zero.

When you paste a formula, Excel will, by default, adjust the formula in exactly the same way that it does when you AutoFill.

**12** Undo the previous paste.

Click the undo button ⟲ on the quick access toolbar.

You are going to learn a lot more about the undo button later in: *Lesson 3-8: Use Undo and Redo.*

**13** Paste again, this time using Paste Values.

Right-click in cell D17 and click: Paste Options→Values from the shortcut menu.

This time the values within the cells (rather than the formulas used to calculate the values) are pasted.

| ⊿ | A | B | C | D | E | F |
|---|---|---|---|---|---|---|
| 15 | Ferrari | LaFerrari | 217 | 349 | 2.6 | 950 |
| 16 | | | | | | |
| 17 | | | | 431.3 | | |
| 18 | | | | 365.3 | | |

**14** Delete the values in cells D17:D28.

Select cells D17:D28 and press the <Delete> key.

**15** Save your work as *The World's Fastest Cars-6*.

# Lesson 3-6: Transpose a range

*Paste Values* is the most used special pasting option but there's another that is often very useful.

If a worksheet has many columns but few rows it may become impossible to print. In this case you may wish to reverse the arrangement so that the worksheet has many rows but few columns.

Transposing allows you to do this automatically.

1 Open *The World's Fastest Cars-6* from your sample files folder (if it isn't already open).

2 Add a new worksheet and name it: *Transposed.*

This skill was covered in: *Lesson 1-9: View, move, add, rename, delete and navigate worksheet tabs.*

3 Select and copy the range A3:H15 on the *World Cars* worksheet.

| ⁄ | A | B | C | D | E | F | G | H |
|---|---|---|---|---|---|---|---|---|
| 1 | The World's Fastest Cars | | | | | | | |
| 2 | | | | | | | | |
| 3 | Make | Model | MPH | KM/H | 0-60 | BHP | Price (USD) | Country |
| 4 | Bugatti | Veyron Super Sport | 268 | 431 | 2.4 | 1,184 | 1,700,000 | Germany |
| 5 | Ferrari | F12 Berlinetta | 227 | 365 | 3.1 | 730 | 330,000 | Italy |
| 6 | Lamborghini | Aventador Super Veloce | 217 | 349 | 2.8 | 690 | 493,095 | Italy |
| 7 | Aston Martin | V12 Vantage S | 205 | 330 | 3.7 | 565 | 123,695 | UK |
| 8 | Ferrari | 488 GTB | 205 | 330 | 2.9 | 661 | 242,737 | Italy |
| 9 | Lamborghini | Huracán | 202 | 325 | 2.5 | 602 | 237,250 | Italy |
| 10 | Porsche | 911 Turbo S Sport+ | 197 | 317 | 3.1 | 560 | 241,105 | Germany |
| 11 | Aston Martin | Vanquish Volante | 197 | 317 | 3.8 | 568 | 299,000 | UK |
| 12 | Mercedes | SLS AMG Black Series | 196 | 315 | 3.5 | 622 | 275,000 | Germany |
| 13 | Lotus | Evora 400 | 186 | 299 | 4.1 | 400 | 89,900 | UK |
| 14 | Tesla | Model S P90D | 155 | 249 | 2.6 | 762 | 130,700 | USA |
| 15 | Ferrari | LaFerrari | 217 | 349 | 2.6 | 950 | 1,690,000 | Italy |

4 Select cell A3 on the *Transposed* worksheet.

5 Click: Home→Clipboard→
Paste (drop down list)→Transpose.

The World's Fastest Cars-6

The cells are copied in a rather interesting way. The columns have now become rows and the rows have become columns.

| | A | B | C | D | E | F | G | H | I | J | K | L | M |
|---|---|---|---|---|---|---|---|---|---|---|---|---|---|
| 1 | | | | | | | | | | | | | |
| 2 | | | | | | | | | | | | | |
| 3 | Make | Bugatti | Ferrari | Lamborgh | Aston Mar | Ferrari | Lamborgh | Porsche | Aston Mar | Mercedes | Lotus | Tesla | Ferrari |
| 4 | Model | Veyron Su | F12 Berlin | Aventado | V12 Vanta | 488 GTB | Huracán | 911 Turbo | Vanquish | SLS AMG E | Evora 400 | Model S P | LaFerrari |
| 5 | MPH | 268 | 227 | 217 | 205 | 205 | 202 | 197 | 197 | 196 | 186 | 155 | 217 |
| 6 | KM/H | 431 | 365 | 349 | 330 | 330 | 325 | 317 | 317 | 315 | 299 | 249 | 349 |
| 7 | 0-60 | 2.4 | 3.1 | 2.8 | 3.7 | 2.9 | 2.5 | 3.1 | 3.8 | 3.5 | 4.1 | 2.6 | 2.6 |
| 8 | BHP | 1,184 | 730 | 690 | 565 | 661 | 602 | 560 | 568 | 622 | 400 | 762 | 950 |
| 9 | Price (USD | ###### | 330,000 | 493,095 | 123,695 | 242,737 | 237,250 | 241,105 | 299,000 | 275,000 | 89,900 | 130,700 | ###### |
| 10 | Country | Germany | Italy | Italy | UK | Italy | Italy | Germany | UK | Germany | UK | USA | Italy |

Notice also that the width of the columns has not been maintained.

In the case of the (very expensive) Bugatti Veyron and Ferrari LaFerrari there isn't even enough space in the cell to display the price and a row of hashes is displayed instead.

(If you're used to calling the hash (#) a *pound sign* or *number sign* see the sidebar in: *Lesson 2-9: Re-size rows and columns* for an explanation).

6　Automatically size all columns in one operation.

1. Select every cell in the workbook by clicking the *select all* button in the top left corner of the worksheet:

2. Hover the mouse cursor over the intersection of any two columns until you see the *re-size* cursor shape ⟷ and then double-click.

3. Every column is now perfectly sized.

| | A | B | C | D |
|---|---|---|---|---|
| 1 | | | | |
| 2 | | | | |
| 3 | Make | Bugatti | Ferrari | Lamborghini |
| 4 | Model | Veyron Super Sport | F12 Berlinetta | Aventador Super Veloce |
| 5 | MPH | 268 | 227 | 217 |
| 6 | KM/H | 431 | 365 | 349 |

7　Save your work as *The World's Fastest Cars-7*.

## note

### About task panes

Task panes are similar to dialogs but there are several important differences.

**1. Task panes are modeless.**

Windows dialogs (with very few exceptions) are *modal*, while task panes are *modeless*.

Until you've dismissed a dialog (usually by clicking an *OK* or *Cancel* button) you can't do anything else.

If you click anywhere on the worksheet or Ribbon when a modal dialog is open, you'll just hear a "ding" noise!

Task panes are modeless.

This means that you can go on working and leave task panes happily sitting in the background.

**2. Task panes can automatically update as you work.**

Task panes can respond dynamically to any actions you take on the worksheet.

You can see this in action with the *Clipboard* task pane.

As you copy new items they automatically update in the task pane.

**3. Task panes can be re-sized and either docked to the left or right of the screen or floated.**

If you click and drag the title bar of a task pane, you can "dock" the pane to the right or left of the screen. This means that the task pane snaps into place and is then re-sized with the Excel window.

If you drag a task pane to the centre of the screen it becomes a "floating" task pane and can be positioned anywhere.

**The World's Fastest Cars-7**

# Lesson 3-7: Use the Multiple Item Clipboard

When you copy items from any non-Office Windows application, the selected item is copied to the *Windows Clipboard*. You are then able to paste this item into any other Windows application.

While the *Windows Clipboard* can only contain one item, Office has its own clipboard that can contain up to 24 items.

Because all Office applications share the same *Office Clipboard*, it is possible to copy and paste up to 24 items between Excel, PowerPoint, Word, Access, Outlook and all other Office applications.

In this lesson, you'll use the *Office Clipboard* to add content to a new worksheet in the workbook. The new worksheet will contain details of the world's fastest *German* cars.

1   Open *The World's Fastest Cars-7* from your sample files folder (if it isn't already open).

2   Insert a new worksheet and name it *German Cars*.

This skill was covered in: *Lesson 1-9: View, move, add, rename, delete and navigate worksheet tabs.*

3   Click: Home→Clipboard→Dialog Launcher.

This is your first experience of using a *dialog launcher* button. The dialog launcher button is situated on the bottom right-hand corner of some Ribbon command groups.

The *Clipboard* task pane is displayed:

This is also your first use of a *Task Pane* (see sidebar for more on task panes).

4   If any items are shown on the Clipboard click the *Clear All* button to remove them.

5   Copy row 3 on the World Cars worksheet to the clipboard.

1.   Click the *World Cars* worksheet tab to select it.

2.  Right-click the row 3 row header and click *Copy* from the shortcut menu.

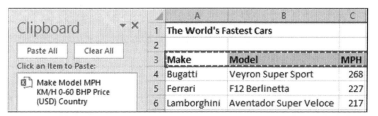

6   Copy row 4 in the *World Cars* worksheet to the clipboard.

7   Copy row 10 in the *World Cars* worksheet to the clipboard.

8   Copy row 12 in the *World Cars* worksheet to the clipboard.

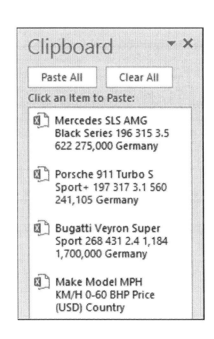

The header row, along with details for the three German cars, are now displayed on the clipboard (see sidebar).

9   Click the *German Cars* tab.

The blank *German Cars* worksheet is displayed.

10  Type **The World's Fastest German Cars** into cell A1 and bold face the text.

11  Click cell A3 to make it the Active Cell.

12  Complete the worksheet with a single click by clicking the *Paste All* button.

It would be possible to achieve the same result by clicking once upon each of the four items on the Clipboard.  Because you want the entire contents of the Clipboard, four clicks are saved by using the *Paste All* button.

When you click the *Paste All* button, all of the items on the clipboard are pasted into adjacent rows:

13  Automatically Re-size all of the columns.

This skill was covered in: *Lesson 2-9: Re-size rows and columns.*

14  Close the clipboard task pane.

Click the *Close* button at the top right-hand corner of the clipboard task pane.

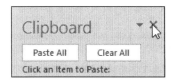

15  Save your work as *The World's Fastest Cars-8.*

# Lesson 3-8: Use Undo and Redo

Excel's (fantastically useful) *Undo* feature enables you to reverse an action when you have made a mistake.

It is only possible to undo the previous 100 actions.

Sometimes you may undo an action and then change your mind. Redo will step through the operations in reverse, in effect "undoing the undo".

1   Close any workbooks that are open and then re-open Excel.

Excel keeps tabs on the last 100 actions taken. By closing and re-opening Excel you'll clear the existing list of actions available for undo.

2   Open *The World's Fastest Cars-8* from your sample files folder and select the *World Cars* worksheet.

3   Type **UK Cars** into cell A17 and bold face the text.

4   Copy row 3 into row 19.

5   Copy row 7 into row 20.

6   Copy row 11 into row 21.

7   Copy row 13 into row 22.

The worksheet should now look like this:

| | A | B | C | D | E | F | G | H |
|---|---|---|---|---|---|---|---|---|
| 1 | The World's Fastest Cars | | | | | | | |
| 2 | | | | | | | | |
| 3 | Make | Model | MPH | KM/H | 0-60 | BHP | Price (USD) | Country |
| 4 | Bugatti | Veyron Super Sport | 268 | 431 | 2.4 | 1,184 | 1,700,000 | Germany |
| 5 | Ferrari | F12 Berlinetta | 227 | 365 | 3.1 | 730 | 330,000 | Italy |
| 6 | Lamborghini | Aventador Super Veloce | 217 | 349 | 2.8 | 690 | 493,095 | Italy |
| 7 | Aston Martin | V12 Vantage S | 205 | 330 | 3.7 | 565 | 123,695 | UK |
| 8 | Ferrari | 488 GTB | 205 | 330 | 2.9 | 661 | 242,737 | Italy |
| 9 | Lamborghini | Huracán | 202 | 325 | 2.5 | 602 | 237,250 | Italy |
| 10 | Porsche | 911 Turbo S Sport+ | 197 | 317 | 3.1 | 560 | 241,105 | Germany |
| 11 | Aston Martin | Vanquish Volante | 197 | 317 | 3.8 | 568 | 299,000 | UK |
| 12 | Mercedes | SLS AMG Black Series | 196 | 315 | 3.5 | 622 | 275,000 | Germany |
| 13 | Lotus | Evora 400 | 186 | 299 | 4.1 | 400 | 89,900 | UK |
| 14 | Tesla | Model S P90D | 155 | 249 | 2.6 | 762 | 130,700 | USA |
| 15 | Ferrari | LaFerrari | 217 | 349 | 2.6 | 950 | 1,690,000 | Italy |
| 16 | | | | | | | | |
| 17 | UK Cars | | | | | | | |
| 18 | | | | | | | | |
| 19 | Make | Model | MPH | KM/H | 0-60 | BHP | Price (USD) | Country |
| 20 | Aston Martin | V12 Vantage S | 205 | 330 | 3.7 | 565 | 123,695 | UK |
| 21 | Aston Martin | Vanquish Volante | 197 | 317 | 3.8 | 568 | 299,000 | UK |
| 22 | Lotus | Evora 400 | 186 | 299 | 4.1 | 400 | 89,900 | UK |

8   Click the undo button on the quick access toolbar.

The Lotus details disappear from row 22.

9   Click the redo button on the quick access toolbar.

The Lotus details re-appear in row 22.

---

## note

### Using the keyboard to undo and redo

It is well worth remembering the undo keyboard shortcut:

**<Ctrl>+<Z>**

I use it all the time. It is also the undo shortcut for the other Office applications.

You'll use the Redo action far less, but for completeness it is:

**<Ctrl>+<Y>**

If you forget them, you'll see the keyboard shortcuts in the tooltip when you hover over the undo and redo buttons.

The World's Fastest Cars-8

10 Click the drop-down arrow to the right of the undo button on the quick access toolbar.

A drop-down menu appears showing all of the actions that have taken place (or the previous 100 actions if more than 100 actions have taken place) since the workbook was opened.

11 Click the Bold action to *Undo 5 Actions*.

Only the text *UK Cars* remains on the worksheet and it is no longer bold faced.

| 14 | Tesla | Model S P90D | | 155 | 249 |
|----|-------|--------------|--|-----|-----|
| 15 | Ferrari | LaFerrari | | 217 | 349 |
| 16 | | | | | |
| 17 | UK Cars | | | | |
| 18 | | | | | |

12 Click the drop-down arrow to the right of the redo button on the quick access toolbar.

A drop-down menu appears showing all of the actions that have been undone and can be potentially re-done.

13 Click the last *Paste* action to redo five actions.

The worksheet reverts to its former state.

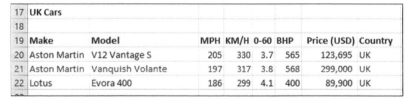

| 17 | UK Cars | | | | | | | |
|----|---------|-------|-----|------|-----|-----|------------|---------|
| 18 | | | | | | | | |
| 19 | Make | Model | MPH | KM/H | 0-60 | BHP | Price (USD) | Country |
| 20 | Aston Martin | V12 Vantage S | 205 | 330 | 3.7 | 565 | 123,695 | UK |
| 21 | Aston Martin | Vanquish Volante | 197 | 317 | 3.8 | 568 | 299,000 | UK |
| 22 | Lotus | Evora 400 | 186 | 299 | 4.1 | 400 | 89,900 | UK |

14 Delete rows 17 to 22.

15 Save your work as *The World's Fastest Cars-9*.

# Lesson 3-9: Insert cell comments

1 Open *The World's Fastest Cars-9* from your sample files folder (if it isn't already open) and select the *World Cars* worksheet.

2 Using Microsoft Word (not Excel), open *Car Descriptions* from your sample files folder.

   1. Open Microsoft Word.

   2. Click: File→Open and open *Car Descriptions* from your sample files folder.

3 Return to Excel without closing Word.

You will notice two buttons on the Windows status bar at the bottom of the screen:

Click the button with the Excel logo to return to Excel.

4 Set up the name that will appear in the comment box.

Whenever you enter a comment, your name is added to the top.

This allows other users to identify the source of each comment if you later distribute the workbook.

   1. Click: File→Options→General.

   2. In the category *Personalize your copy of Microsoft Office* type your name into the *User Name* box.

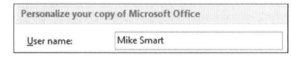

   3. Click the OK button.

5 Copy the text for the Mercedes SLS from the Word document.

   1. Return to Word.

   2. Click and drag across the Mercedes SLS text with the mouse cursor.

   3. Right-click within the selected text and click *Copy* from the shortcut menu.

6 Add the comment text to the Mercedes SLS model cell (cell B12).

---

**note**

### Excel uses your log in user name by default

If you don't set up your user name as described, Excel will use your Windows log-in user name instead.

This is the reason you'll often see cryptic user names (like JSmith93) in other people's worksheets.

---

**note**

### Other ways to insert a comment

Click: Review→Comments→ New Comment.

**OR**

Press: <Shift>+<F2>

---

Car Descriptions

The World's Fastest Cars-9

---

© 2018 The Smart Method® Ltd

## note

### How to put a picture into a comment box

Microsoft probably never intended that you put pictures into comments but there is a way to do this. Here's an example:

Here's the (rather long-winded) way in which you can do this:

1. Right-click into any cell and click: *Insert Comment…* on the shortcut menu.

2. Remove any name text currently inside the cell.

3. Hover over the border of the comment until you see the four-headed arrow cursor shape.

4. Right-click and then click: *Format Comment…* on the shortcut menu.

5. Click the *Colors and Lines* tab and then the drop-down arrow next to Fill→Color.

6. Click: Fill Effects…

7. Click the *Picture* tab.

8. Click: Select Picture...

9. Click the Browse… button next to *From a file*.

10. Select the *SmallMediumLarge* graphic from your sample files folder (or any other picture).

11. Click Insert, OK, OK to close all of the dialogs.

12. Re-size the comment box to display the graphic correctly.

---

1. Return to Excel.

2. Right-click cell B12 and click *Insert Comment* on the shortcut menu.

   A comment box with your name at the top is shown next to cell B4.

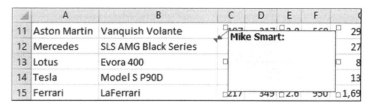

3. Paste into the comment box.

   The text that you copied from the Word document appears in the box.

7   Enlarge the comment box, using the sizing handles, so that all text is visible.

The sizing handles are the small white dots that appear on the corners and edges of the comment box. When you hover over a sizing handle, the cursor shape changes to a double headed arrow.

1. Hover carefully over the bottom-right sizing handle until you see the double-headed arrow cursor shape.

2. Click and drag the re-size handles to re-size the comment box.

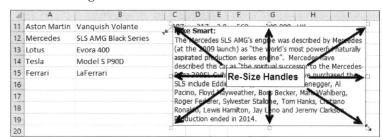

8   Click anywhere in the worksheet.

The comment disappears but a small red triangle has appeared in the top right corner of the cell.

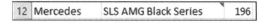

9   Add two more comments for the Tesla and Ferrari 488 GTB.

10   Save your work as *The World's Fastest Cars-10*.

# Lesson 3-10: View cell comments

1   Open *The World's Fastest Cars-10* from your sample files folder (if it isn't already open) and select the *World Cars* worksheet.

Cells with comments show a small red triangle in their top right-hand corner.

2   View the comment behind a single cell.

Hover the mouse cursor over any of the cells with a red triangle. The cell comment is displayed.

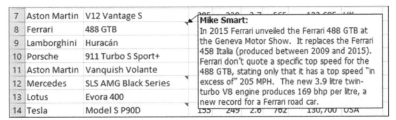

3   View all of the comments in a worksheet at the same time.

Click: Review→Comments→Show All Comments.

Every comment on the worksheet is displayed.

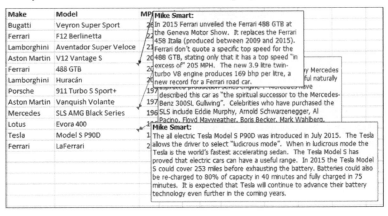

Unfortunately, the comments overlap so you are unable to read them all at the same time. It is possible to view each comment by clicking it, as this brings the window to the front, but it isn't very elegant.

4   Move and re-size the comments so that they do not overlap.

Click a comment and then hover anywhere on the border *but not on a sizing handle* until you see a four-headed arrow. When you see the four-headed arrow, click and drag to move the comment.

The World's Fastest Cars-10

| ⊿ | A | B | C | D | E | F | G | H | I | J | K |
|---|---|---|---|---|---|---|---|---|---|---|---|
| 1 | The World's Fastest Cars | | | | | | | | | | |
| 2 | | | | **Mike Smart:** | | | | | | | |
| 3 | Make | Model | MPH | In 2015 Ferrari unveiled the Ferrari 488 GTB at the Geneva Motor Show. It replaces the Ferrari 458 Italia (produced between 2009 and 2015). Ferrari don't quote a specific top speed for the 488 GTB, stating only that it has a top speed "in excess of" 205 MPH. The new 3.9 litre twin-turbo V8 engine produces 169 bhp per litre, a new record for a Ferrari road car. | | | | | | | |
| 4 | Bugatti | Veyron Super Sport | 268 | | | | | | | | |
| 5 | Ferrari | F12 Berlinetta | 227 | | | | | | | | |
| 6 | Lamborghini | Aventador Super Veloce | 217 | **Mike Smart:** | | | | | | | |
| 7 | Aston Martin | V12 Vantage S | 205 | The Mercedes SLS AMG's engine was described by Mercedes (at the 2009 launch) as "the world's most powerful naturally aspirated production series engine". Mercedes have described this car as "the spiritual successor to the Mercedes-Benz 300SL Gullwing". Celebrities who have purchased the SLS include Eddie Murphy, Arnold Schwarzenegger, Al Pacino, Floyd Mayweather, Boris Becker, Mark Wahlberg, Roger Federer, Sylvester Stallone, Tom Hanks, Cristiano Ronaldo, Lewis Hamilton, Jay Leno and Jeremy Clarkson. Production ended in 2014. | | | | | | | |
| 8 | Ferrari | 488 GTB | 205 | | | | | | | | |
| 9 | Lamborghini | Huracán | 202 | | | | | | | | |
| 10 | Porsche | 911 Turbo S Sport+ | 197 | | | | | | | | |
| 11 | Aston Martin | Vanquish Volante | 197 | | | | | | | | |
| 12 | Mercedes | SLS AMG Black Series | 196 | | | | | | | | |
| 13 | Lotus | Evora 400 | 186 | **Mike Smart:** | | | | | | | |
| 14 | Tesla | Model S P90D | 155 | The all electric Tesla Model S P90D was introduced in July 2015. The Tesla allows the driver to select "ludicrous mode". When in ludicrous mode the Tesla is the world's fastest accelerating sedan. The Tesla Model S has proved that electric cars can have a useful range. In 2015 the Tesla Model S could cover 253 miles before exhausting the battery. Batteries could also be re-charged to 80% of capacity in 40 minutes and fully charged in 75 minutes. It is expected that Tesla will continue to advance their battery technology even further in the coming years. | | | | | | | |
| 15 | Ferrari | LaFerrari | 217 | | | | | | | | |
| 16 | | | | | | | | | | | |
| 17 | | | | | | | | | | | |
| 18 | | | | | | | | | | | |
| 19 | | | | | | | | | | | |
| 20 | | | | | | | | | | | |

5    Hide all of the comments.

Click: Review→Comments→Show All Comments.

The comments disappear.

6    Make the Ferrari 488 GTB comment display all of the time.

Sometimes you will want to send somebody a worksheet and make sure that an important comment is on view when they open it.

Right click cell B8 and choose *Show/Hide Comments* from the shortcut menu.

The comment remains on display all of the time (even if you are not hovering over the comment cell).

7    Hide the Ferrari 488 GTB comment.

Right click cell B8 and choose *Hide Comment* from the shortcut menu.

8    Save your work as *The World's Fastest Cars-11*.

# Lesson 3-11: Print cell comments

One of the most common comment-related questions asked in my Excel classroom courses is: "how can I print a list of comments at the end of a worksheet"? Excel can do this but the feature is hidden away in the *Page Setup* dialog and missed by most users.

1   Open *The World's Fastest Cars-11* from your sample files folder (if it isn't already open) and select the *World Cars* worksheet.

2   Tell Excel to print comments at the end of the worksheet.

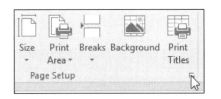

1.   Click: Page Layout→Page Setup→Dialog Launcher.

The *Dialog Launcher* is the small button on the bottom-right corner of the *Page Setup* group.

The *Page Setup* dialog is displayed.

2.   Click the *Sheet* tab.

3.   Click the *Comments* drop-down and select: *At end of sheet.*

3   Click the *Print Preview* button to view the comments as they would print.

You can either click the *Print Preview* button on the *Page Setup* dialog or close the dialog and click: File→Print.

Whichever way you choose, the *Backstage* view opens and displays a print preview of the worksheet in the right-hand pane.

Click the *Next Page* button 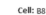 to view Page 2 of the preview. The comments are displayed exactly as they would print.

---

**Cell:** B8
**Comment:** Mike Smart:
In 2015 Ferrari unveiled the Ferrari 488 GTB at the Geneva Motor Show. It replaces the Ferrari 458 Italia (produced between 2009 and 2015). Ferrari don't quote a specific top speed for the 488 GTB, stating only that it has a top speed "in excess of" 205 MPH. The new 3.9 litre twin-turbo V8 engine produces 169 bhp per litre, a new record for a Ferrari road car.

**Cell:** B12
**Comment:** Mike Smart:
The Mercedes SLS AMG's engine was described by Mercedes (at the 2009 launch) as "the world's most powerful naturally aspirated production series engine". Mercedes have described this car as "the spiritual successor to the Mercedes-Benz 300SL Gullwing". Celebrities who have purchased the SLS include Eddie Murphy, Arnold Schwarzenegger, Al Pacino, Floyd Mayweather, Boris Becker, Mark Wahlberg, Roger Federer, Sylvester Stallone, Tom Hanks, Cristiano Ronaldo, Lewis Hamilton, Jay Leno and Jeremy Clarkson. Production ended in 2014.

**Cell:** B14
**Comment:** Mike Smart:
The all electric Tesla Model S P90D was introduced in July 2015. The Tesla allows the driver to select "ludicrous mode". When in ludicrous mode the Tesla is the world's fastest accelerating sedan. The Tesla Model S has proved that electric cars can have a useful range. In 2015 the Tesla Model S could cover 253 miles before exhausting the battery. Batteries could also be re-charged to 80% of capacity in 40 minutes and fully charged in 75 minutes. It is expected that Tesla will continue to advance their battery technology even further in the coming years.

---

**The World's Fastest Cars-11**

4   Click the Back button  to return to the worksheet.

---

5    Make the Tesla comment display all of the time.

Right click cell B14 and click: *Show/Hide Comments* from the shortcut menu.

6    Move the Tesla comment so that it doesn't obscure the data in the worksheet.

This was covered in: *Lesson 3-10: View cell comments.*

7    Tell Excel to print comments exactly as they are displayed on the worksheet.

1.  Click: Page Layout→Page Setup→Dialog Launcher.

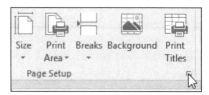

The *Page Setup* dialog is displayed.

2.  Click the *Sheet* tab.

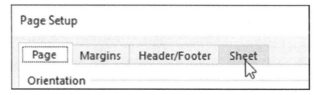

3.  Click the *Comments* drop-down and select: *As displayed on sheet.*

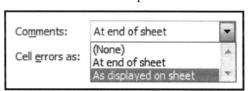

8    Click the *Print Preview* button to view the comment as it would print.

9    Click the *Back Button* ⟵ on the ribbon to return to the worksheet.

10   Hide the comment.

Right click cell B14 and click: *Hide Comment* from the shortcut menu.

11   Save your work as: *The World's Fastest Cars-12.*

# Lesson 3-12: Understand absolute and relative cell references

You've seen how useful Excel's AutoFill is when copying formulas. Most of the time things work perfectly, as you normally want to increment row and column references when you AutoFill down and across.

Sometimes AutoFill can be a little too helpful when it adjusts cell references that you would like to be left alone. This lesson will illustrate the type of worksheet that requires *absolute cell references* as we convert USD (US Dollar) prices to GBP (Great Britain Pounds).

1   Open *The World's Fastest Cars-12* from your sample files folder (if it isn't already open) and select the *World Cars* worksheet.

2   Insert a column to the left of column H.

   This skill was covered in: *Lesson 3-1: Insert and delete rows and columns.*

3   Type **Price (GBP)** into cell H3.

4   Type **USD/GBP** into cell G1.

5   Type **0.66519** into cell H1.

   Don't worry if the cell remains blank for the moment. This exchange rate will have changed by the time you read this book.

   If you want more realism you can get the current exchange rate from http://oanda.com. If you are not in England or America it might be fun to change the exchange rate to match your own currency.

6   If necessary, adjust the number of decimal places to show all five decimal places.

   You learned how to do this in: *Lesson 3-5: Use Paste Values and increase/decrease decimal places displayed.*

7   Make the text in cells G1 and H1 bold.

8   Place a formula in cell H4 that will calculate the price of a Bugatti Veyron in GBP (Great Britain Pounds).

   Formulas were covered in: *Lesson 2-12: Create your own formulas.*

   The correct formula is:

   **=G4*H1**

   You can now see that the Bugatti costs £1,130,823 in Great Britain Pounds.

| | G | H | I |
|---|---|---|---|
| 1 | USD/GBP | 0.66519 | |
| 2 | | | |
| 3 | Price (USD) | Price (GBP) | Country |
| 4 | 1,700,000 | 1,130,823 | Germany |
| 5 | 330,000 | | Italy |

The World's Fastest Cars-12

**9** Consider what will happen if you AutoFill this formula.

AutoFill was covered in: *Lesson 2-15: Use AutoFill to adjust formulas.*

As the formula is AutoFilled downward the number part of each formula will be incremented like this:

| | H |
|---|---|
| 1 | 0.66519 |
| 2 | |
| 3 | Price (GBP) |
| 4 | =G4*H1 |
| 5 | =G5*H2 |
| 6 | =G6*H3 |

Consider cell H5 (the price of the Ferrari F12 Berlinetta). The formula in this cell is **=G5*H2**.

AutoFill has done a wonderful job with G5. It has changed the reference from the Bugatti's price to the Ferrari F12, and that's exactly what you wanted.

But AutoFill has seriously messed up with the H2 reference. The exchange rate is always in cell H1. It never moves.

To express this in Excel terminology: G4 is a **relative reference** (ie you want AutoFill to adjust it) while H1 is an **absolute reference** (ie you want AutoFill to leave it alone).

**10** Change the formula in cell H4 to make H1 into an absolute reference.

To make a reference absolute you simply add a dollar sign in front of both the letter and number.

So: H1 becomes $H$1.

Click in cell H4 and then edit the formula (shown in the formula bar) so that it now reads:

**=G4*$H$1**

**11** AutoFill the formula in cell H4 to the end of the list.

(AutoFill was covered in: *Lesson 2-15: Use AutoFill to adjust formulas*).

The price of each car is now displayed in both US Dollars and Great Britain Pounds.

Click on each of the GBP prices and observe the formula shown in the formula bar at the top of the screen.

In each cell Excel has adjusted the G4 part of the formula but left the H1 part of the formula alone.

| H5 | ▼ | | ✕ | ✓ | *fx* | =G5*$H$1 |
|---|---|---|---|---|---|---|

| | C | D | E | F | G | H |
|---|---|---|---|---|---|---|
| 3 | MPH | KM/H | 0-60 | BHP | Price (USD) | Price (GBP) |
| 4 | 268 | 431 | 2.4 | 1,184 | 1,700,000 | 1,130,823 |
| 5 | 227 | 365 | 3.1 | 730 | 330,000 | 219,513 |

**12** Save your work as *The World's Fastest Cars-13*.

| | G | H | I |
|---|---|---|---|
| 3 | Price (USD) | Price (GBP) | Country |
| 4 | 1,700,000 | 1,130,823 | Germany |
| 5 | 330,000 | 219,513 | Italy |
| 6 | 493,095 | 328,002 | Italy |

**note**

**Don't worry if you're unable to understand this concept at first**

In my "Essential Skills" classroom courses I've found that many students find mixed cell references a very difficult concept to understand.

I never waste a lot of time on this lesson if some students are unable to easily follow the logic.

I'd advise that you take the same approach and don't waste a lot of time on this lesson if you find it difficult to follow.

You won't need to use mixed cell references anywhere else in the *Essential Skills* course and it's a skill that most office workers don't have.

If you do skip this lesson it's well worthwhile returning to it later, when you've completed the course and have been using Excel for a few months.

By then you will probably have encountered some of the real-world business problems that are more efficiently solved using mixed cell references.

# Lesson 3-13: Understand mixed cell references

Before you tackle mixed cell references I must warn you that this subject is a bit of a brain teaser (see sidebar). The skill is well worth mastering as you'll find it extremely useful in many types of real-world worksheets.

1   Open *International Price List* from your sample files folder.

This worksheet will calculate the price of each car in five different currencies. The exchange rates are shown in row 4.

The real-world exchange rates will have changed by the time you read this book. If you would like more realism you can obtain the current exchange rates from http://oanda.com.

2   Add a formula to cell D6 that will calculate the UK price of a Bugatti Veyron.

Formulas were covered in: *Lesson 2-12: Create your own formulas.*

The correct formula is:

**=C6*D4**

You can see that the Veyron costs £1,130,823.

| | C | D | E | F | G | H |
|---|---|---|---|---|---|---|
| 3 | | GBP | EUR | JPY | CAD | CHF |
| 4 | | 0.66519 | 0.94522 | 122.93 | 1.33668 | 1.02979 |
| 5 | USA $ | UK £ | Euros € | Japan ¥ | Canada $ | Switzerland fr. |
| 6 | 1,700,000 | 1,130,823 | | | | |

3   Consider what will happen if you AutoFill this formula.

AutoFill was covered in: *Lesson 2-15: Use AutoFill to adjust formulas.*

As the formula is AutoFilled downward, the number part of each formula is incremented like this:

| | C | D |
|---|---|---|
| 6 | 1700000 | =C6*D4 |
| 7 | 330000 | =C7*D5 |
| 8 | 493095 | =C8*D6 |

The reference to cell C6 is being correctly adjusted to point to the price of each car in the list. There is a problem with the reference to cell D4 as it should not be adjusted.

You may be thinking that this problem is exactly the same as the one solved in: *Lesson 3-12: Understand absolute and relative cell references.*

Why not simply make D4 into an absolute reference? Like this:

| | C | D |
|---|---|---|
| 3 | | GBP |
| 4 | | 0.66519 |
| 5 | USA $ | UK £ |
| 6 | 1700000 | =C6*$D$4 |

This will work just fine for the GBP prices, but think carefully about what will then happen when you AutoFill to the right.

AutoFill knows that when you fill right you *usually* want the letter part of each formula incremented like this:

| | C | D | E |
|---|---|---|---|
| 3 | | GBP | EUR |
| 4 | | 0.66519 | 0.94522 |
| 5 | USA $ | UK £ | Euros € |
| 6 | 1700000 | =C6*$D$4 | =D6*$D$4 |
| 7 | 330000 | =C7*$D$4 | |
| 8 | 493095 | =C8*$D$4 | |

This will not correctly calculate the Euro price. AutoFill has made two errors:

1.  It is still using the GBP exchange rate for the EUR prices because you made D4 an absolute reference.

2.  It is referencing the UK price of the Bugatti instead of the US dollar price because C6 is a relative reference.

Here is how each problem can be solved using mixed cell references:

1.  You want the GBP exchange rate to adjust to the EUR exchange rate as the formula is filled to the right. In this case the D part of D4 should be relative but the 4 part should be absolute. This can be denoted by D$4 instead of $D$4.

2.  You want the US Dollar price to always be used against the US Dollar Exchange rates in Row 4. Therefore, you want the C part of C6 to be absolute. As AutoFill fills downward you need the price to be adjusted to the relevant car so the 6 part of C6 needs to be relative. This can be denoted by $C6 instead of $C$6.

4   Correct the formula so that it will AutoFill correctly.

Enter the formula =$C6*D$4 into cell D6.

This will AutoFill correctly like this:

| | C | D | E | F |
|---|---|---|---|---|
| 3 | | GBP | EUR | JPY |
| 4 | | 0.66519 | 0.94522 | 122.93 |
| 5 | USA $ | UK £ | Euros € | Japan ¥ |
| 6 | 1700000 | =$C6*D$4 | =$C6*E$4 | =$C6*F$4 |
| 7 | 330000 | =$C7*D$4 | =$C7*E$4 | =$C7*F$4 |
| 8 | 493095 | =$C8*D$4 | =$C8*E$4 | =$C8*F$4 |

5   AutoFill across to cell H6.

The correct Bugatti prices are shown in five currencies.

6   AutoFill down to cell H17.

The correct prices are shown for all cars and all currencies.

7   Make the columns wide enough to display the prices.

8   Save your work as *International Price List-1*.

## tip

### A faster way to add dollar signs to create mixed references

1.  Click on the formula bar so that the cursor is touching the cell reference you want to convert to mixed:

2.  Press the <F4> key repeatedly on the keyboard.

Each time you press <F4> Excel cycles through all possible absolute and mixed references:

## note

### Templates and cloud computing

Until you've completed: *Session Eight: Cloud Computing,* you may not completely understand this sidebar as you'd be getting a little ahead of yourself.

In: *Session Eight: Cloud Computing,* you'll learn how you can store your files on a OneDrive so that you can work on the same files from any device (computer, smartphone or pad), at any location.

This way of working is called *Cloud Computing.*

If you do decide to move your files to the cloud, you'll also want your custom templates to reside in the cloud so that they are available on all of your devices.

In this case you'd set the default custom template folder to a location in your local synchronized OneDrive folder.

## note

### VBA code and Excel

If you search the Internet looking for a solution to an Excel problem, it won't be long before you'll find a well-intentioned user suggesting the use of VBA program code.

Most of the problems that users imagine requires custom VBA code can be better (and more easily) solved by the correct use of Excel features you've learned about in this book (or will learn about in the *Expert Skills* book in this series).

My advice is to avoid VBA code in your projects. When Excel is being used for its intended purpose (as an analytical tool) there are very few real-world business problems that truly need custom VBA code.

# Lesson 3-14: Understand templates and set the default custom template folder

A template is simply a partially completed, normal workbook that contains the starting point for a task that you often need to do. You can put anything into a template that you can put into a regular workbook.

## What are sample templates?

A sample template is a template that was created by Microsoft or another third-party. Sample templates aim to give you a starting point to solve common problems with Excel.

Several sample templates are shown on the *New* dialog (the dialog you see when you first start Excel), such as a *Wedding Budget* and *Inventory List.*

There are many thousands more sample templates available online.

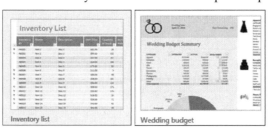

It may seem, at first, as if sample templates are a replacement for having to learn Excel but they are not quite as useful as they first promise to be.

There are three potential problems in using them:

1.  Sample templates often appear to provide a solution that is *almost* what you need. You may find that the work involved in converting them to *exactly* what you need takes longer than starting with a blank worksheet.

2.  Some templates include very advanced Excel features that non-expert users will find difficult to understand.

3.  Some templates include VBA (Visual Basic for Applications) custom program code to extend Excel's normal features. It can be impossible to maintain or customize workbooks containing program code unless you have access to a competent VBA programmer (see sidebar).

## What is a custom template?

A custom template is a template that you have created yourself. Because you completely understand how custom templates work, you may find them far more useful than sample templates.

You'll often find yourself making copies of older workbooks that are nearly the same as the one you need. You then delete the bits you don't need and add the bits that you do.

If you find this happening, it's time to make a custom template. You'll learn how to make your first custom template later, in: *Lesson 3-15: Create a template.*

## note

### How do I create a subfolder?

The concept of folders, subfolders and files is a very fundamental Windows skill rather than an Excel skill.

If you do not have basic Windows skills (an understanding of how Windows organizes files) you would get good value from a Windows book to give you the foundation skills you need to use any Windows program.

Here's how you create a new subfolder:

1. Right-click on the *Custom Office Templates* folder.

2. Click *New Folder* from the shortcut menu.

A new folder will appear called *New Folder.*

3. You will now be able to type: **Excel** in order to name the folder.

If this doesn't work for you, right-click the new folder and select *Rename* from the shortcut menu. You'll then be able to type: **Excel** to rename the folder.

## What is the custom template folder?

The custom template folder is where custom templates are stored on your computer.

By default, all templates, for all Office applications (such as Excel, Word and PowerPoint), are stored in the same folder. This isn't a great idea as you may create a large number of templates and they will be easier to work with if you organize them. For this reason, Excel 2013 introduced a new ability to set a different default custom template location for each Office application.

You're going to organize your templates properly, so you need a folder that will contain only *Excel* custom templates. If you work with Word and PowerPoint, you can use the same technique to create different folders for Word and PowerPoint custom templates.

1     Create an *Excel* folder beneath the *Custom Office Templates* folder.

      1.   Use *Windows File Explorer* to navigate to the folder:

         C:\Users\[Your Windows Log-in Name]\Documents\ Custom Office Templates

         Note that in versions of Windows versions that are older than Windows 10 you may find that the *Documents* folder referred to above is actually called *My Documents.*

      2.   Create a sub-folder beneath the *Custom Office Templates* folder named *Excel.*

         Your folder will look similar to the one shown in the sidebar. You should see your own Windows log-in name instead of *Mike.*

2     Open a new blank workbook.

      When you open a blank workbook, you are actually creating a workbook using the *Blank workbook* standard template.

3     Set the default *Custom Office Templates* folder so that it points to the new Excel folder you have just created.

      Click: File→Options→Save.

      In the *Save Workbooks* section, assuming that you are logged into Windows, you'll probably see that the current *Default personal templates folder* is set to a value similar to:

      | Default personal **t**emplates location: | C:\Users\Mike\Documents\Custom Office Templates\ |
| --- | --- |

      (If the box is blank you may have to type this manually).

      Click at the end of the location path and type: **Excel**

      | Default personal **t**emplates location: | C:\Users\Mike\Documents\Custom Office Templates\Excel |
| --- | --- |

4     Click OK and close Excel.

# Lesson 3-15: Create a template

1 Open *First Quarter Sales and Bonus* from your sample files folder.

| | A | B | C | D | E |
|---|---|---|---|---|---|
| 1 | First quarter sales and bonus | | | | |
| 2 | | | | | |
| 3 | Sales | | | | |
| 4 | | | | | |
| 5 | First Name | Last Name | Sales | Target | Over Target Sales |
| 6 | Andrew | Fuller | 7,639.30 | 5,000 | 2,639.30 |
| 7 | Anne | Dodsworth | 2,979.30 | 5,000 | - 2,020.70 |
| 8 | Janet | Leverling | 29,658.60 | 5,000 | 24,658.60 |
| 9 | Laura | Callahan | 19,271.60 | 5,000 | 14,271.60 |
| 10 | Margaret | Peacock | 44,795.20 | 5,000 | 39,795.20 |
| 11 | Michael | Suyama | 4,109.80 | 5,000 | - 890.20 |
| 12 | Nancy | Davolio | 15,330.10 | 5,000 | 10,330.10 |
| 13 | Robert | King | 21,461.60 | 5,000 | 16,461.60 |
| 14 | Steven | Buchanan | 2,634.40 | 5,000 | - 2,365.60 |
| 15 | | Total: | 147,879.90 | | |
| 16 | | | | | |
| 17 | Bonus | | | | |
| 18 | | | | | |
| 19 | First Name | Last Name | Salary | Bonus | Total |
| 20 | Andrew | Fuller | 2,500 | 131.97 | 2,631.97 |
| 21 | Anne | Dodsworth | 2,000 | - | 2,000.00 |
| 22 | Janet | Leverling | 2,600 | 1,232.93 | 3,832.93 |
| 23 | Laura | Callahan | 2,800 | 713.58 | 3,513.58 |
| 24 | Margaret | Peacock | 3,000 | 1,989.76 | 4,989.76 |
| 25 | Michael | Suyama | 1,800 | - | 1,800.00 |
| 26 | Nancy | Davolio | 4,500 | 516.51 | 5,016.51 |
| 27 | Robert | King | 2,000 | 823.08 | 2,823.08 |
| 28 | Steven | Buchanan | 3,000 | - | 3,000.00 |
| 29 | | Total: | 24,200 | 5,407.82 | 29,607.82 |

This is exactly the type of workbook you'd probably want to convert into a template. Only the data in cells C6:D14 will change each quarter.

Every quarter you could simply open last quarter's workbook, save it with a new name and then delete the old values in cells C6:D14. But you'd have to do that every quarter and then, one day, you might forget the *save it with a new name* step and end up overwriting the old file.

A much more efficient solution would be to save a copy of the workbook, with blank values in cells C6:D14, as a template.

2 Delete the contents of cells *C6:D14.*

This is the data that changes every quarter. Deleting it will provide an empty template, ready to be populated with each quarter's figures.

**First Quarter Sales and Bonus**

3 Replace the text in cell A1 with the words: *Bonus Calculator.*

This is a more generic title that can be used for any quarter.

4   Save your work as: *Bonus Calculator*.

5   Save the workbook again, this time as a template.

1.  Click: File→Save As→Browse.

2.  Click the drop-down list arrow labeled *Save as Type* at the bottom of the *Save As* dialog.

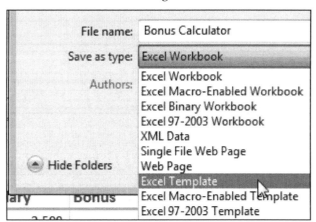

3.  The best choice for this workbook is: *Excel Template*.

If this template needed to be used by users with very old versions of Excel, you'd choose *Excel 97-2003* template.

If the workbook contained macros (working with macros is an Expert level skill covered fully in the *Expert Skills* book in this series) you'd need to choose *Excel Macro-Enabled Template*.

4.  Click the *Save* button to save the template to the default template folder that you created in: *Lesson 3-14: Understand templates and set the default custom template folder*.

The existing name: *Bonus Calculator* is fine.

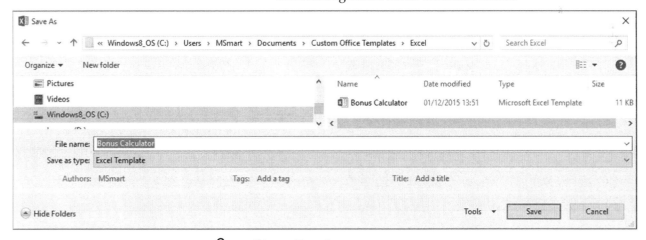

6   Close Excel.

## note

### How to make your custom template appear at the top of the Featured Templates list

Sometimes you may have a template that you use very often.

You may find it tedious to have to click:

File→New→Personal

… every time that you need to use it.

To save time you can *pin* the template. This means that it will appear at the top of the *Featured Templates* list.

The template will then be easy to find, and you'll also save a click every time you create a new worksheet based upon it.

To pin a template, click the pin icon at the bottom-right of the template icon:

The unpinned icon: will then change to a pinned icon: .

The template will then appear at the top of the *Featured Templates* list.

# Lesson 3-16: Use a template

1   Open Excel.

2   Display your own custom templates.

Notice that there are two links above the templates labelled *Featured* and *Personal*. The Personal templates are your own custom templates.

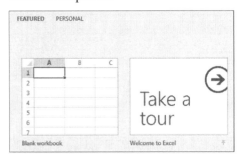

Click the *Personal* link

A dialog appears showing all of the templates in your custom templates folder:

At the moment, the only custom template is the *Bonus Calculator* template you saved in: *Lesson 3-15: Create a template.*

3   Click the *Bonus Calculator* template.

A new workbook is created from the template.

Notice that the workbook has been named *Bonus Calculator1*. You are not looking at the template but a new workbook created from the template.

4 **Use a sample template.**

A set of Microsoft sample templates are included with every copy of Excel.

1. Click: File→New.

   The start-up screen is displayed showing a number of standard Excel templates.

2. Click one of Microsoft's sample templates.

3. Click the *Create* button if necessary (for some templates the workbook may be created without any interim dialog).

   A workbook is created from the template.

   Some of Microsoft's sample templates may seem a little overwhelming at the moment but they'll seem far less intimidating by the time you reach the end of this book.

5 **Create a workbook from Microsoft's library of online templates.**

You'll need to be connected to the Internet to use an online template.

Microsoft have a huge library containing thousands of templates that they add to all the time and make available to you for free.

1. Click: File→New.

2. Type: **Calendar** in the *Search for online templates* box at the top of the screen.

3. Press the **<Enter>** key.

   After a few moments, a huge scrolling list of calendars appears on the screen.

4. Click on any of the calendar templates.

5. Click the *Create* button.

   A workbook (containing a nicely formatted calendar) is created from the template.

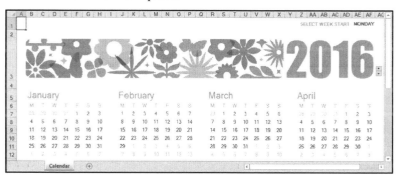

# Lesson 3-17: Understand Office Add-Ins

For many years Excel has supported add-ins. Add-ins allow programmers to create new components that you can add to a workbook. These components can add functionality that isn't present in the standard Excel product.

The traditional add-in was installed on your local hard drive and added new functionality to your copy of Excel. The *Expert Skills* book in this series comprehensively covers this type of add-in.

Office 2013 introduced two new types of add-in that were originally all called: *Excel Apps*. In the Excel 2016 release the two new add-in types are individually called *Task Pane Add-ins* and *Content Add-ins* and are collectively referred to as *Office Add-ins*.

*Office Add-ins* can only be accessed from the Microsoft Store (though many are free of charge).

Office Add-Ins do not require any installation as they are usually hosted on a remote web site (though it is also possible for an IT department to host them on a local network). This means that you normally require an Internet connection in order to use an Office Add-In. If you are disconnected from the Internet, the add-in may stop working.

## Task Pane Add-Ins

You are already familiar with the *Clipboard* task pane that you used in: *Lesson 3-7: Use the Multiple Item Clipboard.*

A good example of a task pane add-in is the *Wikipedia* add-in (free at time of writing in August 2018). The Wikipedia add-in provides a task pane that can be used to research any subject via the Wikipedia application on the Internet and then to copy and paste data from any Wikipedia article into a worksheet.

In this example, I have used the Wikipedia add-in to research the average *GDP per hour worked* by country. I've then copied and pasted the table from the task pane onto my worksheet for further analysis:

## note

### What are Office Add-Ins useful for?

Task Pane and Content Add-Ins are a relatively new feature (introduced in Excel 2013) and it is likely that thousands of new add-ins of this type will become available over the coming years.

Three add-in categories seem to be the most useful:

**New Chart types**

As you'll discover in: *Session Five: Charts and Graphics*, Excel already has a huge range of chart types. If the built-in chart types do not address a specific business need, it is now possible to pay a programmer to create any chart type that can be described as an *Excel Content Add-in.*

The *Gauge* content add-in shown in the lesson is a good example of this.

**Interfacing with real-time data**

Many users will need to interface with current real-time data (data that is constantly changing). Examples would include exchange rates or share and commodity prices.

There are many add-ins available to provide current currency exchange rates and stock prices.

**Interfacing with databases**

One of my favourite free content add-ins is the *Bing Maps content add-in.*

This allows you to reference place names (for example *London* or *New York*) and associated data (for example the population of each city) in a worksheet range.

The location is then found in the Bing maps database and displayed as a map embedded within the worksheet. Hotspots on the map can then be clicked to display the associated data.

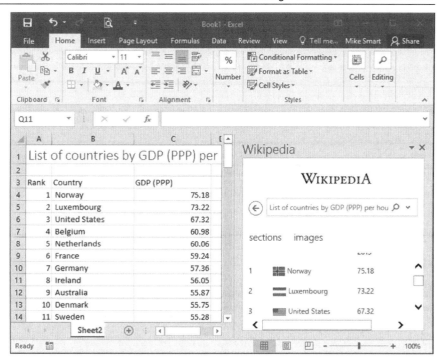

You'll learn how to add a *Task Pane Add-in* to a workbook later, in: *Lesson 3-18: Add an Office Add-In to a workbook.*

## Content Add-Ins

Content add-ins float within the Excel grid (in a similar way to charts, which you will learn about later, in: *Session Five: Charts and Graphics*).

Content add-ins are useful for adding components to a worksheet. A good example of a content add-in is the *Gauge* add-in. This allows a value to be graphically represented on a dial gauge:

Excel does not support dial gauges. The above worksheet was created by adding a *Gauge* content add-in to a worksheet.

# Lesson 3-18: Add an Office Add-In to a workbook

You will need to be connected to the Internet and logged in to a *Microsoft Account* in order to follow-through with this lesson (You'll learn more about Microsoft accounts in: *Session Eight: Cloud Computing*).

1  Open a new blank workbook.

2  Add the *Merriam Webster dictionary* add-in to the workbook.

1.  Click: Insert→Add-ins→Store.

    The *Office Add-ins* dialog appears.

    A dialog opens and displays a list of add-ins available at the Office Store.

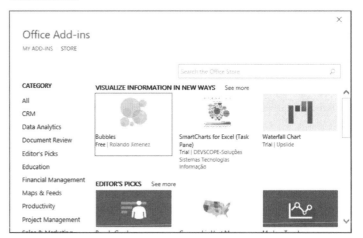

2.  Type: **dictionary** into the search box and press the **<Enter>** key.

    Several dictionary add-ins are displayed:

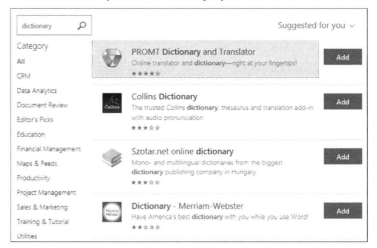

    Note that, because this is an online facility, you'll probably see a different list on your screen (see sidebar).  The above screen-grab was taken in August 2018.

3.  Click the *Dictionary-Merriam-Webster* add-in (or another free dictionary add-in if this is no longer available).

4.  Click the *Trust It* button if asked to.

The *Merriam-Webster Dictionary* task pane appears on the right of your screen.

3   Use the Merriam-Webster Dictionary to research the meaning of the word: **Computer**.

1.   Type the word: **Computer** into the search box.

2.   Press the **<Enter>** key.

The dictionary displays its definition:

# Lesson 3-19: Freeze columns and rows

1 Open *Sales First Quarter 2016* from your sample files folder.

Notice that it is easy to see which data is in each column when you are at the top of the worksheet and can see the top row:

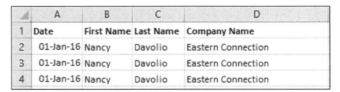

But things get confusing when you scroll further down the list:

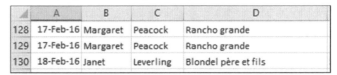

It is no longer clear what information is contained in each column because the top row has disappeared.

2 Press **<Ctrl>+<Home>** to quickly move to cell A1.

3 Click: View→Window→Freeze Panes.

A rich menu is displayed:

With Excel's rich menus, the meaning of each option is quite clear.

4 Click the *Freeze Top Row* menu item.

A small black line appears beneath the first row.

5 Scroll down the list.

Notice that as you scroll down, the top row now remains in place.

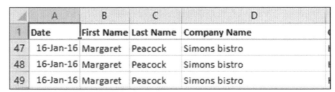

6 Unfreeze the top row.

**note**

Another way to freeze the top row would be to convert the range into a table.

Excel automatically freezes column headers in tables.

Working with tables is an Expert level skill covered fully in the *Expert Skills* book in this series.

**Sales First Quarter 2016**

Click: View→Window→Freeze Panes once more.

The first choice has now changed to *Unfreeze Panes*. Click this menu item to put things back to normal.

7   Freeze the first column.

Do exactly as you did before but this time select *Freeze First Column* from the rich menu.

Notice that the date column is now locked into place. As you scroll to the right, the date remains in the first column.

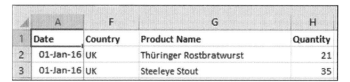

| | A | F | G | H |
|---|---|---|---|---|
| 1 | Date | Country | Product Name | Quantity |
| 2 | 01-Jan-16 | UK | Thüringer Rostbratwurst | 21 |
| 3 | 01-Jan-16 | UK | Steeleye Stout | 35 |

8   Unfreeze the panes.

9   Freeze the first two rows and the left most three columns.

While a simple freezing of the top row or first column will usually be all you need, you may sometimes want to freeze both columns *and* rows.

You may also want to freeze more than one column and/or row.

1.   Click in cell D3 to make it the active cell.

     This is your way of telling Excel that you want to freeze all cells above, and to the left of, cell D3.

2.   Click: View→Window→Freeze Panes again but, this time, select the first option from the rich menu: *Freeze Panes*.

3.   The first two rows and first three columns are frozen.

| | A | B | C | G | H |
|---|---|---|---|---|---|
| 1 | Date | First Name | Last Name | Product Name | Quantity |
| 2 | 01-Jan-16 | Nancy | Davolio | Thüringer Rostbratwurst | 21 |
| 8 | 01-Jan-16 | Nancy | Davolio | Fløtemysost | 60 |
| 9 | 02-Jan-16 | Laura | Callahan | Tunnbröd | 60 |

10  Unfreeze the panes.

# Lesson 3-20: Split the window into multiple panes

1   Open *Sales First Quarter 2016* from your sample files folder (if it isn't already open).

2   Press **<Ctrl>+<End>** to quickly move to the end of the worksheet (cell J242).

This is quite a long list. Imagine that you need to compare sales for 3rd February 2016 to sales for 3rd March 2016.

This could involve a lot of scrolling unless you split the window into two panes.

3   Split the window into two horizontal panes.

1.  Click in a cell in column A that is positioned around half way down the screen.

As you'll see later in this lesson, the active cell determines whether the window will be split horizontally, vertically, or both horizontally and vertically.

For a horizontal split, the active cell needs to be a cell within column A.

The position of the active cell also determines where the screen will be split. By positioning it half way down the screen we will split the screen into two equally sized panes.

2.  Click: View→Window→Split.

The screen is split into two independently scrolling horizontal panes.

4   Scroll the lower pane so that the first sale on 3rd March 2016 is shown on the first line.

5   Scroll the upper pane so that the first sale on 3rd February 2016 is shown on the first line.

Sales First Quarter 2016

6   Remove the split window view.

Click: View→Window→Split.

**OR**

Position the mouse cursor over the split bar and double-click.

7   Split the window into two vertical panes.

1.   Click in cell D1.

If the active cell is in row 1, the screen will be split into two *vertical* panes.

2.   Click: View→Window→Split.

The window is split into two vertical panes

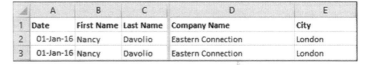

8   Move the split bar so that the left pane shows columns A to E.

Click and drag the split bar to its new location:

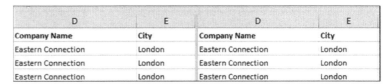

9   Remove the split window view.

10  Split the window into four panes.

If the active cell is not in row 1 or column A, the screen will split into four panes at the cursor position.

1.   Click in a cell towards the center of the screen

2.   Click: View→Window→Split.

The screen is split into four windows.

11  Remove the split window view.

# Lesson 3-21: Check spelling

## anecdote

### Fun with dictionaries

I used to tell my students that the Australian English dictionary included such words as G'day, which I thought was a joke.

One day, one of my students checked it out in a coffee break and it's actually true!

Excel shares the same powerful spell checker that is included with Word and other Office applications.

Most European companies have a corporate standard for their spelling, often American English or British English. Excel also includes standard support for eighteen different dialects of English as well as other languages.

While most words are included in Excel's dictionary, you will often be warned that a correct spelling is misspelled. When this is the case you can add the word to the dictionary so that Excel doesn't keep bothering you about it in the future.

1   Open *Empire Car Sales Stock List* from your sample files folder.

| | F | G |
|---|---|---|
| 5 | Colour | Selling points |
| 6 | Black | Can accelarate faster than most sports cars. |
| 7 | Topaz Blue | One concientous owner from new. |
| 8 | Yellow | Acheives nearly 50 miles to the gallon. |
| 9 | Silver | Particulaly clean example of this executive coupe. |
| 10 | Blue | Reconised as one of the safest cars on the road. |
| 11 | Brown | A collector's car strictly for connisseurs. |

The *Selling points* column contains many frequently incorrectly spelled words.

You may find it fun to try to identify the spelling errors before we set the Spell Checker loose on the job.

2   Check the spelling for the words in the range F5:G7.

If you select a range of cells before invoking the spell checker, only the selected range will be checked.

1.   Select the range: F5:G7

2.   Click: Review→Proofing→Spelling to start the spell checker.

## note

### Another way to start the spell checker

Press the <F7> key.

If all of the words are spelled correctly the spell checker does not display. In this case there are errors, so the *Spelling* dialog is displayed.

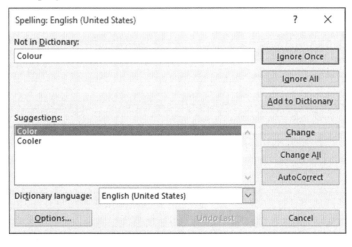

In the example above note that the *Dictionary language* was set to English (United States). The British spelling of the word *colour* does not appear in the American English dictionary because, in America, it is spelled: *color*.

If your dictionary is set to English (United Kingdom) you will not see this error because *colour* is the correct UK English spelling.

See the sidebar if you want to change your dictionary to a different language.

3   Click *Change* to accept Excel's suggested correction.

4   Click *Change* twice more to accept Excel's suggestions for *accelerate* and *conscientious*.

The Spell checker exits and advises that the spell check is complete.

5   Click the OK button to dismiss the dialog.

6   Spell check the single word *Particulaly* in cell G9.

Sometimes you'll type a single word and be unsure that it is correctly spelled. You will want to be able to quickly check the single word.

1. Click cell G9 and then select the word: *Particulaly* in the formula bar at the top of the window.

2. Click: Review→Proofing→Spelling to start the Spell Checker.

3. Click the *Change* button to accept the correct spelling.

4. Click the OK button to dismiss the dialog.

7   Spell check the entire worksheet.

1. Click in any cell on the worksheet. When you don't select a range, or a single word, the spell checker checks the entire worksheet.

   If you don't click cell A1, cells to the right and beneath the selected cell are checked first and then Excel asks: *Do you want to continue checking at the beginning of the sheet?*

2. Click: Review→Proofing→Spelling to start the Spell Checker.

8   Click: *Change* to accept each change until you are prompted for Alfasud.

Alfasud is a real word for a car (a model produced by Alfa Romeo between 1976 and 1989) but it isn't in the Excel dictionary. Perhaps Empire sells a lot of Alfasuds and don't want to be pulled up by the spell checker every time the word is used.

To prevent this from happening, click the *Add to Dictionary* button so that Excel will recognize the word in the future.

When the spell check has ended, a dialog will display advising that the spell check is complete.  Click the OK button to dismiss the dialog.

9   Save your work as *Empire Car Sales Stock List-1*.

## Session 3: Exercise

**1** Open *The Best Selling Albums of All Time* from your sample files folder.

**2** Insert one row above row 7, type *AC/DC* for the Artist and *Back in Black* for the Album.

**3** Use AutoComplete to put the text *Hard Rock* into cell C7 and type *50* for copies sold (millions).

**4** Delete rows 11 and 12 to remove the *Eagles* and *Bee Gees* from the list.

**5** Insert a formula in cell E6 to calculate how much revenue the album sales would have generated if sold at the Average Album Price shown in cell E3.

Don't forget that the reference to cell E3 will have to be an absolute reference.

**6** AutoFill the formula to the end of the list to see the estimated revenue for the top five selling albums.

**7** Use AutoSum to add a value for total copies sold and total revenue to cells D11 and E11.

**8** Remove the decimal places displayed in cells E6:E11 so that the revenue is rounded to the nearest million.

**9** Add a comment to cell B6 saying "Thriller was Michael Jackson's sixth studio album and was produced with a budget of $750,000."

**10** Save your work as *The Best Selling Albums of All Time-1*.

| | A | B | C | D | E |
|---|---|---|---|---|---|
| 1 | Best Selling Albums of All Time | | | | |
| 2 | | | | | US$ |
| 3 | | | Average Album Price | | 14.99 |
| 4 | | | | | |
| 5 | Artist | Album | Genre | Copies Sold (millions) | Revenue (Million USD) |
| 6 | Michael Jackson | Thriller | Pop/R&B | 65 | 974 |
| 7 | AC/DC | Back in Black | Hard Rock | 50 | 750 |
| 8 | Pink Floyd | Dark Side of the Moon | Rock | 45 | 675 |
| 9 | Whitney Houston | The Bodyguard | Pop/R&B | 44 | 660 |
| 10 | Meat Loaf | Bat Out of Hell | Hard Rock | 43 | 645 |
| 11 | | Total: | | 247 | 3703 |
| 12 | | | | | |
| 13 | | | | | |
| 14 | | | | | |
| 15 | | | | | |

**Mike Smart:**
Thriller was Michael Jackson's sixth studio album and was produced with a budget of $750,000.

The Best Selling Albums of All Time

If you need help slide the page to the left

## Session 3 Exercise answers

These are the questions that students find the most difficult to answer:

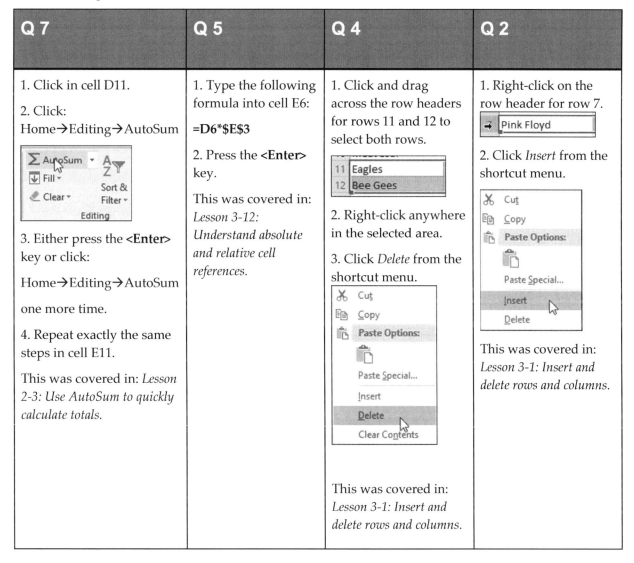

| Q 7 | Q 5 | Q 4 | Q 2 |
|---|---|---|---|
| 1. Click in cell D11.<br><br>2. Click:<br>Home→Editing→AutoSum<br><br>3. Either press the **<Enter>** key or click:<br>Home→Editing→AutoSum<br>one more time.<br><br>4. Repeat exactly the same steps in cell E11.<br><br>This was covered in: *Lesson 2-3: Use AutoSum to quickly calculate totals.* | 1. Type the following formula into cell E6:<br><br>**=D6*$E$3**<br><br>2. Press the **<Enter>** key.<br><br>This was covered in: *Lesson 3-12: Understand absolute and relative cell references.* | 1. Click and drag across the row headers for rows 11 and 12 to select both rows.<br><br>2. Right-click anywhere in the selected area.<br><br>3. Click *Delete* from the shortcut menu.<br><br>This was covered in: *Lesson 3-1: Insert and delete rows and columns.* | 1. Right-click on the row header for row 7.<br><br>2. Click *Insert* from the shortcut menu.<br><br>This was covered in: *Lesson 3-1: Insert and delete rows and columns.* |

If you have difficulty with the other questions, here are the lessons that cover the relevant skill:

**1**   Refer to: Lesson 1-5: Download the sample files and open/navigate a workbook.

**3**   Refer to: Lesson 3-2: Use AutoComplete and fill data from adjacent cells.

**6**   Refer to: Lesson 2-15: Use AutoFill to adjust formulas.

**8**   Refer to: Lesson 3-5: Use Paste Values and increase/decrease decimal places displayed.

**9**   Refer to: Lesson 3-9: Insert cell comments.

**10**  Refer to: Lesson 1-6: Save a workbook.

# Session Four: Making Your Worksheets Look Professional

> It is only shallow people who do not judge by appearances.
>
> *Oscar Wilde, writer, poet and playwright (1854 - 1900)*

Never under-estimate the importance of presentation. In many areas of life, it is valued more than content. This session will enable you to make your worksheets get noticed.

By the end of this session your worksheets will be visually excellent.

## Session Objectives

By the end of this session you will be able to:

- Format dates
- Understand date serial numbers
- Format numbers using built-in number formats
- Create custom number formats
- Horizontally and Vertically align the contents of cells
- Merge cells, wrap text and expand/collapse the formula bar
- Unmerge cells and Center Across Selection
- Understand themes
- Use cell styles and change themes
- Add color and gradient effects to cells
- Add borders and lines
- Create your own custom theme
- Create your own custom cell styles
- Use a master style book to merge styles
- Use simple conditional formatting
- Manage multiple conditional formats using the Rules Manager
- Bring data alive with visualizations
- Create a formula driven conditional format
- Insert a Sparkline into a range of cells
- Apply a common vertical axis and formatting to a Sparkline group
- Apply a date axis to a Sparkline group and format a single Sparkline
- Use the Format Painter
- Rotate text

# Lesson 4-1: Format dates

You may notice that I've been very careful to use internationally safe date formats throughout this book.

A classic cause of errors when dealing with international worksheets is the use of a date such as the following:

10/03/2016

This means *10th March 2016* in some countries (such as the UK) and *3rd October 2016* in others (such as the USA).

If your work may be viewed by an international audience, it is far better to use a date format that cannot possibly cause confusion.

In this lesson, you'll re-format a date into the compact and universally readable format of: *10-Mar-16*.

1    Open *Sales Week Ended 14th March 2016* from your sample files folder.

Notice the hashes in the date column. This tells you that the column isn't wide enough to display the date.

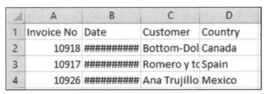

If you're used to calling the hash (#) a **pound sign** or **number sign**, see the sidebar in: *Lesson 2-9: Re-size rows and columns* for an explanation.

2    Auto-resize cells A1:G17 so that their contents are fully visible.

You learned how to do this in: *Lesson 2-9: Re-size rows and columns.*

3    Format the dates in column B so that they display in the format: *10-Mar-16*

At present the dates are formatted with the month spelled out in full:

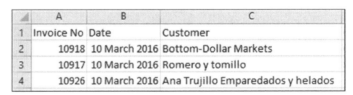

You're going to re-format them to the shorter form: *10 Mar 16*.

1.   Select cells B2:B17.

2.   Right-click anywhere in the selected range and choose *Format Cells...* from the shortcut menu.

You can also do this from the Ribbon (see sidebar).

The *Format Cells* dialog appears.

3.   Click the *Number* tab (if it isn't already selected) and then choose *Date* from the *Category* list box.

**note**

**Launching the Format Cells dialog from the Ribbon**

Click:

Home→Number→ Dialog Launcher

The dialog launcher is the small button on the bottom right of the *Number* group.

**Sales Week Ended 14th March 2016**

The dates you see may be different from those shown above (see sidebar).

I wanted the format *14-Mar-2016* but that isn't in the list. When you need a special format, it is worth checking the *Custom* category to see whether there is a pre-defined format available.

4. Click *Custom* in the category list box.

5. Click on one of the list entries in the *Type* list box and then use the <UpArrow> and <DownArrow> keys to move through the list, keeping your eye on the preview in the *Sample* box.

Depending upon the country you are in (see sidebar), you may see the format *dd-mmm-yy.* In this case you will also see *10-Mar-16* in the sample box.

If the format *dd-mmm-yy* isn't shown for your country, you'll need to manually type it into the *Type* box.

6. Click the OK button.

4    Save your work as *Sales Week Ended 14th March 2016-1.*

## trivia

### The Julian and Gregorian calendars

When you work with very old dates you can run into a problem with the Julian and Gregorian calendars.

In 1582 it was noticed that the seasons had drifted by 10 days because the Julian system (named after Julius Caesar who adopted it in 45 BC) had incorrectly miscalculated a year as being 365 ¼ days. A year is actually slightly shorter than this.

Pope Gregory XIII decreed that, in order to put things right, the world had to lose 10 days to make up for all of those extra leap years.

The reformed Gregorian calendar also adopted a new leap year rule to keep things on track in future years.

It took nearly 200 years for everybody to get on board with the Gregorian calendar. The Catholic countries of Spain, Italy and Portugal adopted it at once but England and parts of America didn't convert until September 14th 1752.

This means that in Spain the dates October 5th 1582 to October 14th 1582 never actually existed. In England it was the dates Sept 3rd 1752 to September 14th 1752.

The strangest case of all was Sweden who decided to "phase it in gradually" between 1700 and 1740 meaning that their calendar was out of step with the rest of the world for 40 years.

If you work with historical data from this era you have to be very careful indeed.

# Lesson 4-2: Understand date serial numbers

Excel stores dates in a very clever way. Understanding Excel's date storage system empowers you to use date arithmetic. You can use date arithmetic to compute the difference between two dates (in days) or to shift date ranges by a given time interval.

## How Excel stores dates

Dates are stored as simple numbers called *date serial numbers*. The serial number contains the number of days that have elapsed since 1st January 1900 (where 1st January 1900 is 1).

## The world began in 1900

An interesting shortcoming of Excel is its inability to easily work with dates before 1900. Excel simply doesn't acknowledge that there were any dates before this time. If you work with older dates you will have to work-around this limitation.

## In Excel every time is a date, and every date is a time

You've already realized that 5th January 1900 is stored as the number 5. What would the number 5.5 mean? It would mean midday on 5th January 1900.

It is possible to format a date to show only the date, only the time, or both a time and a date.

When you enter a time into a cell without a date, the time is stored as a number less than one. Excel regards this as having the non-existent date of: 00 January 1900

When you enter a date into a cell without a time, the time is stored as midnight at the beginning of that day.

1    Create a new blank workbook and put the numbers 1 to 5 in cells A1:A5.

2    Type the formula **=A1** into cell B1 followed by the **<Enter>** key, and then AutoFill the formula to the end of the list.

AutoFill was covered in: *Lesson 2-14: Use AutoFill for text and numeric series.*

| | A | B |
|---|---|---|
| 1 | 1 | 1 |
| 2 | 2 | 2 |
| 3 | 3 | 3 |
| 4 | 4 | 4 |
| 5 | 5 | 5 |

## trivia

### The peculiar case of the Excel date bug and Lotus 1-2-3

Here's the Gregorian leap year rule defined by Pope Gregory XIII in 1582:

*Every year that is exactly divisible by four is a leap year, except for years that are exactly divisible by 100; the centurial years that are exactly divisible by 400 are still leap years.*

This means that the year 1900 wasn't a leap year but 2000 was (causing many millennium software bugs).

Lotus 1-2-3 was a spreadsheet product that was the market leader until Excel overtook it in the early 1990's.

The designers of Lotus 1-2-3 weren't paying enough attention to Pope Gregory's rules. Their DATE() function thought that 1900 was a leap year and thus recognised the non-existent date: February 29th 1900.

Because Excel needed to be compatible with Lotus 1-2-3, Microsoft had to replicate the Lotus bug when they designed Excel.

Try entering **29th Feb 1900** into a worksheet and Excel will gladly accept it.

This bug has the effect of introducing a one-day error into any date arithmetic you may do that spans 29th February 1900.

3 Apply a date format to column A that will show a four-digit year.

This was covered in: *Lesson 4-1: Format dates.*

| | A | B |
|---|---|---|
| 1 | 01 January 1900 | 1 |
| 2 | 02 January 1900 | 2 |

This reveals that the whole numbers 1 to 5 represent the dates 1-Jan-1900 to 05-Jan-1900.

4 Change the date format in column A again so that it shows both dates and times.

Setting a custom format was covered in: *Lesson 4-1: Format dates.*

Choose the custom format: **dd mmm yyyy hh:mm** (if it isn't shown in the list you will need to type it into the *Type* box).

Notice that when a date serial number is a whole number, the time is set to midnight at the beginning of that day.

| | A | B |
|---|---|---|
| 1 | 01 Jan 1900 00:00 | 1 |
| 2 | 02 Jan 1900 00:00 | 2 |

5 Change the time in cell A2 to 12:00.

Notice that the number in cell B2 has changed to 2.5 revealing that times are stored by Excel as the decimal part of the date serial number.

| | A | B |
|---|---|---|
| 1 | 01 Jan 1900 00:00 | 1 |
| 2 | 02 Jan 1900 12:00 | 2.5 |

6 Compute the number of days that occurred between 01 Jan 1900 and 01 Jan 2000.

Now that you have a good grasp of Excel's serial numbers, this task is easy.

1. Enter the two dates in cells D1 and D2, one beneath the other.

2. Click in cell D3 to make it the active cell.

3. Click: Home→Number→Comma Style. 

    You'll be learning more about the comma style in: *Lesson 4-3: Format numbers using built-in number formats.* You have told Excel to display a number in cell D3 instead of a date.

4. Subtract one date from the other by entering the formula: **=D2-D1** into cell D3.

    You now know that 36,525 days occurred during the twentieth century (actually 36,524 due to the Lotus 1-2-3 bug – see sidebar).

7 Close the workbook without saving.

# Lesson 4-3: Format numbers using built-in number formats

## note

### The Comma[0] and Currency[0] styles

With pre-2007 versions of Excel, I was forever applying the comma style and then removing the decimal places as a quick way to add the thousand separators to whole numbers. This used to take three clicks (comma style|decrease decimal|decrease decimal).

Excel 2016 saves a click with the Comma[0] and Currency[0] styles.

To apply these styles, you'll need to display the *Cell Styles Gallery*.

Look in the Home→Styles group. Notice that there's a gallery button towards the bottom-right of the pane:

When you click the gallery button you'll see the *Comma[0]* and *Currency[0]* styles at the bottom of the pane:

You'll be learning a lot more about cell styles later in this session.

**Sales Week Ended 14th March 2016-1**

## Formatting fundamentals

When you format a number you never change its value. For example, if you format the number:

483.45495

... so that it only displays two decimal places, the number displays like this:

483.45

It is important to realize that the actual value in the cell remains at the old value of 483.45495. All you have done is to change the way in which the value is presented to the user.

1  Open *Sales Week Ended 14th March 2016-1* from your sample files folder.

2  Apply the comma style to column E.

There is an extremely useful quick format button called the *comma style*. This is perfect for formatting monetary values with a single click. The comma style places a comma after thousands and displays exactly two decimal places.

1.  Select all of column E.

2.  Click: Home→Number→Comma Style.

3.  Widen column E if necessary so that it is wide enough to display the contents.

All of the values in column E now display correctly.

| | D | E | F | G |
|---|---|---|---|---|
| 1 | Country | Amount | Tax | Total |
| 2 | Canada | 1,447.50 | 0.175 | 1700.8125 |
| 3 | Spain | 365.89 | 0.175 | 429.92075 |

Note that you can also use the *Accounting Number Format* style.

## note

### Solutions to the "penny rounding" problem

Formatting a floating-point number to two decimal places often results in the *penny rounding problem* when you sum a column of numbers.

There are two solutions to the problem. One is a very good solution, the other can cause problems.

### Best practice

The best solution to the problem is to address it when the column is first calculated.

In this lesson's example worksheet, the formula used to calculate the value in cell G2 is:

=E2*(F2+1)

Excel has a ROUND() function that can be used to round the result to two decimal places at the point of calculation.

The new formula would become:

=ROUND(E2*(F2+1),2)

### Changing precision

Click:

File→Options→Advanced

In the *When Calculating This Workbook* group click the *Set precision as displayed* check box.

This alters the default behaviour of Excel so that each value in the worksheet is regarded as being precisely the same as its display value when performing calculations.

Using this option can cause data to become inaccurate as it is a global setting, affecting the entire worksheet (and any other worksheets you may open before turning it off).

Use this feature with extreme caution, or better still, don't use it at all!

This is very similar to the comma style but adds a leading currency symbol and an appropriate number of decimal places. The *More Accounting Formats…* option supports a vast number of international currency styles.

Try the *Accounting Number Format* style out to see how it works. I've found that the comma style is more appropriate for most of my work, as I'm usually working in one country and one currency, making the currency type obvious.

3   Apply the comma style to column G.

Column G has many decimal places in some cases, as the sales tax calculation results in as many as six decimal places.

Apply the comma style to column G and notice how all of the values are displayed rounded to the nearest two decimal places.

| 1380.33125 | Becomes | 1,380.33 |
| 879.82825 | Becomes | 879.83 |

It is a key concept (as discussed in the introduction to this lesson) to realize that the values in the cells have not changed. For example, if you add two cells containing the value 1.4, the result will be 1.4+1.4=2.8. If you then format the cells as whole numbers you'll see that 1+1=3 as each number is rounded up or down.

See the sidebar for potential solutions to this problem.

4   Apply the percentage style to column F.

The example sales tax rate is 17.5%. When working with percentages, it is useful to enter them so that you can calculate a percentage simply by multiplying by the cell.

Instead of 17.5 (more readable) the values are entered as 0.175 (easier to use in formulas). In order to make percentages both readable and easy to use, Microsoft has created the percentage style. If you type 17.5% into a cell, the actual value within the cell will be 0.175.

1.   Select column F.

2.   Click: Home→Number→Percentage Style.

3.   Click: Home→Number→Increase Decimal once, to make the values in column F display one decimal place.

| | D | E | F | G |
|---|---|---|---|---|
| 1 | Country | Amount | Tax | Total |
| 2 | Canada | 1,447.50 | 17.5% | 1,700.81 |
| 3 | Spain | 365.89 | 17.5% | 429.92 |

5   Save your work as *Sales Week Ended 14th March 2016-2*.

# Lesson 4-4: Create custom number formats

The built-in number formats are very quick and convenient but are also quite limited. For example, there was a credit note on 11-Mar-16 for 637.49 plus tax. You could easily miss the little minus sign to the left of the amount.

| | D | E | F | G |
|---|---|---|---|---|
| 6 | Germany | 500.00 | 17.5% | 587.50 |
| 7 | Italy | 637.49 | 17.5% | 749.05 |
| 8 | Italy | - 637.49 | 17.5% - | 749.05 |

Accountants often prefer to show brackets around negative values as bracketed numbers are far more visible. Here's what you want to see:

| | D | E | F | G |
|---|---|---|---|---|
| 6 | Germany | 500.00 | 17.5% | 587.50 |
| 7 | Italy | 637.49 | 17.5% | 749.05 |
| 8 | Italy | (637.49) | 17.5% | (749.05) |

There's one little problem with this requirement. For many locales, Excel 2016 doesn't have this style in any of the built-in or pre-defined custom formats. Fortunately, it is possible to create your own custom format when none of the built-in styles fit your requirement.

## Overview of custom formats

There's plenty of documentation in the help system and on the Internet about the rather cryptic formatting codes provided with Excel 2016. Just about everything is possible once you've got to grips with the basic concepts.

To communicate the custom format to Excel, you must construct a custom format string.

Zeros mean "Display significant zeros". You tell Excel how many you want within the format string. For example, 0.00 means *display at least one leading zero and two decimal places*. The following examples should make things clear:

| Custom Format String | Value | Display |
|---|---|---|
| 0 | 1234.56 | 1235 |
| 0.0 | 1234.56 | 1234.6 |
| | 1234.5 | 1234.5 |
| | .5 | 0.5 |
| 0.00 | 1234.56 | 1234.56 |
| | 1234.5 | 1234.50 |
| | .5 | 0.50 |
| 00.000 | 4.56 | 04.560 |
| 0.000 | 1234.56 | 1234.560 |

## note

### Use the ? custom format string symbol to make number values line up

The question mark inserts a space (when needed) in order to make sure that values that do not display a fixed number of decimal places line up properly.

I must admit that I've never had to use it in a real-world worksheet as I much prefer to pad numbers with trailing zeros.

For example, here's two numbers formatted with the default *General* format:

| |
|---|
| 15.5 |
| 17.775 |

The decimal points don't line up because both numbers are, by default, right aligned.

The custom format:

0.??

Will cause the numbers to round to two places and display as follows:

| |
|---|
| 15.5 |
| 17.78 |

**Sales Week Ended 14th March 2016-2**

# note

## More about custom number formats

It is only possible to give you a broad overview of custom number formats in a single lesson. This should be all that you need to discover more using Excel's help system or the Internet.

Here are a couple of other insights that may help if you want to explore them further:

- You can embed colors into number formats. For example, to make every negative value red you could use:

**0.00;[Red]0.00**

- There are four possible parts to a number format:

Positive format; Negative format; Zero format; Text format. Applying the custom format string:

**0.00;-0.00;"Zero";[Blue]**

To these cells:

| Mike | 0 | 120.119 | -345.5744 |

Would result in:

| Mike | Zero | 120.12 | -345.57 |

(Text in first cell is colored blue).

# note

## Hiding values with the three-semicolon format

You will often want to hide the values in specific cells, even though you want other values in the same column to display.

A common way of doing this is to format the cell with a white foreground color upon a white background. A better solution is to create a custom format consisting of three semicolons:

;;;

The hash symbol (#) is mainly used to add comma separators to thousands and millions.

| Custom Format String | Value | Display |
|---|---|---|
| # | 123.4500 | 123 |
| #.## | 123.45 | 123.45 |
| | 123.50 | 123.5 |
| #,# | 1234.56 | 1,236 |
| #,#.## | 1234.56 | 1,234.56 |
| | 1234.50 | 1,234.5 |
| | 12341234.56 | 12,341,234.56 |

Because the hash symbol can be used in conjunction with zeroes it is also possible to indicate that you want both thousand separators *and* a specific number of leading or trailing zeroes.

| Custom Format String | Value | Display |
|---|---|---|
| #,#0.00 | 12341234.5 | 12,341,234.50 |

You can also specify two different format strings separated by a semi colon. The first provides formatting for positive values and the second for negative values. This information enables us to construct the bracketed custom format string discussed earlier in this lesson.

| Custom format string | Value | Display |
|---|---|---|
| #,#0.00;(#,#0.00) | 12341234.5 | 12,341,234.50 |
| | -12341234.5 | (12,341,234.50) |

1 Open *Sales Week Ended 14th March 2016-2* from your sample files folder (if it isn't already open).

2 Select columns E and G (but not column F).

This was covered in: *Lesson 2-6: Select adjacent and non-adjacent rows and columns.*

3 Right-click anywhere in column E or G and then select *Format Cells…* from the shortcut menu.

4 Select *Custom* from the *Category* list on the left of the dialog.

5 Type the custom format: **#,#0.00;(#,#0.00)** into the box labeled *Type* and click the OK button.

```
Type:
#,#0.00;(#,#0.00)
```

The negative values on the worksheet are now surrounded by brackets.

| Italy | 637.49 | 17.5% | 749.05 |
| Italy | (637.49) | 17.5% | (749.05) |

6 Save your work as *Sales Week Ended 14th March 2016-3*.

# Lesson 4-5: Horizontally align the contents of cells

| Icon | Description | What it does | Example |
|------|-------------|--------------|---------|
| General ▾ | General (the default) | Aligns numbers and dates to the right and text to the left. | Canada 1,447.50 / Spain 365.89 |
| ☰ | Align Left | Aligns cell contents left. If the cell contains text and the adjacent cell is empty, text spills to the right. | Bottom-Dollar Markets / Bottom-Dollar Markets / Bottom-Dollar M Canada |
| | | If the cell contains text and the adjacent text isn't empty, text is truncated. | |
| ☰ | Align Center | Aligns cell contents to the center. If the cell contains text and the adjacent cells are empty, text spills to the left and right. | Bottom-Dollar Markets / Bottom-Dollar Markets / 10-Mar-08 om-Dollar Mar Canada |
| | | If the cell contains text and the adjacent cells are not empty, text is truncated. | |
| ☰ | Align Right | Aligns cell contents to the right. If the cell contains text and the adjacent cell is empty, text spills to the left. | Bottom-Dollar Markets / Bottom-Dollar Markets / 10-Mar-08 om-Dollar Markets C |
| | | If the cell contains text and the adjacent cell isn't empty, text is truncated. | |
| ☰ | Justify | Text lines up to the left and right of the cell (like a newspaper) | to be or not to be, that is the question. |
| ↔ | Distributed | Words are distributed evenly across the cell. | City   of   London |

**Sales Week Ended 14th March 2016-3**

## note

### How to access the Justify and Distributed options

The *Justify* and *Distributed* options are not included in the Ribbon's *Alignment* group as most users wouldn't every find a use for them.

If you find them useful you can add buttons to the Quick Access Toolbar.

Refer to: *Lesson 1-14: Customize the Quick Access Toolbar and preview the printout.*

The table on the facing page summarizes Excel's different horizontal alignment options.

1   Open *Sales Week Ended 14ᵗʰ March 2016-3* from your sample files folder (if it isn't already open).

2   Notice that the text in row 1 doesn't align with the column contents.

Numerical and date values are, by default, right aligned.

Columns E, F and G contain numerical data but the text headings of their columns are left aligned.

You can see the problem more clearly if the columns are widened:

| E | F | G |
|---|---|---|
| Amount | Tax | Total |
| 1,447.50 | 17.5% | 1,700.81 |
| 365.89 | 17.5% | 429.92 |

3   Right-align the column headers for columns E, F and G.

   1.   Select cells E1:G1.

   2.   Click: Home→Alignment→Align Right

       The column headers now look much better.

| E | F | G |
|---|---|---|
| Amount | Tax | Total |
| 1,447.50 | 17.5% | 1,700.81 |
| 365.89 | 17.5% | 429.92 |

4   Right-align cell B1.

Column B also has a problem as the dates and column header do not align.

   1.   Select cell B1.

   2.   Click: Home→Alignment→Align Right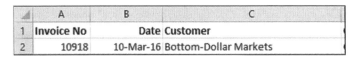

| | B | C |
|---|---|---|
| 1 | Date | Customer |
| 2 | 10-Mar-16 | Bottom-Dollar Markets |
| 3 | 10-Mar-16 | Romero y tomillo |

       You will normally align column headers to the right for numeric/date columns, and to the left for text columns.

5   Bold-face row 1.

   1.   Select row 1.

   2.   Click: Home→Font→Bold. **B**

| | A | B | C |
|---|---|---|---|
| 1 | **Invoice No** | **Date** | **Customer** |
| 2 | 10918 | 10-Mar-16 | Bottom-Dollar Markets |

6   Save your work as *Sales Week Ended 14ᵗʰ March 2016-4.*

## note

### The Merge Cells feature taught in this lesson should generally be avoided

Excel has a newer feature called: *Center Across Selection* that does almost the same thing as *Merge Cells*.

You'll learn about the *Center Across Selection* feature later, in: *Lesson 4-7: Unmerge cells and Center Across Selection.*

For new work, it is usually better to use the newer *Center Across Selection* feature in place of *Merge Cells*.

You still need to know how to use *Merge Cells* as you'll find that a huge number of existing workbooks use the *Merge Cells* feature extensively.

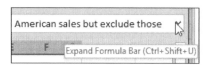

**Sales Week Ended 14th March 2016-4**

# Lesson 4-6: Merge cells, wrap text and expand/collapse the formula bar

1   Open *Sales Week Ended 14th March 2016-4* from your sample files folder (if it isn't already open).

2   Insert three blank rows above row 1.

   This was covered in: *Lesson 3-1: Insert and delete rows and columns.*

3   In cell A1 type: **Sales Week Ended 14th March 2016**

4   Center the title across columns A to G.

   The title cell (A1) doesn't look bad, but wouldn't it be nice to center it above the transactions listed beneath? You could simply copy and paste the title text into cell D1 but that wouldn't be perfectly central.

   The solution is to merge cells A1:G1 so that they turn into one big cell. It will then be possible to center the text inside the merged cell. Excel provides a handy *Merge and Center* button to do this in one click.

   1.   Select cells A1:G1.

   2.   Click: Home→Alignment→Merge & Center. 🔲

   The title appears at the center of the merged cell.

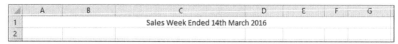

5   View the text in cell A22.

   There is a long description in cell A22. You probably can't see all of it on your screen.

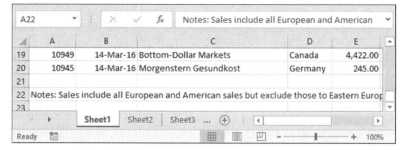

   Re-sizing the formula bar allows all of the text to be read.

   Click cell A22 and then click the *Expand Formula Bar* button. 🔽

   The text becomes visible in the enlarged formula bar:

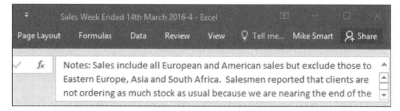

6   Resize the formula bar.

Sometimes there isn't enough space in the expanded formula bar to view all of the text.

If this is the case hover the mouse over the bottom border of the formula bar until you see the double-headed arrow cursor shape.

When the double-headed arrow is visible, click and drag downward or upward to resize the formula bar as required.

7   Collapse the formula bar.

After you have read the text there is no need to keep the formula bar expanded. Click the same button used to expand the formula bar ⌃ and the bar will collapse.

8   Merge cells A22:G22.

Expanding the formula bar isn't a great solution. You will create a box at the bottom of the report to display all of the text.

1.   Select cells A22:G22.

2.   Click: Home→Alignment→Merge & Center (drop-down).

A drop-down menu is displayed.

3.   Click *Merge Cells* to make all of the selected cells into one large cell.  (This is just like *Merge & Center* but without centering).

9   Make row 22 deep enough to display all of the text.

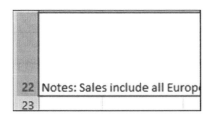

This was covered in: *Lesson 2-9: Re-size rows and columns.*

The cell is now deep enough to display the text, but you can still only see one line.  This is because the text isn't *wrapping.*

10   Wrap the text within the merged cells.

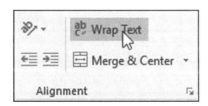

Click: Home→Alignment→Wrap Text.

The text now displays well, except that it appears at the bottom of the cell. You'll discover how to fix this later, in: *Lesson 4-8: Vertically align the contents of cells.*

Notes: Sales include all European and American sales but exclude those to Eastern Europe, Asia and South Africa.  Salesmen reported that clients are not ordering as much stock as usual because we are nearing the end of the first quarter.

11   Save your work as *Sales Week Ended 14th March 2016-5.*

## note

### Problems caused by merged cells

1. If you apply a format to a single column it will not be applied to a merged cell that spans the column.

2. You cannot AutoFill across a merged cell.

3. You cannot select a range within a single column if it contains a merged cell. This is the problem that you encounter at the beginning of this lesson.

4. When working with values it can be unclear which cell a merged value belongs to. This can cause errors when the values in a column that contain a merged cell are totalled.

| | A | B |
|---|---|---|
| 1 | Joe | Bill |
| 2 | | 5 |
| 3 | 10 | 10 |
| 4 | 15 | 10 |

In the example above cells A2:B2 are merged and the merged cell has been right-aligned. The value of 5 is actually in column A causing the totals in row 4 to seem incorrect.

5. If you copy and paste a merged cell the destination cells will also merge.

6. When you merge cells only the data in the left-most cell remains. Values in all other cells are discarded.

7. You cannot *Fill Down* a cell if it is part of a merged set of cells.

8. If you progress to the *Expert Skills* book in this series you will learn how to sort data. Any merged cells in a data set will interfere with sort results.

# Lesson 4-7: Unmerge cells and Center Across Selection

In: *Lesson 4-6: Merge cells, wrap text and expand/collapse the formula bar,* you learned how to merge cells.

The *Merge Cells* feature is a widely used Excel feature. You'll often encounter merged cells in workbooks that were created by other Excel users. Perhaps after reading this lesson you will decide not to use the *Merge Cells* feature in your own worksheets.

Unfortunately, the *Merge Cells* feature can cause a number of problems (see sidebar). For this reason, many Excel professionals advise against ever using the *Merge Cells* feature. That's because there is a very similar Excel feature called *Center Across Selection* that doesn't cause any of the problems associated with *Merge Cells.*

Some Excel professionals even advise that existing workbooks containing merged cells should be converted to use *Center Across Selection* instead.

In this lesson, you will take a workbook that has many merged cells and then unmerge them before achieving the same effect using *Center Across Selection.*

1   Open *Cash and Credit Sales Analysis* from your sample files folder.

| | A | B | C | D |
|---|---|---|---|---|
| 1 | | | | |
| 2 | | | Total | |
| 3 | | Analysis Type | Cash | Credit |
| 4 | | London | | |
| 5 | | Beverages | 22,998 | 30,319 |
| 6 | | Meat/Poultry | 63,452 | 55,030 |
| 7 | | Vegetables | 33,351 | 42,196 |
| 8 | | Paris | | |
| 9 | | Oct | 42,972 | 55,220 |
| 10 | | Nov | 34,472 | 42,216 |
| 11 | | Dec | 42,357 | 51,150 |
| 12 | | New York | | |
| 13 | | UK | 53,847 | 48,230 |
| 14 | | USA | 40,040 | 51,196 |
| 15 | | Canada | 25,914 | 32,215 |

This workbook has been formatted using Excel's *Merge Cells* feature. You learned how to merge cells in: *Lesson 4-6: Merge cells, wrap text and expand/collapse the formula bar.*

To make the merged cells easier to identify they have been shaded.

You can see that this worksheet has had border lines added to enhance appearance. You'll learn to use border lines to create a very similar worksheet later, in: *Lesson 4-12: Add borders and lines.*

2   Appreciate some of the problems caused by merged cells

In: *Lesson 2-7: Select non-contiguous cell ranges and view summary information,* you learned that it is simple and convenient to view the total value of several cells by selecting them with the mouse.

## note

### The Center Across Selection feature cannot be easily added to the Quick Access Toolbar

In: *Lesson 1-14: Customize the Quick Access Toolbar and preview the printout,* you learned that just about every Excel feature can be quickly and easily added to *the Quick Access Toolbar.*

Unfortunately, *Center Across Selection* is one of the very few Excel features that cannot be easily added to the *Quick Access Toolbar* in the normal way.

The *Expert Skills* book in this series provides a full understanding of Excel's *macro* feature and also teaches how to customize the Ribbon. With this knowledge, it is possible to work-around Excel's usual limitations and add a button to the *Ribbon* or *Quick Access Toolbar* using a different (macro based) technique.

The total value of the selected cells is then shown on the status bar at the bottom-right of the screen.

Try to select cells C5:C15 to report the combined cash sales for London, Paris and New York. You will find this impossible to do because of the merged cells in rows 4, 8 and 12.

3   Remove merged cells.

   1.   Select cell C2. This selects the merged cell range C2:D2.

   2.   Click Home→Alignment→Merge & Center.

       The *Merge & Center* button is no longer highlighted and cells C2 and D2 are unmerged.

   3.   Do the same thing to unmerge cells B4, B8 and B12.

       All worksheet cells are now unmerged. You will now find no difficulty in selecting cells C5:C15.

4   Use Center Across Selection to merge cells C2:D2.

   1.   Select cells C2:D2.

   2.   Right-click anywhere in the selected range and choose *Format Cells…* from the shortcut menu.

       The *Format Cells* dialog appears.

   3.   Click the *Alignment* tab.

   4.   Click the drop-down arrow on the side of the *Text Alignment →Horizontal* box.

   5.   Click: *Center Across Selection* from the drop-down list.

   6.   Click the OK button to dismiss the dialog.

       The text in cells C2:D2 now looks the same as when the two cells were merged. The key difference is that you are now able to individually select cell C2 or D2.

       This may only seem like a small difference, but it avoids all of the problems listed in the facing-page sidebar.

5   Use Center Across Selection to merge cells B4:D4, B8:D8 and B12:D12.

The worksheet now looks exactly as it did at the beginning of this lesson. The worksheet also no longer contains any merged cells.

6   Select cells C5:C15 to report the combined cash sales of the London, Paris and New York branches.

This time there is no difficulty selecting the cells and you can read the combined cash sales figure from the status bar (359,403).

> Average: 39,934   Count: 9   Min: 22,998   Max: 63,452   Sum: 359,403

7   Save your work as *Cash and Credit Sales Analysis-1.*

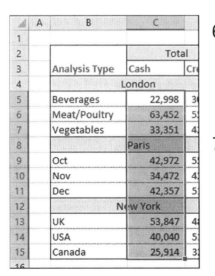

# Lesson 4-8: Vertically align the contents of cells

This table summarizes Excel's different vertical alignment options.

| Icon | Description | What it does | Example |
|---|---|---|---|
| General ▾ | General (the default) | Aligns cell contents to the bottom of the cell. | Bottom-Dollar Markets |
| ☰ | Top Align | Aligns cell contents to the top of the cell | Bottom-Dollar Markets |
| ☰ | Middle Align | Aligns cell contents to the middle of the cell. | Bottom-Dollar Markets |
| ☰ | Bottom Align | Aligns cell contents to the bottom of the cell | Bottom-Dollar Markets |
| No icon | Justify | Lines of text are spread out so that the space between each is equal, the first line is at the top and the last line is at the bottom. | to be or not to be, that is the question. |
| No Icon | Distributed | The same as Justify! | to be or not to be, that is the question. |

1   Open *Sales Week Ended 14th March 2016-5* from your sample files folder (if it isn't already open).

2   Top align the contents of cell A22.

The contents of cell A22 are currently bottom aligned (the default).

> 22  Note: Sales include all European and American sales but exclude those to Eastern Europe, Asia and South Africa.  Salesmen reported that clients are not ordering as much stock as usual because we are nearing the end of the first quarter.

When you place a block of text into a cell in this way, you will typically want it to be top-aligned.

1.   Select cell A22.

**Sales Week Ended 14th March 2016-5**

2. Click: Home→Alignment→Top Align  to align the text to the top of the cell.

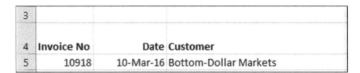

3    Increase the height of row 4 so that it is about twice its present height.

This was covered in: *Lesson 2-9: Re-size rows and columns.*

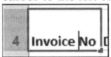

You can see why the default vertical alignment is *bottom align*. This alignment works really well for title rows.

4    Wrap the text in cell A4.

This was covered in: *Lesson 4-6: Merge cells, wrap text and expand/collapse the formula bar.*

5    Split the words *Invoice* and *No* so that they appear on separate lines.

1. Double-click cell A4 to enter Edit mode and then position the cursor to the left of the word *No*.

2. Press **<Alt>+<Enter>**.

3. Press the **<Enter>** key again to exit Edit mode.

The two words now appear on separate lines.

6    Horizontally right-align the text in cell A4.

This was covered in: *Lesson 4-5: Horizontally align the contents of cells.*

7    Automatically resize columns A to G so that each column is just wide enough for the cell contents.

This was covered in: *Lesson 2-9: Re-size rows and columns.*

8    Save your work as *Sales Week Ended 14<sup>th</sup> March 2016-6.*

## note

### What are serifs?

Serifs are the little lines at the edges of text that allow the eye to more easily scan words.

Serifs

Sans Serif

## note

### Can I change the default theme?

The default theme is simply the theme applied to the *Blank Workbook* template.

If you want to use a different default theme (or change any of the standard Excel options) you will need to create an empty workbook, apply the new theme to it, and then save it as a template (for example: *My Blank Workbook*). You learned how to do this in: *Lesson 3-14: Understand templates and set the default custom template folder.*

If you pin the *My Blank Workbook* template, it will then appear at the top of the list when you open Excel.

When you create new blank workbooks in future, you can then use your own customized *My Blank Workbook* custom template in place of Microsoft's *Blank Workbook* template.

# Lesson 4-9: Understand themes

A theme is simply a set of fonts, colors and effects that go very nicely together.

## Font sets

A font set consists of two complementary fonts that work well as a pair.

A golden rule of typesetting is to never have more than two fonts in a document. Old school typesetters would always use a serif font for the body text (also called the *Normal* text) and a sans-serif font for the titles (just as this book does). See sidebar for the difference between serif and sans-serif fonts.

There's a modern school of thought that suggests that breaking this rule is cool and Microsoft have done just that with their default set for Excel 2016 (called the *Office* set) by choosing a sans-serif font (Calibri Light) for titles and a sans-serif font (Calibri) for normal text.

You can see all 25 pre-defined font sets by clicking:

Page Layout→Themes→Fonts

You can also create your own font sets if you don't like any of the pre-defined ones. You'll learn how to do this in: *Lesson 4-13: Create your own custom theme.*

## Color sets

If you click: Home→Font→Fill Color (drop down), you will see this dialog:

# trivia

Color sets are a little more involved than font sets

The ten colors along the top row are the *Theme colors*. The leftmost four are used for *Text and Background colors* and the other six are *Accent colors*. This set of colors has been selected by design professionals to work well together. There are actually twelve theme colors but you can only see ten of them. The two hidden theme colors are used for hyperlinks.

The *Standard colors* are best avoided. They are colors that will remain the same no matter what theme is in use. If you use standard colors (or the *More Colors…* option) the worksheet may look odd if the theme needs to be changed in the future. You can see all 23 pre-defined color sets by clicking:

Page Layout→Themes→Colors

## Effects

You'll only notice a change in theme effects if you have graphic elements on your worksheet, such as drawing shapes or chart objects. We'll see this working later in: *Lesson 5-8: Format 3-D elements and add drop shadows.*

Theme effects are applied to the outline and fill of shapes. You can see all 15 pre-defined effects by clicking:

Page Layout→Themes→Effects

## Themes

Themes are simply a group of one *color* set, one *font* set and one *effects* set.

Because Microsoft have consistently named their Colors, Fonts, Effects and Themes, the *Office* theme consists of the *Office* color set, the *Office* font set and the *Office* effects set.

## Themes aren't just for Excel

The Themes feature is also included in Word, PowerPoint and Outlook.

Choosing the same theme for your documents, spreadsheets, presentations and Emails can give all of your communications a consistent and professional appearance.

# Lesson 4-10: Use cell styles and change themes

In order for themes to work their magic, you must get into the habit of using cell styles to format cells based only upon the options available in the current theme.

For many years, expert Word users have used styles to quickly produce professional documents. Their mortal sin would be to apply a font size or color directly to a document.

Now that Excel also supports styles (they were introduced in Excel 2007), professional Excel users should adopt the same discipline.

1 Open *Sales Week Ended 14th March 2016-6* from your sample files folder (if it isn't already open).

2 Apply the *Title* style to cell A1.

Even though cell A1 now encompasses cells A1:G1 it retains the cell reference A1.

A novice user might apply a font and color directly to cell A1 but you're going to do things the professional way and use the *Title* style.

1. Select cell A1.

2. Click: Home→Styles→Cell Styles.

The styles gallery appears.

3. Click *Title* to apply the Title style to cell A1.

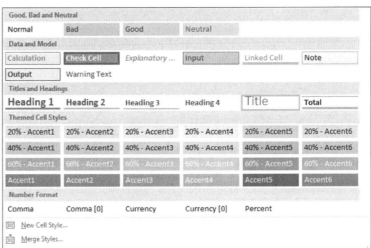

Cell A1 is formatted with the *Title* style.

3 Apply the *Heading 3* style to cells A4:G4.

1. Select cells A4:G4.

2. Click: Home→Styles→Cell Styles→Heading 3.

4 Apply the *Note* style to cell A22.

1. Select cell A22.

2. Click: Home→Styles→Cell Styles→Note.

**Sales Week Ended 14th March 2016-6**

## note

### Microsoft's suggested use for the built-in cell styles

In: *Lesson 4-14: Create your own custom cell styles*, you'll learn how to create your own cell styles.

While you can use the built-in cell styles for any purpose you can see that Microsoft are suggesting the following usage:

**Good, Bad and Neutral** – to mark particularly good or bad results.

**Data and Model** – usually used in a worksheet containing formulas to mark cells that require user input or contain formula results.

**Titles and Headings** – for section titles and column headers.

**Themed Cell Styles** – to color cells based upon the theme colors.

**Number Format** – to quickly apply number formats.

| | | | |
|---|---|---|---|
| Argentina | 644.80 | 17.5% | 757.64 |
| UK | 220.00 | 17.5% | 258.50 |
| UK | 920.60 | 17.5% | 1,081.71 |
| Germany | 2,731.87 | 17.5% | 3,209.95 |
| Canada | 4,422.00 | 17.5% | 5,195.85 |
| Germany | 245.00 | 17.5% | 287.88 |
| | | | **18,137.37** |

**5** Apply the *20% - Accent 1* style to cells A5:D20.

1. Select cells A5:D20

2. Click: Home→Styles→Cell Styles→20% - Accent 1.

**6** Apply the *20% - Accent 2* style to cells E5:G20.

1. Select cells E5:G20.

2. Click: Home→Styles→Cell Styles→ 20% - Accent 2.

The worksheet now looks very different:

**7** Insert a row above row 21.

This was covered in: *Lesson 3-1: Insert and delete rows and columns.*

**8** Use AutoSum to place a total in cell G21.

This was covered in: *Lesson 2-3: Use AutoSum to quickly calculate totals.*

**9** Apply the *Total* style to cell G21.

1. Select cell G21.

2. Click: Home→Styles→Cell Styles→Total.

**10** Re-size column G if necessary so that it is wide enough to display the total.

The total cell is neatly formatted.

**11** Preview your finished work under different themes.

Because you did things the professional way, using styles instead of directly formatting cells, it is now possible to cycle through the themes. You may find one of the other themes more attractive.

1. Click: Page Layout→Themes→Themes.

   The *Themes* gallery appears.

2. Hover over each theme in turn. You'll be amazed at how the appearance of the worksheet completely changes as each theme's style set is applied.

**12** Save your work as *Sales Week Ended 14ᵗʰ March 2016-7.*

# Lesson 4-11: Add color and gradient effects to cells

Most of the time solid colors are all you need, but you may want to make data look more interesting for a PowerPoint presentation, or for publication in a newsletter or a web page.

When you add colors, it is usually best to stay within those of the current theme. This enables you to quickly change the appearance of the worksheet to match that of a PowerPoint presentation or Word document that uses a different theme (see sidebar for an example of this in action).

In this lesson, you'll add a gradient to the sharp transition between the orange totals section and the blue transaction details section of the worksheet.

1   Open *Sales Week Ended 14th March 2016-7* from your sample files folder (if it isn't already open).

2   Check the colors that are currently being used for the transaction and totals section in your worksheet.

1.   Click anywhere in the blue area of your worksheet (cells A5:C21).

2.   Click the drop-down arrow next to: Home→Font→Fill Color.

Notice that one color has a small square around it. When you hover over this button you will see that the fill color for the left-hand side of the worksheet is *Blue, Accent 1, Lighter 80%.*

3.   Do the same for the orange colored cells (cells D5:G21). You'll find that they are *Orange, Accent 2, Lighter 80%.*

3   Set a gradient fill in column D.

1.   Select cells D5:D21.

2.   Right-click inside the selected range and click *Format Cells…* from the shortcut menu.

3.   Click the *Fill* Tab.

Sales Week Ended
14th March 2016-7

4. Click the *Fill Effects...* button.

5. In the *Colors* frame, choose *Blue, Accent 1, Lighter 80%* for *Color 1*.

6. In the *Colors* frame, choose *Orange, Accent 2, Lighter 80%* for *Color 2*.

7. Select the *Vertical* shading style.

8. Select the top left variant.

| Country | Amount |
|---------|--------|
| Canada | 1,447.50 |
| Spain | 365.89 |
| Mexico | 514.40 |
| Germany | 1,174.75 |
| Germany | 500.00 |
| Italy | 637.49 |
| Italy | (637.49) |
| Brazil | 475.14 |
| Canada | 1,025.32 |
| France | 748.79 |
| Argentina | 644.80 |
| UK | 220.00 |

9. Click OK and then OK again.

A smooth gradient fill has been added to column D.

4 Save your work as *Sales Week Ended 14ᵗʰ March 2016-8.*

# Lesson 4-12: Add borders and lines

1   Open *Sales Analysis* from your sample files folder.

You're going to use the powerful *borders and lines* feature to make this worksheet more readable.

| Before | After |
|---|---|

**Before**

| | A | B | C | D | E |
|---|---|---|---|---|---|
| 1 | | | | | |
| 2 | | | Total | | |
| 3 | | Analysis Type | Cash | Percent | |
| 4 | | By Category | | | |
| 5 | | Beverages | 25,326 | 20% | |
| 6 | | Meat/Poultry | 65,780 | 52% | |
| 7 | | Vegetables | 35,679 | 28% | |
| 8 | | Total | 126,785 | | |
| 9 | | By Month | | | |
| 10 | | Oct | 45,300 | 36% | |
| 11 | | Nov | 36,800 | 29% | |
| 12 | | Dec | 44,685 | 35% | |
| 13 | | Total | 126,785 | | |
| 14 | | By Country | | | |
| 15 | | UK | 56,175 | 44% | |
| 16 | | USA | 42,368 | 33% | |
| 17 | | Canada | 28,242 | 22% | |
| 18 | | Total | 126,785 | | |
| 19 | | | | | |

**After**

| | A | B | C | D | E |
|---|---|---|---|---|---|
| 1 | | | | | |
| 2 | | | Total | | |
| 3 | | Analysis Type | Cash | Percent | |
| 4 | | By Category | | | |
| 5 | | Beverages | 25,326 | 20% | |
| 6 | | Meat/Poultry | 65,780 | 52% | |
| 7 | | Vegetables | 35,679 | 28% | |
| 8 | | Total | 126,785 | | |
| 9 | | By Month | | | |
| 10 | | Oct | 45,300 | 36% | |
| 11 | | Nov | 36,800 | 29% | |
| 12 | | Dec | 44,685 | 35% | |
| 13 | | Total | 126,785 | | |
| 14 | | By Country | | | |
| 15 | | UK | 56,175 | 44% | |
| 16 | | USA | 42,368 | 33% | |
| 17 | | Canada | 28,242 | 22% | |
| 18 | | Total | 126,785 | | |
| 19 | | | | | |

## note

### This worksheet contains a merged cell

In: *Lesson 4-7: Unmerge cells and Center Across Selection,* you learned that some Excel professionals like to avoid merged cells in their worksheets.

In this worksheet cells C2:D2 are merged.

You could unmerge these cells and then center the **Total** text using the **Center Across Selection** feature. If you did this, the appearance of the worksheet would be entirely unchanged.

**Sales Analysis**

2   Add cell styles to rows 2, 3, 4, 9 and 14.

1.   Select cells B2:D3.

2.   Click: Home→Styles→Cell Styles→40% Accent 6.

3.   Select cells B4:D4, B9:D9 and B14:D14.

This was covered in: *Lesson 2-7: Select non-contiguous cell ranges and view summary information.*

4.   Click: Home→Styles→Cell Styles→20% Accent 6.

5.   Select cells B2:D3.

6.   Click: Home→Styles→Cell Styles→Heading 4.

3   Switch off the worksheet gridlines.

When you are working with borders it is always a good idea to switch off the gridlines so that you can have a better idea of how the worksheet will print.

This feature appears in two different places on the Ribbon. Uncheck either of the following check boxes:

View→Show→Gridlines

**OR**

Page Layout→Sheet Options→Gridlines→View

4   Add a solid border around the entire range.

1. Select cells B2:D18.

2. Click: Home→Font→Borders drop-down→ Outside Borders.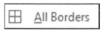

## tip

### Use the draw border tool to quickly add complex borders

The fastest way to quickly add borders is to simply draw them into place using the *Draw Border* tool.

Click:

Home→Font→ Borders drop-down→ Draw Border

You can then simply draw borders straight onto the grid. There's also an *Erase Border* tool available on the same menu.

## note

### Changing the border line style or color from the drop-down menu

The ability to change line style and color from the menu means you'll rarely have to resort to using the *Format Cells* dialog for borders.

To change line style or color from the *Borders* drop-down menu, select *Line Color or Line Style*.

The selected color and/or style will remain active until you close Excel. Next time you open Excel it will have returned to the default.

5  Add solid borders inside cells C2:D3.

1. Select cells C2:D3.

2. Click: Home→Font→Borders drop-down→All Borders.

6  Add top and bottom borders to *By Category*, *By Month* and *By Country*.

1. Select cells B4:D4, B9:D9 and B14:D14.

2. Click: Home→Font→Borders drop-down→ Top and Bottom Border.

   [Top and Bottom Border]

7  Add dotted outlines to the borders of cells B5:D8, B10:D13 and B15:D18.

1. Select cells B5:D8, B10:D13 and B15:D18.

2. Right-click any of the selected cells and click *Format Cells…* from the shortcut menu.

   The *Format Cells* dialog appears.

3. Click the *Border* tab of the *Format Cells* dialog.

4. Click the *Dotted Line* style.

5. Click the *Inside* button.

6. Click the OK button.

   The dotted lines are displayed within the cells.

8  Add left and right borders to cells C5:C8, C10:C13 and C15:C18.

1. Select cells C5:C8, C10:C13 and C15:C18.

2. Click: Home→Font→Borders→Left Border.

   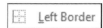 [Left Border]

3. Click: Home→Font→Borders→Right Border.

   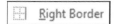 [Right Border]

9  Save your work as *Sales Analysis-1*.

# Lesson 4-13: Create your own custom theme

If none of the 35 built-in themes suffice, you can create your own.

Some clients have a defined corporate style and are extremely particular that colors, fonts and other layout items reinforce their corporate identity.

When individuality is important, you need your own custom theme.

1 Open *Sales Week Ended 14th March 2016-8* from your sample files folder (if it isn't already open).

2 Select a different set of theme colors.

    1. Click: Page Layout→Themes→Colors.

       All of the pre-defined sets of colors are displayed (see sidebar). Try hovering your mouse over them one at a time, to see how your worksheet would look if you changed the theme colors.

    2. Choose a different set that you think look attractive.

3 Create a custom set of theme colors.

    1. Click: Page Layout→Themes→Colors→Customize Colors.

       The *Create New Theme Colors* dialog appears (displaying the color set for the currently selected theme).

    2. Click any of the colors on the left of the dialog and select a different color. Notice that, as you do, the *Sample* frame shows a preview of how your theme looks. Let your imagination run wild and create your own custom color theme.

    3. Type: **TSM Corporate** into the *Name* box.

    4. Click the *Save* button to create your own personalized set of custom colors.

4 Select a different set of fonts.

    As discussed in: *Lesson 4-9: Understand themes*, a theme consists of a *color set*, a *font set* and an *effects set*.

## note

### Can I change the default theme?

If you've adopted a custom theme as your corporate standard, you will probably want to use this when creating new blank workbooks.

To do this, refer to the sidebar in: *Lesson 4-9: Understand themes*.

Sales Week Ended
14th March 2016-8

A font set consists of two fonts: a heading font and a body font.

1.  Click: Page Layout→Themes→Fonts.

    All of the pre-defined sets of fonts are displayed (see sidebar). Try hovering your mouse over them one at a time, to see how your worksheet would look if you changed the theme fonts.

2.  Choose a different set that you think look attractive.

5   **Create a custom set of theme fonts.**

1.  Click: Page Layout→Themes→Fonts→Customize Fonts.

    The *Create New Theme Fonts* dialog appears (displaying the font set for the currently selected theme).

2.  Select two complimentary fonts. Ideally the body font should be a serif font and the heading font should be a sans-serif font (this issue is discussed in: *Lesson 4-9: Understand themes*).

3.  Type: **TSM Corporate** into the *Name* box.

4.  Click the *Save* button to create your own personalized set of custom fonts.

6   **Select a different set of effects.**

Unlike colors and fonts, you can't create a custom set of effects. You have to choose from the pre-defined ones.

Effects change the appearance of drawing objects and you haven't yet covered these (they will make an appearance in: *Lesson 5-8: Format 3-D elements and add drop shadows*).

1.  Click: Page Layout→Themes→Effects.

2.  Choose a different set of effects.

7   **Save the corporate theme.**

1.  Click: Page Layout→Themes→Themes→Save Current Theme.

2.  Enter the name: **TSM Corporate** in the *File Name* text box.

3.  Click the *Save* button.

8   **Revert to the standard *Office* theme.**

1.  Click: Page Layout→Themes→Themes.

    Notice that your custom theme is listed at the top in the *Custom* group.

2.  Click the *Office* theme to put things back the way they were.

9   **Close the workbook without saving.**

# Lesson 4-14: Create your own custom cell styles

In: *Lesson 4-10: Use cell styles and change themes*, you learned how to use Excel's built-in cell styles.  You can also create your own custom styles.

Custom styles are only available in the workbook in which they were originally created. In order to use them in another workbook, you need to use Excel's *merge styles* feature. The *merge styles* feature will be covered later, in: *Lesson 4-15: Use a master style book to merge styles*.

1   Open *Sales Week Ended 14ᵗʰ March 2016-8* from your sample files folder (if it isn't already open).

2   Modify an existing cell style.

Click cell A23 to make it the active cell.  This is the cell containing the *Note* text.

> Note: Sales include all European and American
> Asia and South Africa.  Salesmen reported that
> 23 because we are nearing the end of the first qua

1.  Click: Home→Styles→Cell Styles.

2.  Right-click the *Note* style and click *Modify* from the shortcut menu.

    The *Style* dialog appears (see sidebar).

3.  Click the *Format…* button. The *Format Cells* dialog appears.

4.  Click the *Fill* tab and select a light green background color:

5.  Click the OK button and then the OK button once more.

6.  If cell A23 isn't green, click: Home→Styles→Cell Styles and click once on the *Note* style.

    Notice that the background color of cell A23 (which has the *Note* style applied to it) has now turned light green.

    You haven't permanently changed the *Office* theme's *Note* style. You've simply changed it for this workbook only.  When you open another workbook that uses the *Office* theme, the *Note* style will be light yellow once again.

3   Duplicate the *Note* built-in cell style.

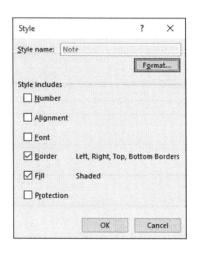

Sales Week Ended
14ᵗʰ March 2016-8

1. Click: Home→Styles→Cell Styles to display the *Cell Styles* gallery.

2. Right-click the *Note* cell style and then click *Duplicate* from the shortcut menu.

3. The *Style* dialog appears, suggesting the name *Note 2* for your new cell style.

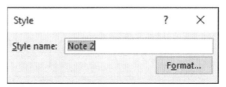

4. Change the style name to *Blue Note* (you're going to change the color in a moment) and click the OK button.

5. Click: Home→Styles→Cell Styles to display the *Cell Styles* gallery once more. Notice that the *Blue Note* style is at the top of the gallery in the *Custom* section.

6. Change the background color of the new *Blue Note* style to light blue using the technique learned in: *Step 2 - Modify an existing cell style*.

4   Create a custom cell style *By Example*.

This is the easiest way to create custom cell styles.

1. Select cell A23.

2. Click: Home→Font→Fill Color Drop-down and choose the *Gold, Accent 4, Lighter 80%* theme color.

3. Click: Home→Styles→Cell Styles→New Cell Style.

The *Style* dialog appears but notice the words: *By Example*. This means that the style already contains all of the formatting information for cell A23.

4. Change the style name to **Gold Note** and click the OK button.

5   Save your work as *Sales Week Ended 14ᵗʰ March 2016-9*.

# Lesson 4-15: Use a master style book to merge styles

When you create custom styles, they are only available within the workbook in which they were created. Sometimes it is useful to have the same set of custom styles available across multiple workbooks.

In this lesson, you'll cater for the following scenario at Empire Car Sales:

Syd Slater, the owner of Empire Car Sales, knows that you have to keep your stock turning over.

His salesmen are allowed to discount 10% of the sticker price on all cars.

If the car has been on the forecourt for more than two weeks they are allowed to discount 15%, after three weeks 20%, and after four weeks the car goes back to auction.

Syd's salesmen need to know the maximum discount they can offer, but Syd doesn't want the customers to find this out, so they use a cunning system of color coding on the stock list:

10% Max Discount:   Blue

15% Max Discount:   Green

20% Max Discount:   Orange

The stock list is produced each week in Excel with three custom cell styles, one for each discount.

To avoid having to constantly re-create custom cell styles, they are stored in a master style book called *Empire Styles* which Syd merges with his worksheets so that the three styles are always available.

1   Open a new blank workbook.

2   Create a custom style called *10% Max Discount* with a background color of *Light Blue*.

> This was covered in: *Lesson 4-14: Create your own custom cell styles.*

3   Create a custom style called *15% Max* Discount with a background color of *Light Green*.

4   Create a custom style called *20% Max* Discount with a background color of *Light Orange*.

Because you have used theme colors for the custom styles, their color will change if the theme is changed.

For example, if you change the theme to *Slate*, the *10% Max Discount* becomes red, *15%* becomes brown and *20%* becomes tan.

For this reason, you could argue that it would be better to set the colors using the *More Colors* option so that the colors remained the same even if the theme is changed.

Empire Car Sales
Stock List-1

For the purposes of this lesson you will assume that Syd will not change from the *Office* theme and will follow the normal rule of restricting color choice to theme colors. (See the sidebar in: *Lesson 4-11: Add color and gradient effects to cells,* for an explanation of why this is best practice).

5    Save the workbook as *Empire Styles* but don't close it.

6    Open *Empire Car Sales Stock List-1* from your sample files folder.

7    Merge the styles from the *Empire Styles* master style book.

     1.   Click: Home→Styles→Cell Styles→Merge Styles…

     2.   The *Merge Styles* dialog appears.

     3.   Select *Empires Styles.xlsx* and then click the OK button.

The three custom styles are now available within the current workbook.

8    Apply the 20% style to the Volkswagen and Mercedes.

9    Apply the 15% style to the BMW and Alfa Romeo.

10   Apply the 10% style to the Volvo and Ford.

Syd's salesmen are now ready to start selling!

11   Save your work as *Empire Car Sales Stock List-2.*

**note**

**You can also apply simple conditional formats using the Quick Analysis button**

Whenever you select a range of cells, a *Quick Analysis* button appears just outside the bottom-right corner of the selected range.

| 24 | USA | 49,190.99 | |
|----|-----|-----------|--|
| 25 | Venezuela | 13,189.98 | |
| 26 | Grand Total | 266,644.33 | |
| 27 | | | |

When you click the *Quick Analysis* button, the *Quick Analysis* dialog appears.

One of the menu options on this dialog is *Formatting*.

When you click the *Formatting* menu option, one of the options is *Greater Than:*

Greater Than

When you click the *Greater Than* icon you will see the same *Greater Than* dialog that you display using the Ribbon in this lesson.

Unfortunately, the *Quick Analysis* button is not as powerful as the Ribbon method used in this lesson.

There is no *Less Than* option, meaning that it would not be possible add the conditional formats described in this lesson using only the *Quick Analysis* feature.

# Lesson 4-16: Use simple conditional formatting

Simple conditional formatting applies a format to a cell based upon the value of the cell. In this lesson, you'll change the cell background color to red if the cell has a value of less than 5,000 and to green if the value is over 30,000.

The same technique learned in this lesson can be used to apply conditional formats based upon text that begins with, ends with, or contains specific characters.

You can also apply conditional formats to cells containing dates. For example, you can highlight dates such as *today, tomorrow, in the last seven days, last week* and *this week*. Conditional formatting will then cause the worksheet to change every time that you open it based upon the current date.

1   Open *Sales Report* from your sample files folder.

2   AutoFit cells A4:A26.

   1.   Select cells A4:A26.

   2.   Click: Home→Cells→Format→AutoFit Column Width.

3   AutoFit cells D4:D13.

4   Apply the *Comma* style to column B and column E.

This was covered in: *Lesson 4-3: Format numbers using built-in number formats.*

5   Merge cells A3:B3, D3:E3 and D18:E18.

This was covered in: *Lesson 4-6: Merge cells, wrap text and expand/collapse the formula bar.*

6   Apply the *Title* style to cell A1.

This was covered in: *Lesson 4-10: Use cell styles.*

7   Apply the *Heading 2* style to cells A3, D3 and D18.

8   Apply the *Heading 3* style to cells A4:B4, D4:E4 and D19:E19.

9   Apply the *Total* style to cells A26:B26, D13:E13 and D26:E26.

The worksheet is now well formatted and has a professional appearance:

| | A | B | C | D | E |
|---|---|---|---|---|---|
| 1 | Sales Report - 6 Months ended March 2016 | | | | |
| 2 | | | | | |
| 3 | Sales By Country | | | Sales by Category | |
| 4 | Country | Total Sales | | Category | Total Sales |
| 5 | Argentina | 762.60 | | Beverages | 70,168.10 |
| 6 | Austria | 33,462.58 | | Condiments | 24,938.06 |

**Sales Report**

10   Select cells B5:B25.

# note

### You can have as many conditional formats as you need

Excel versions prior to Excel 2007 were limited to three conditional formats per cell.

In Excel 2016 you can define an infinite number of conditional formats.

| 3 | Sales By Country | |
|---|---|---|
| 4 | Country | Total Sales |
| 5 | Argentina | 762.60 |
| 6 | Austria | 33,462.58 |
| 7 | Belgium | 6,109.48 |
| 8 | Brazil | 20,524.42 |
| 9 | Canada | 21,306.29 |
| 10 | Denmark | 16,658.80 |
| 11 | Finland | 5,525.00 |
| 12 | France | 26,155.54 |
| 13 | Germany | 28,361.38 |
| 14 | Ireland | 6,157.76 |
| 15 | Italy | 2,585.69 |
| 16 | Mexico | 3,524.30 |
| 17 | Norway | 1,058.40 |
| 18 | Poland | 459.00 |
| 19 | Portugal | 5,584.13 |

| 3 | Sales By Country | |
|---|---|---|
| 4 | Country | Total Sales |
| 5 | Argentina | 762.60 |
| 6 | Austria | 33,462.58 |
| 7 | Belgium | 6,109.48 |
| 8 | Brazil | 20,524.42 |
| 9 | Canada | 21,306.29 |
| 10 | Denmark | 16,658.80 |
| 11 | Finland | 5,525.00 |
| 12 | France | 26,155.54 |
| 13 | Germany | 28,361.38 |
| 14 | Ireland | 6,157.76 |
| 15 | Italy | 2,585.69 |

**11** Conditionally format the selected range so that any country with sales below 5,000 has a light red fill with dark red text.

1. Click: Home→Styles→Conditional Formatting→Highlight Cells Rules→Less Than…

   The *Less Than* dialog appears.

2. Type 5,000 in the left-hand text box and choose *Light Red Fill with Dark Red Text* for the font and fill color.

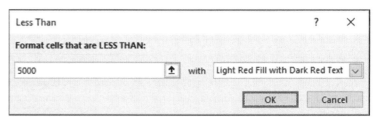

Notice that when you change the value in the text box, the worksheet adjusts in the background to preview what will happen with this conditional format.

Note also that there's a *Custom Format…* option (in the drop-down list) which enables you to choose effects such as underlines as well as any color.

3. Click the OK button.

   Cells that have a value of less than 5,000 are now highlighted in red (see sidebar).

**12** Add another conditional format to the same range, so that any country with sales above 30,000 has a green fill with dark green text.

Both conditional formats now display with the two sales values over 30,000 displayed in green (see sidebar).

**13** Remove both conditional formats.

1. Select cells B5:B25.

2. Click: Home→Styles→Conditional Formatting→Clear Rules→Clear Rules from Selected Cells.

   The conditional formats are removed.

**14** Save your work as *Sales Report-1.*

# Lesson 4-17: Manage multiple conditional formats using the Rules Manager

The conditional formats applied in the previous lesson depended upon the value of a single cell.

Often you will want a cell to be formatted based upon its relationship to other cells in a range.

In this lesson you'll color the top 25% of sales green, the middle 50% yellow and the bottom 25% red.

This lesson also introduces the *Rules Manager* that allows you to edit conditional format rules and to specify the order in which conditional formats are applied.

1 Open *Sales Report-1 from* your sample files folder (if it isn't already open).

2 Select cells B5:B25.

3 Conditionally format the selected range so that any country whose sales are in the top 25% has a green fill with dark green text.

    1. Click: Home→Styles→Conditional Formatting→ Top/Bottom Rules→Top 10%.

    The *Top 10%* dialog appears.

    2. Change the value to 25% and choose *Green fill with Dark Green Text* for the fill.

    3. Click the OK button.

| 3 | Sales By Country | |
|---|---|---|
| 4 | **Country** | **Total Sales** |
| 5 | Argentina | 762.60 |
| 6 | Austria | 33,462.58 |
| 7 | Belgium | 6,109.48 |
| 8 | Brazil | 20,524.42 |
| 9 | Canada | 21,306.29 |
| 10 | Denmark | 16,658.80 |
| 11 | Finland | 5,525.00 |
| 12 | France | 26,155.54 |
| 13 | Germany | 28,361.38 |
| 14 | Ireland | 6,157.76 |
| 15 | Italy | 2,585.69 |

4 Conditionally format the selected range so that any country whose sales are in the bottom 25% has a light red fill with dark red text.

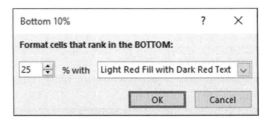

The top and bottom 25% of sales are now highlighted as specified in the two conditional formats (see sidebar).

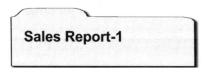
**Sales Report-1**

5 Add another conditional format so that any country with sales greater than zero has a yellow fill with dark yellow text.

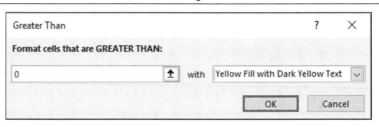

Remember that the specification was to color the middle 50% of sales yellow.

Unfortunately, all sales are now yellow because the yellow cells are over-writing the red and green cells.

6 Use the *Rules Manager* to control the order in which conditional formats are applied.

1. Select cells B5:B25.

2. Click: Home→Styles→Conditional Formatting→Manage Rules.

   The *Conditional Formatting Rules Manager* dialog is displayed.

3. Click the first rule (the *Cell Value > 0* rule).

4. Use the *Move Down* button to move the *Cell Value > 0* rule to the bottom of the list (if you don't see the *Move Down* button it is because you haven't selected the rule).

5. Click the OK button.

   The red, green and yellow formatting rules are now applied as required. This works because of the conflict resolution rules (see sidebar).

7 Use the *Rules Manager* to edit the rules so that the top and bottom 30% values are now highlighted.

1. Select cells B5:B25.

2. Click: Home→Styles→Conditional Formatting→Manage Rules.

3. Select the *Bottom 25%* rule.

4. Click the *Edit Rule...* button and change the criteria to: *30%*.

5. Edit the *Top 25%* rule in the same way so that it will show the top 30% values.

8 Remove all three conditional formats.

   This was covered in: *Lesson 4-16: Use simple conditional formatting.*

# Lesson 4-18: Bring data alive with visualizations

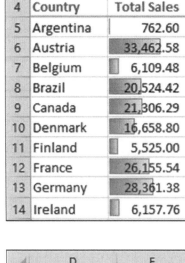

Visualizations are a half-way house between raw data and charts. With a few clicks of the mouse they allow you to express numbers in a visual manner.

1   Open *Sales Report-1* from your sample files folder (if it isn't already open).

2   Add a data bar visualization to the *Sales by Country* figures.

1.   Select cells B5:B25.

2.   Click: Home→Styles→Conditional Formatting→ Data Bars→Gradient Fill→Red Data Bar.

The visualization is applied (see sidebar).

3   Add a color scale visualization to the *Sales by Category* figures.

1.   Select cells E5:E12.

2.   Click: Home→Styles→Conditional Formatting→ Color Scales→Green-Yellow Color Scale.

The visualization is applied (see sidebar).

4   Add an icon set visualization to the *Sales by Month* figures.

1.   Select cells E20:E25.

2.   Click: Home→Styles→Conditional Formatting→Icon Sets→ Indicators→3 Flags.

3.   Re-size column E so that it is wide enough to display the values.

The visualization is applied (see sidebar).

When the icon set contains three icons, Excel assigns the relative icons to the top third, middle third, and bottom third of the value range.

You will often need to change these arbitrary values.

5   Use the *Rules Manager* to modify the *Sales by Month* visualization so that three green flags are shown.

The *Sales by Month* visualization may discourage your salesmen because only one month is flagged as green, with four months flagged red. You will now adjust the criteria for flag allocation so that three months are shown as green.

1.   Select cells E20:E25.

2.   Click: Home→Styles→Conditional Formatting→ Manage Rules…

The *Conditional Formatting Rules Manager* dialog is displayed.

3.   Click the *Edit Rule* button. 

Sales Report-1

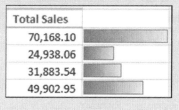

4. Change the criteria in the dialog so that values over 45,000 are green, values over 38,000 are yellow and values under 38,000 are red.

You'll need to set the criteria as follows:

5. Click OK and OK again.

The flags are displayed as required, with three green flags (see sidebar).

**6** Use the *Rules Manager* to show the visualizations for *Sales by Country* without the underlying data.

1. Select cells B5:B25.

2. Click: Home→Styles→Conditional Formatting→Manage Rules.

The *Conditional Formatting Rules Manager* dialog is displayed.

3. Click the *Edit Rule* button.

4. Check the *Show Bar Only* check box.

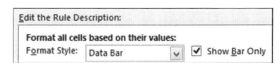

5. Click the OK button on each dialog to close them.

The bars are shown without the values (see sidebar).

**7** Use the *Rules Manager* to bring back the values for *Sales by Country*.

Follow the same procedure as in the previous step to uncheck the *Show Bar Only* check box.

**8** Save your work as *Sales Report-2*.

## note

### A more expert solution using mixed cell references

In my classroom courses, I always teach this lesson as presented here.

I like to keep things simple by solving the problem using a simple formula.

The reason I do this is that many students find mixed cell references challenging (the subject of: *Lesson 3-13: Understand mixed cell references*).

If you completely understood *Lesson 3-13: Understand mixed cell references,* you might find it interesting to solve this problem in a more efficient way.

You can apply a single mixed cell reference to all four columns in a single operation:

1.  Select columns A to D.

2.  Click: Home→Styles→ Conditional Formatting→ New Rule...

3.  Select: *Use a formula to determine which cells to format.*

4.  Type this formula (note the use of a mixed cell reference) into the *Format values where this formula is true* box:

    =$C1="USA"

5.  Click the *Format...* button.

6.  Click the *Fill* tab and select a light orange color for the conditional fill.

7.  Click OK and OK again.

# Lesson 4-19: Create a formula driven conditional format

While the built-in conditional format options are very powerful, you will occasionally have a conditional format requirement that is not catered for.

For example, I've lost count of the number of times I have been asked if it is possible to highlight an entire row, rather than a single cell within a row, based upon the value in one of the row's cells.

This lesson will show you how to achieve this using a formula-driven conditional format.

1   Open *Sales Summary First Quarter 2016* from your sample files folder.

Our challenge will be to highlight the entire row when the Country column contains the value: *USA*.

2   Apply a conditional format to column C to change the background color to light orange when the cell contains the text: USA.

1.  Select column C and apply a *Text that Contains...* conditional formatting rule selecting *Custom Format* as the fill color:

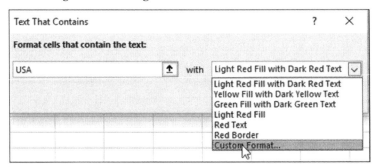

This was covered in: *Lesson 4-16: Use simple conditional formatting.*

2.  Click the *Fill* tab and select a light orange color for the conditional fill.

3.  Click the OK button once, and then again, to close both dialogs.

Every cell in column C that contains the text *USA* is now shaded light orange.

| | B | C | D |
|---|---|---|---|
| 40 | Familia Arquibaldo | Brazil | 100.00 |
| 41 | Hungry Coyote Import Store | USA | 62.40 |
| 42 | Hungry Coyote Import Store | USA | 40.00 |
| 43 | Wartian Herkku | Finland | 146.00 |

**Sales Summary First Quarter 2016**

3    Apply a formula-driven conditional format to column B so that the same rows are highlighted.

This is a lot more difficult than the simple conditional format applied to column C.

1.  Select column B.

2.  Click: Home→Styles→Conditional Formatting→New Rule…

    The *New Formatting Rule* dialog appears.

3.  Select *Use a formula to determine which cells to format* from the *Select a Rule Type* list.

4.  Type the formula **=C1="USA"** into the formula text box.

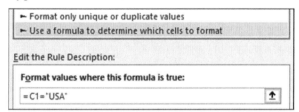

See sidebar for a discussion of this formula.

5.  Click the *Format* button, then the *Fill* tab and apply the same light orange fill color.

6.  Click the OK button once, and then again, to close both dialogs.

    Both columns now have a light orange fill when the country is USA.

| | A | B | C | D |
|---|---|---|---|---|
| 40 | 14-Jan-08 | Familia Arquibaldo | Brazil | 100.00 |
| 41 | 15-Jan-08 | Hungry Coyote Import Store | USA | 62.40 |
| 42 | 15-Jan-08 | Hungry Coyote Import Store | USA | 40.00 |
| 43 | 16-Jan-08 | Wartian Herkku | Finland | 146.00 |

4    Apply the same formula-driven conditional format to columns A and D so that the whole row is highlighted.

| | A | B | C | D |
|---|---|---|---|---|
| 40 | 14-Jan-08 | Familia Arquibaldo | Brazil | 100.00 |
| 41 | 15-Jan-08 | Hungry Coyote Import Store | USA | 62.40 |
| 42 | 15-Jan-08 | Hungry Coyote Import Store | USA | 40.00 |
| 43 | 16-Jan-08 | Wartian Herkku | Finland | 146.00 |

5    Save your work as *Sales Summary First Quarter 2016-1*.

## tip

### Why does the formula relate to cell C1?

At first it seems rather odd that you refer to cell C1 in the conditional formatting formula.

C1 is in the title row so how can this be right?

The answer is to be found in Excel's treatment of absolute and relative cell references (originally explained in: *Lesson 3-12: Understand absolute and relative cell references*).

Excel regards the cell reference to be relative to the first row in the selected range.

Since you selected an entire column, row 1 is the reference row used to adjust the formula for every other row within the column.

In other words, Excel will look at cell C2 when applying conditional formatting to row 2, C3 when applying to row 3… and so on.

This is exactly what you want to happen.

# Lesson 4-20: Insert a Sparkline into a range of cells

Sparklines were introduced for the first time in Excel 2010. They solve a very common worksheet problem.

In *Lesson 4-18: Bring data alive with visualizations,* you discovered how visualizations can illustrate the differences between values in a single column of data (see example in sidebar).

In: *Session Five: Charts and Graphics,* you will discover Excel's ability to create fantastic charts of all descriptions. These are especially useful when your data has two dimensions (several columns per row). You'll create this chart:

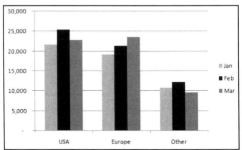

## important

### Sparklines will not display in Excel versions older than Excel 2010

Sparklines were introduced in Excel 2010 and are not compatible with earlier versions.

Sparklines appear as blank cells when opened with an earlier Excel version than Excel 2010 (such as Excel 2007).

But imagine you had a large number of rows of two dimensional data to compare. This is the case in the sample worksheet for this lesson, where there are 36 rows (one for each branch), each having six values (Jan-Jun):

| | A | B | C | D | E | F | G | H |
|---|---|---|---|---|---|---|---|---|
| 4 | Country | Branch | Jan | Feb | Mar | Apr | May | Jun |
| 5 | USA | Chicago | 671,185 | 359,811 | 745,471 | 685,637 | - 16,562 | 711,009 |
| 6 | USA | Dallas | 708,157 | 276,972 | 227,227 | 482,136 | 377,175 | 198,273 |

The worksheet contains data for 36 branches and would produce a very confusing chart (with 36 data series, one for each branch):

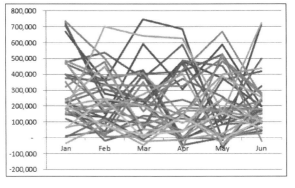

A *Sparkline* is a chart that can be inserted into a single cell, typically charting the values on its left hand side.

Sparklines provide an elegant way to present users with a visual depiction of large two-dimensional data sets, even when they contain thousands of rows.

First Half-Year Profit Report

| | A | B | C | D | E | F | G | H | I |
|---|---|---|---|---|---|---|---|---|---|
| 4 | Country | Branch | Jan | Feb | Mar | Apr | May | Jun | |
| 5 | USA | Chicago | 671,185 | 359,811 | 745,471 | 685, *Sparklines* | | 711,009 | |
| 6 | USA | Dallas | 708,157 | 276,972 | 227,227 | 482,136 | 377,175 | 198,273 | |

https://TheSmartMethod.com

# note

## You can also add Sparklines using the Quick Analysis button

Whenever you select a range of cells, a *Quick Analysis* button appears just outside the bottom-right corner of the selected range.

| Apr | May | Jun |
|---|---|---|
| 685,637 | - 16,562 | 711,009 |
| 482,136 | 377,175 | 198,273 |
| - 2,625 | 86,518 | 96,686 |

When you click the *Quick Analysis* button, the *Quick Analysis* dialog appears.

One of the menu options on this dialog is *Sparklines*.

It is possible to add *Line, Column* and *Win/Loss* Sparklines using this dialog.

# important

## Win/Loss Sparklines depict zero values with a blank space

In the example data for this lesson, all of the branches have either made a profit or a loss.

If you have a data set with zero values, the Win/Loss Sparkline will show blank spaces in the chart to illustrate zero values.

| | M | N | O | P | Q |
|---|---|---|---|---|---|
| 5 | 20 | 0 | 15 | -10 | |
| 6 | -22 | 34 | 0 | -15 | |

1  Open *First Half-Year Profit Report* from your sample files folder.

2  Create a *Line Sparkline* in cell I5 that charts the data in cells C5:H5.

   1. Click in cell I5.

   2. Click: Insert→Sparklines→Line.

   The *Create Sparklines* dialog appears.

   3. Click in the *Data Range:* box and then select cells C5:H5

   4. Click the OK button.

   A Sparkline appears in cell I5:

| | H | I |
|---|---|---|
| 4 | Jun | |
| 5 | 711,009 | |

3  AutoFill the Sparkline to cells I6:I40.

   You learned how to do this in: *Lesson 2-14: Use AutoFill for text and numeric series.*

   You can now see how Sparklines visualize each branch's performance in a way that is beyond the scope of Visualizations and Charts.

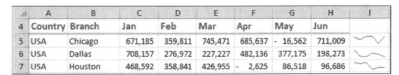

| | A | B | C | D | E | F | G | H | I |
|---|---|---|---|---|---|---|---|---|---|
| 4 | Country | Branch | Jan | Feb | Mar | Apr | May | Jun | |
| 5 | USA | Chicago | 671,185 | 359,811 | 745,471 | 685,637 | - 16,562 | 711,009 | |
| 6 | USA | Dallas | 708,157 | 276,972 | 227,227 | 482,136 | 377,175 | 198,273 | |
| 7 | USA | Houston | 468,592 | 358,841 | 426,955 | - 2,625 | 86,518 | 96,686 | |

4  Use the same technique to place a *Column Sparkline* in cells J5:J40 that charts the same data range (C5:H5).

5  Use the same technique to place a *Win/Loss Sparkline* in cells K5:K40 that charts the same data range (C5:H5).

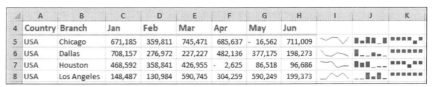

| | A | B | C | D | E | F | G | H | I | J | K |
|---|---|---|---|---|---|---|---|---|---|---|---|
| 4 | Country | Branch | Jan | Feb | Mar | Apr | May | Jun | | | |
| 5 | USA | Chicago | 671,185 | 359,811 | 745,471 | 685,637 | - 16,562 | 711,009 | | | |
| 6 | USA | Dallas | 708,157 | 276,972 | 227,227 | 482,136 | 377,175 | 198,273 | | | |
| 7 | USA | Houston | 468,592 | 358,841 | 426,955 | - 2,625 | 86,518 | 96,686 | | | |
| 8 | USA | Los Angeles | 148,487 | 130,984 | 590,745 | 304,259 | 590,249 | 199,373 | | | |

   The *Column Sparkline* is very similar to the *Line Sparkline* but represents data as a bar chart.

   Notice how the *Win/Loss Sparkline* enables you to see at a glance that Chicago and Houston had one loss-making month while Dallas and Los Angeles made a profit every month.

6  Save your work as *First Half Year Profit Report-1*.

# Lesson 4-21: Apply a common vertical axis and formatting to a Sparkline group

Consider the following column Sparklines:

| | A | B | C | D | E | F | G | H | J |
|---|---|---|---|---|---|---|---|---|---|
| 4 | Country | Branch | Jan | Feb | Mar | Apr | May | Jun | |
| 5 | USA | Chicago | 671,185 | 359,811 | 745,471 | 685,637 | - 16,562 | 711,009 | ▮▪▮▮_▮ |
| 28 | UK | Manchester | 180,988 | 209,763 | 203,761 | 2,201 | 165,328 | 124,392 | ▮▮▮_▮▪ |

If you only looked at the Sparklines (and not the values) you'd guess that Manchester made more profit in the first three months than Chicago.

A glance at the actual profit values shows that Chicago actually made about three times more profit than Manchester.

The *Column* Sparklines are misleading because, by default, Excel only considers each row's values when setting the *Maximum* and *Minimum* values for the bars (also called the *Vertical Axis* values).

In this lesson, you'll change this behavior so that the size of the bars gives a true indication of each branch's profit relative to the other branches in the list.

1 Open *First Half-Year Profit Report-1* from your sample files folder (if it isn't already open).

2 Delete columns I and K so that only the Column Sparklines remain.

> You learned how to do this in: *Lesson 3-1: Insert and delete rows and columns*. Removing the two other Sparklines will help to focus upon the *Column Sparkline*.

3 Set a common Maximum and Minimum value for all Sparklines.

1. Click on any of the Sparklines in column I.

   Notice that a thin blue line has appeared around all of the Sparklines in column I. This happens because Excel views all of the Sparklines as a *Sparkline Group*. This means that when you use any of the *Sparkline Design Tools* on the Ribbon, the settings will apply to all Sparklines in the group.

2. Click: Sparkline Tools→Design→Group→Axis drop-down.

3. Click: Vertical Axis Minimum Value Options→ Same for All Sparklines.

4. Click: Vertical Axis Maximum Value Options→ Same for All Sparklines.

5. Notice the change in the Chicago and Manchester Sparklines:

| | F | G | H | I |
|---|---|---|---|---|
| 4 | Apr | May | Jun | |
| 5 | 685,637 | - 16,562 | 711,009 | ▮▪▮▮_▮ |
| 28 | 2,201 | 165,328 | 124,392 | _ _ _ _ _ _ |

## important

### Deleting Sparklines

In this lesson, you deleted two Sparkline groups by deleting the columns that contained them.

Sometimes you will need to delete a Sparkline group without deleting the column that contains them.

To do this:

1. Select the Sparkline group.

2. Click:

   Sparkline Tools→Design→ Group→Clear→ Clear Selected Sparkline Groups

First Half-Year Profit Report-1

## note

### You can change the size of a Sparkline by re-sizing the cell that contains it

In the lessons in this session, the Sparkline cells have been left at their default size for neatness and to keep the worksheet compact.

If you resize a cell that contains a Sparkline it will automatically resize to fill the cell:

It is now clear, from looking at the bars alone, that in every month (except May) Manchester produced far less profit than Chicago.

4   Explore Sparkline formatting options.

The *Sparkline Tools Design* tab on the Ribbon provides many ways in which you can change the appearance of a group of Sparklines. Try experimenting with them.

1.  Use the *Show* and *Style→Marker Color* options.

    The *Show* check boxes allow you to apply a chosen color to any of the following points on a Sparkline.

    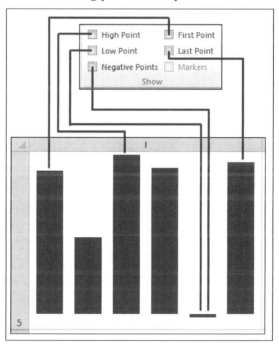

    You can choose a color for each of the points you check from the *Style→Marker Color* drop down.

2.  Choose a new *Sparkline Style* from the *Style* gallery.

    Styles allow you to change the color scheme for your Sparkline. Note that the styles use theme colors and will change if you change the current theme. (You learned about themes in: *Lesson 4-9: Understand themes*).

3.  Change the *Sparkline Type* to *Line* by clicking: Type→Line.

4.  Add *Markers*.

    Click: Sparkline Tools→Design→Show→Markers.

    When the *Sparkline Type* is *Line*, you are able to select the *Markers* option in the *Show* group. Each data point on the Sparkline is then marked with a dot.

5.  Click: Sparkline Tools→Design→Style→Sparkline Color.

6.  Change the line color.

7.  Change the line thickness by clicking *Weight* (at the bottom of the Sparkline Color dialog).

5   Close *First Year Profit Report-1* without saving.

# Lesson 4-22: Apply a date axis to a Sparkline group and format a single Sparkline

Sometimes you will encounter data that is attached to dates with uneven time intervals. Here's some of the sample data for this lesson:

| | A | B | C | D | E | F | G | H |
|---|---|---|---|---|---|---|---|---|
| 1 | Number of Rings to Answer Phone Survey | | | | | | | |
| 2 | | | | | | | | |
| 3 | Country | Branch | 01-Mar-16 | 03-Mar-16 | 04-Mar-16 | 07-Mar-16 | 08-Mar-16 | 09-Mar-16 |
| 4 | USA | Chicago | 3 | 1 | 1 | 2 | 3 | 2 |
| 5 | USA | Dallas | 2 | 3 | 1 | 3 | 2 | 1 |
| 6 | USA | Houston | 10 | 8 | 11 | 7 | 11 | 5 |
| 7 | USA | Los Angeles | 1 | 3 | 2 | 3 | 3 | 1 |

This company has a policy that the telephone should be answered within three rings. To make sure the staff are hitting this target, head office phone each branch occasionally and record the number of rings taken to answer. You can see that Chicago, Dallas and Los Angeles are doing well but Houston is performing well below standard.

Head office don't phone every day – only when they have time to do so. This means that they didn't phone at all on 2nd, 5th and 6th March.

By default, a Sparkline will assume that the data is at equal intervals and chart like this:

| | C | D | E | F | G | H | I |
|---|---|---|---|---|---|---|---|
| 3 | 01-Mar-16 | 03-Mar-16 | 04-Mar-16 | 07-Mar-16 | 08-Mar-16 | 09-Mar-16 | |
| 4 | 3 | 1 | 1 | 2 | 3 | 2 | ▮_ _ ▮▮ |
| 5 | 2 | 3 | 1 | 3 | 2 | 1 | _▮▮_▮_ |
| 6 | 10 | 8 | 11 | 7 | 11 | 5 | ▮▮▮▮▮_ |
| 7 | 1 | 3 | 2 | 3 | 3 | 1 | _▮▮▮▮_ |

… but you'd like the Sparklines to have a common vertical axis and show a gap for the missing dates like this:

| | E | F | G | H | I |
|---|---|---|---|---|---|
| 3 | 04-Mar-11 | 07-Mar-11 | 08-Mar-11 | 09-Mar-11 | |
| 4 | 1 | 2 | 3 | 2 | _ __ _▪_ |
| 5 | 1 | 3 | 2 | 1 | _ __ ▪__ |
| 6 | 11 | 7 | 11 | 5 | ▮ ▪▮ ▪▮▪ |
| 7 | 2 | 3 | 3 | 1 | _ __ __▪ |

1   Open *Phone Survey* from your sample files folder.

2   Insert a Column Sparkline in cell I4 to chart data in cells C4:H4 and AutoFill it down to the end of the range.

> You learned how to do this in: *Lesson 4-20: Insert a Sparkline into a range of cells.*

3   Set the *Vertical Axis Minimum Value* and *Vertical Axis Maximum Value* to be the same for all Sparklines.

> You learned how to do this in: *Lesson 4-21: Apply a common vertical axis and formatting to a Sparkline group.*

Phone Survey

# note

## Options for worksheets that contain Hidden and Empty cells

In:

*Lesson 5-15: Chart non-contiguous source data by hiding rows and columns*

And:

*Lesson 5-17: Deal with empty data points*

… you will learn the concept of hidden rows and columns, and also learn how to use Excel's *Hidden and Empty Cells* dialog.

You'll then also be able to use these options when you add a Sparkline to worksheets that contain empty cells or hidden rows and columns.

Your worksheet should now look like this:

| | D | E | F | G | H | I |
|---|---|---|---|---|---|---|
| 3 | 03-Mar-16 | 04-Mar-16 | 07-Mar-16 | 08-Mar-16 | 09-Mar-16 | |
| 4 | 1 | 1 | 2 | 3 | 2 | _ _ _ _ _ _ |
| 5 | 3 | 1 | 3 | 2 | 1 | _ _ _ _ _ _ |
| 6 | 8 | 11 | 7 | 11 | 5 | ▪▪▪▪▪▪ |
| 7 | 3 | 2 | 3 | 3 | 1 | _ _ _ _ _ _ |

4   Set the *Sparkline Date Range* to C3:H3.

   1. Click any Sparkline in column I to select the Sparkline group.

   2. Click:

      Sparkline Tools→Design→Group→Axis→Date Axis Type…

      The *Sparkline Date Range* dialog appears.

   3. Select cells C3:H3 with the mouse.

   4. Click the OK button.

      The Sparklines are now shown with gaps for the missing dates:

| | E | F | G | H | I |
|---|---|---|---|---|---|
| 3 | 04-Mar-11 | 07-Mar-11 | 08-Mar-11 | 09-Mar-11 | |
| 4 | 1 | 2 | 3 | 2 | _ _ _ _ _ |
| 5 | 1 | 3 | 2 | 1 | _ _ _ _ _ |
| 6 | 11 | 7 | 11 | 5 | ▪ ▪▪ ▪▪▪ |
| 7 | 2 | 3 | 3 | 1 | _ _ _ _ _ |

5   Format the *Houston* Sparkline (in cell I6) so that all bars are orange.

   To format a single Sparkline, it is necessary to *Ungroup* the Sparklines. When Sparklines are ungrouped, it is possible to format them individually.

   1. Click in cell I6.

   2. Click: Sparkline Tools→Design→Group→Ungroup.

   3. Click:

      Sparkline Tools→Design→Style→Sparkline Color→ Orange Accent 2

      The *Houston* Sparkline is now colored orange, while all other Sparklines remain black.

6   Save your work as *Phone Survey-1*.

# Lesson 4-23: Use the Format Painter

The format painter is one of the most useful tools in Microsoft Office.

You can use the format painter in PowerPoint, Word and all other Office applications.

I find that at least half of the experienced Excel users who attend my classroom courses have never discovered the format painter. I love it when they gasp in amazement at the enormous amount of time and effort they will save in future when using this tool.

In this lesson, you're going to take a worksheet that is partially formatted and use the format painter to quickly copy formatting information (as opposed to values) from one cell to another.

1    Open *Sales Report-FP* from your sample files folder.

This worksheet has been partially formatted.

| | A | B | C | D | E |
|---|---|---|---|---|---|
| 1 | Sales Report - 6 Months ended March 2016 | | | | |
| 2 | | | | | |
| 3 | Sales By Country | | | Sales by Category | |
| 4 | Country | Total Sales | | Category | Total Sales |
| 5 | Argentina | 762.6 | | Beverages | 70168.1 |
| 6 | Austria | 33462.58 | | Condiments | 24938.055 |
| 7 | Belgium | 6109.48 | | Confections | 31883.54 |
| 8 | Brazil | 20524.42 | | Dairy Products | 49902.95 |
| 9 | Canada | 21306.29 | | Grains/Cereals | 19570.36 |
| 10 | Denmark | 16658.8 | | Meat/Poultry | 35767.63 |
| 11 | Finland | 5525 | | Produce | 17109.18 |
| 12 | France | 26155.54 | | Seafood | 17304.51 |
| 13 | Germany | 28361.38 | | Grand Total | 266644.325 |
| 14 | Ireland | 6157.755 | | | |

2    Apply the comma style to all of the values in column B.

This was covered in: *Lesson 4-3: Format numbers using built-in number formats*.

Values are now formatted with two decimal places and a thousand comma separator.

| | A | B |
|---|---|---|
| 9 | Canada | 21,306.29 |
| 10 | Denmark | 16,658.80 |
| 11 | Finland | 5,525.00 |

3    Use the format painter to copy formatting from the values in column B to the ranges E5:E13 and E20:E26.

   1.   Click any value in column B.

   2.   Click: Home→Clipboard→Format Painter. [Format Painter]

   The cursor shape changes to a paint brush.

**Sales Report-FP**

# note

## Autofill and Paste are also able to match formatting in the same way as the Format Painter

The Format Painter is the fastest and most convenient way to match formatting when you only have to deal with a small range of cells.

Sometimes you'll need to match formatting in very large ranges containing thousands of cells. This would take a long time using the Format Painter but can be quickly achieved using *AutoFill,* or by using *Paste* along with the skills you learned in: *Lesson 2-8: AutoSelect a range of cells.*

## AutoFill

AutoFill options were covered in depth in: *Lesson 2-16: Use AutoFill options.*

When you AutoFill using a right-click and drag (or AutoFill and then look at the Smart tag options) you'll notice that there's a *Fill Formatting Only* option.

## Paste

Copy and Paste were covered in depth in: *Lesson 3-3: Cut, copy and paste.*

When you paste there's also a *Formatting* option in the *Paste Options.*

3.   Click and drag across cells E5:E13.

The format of cells E5:E13 changes to match those of the values in column B.

|  | D | E |
|---|---|---|
| 4 | Category | Total Sales |
| 5 | Beverages | 70,168.10 |
| 6 | Condiments | 24,938.06 |

4.   Click on any value in column B.

5.   Click: Home→Clipboard→Format Painter.

6.   Drag across cells E20:E26.

All values in this worksheet are now formatted with the comma style.

**4**   Use the format painter to copy formatting from cell A3 to cells D3 and D18.

This time you will use the format painter in a slightly different way. If you double-click the format painter icon  a *sticky format painter* results. This will stay switched on until you click the format painter icon again to switch it off.

1.   Click on cell A3 to make it the active (source) cell.

2.   Double-click: Home→Clipboard→Format Painter.

The cursor shape changes to a paint brush. 

3.   Click cell D3. The format now matches cell A3 but the cursor remains the same. 

4.   Click cell D18. The format now matches cell A3 but the cursor remains the same. 

5.   Click: Home→Clipboard→Format Painter to switch off the format painter. The cursor reverts to the normal shape.

**5**   Copy formatting from cell A4 to cells D4:E4 and D19:E19 using the format painter.

**6**   Apply the *Total* style to cell B26.

This was covered in: *Lesson 4-10: Use cell styles and change themes.*

**7**   Copy the total style from cell B26 to cells E13 and E26 using the format painter.

**8**   Save your work as *Sales Report-FP-1.*

# Lesson 4-24: Rotate text

1    Open *Top 20 Films* from your sample files folder.

2    Insert a new column to the left of column A.

You learned how to do this in: *Lesson 3-1: Insert and delete rows and columns.*

3    Cut and paste the contents of cell B1 to cell A1.

You learned how to do this in: *Lesson 3-3: Cut, copy and paste.*

4    Apply the *Title* style to cell A1, the *Heading 2* style to cells A3:E3 and the *Heading 4* style to cell D25.

You learned how to do this in: *Lesson 4-10: Use cell styles and change themes.*

5    Type: **Over 1,500M** into cell A4, **Over 1,100M** into cell A9 and **Over 1,000M** into cell A18.

6    Make column A slightly wider so that all text in the column is visible.

You learned how to do this in: *Lesson 2-9: Re-size rows and columns.*

7    Select cells A4:A8.

| | A | B | C |
|---|---|---|---|
| 3 | | Title | Year |
| 4 | Over 1,500M | Avatar | 2009 |
| 5 | | Titanic | 1997 |
| 6 | | Jurassic World | 2015 |
| 7 | | The Avengers | 2012 |
| 8 | | Furious 7 | 2015 |
| 9 | Over 1,100M | Avengers: Age of Ultron | 2015 |

8    Merge the selected cells.

This was covered in: *Lesson 4-6: Merge cells, wrap text and expand/collapse the formula bar.*

9    Rotate the text through ninety degrees.

1.   Click: Home→Alignment→Orientation.

2.   Select *Rotate Text Up* from the drop-down list.

## note

### Other ways to rotate text

You can also rotate text using the *Format Cells* dialog, though you'll nearly always find the Ribbon method faster and more convenient.

The *Format Cells* dialog is slightly more powerful as it allows you to rotate text by any angle.

1.   Right-click a cell or range and click *Format Cells* from the shortcut menu.

2.   Click the *Alignment* tab.

3.   In the *Orientation* pane either type in the number of degrees of rotation or click and drag the red diamond to set it visually.

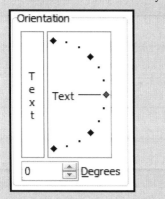

**Top 20 Films**

| | A |
|---|---|
| 3 | Title |
| 4 | Avatar |
| 5 | Titanic |
| 6 | Jurassic World |
| 7 | The Avengers |
| 8 | Furious 7 |
| 9 | Avengers: Age of |
| 10 | Harry Potter and |
| 11 | Frozen |
| 12 | Iron Man 3 |
| 13 | Minions |
| 14 | Transformers: Da |
| 15 | The Lord of the R |
| 16 | Skyfall |
| 17 | Transformers: Ag |
| 18 | The Dark Knight |
| 19 | Pirates of the Ca |
| 20 | Toy Story 3 |
| 21 | Pirates of the Ca |
| 22 | Jurassic Park |
| 23 | Star Wars Episod |

(Rows 4–8: Over 1,500M; Rows 9–17: Over 1,100M; Rows 18–23: Over 1,000M)

10   Merge and rotate the text in cells A9:A17 and A18:A23.

Your worksheet should now look like the sidebar.

11   Select cells A4:A18 and set the horizontal alignment to *center* and the vertical alignment to *middle.*

You learned how to do this in: *Lesson 4-5: Horizontally align the contents of cells* and *Lesson 4-8: Vertically align the contents of cells.*

12   Apply the *Heading 4* style to cells A4:A18.

13   AutoFit cells A4:A18 so that they are just wide enough for the text.

You learned how to do this in: *Lesson 2-9: Re-size rows and columns.*

14   Apply the *40% Accent 3* style to cell A4.

You learned how to do this in: *Lesson 4-10: Use cell styles and change themes.*

Note that the cell reference for the old range A4:A8 is now the single cell reference A4.

15   Apply the *40% Accent 6* style to cell A9.

16   Apply the *40% Accent 2* style to cell A18.

17   Re-size row 3 so that it is about three times the normal height.

18   Rotate the text in row 3 by 45 degrees.

1.   Select row 3.

2.   Click: Home→Alignment→Orientation → Angle Counterclockwise.

19   Make columns C and E a little wider.

| | A | B | C | D | E |
|---|---|---|---|---|---|
| 1 | Top 20 Films By USA Box Office Takings | | | | |
| 2 | | | | | |
| 3 | | Title | Year | Studio | Gross* |
| 4 | Over 1,500M | Avatar | 2009 | 20th Century Fox | 2,788 |
| 5 | | Titanic | 1997 | 20th Century Fox/Paramount | 2,187 |
| 6 | | Jurassic World | 2015 | Universal | 1,669 |
| 7 | | The Avengers | 2012 | Walt Disney | 1,520 |
| 8 | | Furious 7 | 2015 | Universal | 1,515 |
| 9 | Over 1,100M | Avengers: Age of Ultron | 2015 | Walt Disney | 1,405 |
| 10 | | Harry Potter and the Deathly Hallows – Part 2 | 2011 | Warner Bros. | 1,342 |
| 11 | | Frozen | 2013 | Walt Disney | 1,280 |
| 12 | | Iron Man 3 | 2013 | Walt Disney | 1,215 |
| 13 | | Minions | 2015 | Universal | 1,157 |
| 14 | | Transformers: Dark of the Moon | 2011 | Paramount Pictures | 1,124 |
| 15 | | The Lord of the Rings: The Return of the King | 2003 | New Line Cinema | 1,120 |
| 16 | | Skyfall | 2012 | MGM/Columbia | 1,109 |
| 17 | | Transformers: Age of Extinction | 2014 | Paramount | 1,104 |
| 18 | Over 1,000M | The Dark Knight Rises | 2012 | Warner Bros. | 1,085 |
| 19 | | Pirates of the Caribbean: Dead Man's Chest | 2006 | Buena Vista Pictures | 1,066 |
| 20 | | Toy Story 3 | 2010 | Walt Disney | 1,063 |
| 21 | | Pirates of the Caribbean: On Stranger Tides | 2011 | Walt Disney | 1,046 |
| 22 | | Jurassic Park | 1993 | Universal | 1,030 |
| 23 | | Star Wars Episode I: The Phantom Menace | 1999 | 20th Century Fox | 1,027 |
| 24 | | | | | |
| 25 | | | | | *USA Box office takings in millions of dollars |

20   Save your work as *Top 20 Films-1.*

## Session 4: Exercise

**1** Open *House Mortgage* from your sample files folder.

**2** Merge and center cells B3:J3.

**3** Apply the *Title* style to cell A1, the *Heading 1* style to cell B3, the *Heading 3* style to cells A4:J4 and the *Heading 3* style to cells A10:C10.

**4** Apply the *Heading 4* style to cells A5:A8 and cells A11:A16.

**5** Apply the *Percentage* style to cells B4:J4.

**6** Apply the *Comma* style to cells B5:J8.

**7** Apply the *Percentage* style to cells B11:C16 and then increase decimals to one place.

**8** Type the word *Average* into cell A17 and use the *Format Painter* to match the formatting to that of the cell above (A16).

**9** Horizontally right-align the text in cell A17.

**10** Use *AutoSum* to place an *Average* function into cells B17 and C17.

**11** Place a thin black border beneath cells A16:C16.

**12** Apply a *20% Accent 1* cell style to cells B4:J4 and B10:C10.

**13** Change the theme to *Celestial*.

**14** Save your work as *House Mortgage-1*.

| ⯅ | A | B | C | D | E | F | G | H | I | J |
|---|---|---|---|---|---|---|---|---|---|---|
| 1 | House Mortgage Monthly Payments - 25 year term | | | | | | | | | |
| 2 | | | | | | | | | | |
| 3 | | | | | Interest rate | | | | | |
| 4 | House Value | 2% | 3% | 4% | 5% | 6% | 7% | 8% | 9% | 10% |
| 5 | 50000 | 211.93 | 237.11 | 263.92 | 292.30 | 322.15 | 353.39 | 385.91 | 419.60 | 454.35 |
| 6 | 100000 | 423.85 | 474.21 | 527.84 | 584.59 | 644.30 | 706.78 | 771.82 | 839.20 | 908.70 |
| 7 | 150000 | 635.78 | 711.32 | 791.76 | 876.89 | 966.45 | 1,060.17 | 1,157.72 | 1,258.79 | 1,363.05 |
| 8 | 200000 | 847.71 | 948.42 | 1,055.67 | 1,169.18 | 1,288.60 | 1,413.56 | 1,543.63 | 1,678.39 | 1,817.40 |
| 9 | | | | | | | | | | |
| 10 | Historical Base/Fed. Fund Rates | UK | USA | | | | | | | |
| 11 | 1990 | 14.8% | 7.0% | | | | | | | |
| 12 | 1995 | 6.7% | 5.8% | | | | | | | |
| 13 | 2000 | 6.0% | 6.2% | | | | | | | |
| 14 | 2005 | 4.7% | 3.2% | | | | | | | |
| 15 | 2010 | 0.5% | 0.2% | | | | | | | |
| 16 | 2014 | 0.5% | 0.9% | | | | | | | |
| 17 | Average | 5.5% | 3.9% | | | | | | | |

House Mortgage

If you need help slide the page to the left

## Session 4: Exercise answers

These are the questions that students find the most difficult to answer:

| Q 13 | Q 11 | Q 10 | Q 8 |
|---|---|---|---|
| 1. Click Page Layout→ Themes→Themes→ Celestial.<br><br>This was covered in: *Lesson 4-10: Use cell styles and change themes.* | 1. Select cells A16:C16.<br><br>2. Click: Home→Font→ Borders→ Bottom Border.<br><br><br><br>This was covered in: *Lesson 4-12: Add borders and lines.* | 1. Select cells B17:C17.<br><br>2. Click:<br><br>Home→Editing→ AutoSum→Average<br><br><br><br>3. Either press the **<Enter>** key or click the AutoSum button again.<br><br>This was covered in: *Lesson 2-11: Use AutoSum to calculate average and maximum values.* | 1. Click in cell A16.<br><br>2. Click:<br><br>Home→Clipboard→ Format Painter<br><br>3. Click in cell A17.<br><br>This was covered in: *Lesson 4-23: Use the Format Painter.* |

If you have difficulty with the other questions, here are the lessons that cover the relevant skills:

**1**    Refer to: Lesson 1-5: Download the sample files and open/navigate a workbook.

**2**    Refer to: Lesson 4-6: Merge cells, wrap text and expand/collapse the formula bar.

**3**    Refer to: Lesson 4-10: Use cell styles and change themes.

**4**    Refer to: Lesson 4-10: Use cell styles and change themes.

**5,6,7** Refer to: Lesson 4-3: Format numbers using built-in number formats.

**9**    Refer to: Lesson 4-5: Horizontally align the contents of cells.

**11**   Refer to: Lesson 4-3: Format numbers using built-in number formats.

**12**   Refer to: Lesson 4-10: Use cell styles and change themes.

**14**   Refer to: Lesson 1-6: Save a workbook to a local file.

# Session Five: Charts and Graphics

In this session, you'll learn to present your data in a chart. You'll also learn some valuable "tricks of the trade" to present your data in the most effective way.

## Session Objectives

By the end of this session you will be able to:

■ Understand chart types, layouts and styles

■ Create a simple chart with two clicks

■ Move, re-size, copy and delete a chart

■ Create a chart using the Recommended Charts feature

■ Add and remove chart elements using Quick Layout

■ Apply a pre-defined chart style and color set

■ Manually format a chart element

■ Format 3-D elements and add drop shadows

■ Move, re-size, add, position and delete chart elements

■ Apply a chart filter

■ Change a chart's source data

■ Assign non-contiguous source data to a chart

■ Understand data series and categories

■ Change source data using the Select Data Source dialog tools

■ Chart non-contiguous source data by hiding rows and columns

■ Create a chart with numerical axes

■ Deal with empty data points and add data labels to a chart

■ Highlight specific data points with color and annotations

■ Add gridlines and scale axes

■ Emphasize data by manipulating pie charts

■ Create a chart with two vertical axes

■ Create a combination chart containing different chart types

■ Work with trend lines and forecast sheets

■ Add a gradient fill to a chart background

■ Create your own chart templates

■ Create a filled map chart

# Lesson 5-1: Understand chart types, layouts and styles

The Excel designers noted that there are three things that control the design of a chart:

## Chart Type

There are many different *types* of chart. The most common are: *Column Charts, Line Charts* and *Pie Charts.*

You'll discover how to choose a suitable *Chart Type* in: *Lesson 5-2: Create a simple chart with two clicks.*

## Chart Layout

The layout of a chart can be thought of as a list of the *elements* that a chart contains.

Elements are artifacts such as a *Title, Axis Titles or Legend.*

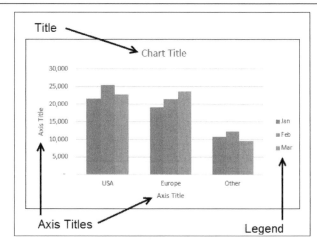

In: *Lesson 5-5: Add and remove chart elements using Quick Layout,* you'll discover how to quickly select a group of common elements for a chart.

## Chart Style

The *Chart Style* determines the font, color and positioning of each chart element. Here are two charts that have an identical *Type* and *Layout* but have different styles:

You can see that both charts are of the same type (*Clustered Column*), and that both have the same elements (that include the *Axis Titles, Chart Title* and *Legend* elements).

The differences in appearance (colors, shading of bars, fonts used and position of legend) are collectively referred to as the chart's *Style.*

You'll learn how to change a chart's style in: *Lesson 5-6: Apply a pre-defined chart style and color set.*

# Lesson 5-2: Create a simple chart with two clicks

1   Open *World Sales* from your sample files folder.

This is a very simple worksheet containing January, February and March sales data for three regions.

|   | A | B | C | D |
|---|---|---|---|---|
| 1 | Month | USA | Europe | Other |
| 2 | Jan | 21,600 | 19,200 | 10,800 |
| 3 | Feb | 25,400 | 21,400 | 12,200 |
| 4 | Mar | 22,800 | 23,600 | 9,600 |

2   Select all of the values and all of the labels (cells A1:D4).

When Excel creates a chart, it needs both values and labels. For this reason, you must always select the labels *as well as* the values before you create your chart.

Missing the labels is one of the most common errors in my classroom courses.

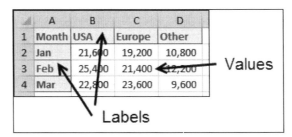

3   Click: Insert→Charts→Insert Column or Bar Chart and hover the mouse pointer over some of the charts in the gallery.

As you hover the mouse cursor over each chart type Excel provides a ScreenTip describing the chart. A preview of how the chart will look is also displayed on the worksheet.

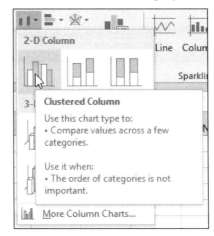

4   Click the left-most 2-D Column chart (the *Clustered Column* chart).

In just two clicks you have created a very presentable chart.

**World Sales**

# note

## Changing the chart type of an existing chart

You may create a chart but later decide that you really need a different chart type.

For example, you might create a *bar chart* but later decide you would have preferred a *pie chart* or *line chart*.

To change the type of an existing chart:

1. Right-click on the chart.

2. Click: *Change Chart Type* from the shortcut menu.

# note

## Create a chart with the Quick Analysis button

Whenever you select a range of cells, a *Quick Analysis* button appears just outside the bottom-right corner of the selected range.

When you click the *Quick Analysis* button, the *Quick Analysis* dialog appears.

One of the menu options on this dialog is *Charts*.

When you click the *Charts* menu option you are presented with a choice of four recommended charts for the range selected. There's also a More... button that gives access to the full *Insert Chart* dialog (that you'd see if you clicked: Charts→Dialog Launcher).

This method isn't as versatile as choosing a chart manually (as described in this lesson).

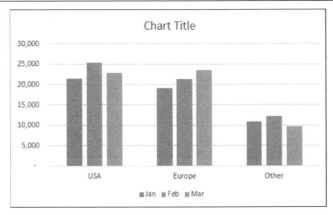

Because you have only specified the chart *Type*, Excel has chosen a default *Layout* and *Style* for you. You'll learn how to change these default choices later in this session.

5   Understand chart activation.

In this example, the worksheet only contains one chart.

It is possible that a worksheet will contain more than once chart.

For this reason, you need to indicate to Excel which chart you want to work on. To do this the chart needs to be *activated*.

To activate a chart, you simply click anywhere inside the chart.

When the chart is activated two things happen:

1.   The *Chart Tools Design* and *Chart Tools Format* tabs appear on the Ribbon:

2.   A frame (with sizing handles) appears around the chart:

6   Save your work as *World Sales-1*.

## tip

### Give charts meaningful names to make them easier to find in the Selection and Visibility task pane

If you have more than one chart embedded in a worksheet, it is a good idea to give them more meaningful names than the default *Chart1, Chart2* etc.

To rename a chart you need to first activate it and then change the name in the *Name Box* (at the left of the formula bar):

When charts have meaningful names it is easy to activate them using the *Selection and Visibility* task pane.

To make this task pane appear, first activate the chart and then click:

Chart Tools→Format→ Arrange→Selection Pane

The selection pane will then appear and can be left on screen to quickly activate specific charts.

It is also possible to show or hide charts by clicking the eyeball symbol to the right of the relevant chart.

# Lesson 5-3: Move, re-size, copy and delete a chart

1 Open *World Sales-1* from your sample files folder (if it isn't already open).

2 Move the chart to a different position on screen.

1. Click just inside the border of the chart to activate it.

When the chart is activated you will see a frame and corner handles around it.

Excel also displays the *Chart Tools* group of Ribbon tabs.

2. Hover with the mouse cursor just inside the border of the selected chart until you see the four-headed arrow cursor shape.

3. Click and drag the chart to the required position.

3 Re-size the chart.

1. Click just inside the border of the chart to activate it.

2. Hover over one of the corner or side sizing handles on the edges of the chart until you see the two-headed arrow cursor shape.

3. When you see the two-headed arrow cursor shape, click and drag to re-size the chart.

If you hold down the **<Shift>** key as you click-and drag one of the corners of the chart, the perspective will remain constant (the chart will get proportionately wider as it gets taller).

4 Create a duplicate chart using copy and paste.

1. Click just inside the border of the chart to activate it.

2. Right-click on the border of the activated chart (just inside the border works too) and click *Copy* from the shortcut menu.

3. Right-click anywhere on the worksheet and click *Paste* from the shortcut menu to create the duplicate chart.

**World Sales-1**

## note

### Another way to copy a chart

1.  Hover the mouse cursor over the border of an embedded chart.

    The cursor shape will change to a four-headed arrow.

2.  Right-click and drag the chart to a new location.

    When you release the mouse button you will see a prompt asking whether to move or copy the chart to the new location.

3.  Click *Copy Here* to copy the chart.

## note

### Advantages of placing charts on chart sheets

*   They are easier to find as you can give each chart sheet a meaningful name.

*   They are easier to view as the chart normally takes up the entire screen. You can re-size a chart on a chart sheet but this isn't often done.

*   They are easier to print as you can simply click the chart sheet tab and print. You can also print an embedded chart in isolation but to do so you must first find and activate the chart.

### The Advantage of embedding charts within worksheets

You are able to print a chart and associated worksheet data on the same page.

If you have no need to print worksheet data alongside your chart, it is usually better to place your charts on chart sheets.

Note that even though the new chart is a duplicate, it is not linked to the original chart in any way. You can freely change any part of either chart and it will never affect the other.

5   Delete one of the charts.

1.  Click just inside the border of either of the charts to activate it.

2.  Press the **<Delete>** key on the keyboard.

6   Move the chart to its own chart worksheet.

Sometimes it is better to keep charts and data separate by placing a chart in its own *chart worksheet*. A chart worksheet is a special worksheet without any cells that can only contain a single chart.

1.  Right-click just inside the border of the chart to activate it and then click *Move Chart...* from the shortcut menu.

2.  Click the *New Sheet* option button, name the new sheet *Sales Summary Chart* and click the OK button.

The chart is now displayed within its own dedicated chart worksheet.

7   Move the chart back to its original location.

1.  Right-click just inside the border of the chart and click *Move Chart...* from the shortcut menu.

2.  Click the *Object in* option button, choose *Sheet1* from the drop-down list and click the OK button.

8   Save your work as *World Sales-2*.

# Lesson 5-4: Create a chart using the Recommended Charts feature

Excel is able to intelligently analyze your data and then try to guess which chart type will do the best job of representing it visually.

1    Open *Hawaii Temperature-1* from your sample files folder.

This worksheet contains temperature data for Honolulu, Hawaii (one of the nicest year-round climates in the world).

2    Use *Recommended Charts* to select a suitable chart type.

1.   Click anywhere inside the data (in a cell somewhere in the range A5:C17).

You could also select the range A5:C17, but when you want to chart an entire range it is only necessary to select a single cell within the range.

2.   Click: Insert→Charts→Recommended Charts.

The *Insert Chart* dialog is displayed with the *Recommended Charts* tab selected.

**Hawaii Temperature-1**

## note

### You can also access the Recommended Charts feature using the Quick Analysis button

Whenever you select a range of cells, a *Quick Analysis* button appears just outside the bottom-right corner of the selected range.

| 31 | 23 | |
|----|----|----|
| 31 | 22 | |
| 29 | 21 | |
| 28 | 19 | |
| | | |
| | | |

When you click the *Quick Analysis* button, the *Quick Analysis* dialog appears.

One of the menu options on this dialog is *Charts*.

When you click the *Charts* menu option you are presented with a choice of five recommended charts for the range selected.

There's also a *More...* button that opens the more powerful *Insert Chart* dialog used in this lesson:

More...

Notice that Excel's first choice for an appropriate chart type is a line chart.

This isn't a bad choice but perhaps Excel's second choice, the *Clustered Column* chart, will work better with this data.

3. Click the *Clustered Column* chart (the second recommended chart in the left-hand list).

A preview of the clustered column chart is shown in the right-hand pane of the dialog.

4. Click OK to create a *Clustered Column* chart.

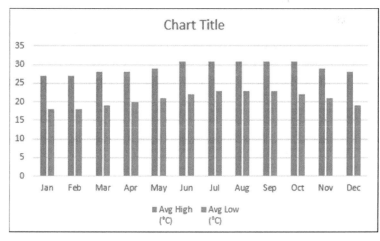

This chart does a very good job of visually showing the temperature range each month in Hawaii.

In: *Lesson 5-5: Add and remove chart elements using Quick Layout*, you'll learn how to change the *Chart Title* element to display appropriate text.

3  Save your work as *Hawaii Temperature-2*.

# Lesson 5-5: Add and remove chart elements using Quick Layout

The term *Layout* can be confusing. It is used to describe the *Elements* that a chart contains. For example, here is a simple chart containing only two elements:

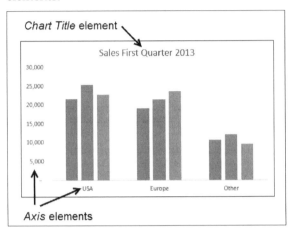

And here's a chart that contains four elements:

Some layouts also include a *Data Table* element showing the source data for the chart:

Don't confuse the *layout* (the elements that a chart contains) with the chart *style* (the colors and appearance of the chart elements).

In this lesson, you will use Excel's *Quick Layout* feature to choose from nine common layouts with a single click.

1   Open *World Sales-2* from your sample files folder (if it isn't already open).

2   Change the *Chart Layout* to: *Layout 9*.

   1.   Click just inside the border of the chart to activate it.

   2.   Click: Chart Tools→Design→Chart Layouts→Quick Layout.

This gallery contains eleven pre-defined chart layouts. Each layout contains a group of elements.

Notice that the chart changes as you hover over each layout so that you can preview how your chart will look if the layout is chosen.

   3.   Click: *Layout 9*.

This layout includes a *Chart Title* element, a *Legend* element, two *Axis* elements, two *Axis Title* elements and a *Gridlines* element.

In: *Lesson 5-9: Move, re-size, add, position and delete chart elements,* you'll learn how to add elements one by one. You'll then appreciate how much faster it is to select all five elements with a single click instead of individually adding each one.

3   Click the *Chart Title* element and type: **Sales First Quarter** followed by the **<Enter>** key.

4   Click the *Vertical Axis Title* element and type: **Sales** followed by the **<Enter>** key.

5   Click the *Horizontal Axis Title* element and type: **Region** followed by the **<Enter>** key.

6   Save your work as: *World Sales-3.*

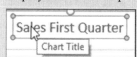

# Lesson 5-6: Apply a pre-defined chart style and color set

1   Open *World Sales-3 from* your sample files folder (if it isn't already open).

2   Change the chart style.

1.   Click just inside the border of the chart to activate it.
2.   Click: Chart Tools→Design→Chart Styles→ Chart Styles Gallery.

Chart Styles

When you click the *Gallery* button ⬇ you are able to choose a new chart style from 14 pre-defined options. Each chart style uses theme colors, so the chart's appearance will change if you later change the workbook's theme (you learned about themes in: *Lesson 4-9: Understand themes*).

Notice that the chart changes as you hover over each style so that you can preview how your chart will look if the style is chosen.

3.   Click a new chart style to change the appearance of your chart.

In the example below I have chosen *Style 8.*

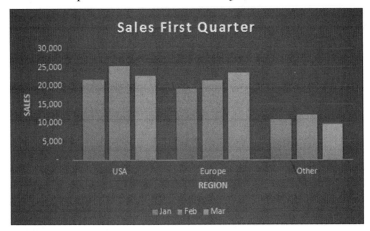

## note

### Preventing the gallery from obscuring the chart

You can hover the mouse cursor over each option in the *Chart Styles* gallery to apply the style to the chart so that you can preview how it looks.

Sometimes the gallery will obscure the chart, making it impossible to preview the new chart style.

To prevent this from happening use the *Next Row* button to view the *Chart Style Gallery* one row at a time.

3   Change the chart's color set.

In: *Lesson 4-9: Understand themes,* you learned that every theme has a related color set.

In: *Lesson 4-11: Add color and gradient effects to cells (sidebar)* you learned why it is good practice to restrict colors to theme colors.

Excel provides a quick and convenient way to choose new set of colors (from the current theme's color set) for your chart.

**World Sales-3**

# note

## Another way to change a chart's style or color set

When you activate a chart (by clicking on it), three small icons appear next to the top-right corner:

The middle icon  provides a different way to select a style or color set.

The other two buttons allow you to select *Chart Elements* and *Chart Filters*.

You'll learn more about Chart Elements later, in: *Lesson 5-9: Move, re-size, add, position and delete chart elements.*

You'll learn about Chart Filters later, in: *Lesson 5-10: Apply a chart filter.*

1. Click just inside the border of the chart to activate it.

2. Click: Chart Tools→Design→Change Colors.

   A set of color palettes (each consisting of six colors) are displayed. All colors belong to the current theme (in this example, the default *Office* theme).

   As you hover the mouse cursor over each palette, the chart changes to preview the effect of choosing the new color set.

3. Click any of the color sets to select one. The new color set is applied to the chart.

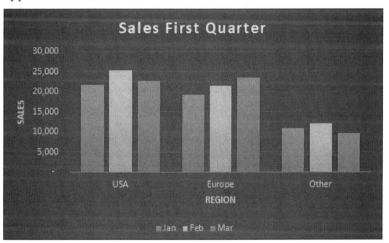

4 Close the workbook without saving.

   You want to stay with the original default style, so close this workbook without saving. The chart will then retain the default style.

## note

### Chart titles can display the contents of a specific worksheet cell

Normally you will simply type the text that you need directly into the *Chart Title* element.

It is also possible to link the *Chart Title* to a worksheet cell so that it displays whatever text is in the specified cell.

Here's how it is done:

1.  Click the *Chart Title* element.

2.  Click inside the formula bar.

3.  Type: = to start the formula.

4.  Click on cell A1 (or the worksheet cell containing the value that you want to be displayed).

5.  Press the **<Enter>** key.

    This will add a fully qualified cell reference such as:

    **=Sheet1!$A$1**

    This is required when you reference a cell from a *Chart Title* element. A simple reference such as:

    **=A1**

    …will not work.

    You'll learn more about fully qualified cell references later, in: *Lesson 6-6: Create cross worksheet formulas.*

    The contents of cell A1 are then displayed in the *Chart Title* element and will change whenever the text in cell A1 changes.

# Lesson 5-7: Manually format a chart element

Up until now you've selected a pre-defined chart style and color set from a gallery.

Sometimes you may have a requirement that is not catered for within the selection of pre-defined styles offered by the *Chart Styles* gallery.

In this case you will need to manually format one or more chart elements.

Once you have the hang of how to format one element it becomes easy to work with any other element, because the options are broadly the same.

In this lesson, you'll manually format the *Chart Title* element.

1   Open *World Sales-3* from your sample files folder (if it isn't already open).

2   Click the *Chart Title* element to select it.

A frame appears:

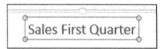

3   Right-Click the *Chart Title* element and click *Format Chart Title…* from the shortcut menu.

The *Format Chart Title* task pane appears.

4   Apply a *Blue Accent 1* fill (background color) to the *Chart Title* element.

1.  Click the *Fill & Line* icon in the *Format Chart Title* task pane.

2.  Click the *Fill* option to display the fly-out menu.

3.  Click the *Solid fill* option button.

4.  Click the *Fill Color* icon.

5.  Click the *Blue, Accent 1* fill color.

6.  Drag the *Transparency* slider to the right to set the transparency to about 80%.

**World Sales-3**

note

**Working with the Format Shape task pane**

The *Format Chart Title* task pane that you have been working with in this lesson is actually an instance of the more generic *Format Shape* task pane.

The name shown at the top of the *Format Shape* task pane changes depending upon which chart element you are working with.

The *Format Shape* task pane (in common with all other Office task panes) is modeless. You learned about the difference between modal dialogs and modeless task panes in: *Lesson 3-7: Use the Multiple Item Clipboard – sidebar.*

This means that you can go on working and leave the *Format Shape* dialog happily sitting in the background. Even better, as you select different chart elements, the *Format Shape* task pane will automatically change to show the appropriate settings for the selected element.

This is a huge time saver, especially if you have a large screen (or multiple monitors) enabling you to "park" the task pane out of the way of the worksheet.

Notice that the background color of the *Chart Title* element becomes lighter as you drag to the right, and darker as you drag to the left.

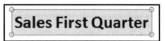

5 Apply a 1pt solid black border to the *Chart Title* element.

1. Click the *Fill & Line*  icon in the *Format Chart Title* task pane.

2. Click the *Border* option to display the fly-out menu.

3. In the *Border* section, click the *Solid Line* option button.

4. Click the *Color* drop-down arrow and select a solid black color.

5. In the *Border* section, set the *Width* to: 1pt

Notice that a solid black border has now been applied to the *Chart Title* element.

6 Close the *Format Chart Title* task pane.

7 Save your work as *World Sales-4*.

# Lesson 5-8: Format 3-D elements and add drop shadows

The use of subtle shadows and 3-D formats will add a professional sheen to your work.

1   Open *World Sales-4* from your sample files folder (if it isn't already open) and click just inside the border of the chart to activate it.

2   Select the *Chart Title* element using *Chart Tools*.

Click: Chart Tools→Format→Current Selection→ Chart Elements drop-down→Chart Title.

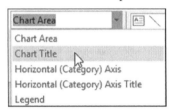

This is an alternative way to select chart elements. The drop-down shows every element in the currently selected chart.

Directly clicking on an element is usually faster but there are some chart elements (such as gridlines) that can sometimes be difficult to select with the mouse.

Here are the elements available in the *Chart Elements* drop-down list for this chart:

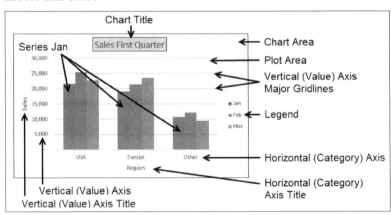

If you do a lot of work with charts it is well worth adding the *Chart Elements drop-down* to the *Quick Access Toolbar* (this was covered in: *Lesson 1-14: Customize the Quick Access Toolbar and preview the printout*).

3   Display the *Format Title* task pane.

Click: Chart Tools→Format→Current Selection→Format Selection.

This is an alternative way to bring up the *Format Chart Title* dialog.

4   Apply an *Offset Diagonal Bottom Right* shadow to the *Chart Title* element.

## note

### More about data series

A data series is a group of data that is associated with a specific category.

For example, the *Series Jan* data series is a group of values, one for each of the categories *USA, Europe* and *Other*.

In this example, there are three data series containing numerical data for each category.

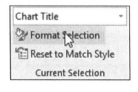

**World Sales-4**

1. Click the *Effects* 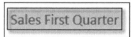 icon in the *Format Chart Title* task pane.

2. Select *Shadow* from the four effects options.

3. Click the *Presets* icon. 

   While you can create your own shadows using the *Transparency, Size, Blur, Angle* and *Distance* sliders, you'll probably find that the presets will suffice. Presets will also maintain uniformity between different chart elements.

4. Click the *Offset Bottom Right* item in the shadow gallery.

   The effect is applied to the *Chart Title* element.

**Sales First Quarter**

5    Apply a *Circle top bevel* 3D effect to the *Chart Title* element

Bevel effects make an element look like a button.

1. Click the *Effects* 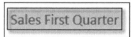 icon in the *Format Chart Title* task pane.

2. Select *3-D Format* from the four effects options.

3. Click the *Top Bevel* preset button to display the Top Bevel gallery and choose a *Round* top bevel.

   Just like shadows, you'll probably find what you need in the 3-D presets rather than creating your own custom 3-D effects.

6    Use *Reset to Match Style* to restore the *Chart Title* element to its default state.

You've added a lot of fancy formatting to the *Chart Title* element but haven't really improved the appearance of the element.

Excel provides the *Reset to Match Style* feature to enable you to restore elements back to their original state.

1. Click on the *Chart Title* element to select it.

2. Click: Chart Tools→Format→Current Selection→ Reset to Match Style.

   The *Chart Title* element is restored to its default state.

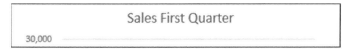

7    Close the *Format Chart Title* task pane.

8    Save your work as *World Sales-5*.

# Lesson 5-9: Move, re-size, add, position and delete chart elements

Several elements such as the *Chart Title*, *Legend* and *Horizontal/Vertical Axis Titles* can be moved by drag and drop.

In this lesson, you'll see how to manually move these elements, and how to automatically restore them to their pixel-perfect locations if you change your mind.

You'll also manually add and remove single chart elements. Once you've got the hang of this you'll be able to custom design charts for any specific requirement.

1  Open *World Sales-5* from your sample files folder (if it isn't already open).

2  Click and drag the *Chart Title* element to the left-hand side of the chart.

1.  Click the *Chart Title* element to select it.

2.  Hover the mouse cursor over the border of the *Chart Title* element until you see a four-headed arrow.

3.  When you see the four-headed arrow, click and drag to move the element to the top left corner of the chart.

3  Move the *Chart Title* element back so that it is above the center of the chart.

You couldn't position this perfectly using the mouse.

1.  Click on the *Chart Title* element to select it.

2.  Click: Chart Tools→Design→Chart Layouts→ Add Chart Element→Chart Title→Above Chart.

The *Chart Title* element is restored to the center.

4  Delete the legend.

1.  Click the *Legend* element to select it:

2.  Press the **<Delete>** key.

5  Display the legend at the top of the screen.

1.  Select the chart.

Notice that a group of three icons appears outside the top right corner of the chart.

**World Sales-5**

2. Click the *Chart Elements*  icon.

A list of all elements available for the chart is displayed. This is almost the same as the dialog shown when you clicked the *Add Chart Element* button on the Ribbon earlier in this lesson.

3. Click the arrow button to the right of the word: *Legend* in the list.

Several options for positioning the legend are shown.

4. Click: *Top*.

The legend appears at the top of the chart.

**6** Add a thin black border to the *Legend* element.

This was covered in: *Lesson 5-7: Manually format a chart element.*

**7** Resize the *Legend* element so that it spans the entire width of the plot area.

1. Click the *Legend* element to select it. Notice the sizing handles on each corner and edge.

2. Hover over the round sizing handle on the right-hand edge of the element. Notice that the cursor shape changes to a two-headed arrow.

3. When you see the two-headed arrow click and drag to re-size the legend so that it is the same width as the plot area. (You'll have to first re-size the right side and then the left).

**8** Increase the size of the font within the *Legend* element.

1. Click the *Legend* element to select it.

2. Click: Home→Font→Font Size Drop-down.

3. Hover the mouse cursor over each font size and note that *Live Preview* allows you to preview the effect of your choice.

4. Select *14 points* for the new text size.

You'll often want to increase text sizes when you create charts for PowerPoint slides.

**9** Save your work as *World Sales-6*.

# Lesson 5-10: Apply a chart filter

The chart that you have been working with contains three data series and three categories:

- The *data series* are Jan, Feb and Mar. Each of these data series contain three different values, one for each category.

- The *categories* are USA, Europe and Other.

The *Chart Filters* feature allows you to show or hide any of the data series or categories.

1 Open *World Sales-6* from your sample files folder (if it isn't already open).

2 Apply a *Chart Filter* to only show sales for Jan and Feb.

1. Click on the chart to activate it.

   A group of three icons appears outside the top right corner of the chart.

2. Click the *Chart Filters* ⧩ icon.

   A list of all of the data series and categories used in the chart is displayed (see sidebar).

   Each data series and category has a check box enabling you to hide or show the relevant item.

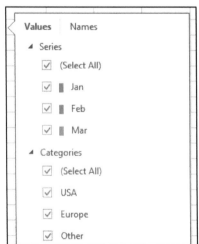

3. Uncheck the *Mar* check box so that only the *Jan* and *Feb* data series will be shown on the chart.

4. Click the *Apply* button to apply the filter.

   The chart changes so that only *Jan* and *Feb* data is displayed.

World Sales-6

3 Apply *Chart Filters* to show sales for all months, but only in the *USA* and *Europe* categories.

1. Click on the chart to activate it.

2. Click the *Chart Filters* ⦣ icon.

3. In the *Series* list check the *(Select All)* check box to select all three months.

4. In the *Categories* list uncheck the *Other* item so that only the *USA* and *Europe* categories will be shown on the chart.

5. Click the *Apply* button to apply the filter.

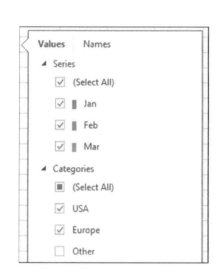

The chart changes so that only *USA* and *Europe* data is displayed for the months *Jan, Feb* and *Mar.*

4 Remove all filters so that all data series and categories are displayed.

1. Select the chart.

2. Click the *Chart Filters* ⦣ icon.

3. Check the *(Select All)* check box in the *Categories* list to select all three categories.

4. Click the *Apply* button to apply the filter.

# Lesson 5-11: Change a chart's source data

You'll often want to chart a small number of columns from a much larger range (that may contain hundreds, or even thousands of columns).

If a range only contains a handful of columns, it may be easier to chart the entire range and then use the *Chart Filters* feature (that you used in: *Lesson 5-10: Apply a chart filter*) to remove the unwanted columns.

When there are a lot of columns, you may find it a lot faster to address the issue in the chart's source data using the technique described in this lesson.

1 Open *World Sales-6* from your sample files folder (if it isn't already open).

**note**

**Another way to display the Select Data Source dialog**

You can also bring up the *Select Data Source* dialog from the Ribbon by clicking:

Chart Tools→
Design→Data→Select Data

2 Display the *Select Data Source* dialog.

Right-click in the *Plot Area* of the chart and click *Select Data…* from the shortcut menu.

The *Select Data Source* dialog appears.

Notice the *Chart data range* shown at the top of the dialog. For the moment, this is all that I want you to concentrate upon.

The range is shown as: *Sheet1!$A$1:$D$4*.

This means the absolute range A1:D4 on the *Sheet1* worksheet.

(Absolute cell references were covered in: *Lesson 3-12: Understand absolute and relative cell references*).

3 Change the *Chart data range* so that only USA sales are charted.

The current range is A1:D4.

| | A | B | C | D |
|---|---|---|---|---|
| 1 | Month | USA | Europe | Other |
| 2 | Jan | 21,600 | 19,200 | 10,800 |
| 3 | Feb | 25,400 | 21,400 | 12,200 |
| 4 | Mar | 22,800 | 23,600 | 9,600 |

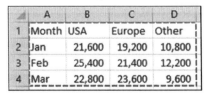

World Sales-6

If you change the range to A1:B4 the *Europe* and *Other* regions will be removed.

You could simply type the new reference into the *Chart data range* text box, but it is less error prone if you visually select the data with the mouse.

1. Delete the current contents of the *Chart data range* text box.

2. With the flashing cursor still inside the empty *Chart data range* text box, click and drag with the mouse across cells A1:B4.

The data range displays in both the *Chart data range* text box and as a marquee on the worksheet.

It is very easy to mess up the data range in the text box. If you get an obscure error message, simply delete all of the contents of the *Chart data range* text box and re-select.

Notice that, in the background, the chart has changed to reflect the new data range.

4 Change the *Chart data range* to A1:C4 to chart sales for the USA and Europe.

5 Click OK to view the new chart.

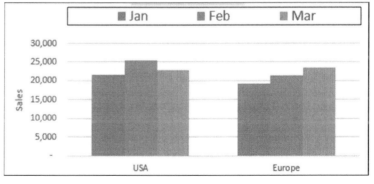

6 Save your work as *World Sales-7*.

# Lesson 5-12: Assign non-contiguous source data to a chart

In the previous lesson it was easy to select the source data because it comprised of a single block (we use the word: *contiguous* for this type of range).

In this lesson, you'll take things a little further by selecting data that isn't in a single block (ie non-contiguous data) to show sales for the *USA* and *Other* categories.

1   Open *World Sales-7* from your sample files folder (if it isn't already open).

2   Chart sales for all months in the *USA* and *Other* categories by changing the source data.

   1.   Right-click in the plot area of the chart and click *Select Data* from the shortcut menu.

      The *Select Data Source* dialog appears.

   2.   Delete the current contents of the *Chart data range* text box.

   3.   With the cursor still flashing inside the empty *Chart data range* text box, click and drag with the mouse across cells A1:B4.

   4.   Release the mouse button.

   5.   Hold down the **<Ctrl>** key.

   6.   Select the range D1:D4.

   7.   Click the OK button.

      Selecting non-contiguous ranges was covered extensively in: *Lesson 2-7: Select non-contiguous cell ranges and view summary information.*

3   Display the total sales for each month in column E.

World Sales-7

Type the word: **Total** into cell E1 and then use AutoSum to place the totals for all regions into cells E2:E4.

AutoSum was covered in: *Lesson 2-3: Use AutoSum to quickly calculate totals.*

4    Change the source data so that only the *Total* category is charted.

1.    Right-click in the plot area of the chart.

2.    Click *Select Data* from the shortcut menu.

3.    Delete the current contents of the *Chart data range* text box.

4.    With the mouse cursor still flashing inside the empty *Chart data range* text box, click and drag with the mouse across cells A1:A4.

5.    Hold down the **<Ctrl>** key.

6.    Select cells E1:E4.

7.    Click OK to close the *Select Data Source* dialog.

5    Change the source data so that sales for *USA*, *Europe* and *Other* regions are shown (but not the total).

1.    Right-click in the plot area of the chart and click *Select Data* from the shortcut menu.

2.    Select cells A1:D4.

3.    Click OK to close the *Select Data Source* dialog.

6    Save your work as *World Sales-8*.

# Lesson 5-13: Understand Data Series and Categories

In order to use the *Select Data Source* dialog in a more advanced way, you will need to understand how Excel automatically divides a range of data into *data series* and *categories*.

## Data series and categories

Here is the data you have been working with for most of this session:

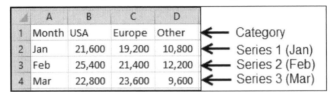

Excel interprets this data as having three data series (Jan, Feb and Mar).

In this example, each data series has three values. For example, the *Jan* data series has the three values 21,600, 19,200 and 10,800.

The values are plotted along the left-hand vertical axis (sometimes referred to as the Y axis).

Each of the values in a data series is associated with a *Category*. This is simply a label that identifies each value in the series. For example, the *Jan* series value of 19,200 belongs to the *Europe* category.

The category is shown along the bottom horizontal axis (sometimes referred to as the X axis).

Showing this on the chart makes things clearer:

## Swapping the Rows and Columns

It is also possible to take a different view of the same data.

The old data series become categories, and the old categories become data series.

**World Sales-8**

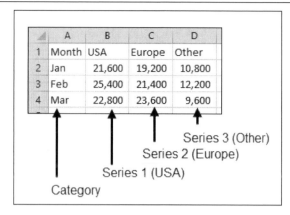

When the data is viewed in this way a different chart will result.

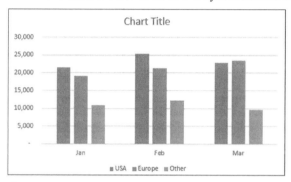

**1** Open *World Sales-8* from your sample files folder (if it isn't already open).

At present Excel regards months as data series, and regions as categories:

**2** Switch the rows and columns so that the X axis shows months instead of regions.

1. Click just inside the border of the chart to select it.

2. Click: Chart Tools→Design→Data→Switch Row/Column

Excel now regards the regions as data series, and the months as categories.

**3** Save your work as *World Sales-9.*

# Lesson 5-14: Change source data using the Select Data Source dialog tools

1 Open *World Sales-9* from your sample files folder (if it isn't already open).

2 Display the *Select Data Source* dialog.

Right-click in the *Plot Area* of the chart and click *Select Data…* from the shortcut menu.

The *Select Data Source* dialog appears.

Notice that there are check boxes next to each series and category.

 lter (a different way to do the same thing that you did in: *Lesson 5-10: Apply a chart filter*).

3 Add a *Total* data series.

Click the *Add* button ![Add] in the *Legend Entries (Series)* pane.

1. Type: **Total** for the series name.

2. Delete any text currently appearing in the *Series values* text box.

3. Select the range E2:E4 for the *Series values*.

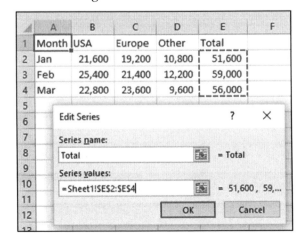

## note

### An alternative method for selecting source data

The *Select Data Source* dialog is by far the best way to set and modify source data for charts.

An alternative (and less intuitive) way is to copy a data range, activate the chart, and then click:

Home→Clipboard→Paste→ Paste Special…

A *Paste Special* dialog is then displayed that is specifically designed for charts:

World Sales-9

4.  Click OK.

The series is added to the dialog.

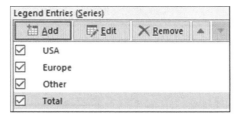

The series also appears on the chart.

**4**   Delete the *Total* data series.

1.  Display the *Select Data Source* dialog (if it isn't already open).

2.  Click the *Total* data series in the *Legend Entries (Series)* list to select it.

3.  Click the Remove button.

The series is removed from both the dialog and the chart.

**5**   Switch the rows and columns so that the X Axis shows regions instead of months.

You learned how to do this using the Ribbon in: *Lesson 5-13: Understand Data Series and Categories.*

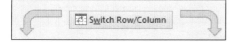

You can do the same thing by clicking the *Switch Row/Column* button on the *Select Data Source* dialog.

**6**   Click the OK button to close the *Select Data Source* dialog.

**7**   Save your work as *World Sales-10.*

---

# Lesson 5-15: Chart non-contiguous source data by hiding rows and columns

In this lesson, you'll look at an alternative method of charting a non-contiguous range simply by hiding the data elements that you don't want to chart.

Excel allows you to hide rows and columns in a worksheet by effectively setting their width to zero. The default behavior of charts is to ignore these hidden rows and columns.

It is also possible to override this default behavior and instruct Excel to chart hidden rows and columns.

1    Open *World Sales-10 from* your sample files folder (if it isn't already open).

2    Remove the *Europe* series from the chart by hiding column C.

    1.   Right-click on the column header button at the top of column C.

    2.   Click *Hide* from the shortcut menu.

                ■  *Format Cells...*
                      *Column Width...*
                      *Hide*
                      *Unhide*

    The *European* sales data is no longer shown on the chart.

3    Remove the *February* data from the chart by hiding row 3.

    1.   Right-click on the row header button to the left of row 3.

    2.   Click *Hide* from the shortcut menu.

    February data is no longer shown on the chart.

4    Display the hidden data in the chart.

Excel allows you to chart hidden data if you want to.

**World Sales-10**

1. Right-click in the plot area of the chart and click *Select Data...* from the shortcut menu.

   The *Select Data Source* dialog appears.

2. Click the *Hidden and Empty Cells* button on the bottom left corner of the dialog.

   The *Hidden and Empty Cell Settings* dialog appears.

3. Check the *Show data in hidden rows and columns* check box.

4. Click the OK button twice to dismiss the dialogs.

   The previously hidden chart data re-appears.

5   Unhide the hidden rows and columns.

   1. Click any cell in the worksheet to de-activate the chart.

   2. Click the *Select All* button at the top left corner of the worksheet to select every cell.

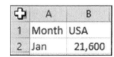

   3. Click: Home→Cells→Format→Hide & Unhide→Unhide Rows.

   4. Click: Home→Cells→Format→Hide & Unhide→Unhide Columns.

6   Save your work as *World Sales-11.*

---

**note**

**The Hidden and Empty Cell Settings dialog can also be used with Sparklines**

If you select a Sparkline group and click:

Sparkline Tools→Design→ Sparkline→Edit Data→ Hidden & Empty Cells

... you will see the same *Hidden and Empty Cell Settings* dialog that is used in this lesson to deal with hidden rows and columns in charts.

You can use it in exactly the same way to deal with hidden rows and columns in Sparklines.

You learned how to create Sparkline groups in: *Lesson 4-20: Insert a Sparkline into a range of cells.*

---

# Lesson 5-16: Create a chart with numerical axes

Sometimes Excel gets a little confused when it attempts to automatically generate a chart.

Problems usually occur when you need to plot numerical information along the horizontal axis. Excel sees the numerical labels and assumes that they are a series.

In this lesson, you'll use such a worksheet to confuse Excel and then fix things up manually using the *Select Data Source* dialog.

1 Open *Annual Sales Summary* from your sample files folder.

2 Display the range as a clustered column chart.

   1. Click on any single cell inside the range.

      Note that it isn't necessary to select the range when you want to chart all of it.

      If you simply click any cell inside the range, Excel will automatically select the entire range for the chart's source data.

   2. Click: Insert→Charts→Insert Column or Bar Chart→ 2D Column→Clustered Column.

   The range is displayed as a chart, but there's a problem. Excel has assumed that the numbers in the *Year* column are a data series.

   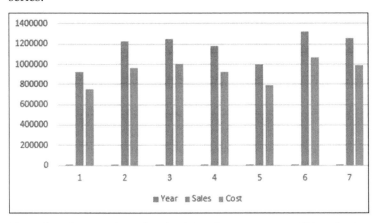

   Note that the numbers for the *Year* data are so small in relation to the *Sales* and *Cost* data that you can hardly see their bars in the bar chart. The bars are there, but they are so short that they are almost invisible.

3 Right-click just inside the plot area of the chart and click *Select Data…* from the shortcut menu.

   The *Select Data Source* dialog is displayed.

**Annual Sales Summary**

The problem is immediately apparent. Excel has wrongly identified the year as series data rather than as category axis labels.

4    Remove the *Year* data series and add the *Year* data as *Horizontal (Category) Axis Labels*.

1.   Click *Year* in the left hand pane of the dialog and then click the Remove button.

2.   Click the *Edit* button on the right hand pane.

3.   Select cells A2:A8 for the *Axis label range* (the year data but not the column header).

4.   Click the OK button twice to close both dialogs.

The chart now displays correctly.

5    Save your work as *Annual Sales Summary-1*.

# Lesson 5-17: Deal with empty data points

| | A | B |
|---|---|---|
| 1 | Date | Weight |
| 2 | 15-Nov-15 | 92.5 |
| 3 | 16-Nov-15 | 92.5 |
| 4 | 17-Nov-15 | 92.5 |
| 5 | 18-Nov-15 | 93.0 |
| 6 | 19-Nov-15 | 91.5 |
| 7 | 20-Nov-15 | 91.5 |
| 8 | 21-Nov-15 | 91.5 |
| 9 | 22-Nov-15 | 91.5 |
| 10 | 23-Nov-15 | |
| 11 | 24-Nov-15 | 93.0 |
| 12 | 25-Nov-15 | 91.0 |
| 13 | 26-Nov-15 | 91.0 |
| 14 | 27-Nov-15 | 91.0 |
| 15 | 28-Nov-15 | 92.0 |
| 16 | 29-Nov-15 | |
| 17 | 30-Nov-15 | |
| 18 | 01-Dec-15 | 91.5 |

Sometimes you'll only have partial data for a series.

In the worksheet used for this lesson I'll share a secret with you. I weigh myself every day and keep a chart on my bathroom wall to make sure that I'm staying at a healthy weight.

Sometimes I'm away travelling and can't weigh in as usual. When I get back I need to fill in the gaps.

If I used a column chart, there would be no problem (see sidebar) as the missing days would have missing columns.

But I use a line chart for my weight, and I'd like the chart to draw a line connecting the last data point recorded before I went away with the first recorded upon my return.  Unfortunately, Excel doesn't do this by default and will leave gaps for the missing data points:

1  Open *Weight 2015* from your sample files folder.

This is a simple worksheet showing my weight in kilograms for each date in July 2015. Notice that there are missing days when I was away from home.

2  Display the range as a *Line with Markers* chart.

1. Click on any of the date values within the range.

2. Click: Insert→Charts→Insert Line or Area Chart→Line with Markers.

The chart displays, but there are gaps for the missing entries.

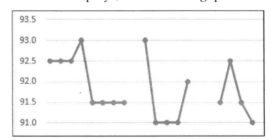

3  Tell Excel to connect the gaps in the chart with a line.

1. Right-click just inside the plot area of the chart and click *Select Data* from the shortcut menu.

The *Select Data Source* dialog is displayed.

2. Click the *Hidden and Empty Cells* button at the bottom left corner of the dialog.

**Weight 2015**

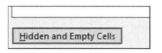

The *Hidden and Empty Cells* dialog appears.

3. Click the *Connect data points with line* option button.

Note the checkbox: *Show #N/A as an empty cell.* #N/A is an error value that Excel displays when a value is not available to a function or formula. Excel's normal behavior when encountering #N/A values is to *Connect data points with line* (even if you select *Gaps* or *Zero*).

The *Show #N/A as an empty cell* option enables you to tell Excel to treat any #N/A errors in the same way it would treat an empty cell. This means that Excel will respect your choice (*Gaps, Zero* or *Connect data points with line*).

The Show *#N/A as an empty cell* feature is only available to Excel 365 users (see sidebar). If you are an Excel 2016 user, you will not see this option.

4. Click the OK button and OK again to dismiss both dialogs

All data points are now connected with a line.

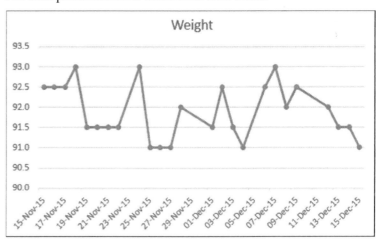

4    Save your work as *Weight 2015-1.*

# Lesson 5-18: Add data labels to a chart

It is possible to approximate the values that are displayed in a chart by looking at the vertical axis.

Sometimes you will need to convey the precise values that are being charted. There are three ways of doing this:

- Embed the chart in the worksheet containing the source data so that the user can see both the chart and data.

- Add data labels to each point on the chart.

- Add a *Data Table* chart element to the bottom of the chart.

1 Open *Annual Sales Summary-1* from your sample files folder.

2 Change the chart's source data so that only sales (not costs) for 2013 to 2016 are charted.

This will allow you to test your understanding of the skills learned in: *Lesson 5-12: Assign non-contiguous source data to a chart, Lesson 5-14: Change source data using the Select Data Source dialog tools,* and *Lesson 5-16: Create a chart with numerical axes.*

1. In the *Select Data Source* dialog select this (non-contiguous) range for the *Chart data range*:

| ▲ | A | B | C | D | E |
|---|---|---|---|---|---|
| 1 | Year | Sales | Cost | | |
| 2 | 2010 | 923,859 | 755,087 | | |
| 3 | 2011 | 1,222,054 | 961,643 | | |
| 4 | 2012 | 1,250,365 | 1,008,292 | | |
| 5 | 2013 | 1,176,787 | 925,430 | | |
| 6 | 2014 | 995,720 | 788,576 | | |
| 7 | 2015 | 1,324,534 | 1,067,627 | | |
| 8 | 2016 | 1,260,340 | 992,272 | | |
| 9 | | | | | |
| 10 | Select Data Source | | | | |
| 11 | Chart data range: | =Sheet1!$A$1:$B$1,Sheet1!$A$5:$B$8 | | | |
| 12 | | | | | |

2. In the *Select Data Source* dialog, select this data range for the *Horizontal (Category) Axis Labels*.

You learned how to do this in: *Lesson 5-16: Create a chart with numerical axes.*

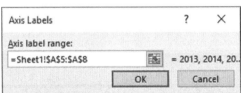

3. In the *Select Data Source* dialog remove the *Year* item from the *Legend Entries (Series)*.

The *Select Data Source* dialog should now look like this:

**Annual Sales Summary-1**

... Resulting in the following chart:

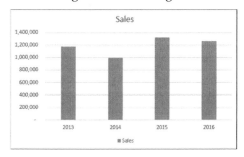

4.   Click the OK button to close the dialog.

3   Add data label elements outside the end of each bar.

1.   Activate the chart by clicking just inside the chart's border.

2.   Click the *Chart Elements* icon ➕ that appears outside the top-right corner of the chart.

3.   Click: Data Labels→Outside End.

Data labels are now shown outside the end of each bar:

4   Switch off the data labels.

1.   Activate the chart by clicking just inside the chart's border.

2.   Click the *Chart Elements* icon ➕ that appears outside the top-right corner of the chart.

3.   Uncheck the *Data Labels* check box.

5   Add a *Data Table* element to the bottom of the chart.

1.   Activate the chart by clicking just inside the chart's border.

2.   Click the *Chart Elements* icon ➕ that appears outside the top-right corner of the chart.

3.   Check the *Data Table* check box.

A table is displayed below the chart:

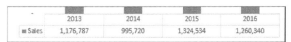

6   Save your work as *Annual Sales Summary-2.*

# Lesson 5-19: Add data labels from a range

In: *Lesson 5-18: Add data labels to a chart*, you added data labels to a column chart to show the precise value represented by each column.

This is the most common use for data labels.

A new feature was added in Excel 2013 that allows you to add data labels capable of displaying any type of information.

The values to be used for the data labels are placed in a range on the worksheet. It is then possible to specify this range as the source for the data labels to be displayed.

In this lesson, you'll use a bar chart to show the actual mark achieved in an examination. Data labels will then be added to show the grade that corresponds to each mark:

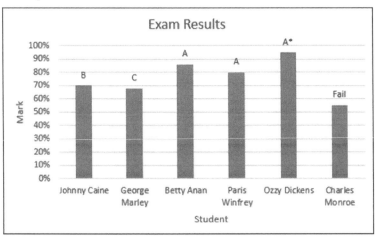

You can see how this adds value to the chart. It is easy to see at a glance that although Betty Annan and Paris Winfrey both achieved a grade A pass, Betty actually had a higher mark.

1   Open *Exam Results-1* from your sample files folder.

2   Create a column chart showing the student name and percentage mark.

    1.   Select the range A3:B9.

    2.   Click: Insert→Charts→Insert Column or Bar Chart→ 2D Column→Clustered Column.

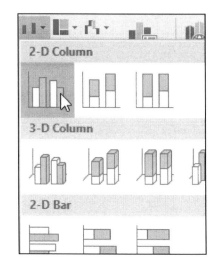

3   Add *Axis Title* elements to the chart.

    You learned how to do this in: *Lesson 5-9: Move, re-size, add, position and delete chart elements.*

4   Change the *Vertical Axis Title* text to: **Mark**, the *Horizontal Axis Title* text to: **Student** and the *Chart Title* text to: **Exam Results**.

Exam Results-1

You learned how to do this in: *Lesson 5-5: Add and remove chart elements using Quick Layout.*

5 Add data labels to show the student grade above each bar.

1. Click anywhere on the chart to activate it.

2. Click the *Chart Elements* icon 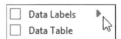 that appears just outside the top right-hand corner of the chart.

3. Click the fly out menu button to the right of *Data Labels.*

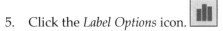

4. Click: *More Options…* from the fly out menu.

The *Format Data Labels* task pane appears.

5. Click the *Label Options* icon.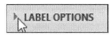

6. Click the fly out menu button to the left of *Label Options.*

LABEL OPTIONS

7. In the *Label Contains* list, uncheck any checked check boxes and then check *Value From Cells.*

8. Click the *Select Range…* button. Select Range…

The *Data Label Range* dialog appears.

9. Click inside the *Select Data Label Range* text box.

10. Select cells C4:C9 with the mouse.

11. Click the OK button.

Your chart should now look like this:

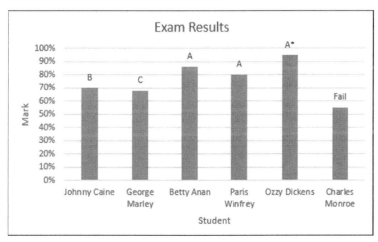

6 Save your work as *Exam Results-2.*

# Lesson 5-20: Highlight specific data points with color and annotations

A single value within a data series is often referred to as a *data point.*

Sometimes you will want to emphasize a specific data point in a series. For example, you may want to color a single column differently to its neighbors to emphasize some special attribute of the data point.

Color alone cannot always convey why the data point is special. You will normally want to also add a text box to the chart to explain the reason for its different color.

In this lesson, you'll imagine that the company is a hotel, and that 2014 was the centenary year in a competing resort, leading to an expectation of decreased sales. To mark this, you'll color the 2014 bar orange and add an annotation saying *Centenary Year* to the bar.

1   Open *Annual Sales Summary-2* from your sample files folder (if it isn't already open).

2   Change the color of the 2014 bar to orange.

   1. Click the 2014 bar once. Notice that the entire data series is selected.

   2. Click the 2014 bar once more. This time only the 2014 bar is selected.

   3. Click: Chart Tools→Format→Shape Styles→ Shape Fill→Orange, Accent 2.

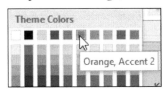

   4. The 2014 bar is now colored orange. The legend has also changed to give a further visual prompt that the orange bar relates to 2014.

3   Add a text box above, and to the right of, the 2014 bar containing the text: **Centenary Year**.

   1. Click just inside the border of the chart to activate it.

2. Click: Chart Tools→Format→Insert Shapes→ Shapes Gallery→Basic Shapes→Text Box.

3. Click on the chart, above the orange 2014 bar, and type **Centenary**, then press **<Shift>+<Enter>** and then type **Year.** (The **<Shift>+<Enter>** key combination moves you to the next line in a text box).

4   Add a border and fill to the text box.

Click the text box to select it and then click:

Drawing Tools→Format→Shape Styles→ Shape Styles Gallery→Subtle Effect – Blue, Accent 1

This effect is the second on row four (see sidebar).

5   Resize the text box.

Click the text box once to select it and then drag the sizing handles to resize the text box so that the text fills the box.

6   Move the text box.

Click the text box once to select it and then hover over any part of the border that is not a sizing handle. You will see the four-headed arrow cursor shape (see sidebar). When you see the four-headed arrow, click and drag to move the text box to an ideal position.

7   Add an arrow pointing from the text box to the orange 2014 bar.

1. Click the chart to activate it. (Make sure that you click just inside the border of the chart and not on the text box. The *Chart Tools* tab will not be displayed when the text box is selected).

2. Click: Chart Tools→Format→Insert Shapes→ Shapes Gallery→Lines→Arrow. (see sidebar).

3. Click and drag to draw an arrow pointing from the text box to the orange bar.

4. With the arrow selected, click: Drawing Tools→Format→ Shape Styles→Gallery drop-down.

5. Choose an attractive style for the arrow.

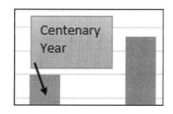

8   Save your work as *Annual Sales Summary-3.*

# Lesson 5-21: Add gridlines and scale axes

In this lesson, you'll manipulate the vertical axis of a sales chart to give two entirely different views of a company's sales. Each chart emphasizes one of the following true statements.

- It is true that sales are increasing every month.

- It is true that sales are almost completely flat.

You'll see how you can manipulate a column chart to visually convey each of these "truths" to an audience. After this session, you'll never look at a chart again without paying close attention to the vertical axis!

1   Open *Sales First Quarter* from your sample files folder.

|   | A | B |
|---|---|---|
| 1 | **Month** | **Sales** |
| 2 | Jan | 80,010 |
| 3 | Feb | 80,040 |
| 4 | Mar | 80,080 |

This worksheet shows sales that are almost completely flat. Sales increased by 0.04% in February and by 0.05% in March.

A twentieth of a percent increase isn't anything at all.

2   Create a chart that illustrates flat sales.

Imagine you are the sales director of the company and need to have a pep talk with your salespeople.

You want to show them a chart that demonstrates the lack of sales growth in order to motivate them to do better in April.

1.   Click inside the data range.

2.   Click: Insert→Charts→Insert Column or Bar Chart→ 2-D Column→Clustered Column.

The following chart is automatically generated:

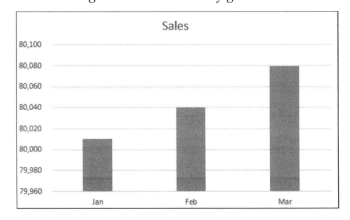

This isn't the chart you want at all. Sales look rather good!

The chart isn't as honest as it should be because the vertical axis begins at 79,960. You're looking at the tips of columns that are very long.

**Sales First Quarter**

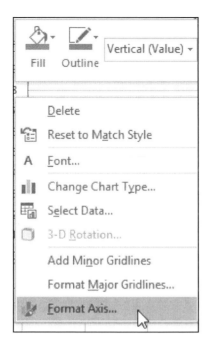

To fix things up you need a more honest vertical axis, one that begins at zero.

3. Right-click the vertical axis and select *Format Axis...* from the shortcut menu.

   The *Format Axis* task pane appears.

4. Change the *Minimum* value to zero and press the **<Enter>** key.

The chart now depicts a more honest representation of flat growth.

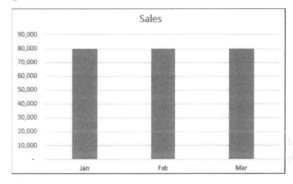

Look at the task pane and notice how Excel has automatically managed the other settings. *Major units* for gridlines (the interval between numbers on the vertical axis) have now changed to 10,000.

5. Change the *Minor Units* gridline value to 5000 (without a comma as Excel has a problem with commas in this task pane). You will enable the display of minor gridline elements in a moment and will see one minor gridline between each major gridline.

## tip

### Use gridlines sparingly

Too many gridlines can make a chart difficult to read.

This lesson's chart looks cluttered with minor gridlines and might even look cleaner without any gridlines.

When you do use gridlines, always choose a light color to focus attention upon foreground elements.

3 Add minor horizontal gridlines to the chart.

1. Activate the chart by clicking just inside the chart's border.

2. Click the *Chart Elements* icon [+] outside the top right of the chart.

3. Click: Gridlines→Primary Minor Horizontal.

Minor gridlines are now displayed on the chart (see sidebar).

4 Save your work as *Sales First Quarter-1.*

# Lesson 5-22: Emphasize data by manipulating pie charts

In the last lesson, you saw how a column chart could visually reinforce different characteristics of the same data.

Pie charts also offer several techniques to present data in a way that will best convey your objectives. Designers of pie charts often use the presentation methods described in this lesson to make one value in a series seem bigger or smaller in relation to its neighbors.

1 Open *Competitor Analysis* from your sample files folder (if it isn't already open).

| | A | B | C |
|---|---|---|---|
| 1 | Splendid Supplies Competitor Analysis | | |
| 2 | | | |
| 3 | Competitor | Annual Sales (Millions) | Market Share |
| 4 | Cheapo discount stores | 22.2 | 28% |
| 5 | Budget supplies | 16.3 | 21% |
| 6 | Lo Cost warehouse | 24.5 | 31% |
| 7 | Splendid Supplies | 16.2 | 20% |

Splendid Supplies have compiled this worksheet to monitor the activity of their three competitors. Splendid aren't doing so well. In fact, they have the lowest market share of the four.

There's a big investor meeting coming up and Splendid would like to make their market share seem a little more impressive!

2 Create a 3-D pie chart for the range A3:B7.

1. Select the range A3:B7.

2. Click: Insert→Charts→Insert Pie or Doughnut Chart→3-D Pie (see sidebar).

A pie chart is displayed, illustrating the market share of the four companies.

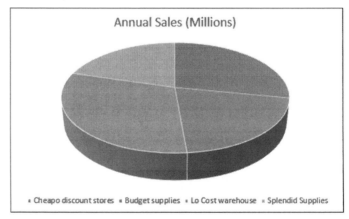

Splendid Supplies don't look very impressive on this chart. You can use a simple presentational technique to make things seem a little better.

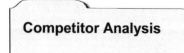

Competitor Analysis

3    Rotate the pie chart so that Splendid Supplies sales are at the front.

Because of the perspective of a 3-D pie, the slice at the front always seems the biggest (especially if you keep the perspective angle high).

1.  Right-click in the plot area of the pie chart. To do this you'll need to click just outside one of the pie chart's slices.

2.  Click *Format Plot Area* on the shortcut menu. If you don't see *Format Plot Area* in the shortcut menu it is because you have right-clicked in the wrong place. In this case try again, making sure that you click just outside one of the pie chart's slices.

    The *Format Plot Area task pane* appears.

3.  Click the *Effects* icon  at the top of the task pane.

4.  In the *3-D rotation* section, click the *X Rotation* spin button until the Splendid Supplies (yellow) slice is at the front of the pie chart (about 220 degrees).

4    Change the pie chart's perspective to emphasize Splendid Supplies' sales.

In the 3-D rotation section, click the *Perspective* spin button to make the Splendid Supplies sales seem as large as possible. I found that a setting of 35 degrees worked well.

5    Pull the Splendid Supplies slice slightly out of the pie.

A very common pie chart presentational technique is to pull the slice that you want to emphasize away from the pie chart. This slice then appears to be larger in relation to the other slices.

1.  Click just inside the chart border to activate the chart.

2.  Click one of the slices on the chart once to select the entire pie.

3.  Click the Splendid Supplies slice once to select it.

4.  Click and drag the slice slightly out of the pie.

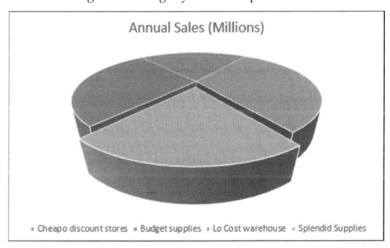

You'd never guess now that Splendid Supplies actually have the lowest market share.

6    Save your work as *Competitor Analysis-1*.

# Lesson 5-23: Create a chart with two vertical axes

Sometimes you'll have two data series that are very different in magnitude but you still want to show them on the same chart.

The examples used in this lesson are *UK Average House Prices* and *Bank Base Rates*. Economists widely believe that when interest rates come down, house and commodity prices go up. Since 2008 many world governments have used low interest rates as a tool to attempt to support asset prices. To test whether this theory has succeeded, you will create a chart showing UK bank base rates and average house prices for the twelve years up to 2015.

During the twelve-year period, house prices ranged from 148,658 to 192,852 while base rates fluctuated between 4.0% and 5.0% before a dramatic reduction to 0.5% in 2009. You need two different vertical axes to make this chart work.

1     Open *UK House Prices* from your sample files folder.

2     Create a default *Line with Markers* chart from the range.

     1.   Click anywhere within the data.

     2.   Click: Insert→Charts→Insert Line or Area Chart→2-D Line→ Line with Markers.

        The default chart is displayed.

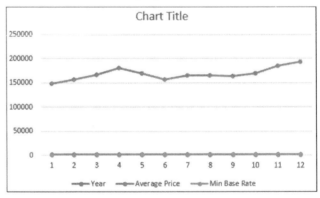

3     Remove the *Year* data series and show the years 2004 to 2015 along the *Horizontal Axis*.

     You learned how to do this in: *Lesson 5-16: Create a chart with numerical axes.*

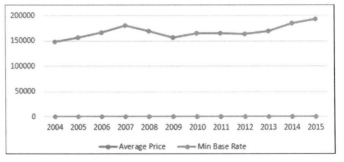

4     Select the *Min Base Rate* series.

UK House Prices

Because the *Min Base Rate* series is in almost the same place as the horizontal axis, this can be difficult with the mouse (though it is possible).

You may find it easier to select the chart and then click:

Chart Tools→Format→Current Selection→
Chart Elements drop down→Series "Min Base Rate"

5    Move the *Min Base Rate* series to a secondary axis.

1.    With the *Min Base Rate* series selected, click:

Chart Tools→Format→Current Selection→Format Selection

The *Format Data Series* task pane is displayed.

2.    Click the *Series Options* icon.

3.    Click the *Secondary Axis* option button.

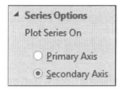

The chart is displayed with two vertical axes and Excel even auto-scales the new axis for you.

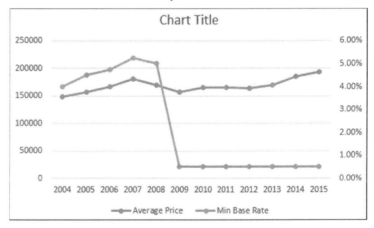

It is now easy to see at a glance that the UK government appears to have succeeded in their objective as the fall in house prices from 2007 to 2009 appears to have been reversed by the fall in interest rates.

6    Save your work as UK House Prices-1.

---

## note

### The secondary axis always appears on top of the primary axis

You can see in the example chart that when the *Min Base Rate* series (the gray line) crosses the *Average Price* series (the orange line), the gray line is on top.

You can change the stacking order of the plot lines by attaching the plot line you need to be on top to the secondary axis (and the other series to the primary axis).

# Lesson 5-24: Create a combination chart containing different chart types

Excel allows you to allocate a different chart type to each data series. This opens up many interesting possibilities such as superimposing a *Clustered Column* chart on top of an *Area* chart.

In this lesson, you'll chart the Hawaii climate as a combination Clustered Column/Area chart with clustered columns for high/low temperature and an area chart for rainfall.

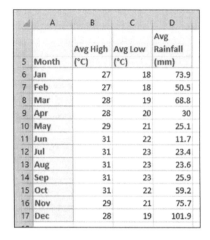

| | A | B | C | D |
|---|---|---|---|---|
| 5 | Month | Avg High (°C) | Avg Low (°C) | Avg Rainfall (mm) |
| 6 | Jan | 27 | 18 | 73.9 |
| 7 | Feb | 27 | 18 | 50.5 |
| 8 | Mar | 28 | 19 | 68.8 |
| 9 | Apr | 28 | 20 | 30 |
| 10 | May | 29 | 21 | 25.1 |
| 11 | Jun | 31 | 22 | 11.7 |
| 12 | Jul | 31 | 23 | 23.4 |
| 13 | Aug | 31 | 23 | 23.6 |
| 14 | Sep | 31 | 23 | 25.9 |
| 15 | Oct | 31 | 22 | 59.2 |
| 16 | Nov | 29 | 21 | 75.7 |
| 17 | Dec | 28 | 19 | 101.9 |

1   Open *Hawaii Climate-1* from your sample files folder.

This workbook documents the temperature range and rainfall in Hawaii for each month of the year.

2   Create a combination chart showing temperature as a *clustered column* chart type and rainfall as an *area* chart type.

1.   Click in any cell within the range.

Because you want to chart the entire data range, there's no need to select the range of cells.

2.   Click: Insert→Charts→Insert Combo Chart→ Create Custom Combo Chart…

The *Insert Chart* dialog appears with the *Combo* chart type chosen in the left-hand menu bar.

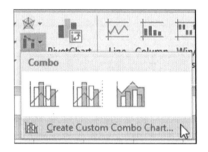

3.   Set the chart types to *Clustered Column* for both *Temperature* series and to *Area* for the *Avg Rainfall (mm)* series.

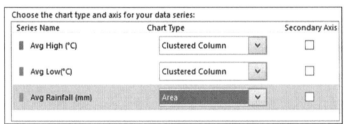

Choose the chart type and axis for your data series:

| Series Name | Chart Type | Secondary Axis |
|---|---|---|
| Avg High (°C) | Clustered Column | ☐ |
| Avg Low(°C) | Clustered Column | ☐ |
| Avg Rainfall (mm) | Area | ☐ |

4.   Click the OK button.

The combination chart is created:

The chart isn't bad but it could be improved. Because there is only one axis, the rainfall's *Area* chart type dominates the chart.

Adding a second vertical axis will solve this problem.

3 Add a secondary axis for rainfall.

You could do this using the technique learned in: *Lesson 5-23: Create a chart with two vertical axes.*

Instead you'll use a different technique by recalling the *Insert Chart* dialog (this time it will be called *Change Chart Type*).

1. Right click anywhere on the chart and click: *Change Chart Type…* from the shortcut menu.

The *Change Chart Type* dialog appears.

2. Click the *Secondary Axis* check box next to *Avg Rainfall (mm).*

3. Click OK.

The chart now looks a lot better with two axes (one for temperature and one for rainfall).

4 Add *Axis Title* elements and give them (along with the *Chart Title* element) appropriate names.

You learned how to do this in: *Lesson 5-9: Move, re-size, add, position and delete chart elements* and *Lesson 5-5: Add and remove chart elements using Quick Layout.*

The chart now looks professional:

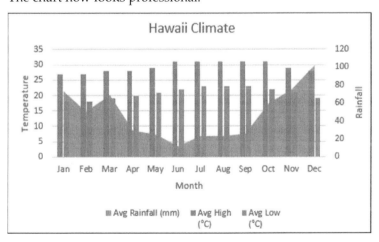

5 Save your work as *Hawaii Climate-2.*

# Lesson 5-25: Add a trend line

It is impossible to demonstrate empirically that a cause produces an effect. Just because the sun has risen every day since the beginning of the Earth does not mean that it will rise again tomorrow. However; it is impossible to go about one's life without assuming such connections, and the best that we can do is to maintain an open mind and never presume that we know any laws of causality for certain.

*David Hume (1711-1776),*
*Scottish philosopher, economist, and historian.*
*From "An Enquiry Concerning Human Understanding".*

Trend analysis applies the science of mathematics to the art of fortune telling.

If a value has been increasing for a long time, trend analysis would suggest that it will go on increasing. Some would say that the reverse is true, but Excel remains healthily optimistic that it is possible to predict the future from the past.

Excel provides several different types of trend analysis. You're going to use a linear trend line and a two-period moving average to decide whether it will be a good idea to buy a house in 2016.

1 Open *UK House Prices-1* from your sample files folder (if it isn't already open).

2 Remove the *Min Base Rate* data series from the chart.

This was covered in: *Lesson 5-14: Change source data using the Select Data Source dialog tools.*

3 Format the Vertical Axis so that it plots values between 145,000 and 205,000.

You learned how to do this in: *Lesson 5-21: Add gridlines and scale axes.*

4 Add a linear trend line element to forecast where property prices will be in the year 2020

1. Activate the chart by clicking just inside the chart's border.

2. Click the *Chart Elements* icon outside the top right of the chart.

3. Click: Trendline→More Options…

The *Format Trendline* task pane appears.

4. Click the *Trendline Options* icon.

5. Make sure that the *Linear* trendline type is selected (this is the default).

6. As 2020 is 5 periods after 2015, enter 5 in the *Forecast Forward* text box and then press the <Enter> key.

**UK House Prices-1**

7. Select the chart and then click and drag one of the right-hand sizing handles to make the chart wider.

Notice the trend line shown on the chart.

Excel isn't very confident that your new house will be a great investment and predicts that it won't be worth any more than you've paid for it in five years' time (though David Hume would have advised you that Excel may well be wrong).

5 Remove the trend line.

1. Click on the trendline to select it.

2. Press the **\<Delete\>** key on the keyboard.

6 Add a two-period moving average.

Moving averages are one of the most loved instruments of speculators who predict the future values of shares, currencies and commodities based entirely upon charts. The theory is that when the price crosses beneath the moving average it is time to sell.

1. Activate the chart.

2. Click the *Chart Elements* icon outside the top right of the chart.

3. Click: Trendline→Two Period Moving Average.

This time the analysis shows that you should have sold in 2008 and then re-purchased in 2010. In 2015, Excel's advice is to hold.

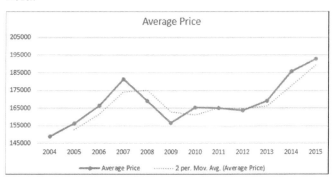

7 Save your work as *UK House Prices-2*.

## note

### Excel's forecast sheets make use of five new Excel 2016 functions

A set of five new FORECAST functions have been added to Excel 2016 in order to support the new *Forecast Sheet* feature.

Fortunately, Excel automatically creates these functions for you when you create a *Forecast Sheet*.

You can see the use of two of these functions on this lesson's forecast sheet:

FORECAST.ETS
FORECAST.ETS.CONFINT

The functions are quite easy to understand as their parameters simply mirror those shown on the *Create Forecast Worksheet* dialog.

In reality, you'll probably never use these functions directly as it is far simpler to use the *Forecast Sheet* feature described in this lesson to create them automatically.

As well as the forecasting functions used in the forecast sheet, Excel 2016 provides three other new functions:

FORECAST.ETS.SEASONALTY
FORECAST.LINEAR
FORECAST.ETS.STAT

You'll probably never use these functions directly. Their main purpose is to provide behind-the-scenes support for Excel forecasting features.

# Lesson 5-26: Add a forecast sheet

*'Tis impossible to be sure of anything but Death and Taxes.*

*Christopher Bullock, from: The Cobler of Preston (1716)*

Excel 2016 introduces a very sophisticated *Forecast Sheet* feature to predict the future more reliably. The new forecast sheets can be used to predict the likely movement of trending data such as currencies, stocks and shares and commodity prices. Just like the weather forecasters, Excel's new forecast sheets allow you to add a confidence factor. Excel can even forecast the future with a 99.9% chance of being correct (at least, this is Excel's bold claim).

This lesson uses the New York average monthly temperature for each month until June 2017. You're going to use Excel 2016's new *Forecast Sheet* feature to predict what the average New York monthly temperature will be in January, February and March 2018. At the end of the lesson you'll discover how accurate Excel's forecast was.

1   Open *Weather Forecast* from your sample files folder (if it isn't already open).

This workbook contains the average monthly temperature recorded in New York's Central Park for the five years up until June 2017. There's also a simple chart to give a visual representation of the data:

You can see that the temperature data is cyclical. You wouldn't be able to predict the average January 2018 temperature with a trend line as a trend line is not sophisticated enough to allow for the cyclical nature of the seasons.

2   Create a forecast sheet that will predict the average monthly temperature for January, February and March 2018.

1.   Select cells A4:B94

A quick way to do this is to place the cursor anywhere in the range and then press the **<Ctrl>+<A>** keys on the keyboard.

2.   Click: Data→Forecast→Forecast Sheet.

The *Create Forecast Worksheet* dialog appears.

3.  Set the *Forecast End date* to 31st March 2018.

4.  Click the *Options* button at the bottom left of the dialog.

5.  Set the *Confidence interval* to 95%.

    This will result in a prediction that Excel is 95% confident will be correct.

    Notice the *Seasonality* setting. This lets you know that Excel has correctly identified a seasonal trend that occurs every 12 months.

    Notice also that there are two icons at the top right of the dialog that enable you to select a *Line* or *Column* chart type. You'll probably find that the line type works best for most forecasts.

6.  Click the *Create* button.

    Excel inserts a new worksheet containing a forecast chart along with the data used to create the chart. The data is presented in an Excel table (see sidebar for more about tables).

## note

### About Excel tables

Microsoft could easily have used a normal Excel range to present the data in the Forecast Sheet. Instead they have chosen to use an Excel table.

The data in the table is used as the source data for the forecast chart.

Tables are an expert-level feature and are covered in depth in the *Expert Skills* book in this series. Tables make some expert-level functions and features easier to use as they have many advanced features.

Forecast sheets don't use any of the advanced features supported by tables. Simply regard the table that supports the forecast chart as a rather colourful range.

You don't need to learn anything about Excel tables to use the *Forecast Sheet* feature.

You can see that Excel has provided both a forecast and the margins of error Excel needs to be 95% sure that the forecast is correct. The chart is advising you:

*In January 2018, the average temperature is forecast to be 32.0 F. There is a 95% probability that the average temperature will be no lower than 21.5 F and no higher than 42.5F.*

If you had set the *Confidence* setting to less than 95%, Excel would have forecast a narrower temperature range to allow for a higher margin of error.

Here are the actual temperatures recorded by the Central Park weather station:

## note

Notice that Excel has got into a bit of a muddle with dates.

Forecasts have been made for both 30-Mar-18 and 31-Mar-18.

You would need to create three different forecast sheets if you wanted forecasts that were slightly more accurate.

| Month | Forecast | Actual | Difference |
|-------|----------|--------|------------|
| Jan 2018 | 32.0 | 31.7 | -1% |
| Feb 2018 | 39.3 | 42.0 | +7% |
| Mar 2018 | 39.7 | 40.1 | -1% |

… so Excel did well with 99% accuracy for two of the months.

3   Save your work as *Weather Forecast-1*.

# Lesson 5-27: Add a gradient fill to a chart background

When you prepare a chart for a PowerPoint presentation, or for inclusion in a high-quality color publication, you want the chart to look professional and interesting. A *Gradient* background fill will put the finishing touch to your chart so that it looks like it was produced by a professional graphic artist.

1   Open *World Sales* from your sample files folder.

2   Create a *Clustered Column* chart from the entire range.

    1.   Click anywhere in the range.

    2.   Click: Insert→Charts→Insert Column or Bar Chart→2-D Column→Clustered Column.

    The chart is created:

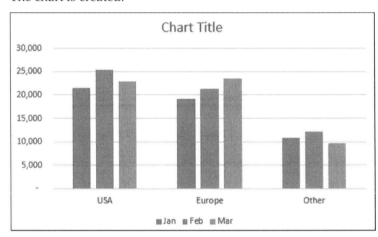

3   Switch Rows/Columns to transpose the *Legend* and *Regions*.

You learned how to do this in: *Lesson 5-13: Understand Data Series and Categories.*

The regions are now listed in the legend and the months are shown along the horizontal axis.

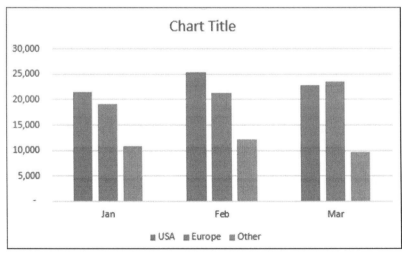

**World Sales**

4    Add a gradient fill to the chart background.

    1.   Right-click on the *Chart Area* element (just inside the border of the chart).

    2.   Click *Format Chart Area* from the shortcut menu.

         The *Format Chart Area* task pane appears.

    3.   Click the *Fill & Line* icon.

    4.   Click the *Fill* menu item.

    5.   Click the *Gradient Fill* option button.

    6.   Choose one of the preset gradients (I chose *Light Gradient – Accent 4*).

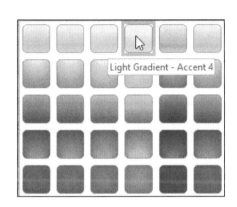

    7.   Explore the *Type/Direction/Angle/Transparency* and other settings until you are happy with the fill.

    8.   Click the *Close* button to close the *Format Chart Area* task pane.

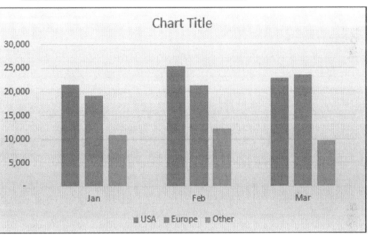

5    Save your work as *Gradient Fill*.

# Lesson 5-28: Create your own chart templates

## note

### You can also change chart text font sizes with the mini toolbar

When you want to change attributes such as font type and size for a single piece of text (such as the Chart Title) it is quicker to use the mini toolbar.

The mini toolbar pops up when you first select text within an element.

If you use charts a lot you may find yourself applying the same fonts, fills, layouts and other attributes over and over again. If you find this happening, it is time to create a chart template.

Chart Templates can be used just like the built-in gallery charts. You can use templates to create a unique, personal, or corporate chart style that will enable you to produce consistently styled work.

In this lesson, you'll develop a useful chart template with larger fonts to enable them to be more readable when incorporated into a PowerPoint presentation. You can then use this template in future for any chart that is destined to be used in a presentation.

1 Open *Gradient Fill* from your sample files folder (if it isn't already open).

2 Increase the font size of the *Chart Title* element to 28 Points.

1. Select the *Chart Title* element

2. Click: Home→Font→Font Size Drop-Down→28 Points.

3 Increase the font size of the *Vertical (Value) Axis*, *Horizontal (Category) Axis* and *Legend* elements to 14 points.

Select each element in turn and set the font size in the same way as in the previous step.

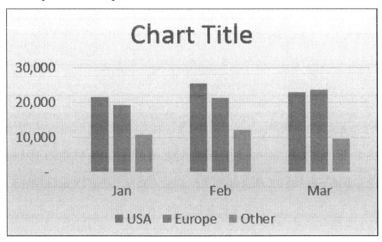

The chart now has labels that will be readable by viewers at the back of the room when projected onto a screen.

4 Save the chart design as a template.

1. Right-click in the *Chart Area* (just inside the border of the chart).

2. Select *Save as Template…* from the shortcut menu.

3. Type **PowerPoint Clustered Column with Title and Gradient Fill** as the *File Name*.

4. Click the *Save* button.

5 Delete the chart.

**Gradient Fill**

Click once, just inside the border of the chart, to select it and then press the **<Delete>** key.

6   Create a new chart from the template.

1.   Click anywhere inside the data range A1:D4.

2.   Click: Insert→Charts→Dialog Launcher.

The *Insert Chart* dialog is displayed.

3.   Click the *All Charts* tab at the top of the *Insert Chart* dialog.

4.   Click the *Templates* category on the left of the dialog.

A single icon is displayed on the right-hand side of the dialog showing a preview of the template that you just saved:

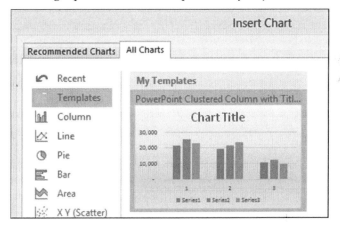

Notice that when you hover the mouse cursor over the icon a larger preview is shown.

5.   Either double-click the template icon, or click it once to select, and then click the OK button.

A chart is displayed with all of the attributes of your template.

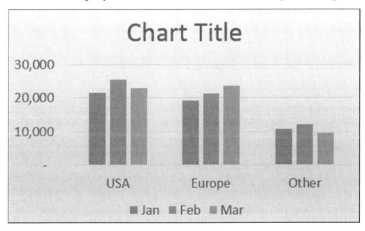

7   Save your work as *PowerPoint Template.*

## important

### The new Filled Map Chart type is only available to Excel 365 subscribers

The *Filled Map* chart type was introduced to Excel 365 subscribers on December 6th, 2016 (in Version 1611).

If you are an Excel 2016 perpetual license holder you will not have access to this feature.

You learned about Excel versions in: *Lesson 1-2: Check that your Excel version is up to date.*

# Lesson 5-29: Create a Filled Map Chart

Microsoft have a database of maps in their *Bing Maps* application. This huge database is now available to you via the Internet enabling you to create a *Filled Map Chart* to visually communicate geographic data.

The *Filled Map Chart* is a very recent addition to Excel 365 (added in December 2016).

1   Open *Vehicle Ownership* from your sample files folder.

2   Create a Filled Map showing vehicle ownership per 1,000 inhabitants for every country in the world.

1.  Click anywhere inside the range containing vehicle ownership data.

2.  Click: Insert→Charts→Maps→Filled Map.

    (See sidebar if you do not see this option on the Ribbon).

    It may take some time for anything to happen as data is being transmitted across the Internet to *Bing Maps* (Microsoft's web mapping service).

    If this is the first time that a *Filled Map Chart* has been created on this computer, you will see a request for Bing to access your data:

    Data needed to create your map chart will be sent to Bing. | I accept |

3.  Click the *I accept* button to send the vehicle ownership data to Bing.

    Provided you are connected to the Internet, a map of the world indicating vehicle ownership appears:

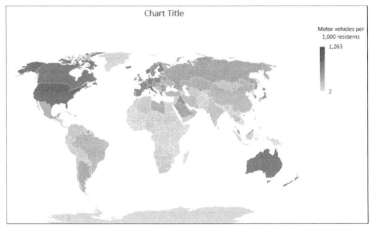

    Instead of having to digest 197 rows of data, the chart enables you to see at a glance that (amongst large countries) North America and Australia/New Zealand have the world's highest vehicle ownership levels.

    In the recent past, this type of chart would have taken a graphic artist many hours to produce.

## important

### You must be connected to the Internet to create a Filled Map chart

Filled Map charts depend upon Microsoft Bing map data. For this reason, they can only be created when you are connected to the Internet.

Once you have created a Filled Map chart it can always be viewed (even when you are not connected to the Internet).

Vehicle Ownership

3    Change the chart title to: **Motor Vehicles per 1,000 Residents**

You learned how to do this in: *Lesson 5-5: Add and remove chart elements using Quick Layout.*

4    Change the colors used by the chart to Red, Yellow and Green.

At the moment, the chart is using different shades of a single color. A darker shade indicates a higher value.

You will now instruct Excel to use red for a low value, yellow for mid values, and green for high values.

1.  Right-click on one of the countries shown on the chart.

2.  Click: *Format Data Series...* from the shortcut menu.

    The *Format Data Series* task pane appears.

3.  Click the *Series Options* icon.

4.  Click the *Series Color* fly-out menu.

    Notice that the chart is currently using a *Sequential (2-color)* series color.

5.  Click the *Series Color* drop-down arrow and click *Diverging (3-color)* in the drop-down list.

6.  Select red, yellow and green standard colors for the *Lowest*, *Midpoint* and *Highest* values.

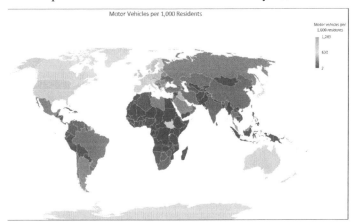

The map now visualizes the data more clearly:

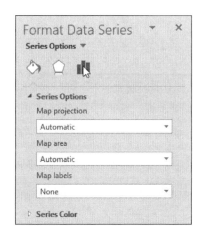

5    Save your work as *Vehicle Ownership-1*.

## note

### What are 3-D Maps?

You may have noticed an icon labeled *3D Map* on the Ribbon.

3D Maps can more correctly be regarded as a separate (and very complex) application rather than an integral part of Excel.

There is a whole session (containing 13 lessons) dedicated to the *3-D Maps* tool in the *Expert Skills* book in this series. 3-D Maps are beyond the scope of this *Essential Skills* book.

3D Maps enable you to create amazing aerial video *tours* of your data (where you can fly around the three-dimensional landscape in a virtual

**279**

## important

### The new Filled Map Chart type is only available to Excel 365 subscribers

The *Filled Map* chart type was introduced to Excel 365 subscribers on December 6th, 2016 (in Version 1611).

If you are an Excel 2016 perpetual license holder you will not have access to this feature.

You learned about Excel versions in: *Lesson 1-2: Check that your Excel version is up to date.*

## note

### Avoid ambiguity

The sample data for this lesson identifies the *Country*, *State* and *Abbreviated State*.

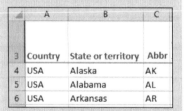

Bing is unable to correctly identify each state correctly without all three geographic data elements (though it can guess some of them).

For example, Bing would incorrectly resolve the abbreviation *VI* (signifying the US Virgin Islands) to Victoria State in south-eastern Australia if only the *Abbreviation* data was present.

USA Population by State

# Lesson 5-30: Add Data Labels to a Filled Map Chart

1  Open *USA Population by State* from your sample files folder.

2  Create a Filled Map chart from the worksheet data.

You learned how to do this in: *Lesson 5-29: Create a Filled Map Chart.*

3  Change the chart title to: **USA Population by State**

You learned how to do this in: *Lesson 5-5: Add and remove chart elements using Quick Layout.*

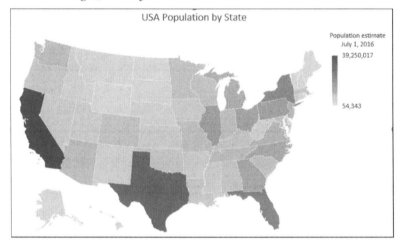

4  Inspect the chart's source data.

Right-click on any of the states shown on the chart and click: *Select Data* from the shortcut menu. The familiar *Select Data Source* dialog is displayed:

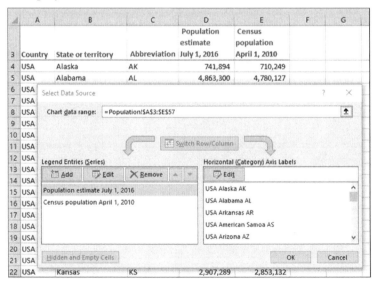

In: *Lesson 5-14: Change source data using the Select Data Source dialog tools,* you learned that *data series* are used as source data for a chart. Because a filled map chart can only map one data series, the chart is using the first data series: *"Population estimate July 1, 2016".*

5  Make the chart use the 2010 population data series.

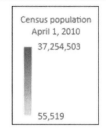

1. Use the *Select Data Source* dialog to remove the *Population estimate July 1, 2016* data series. You learned how to do this in: *Lesson 5-16: Create a chart with numerical axes.*

   The chart now visualizes the April 1, 2010 population.

2. Click the OK button to dismiss the dialog.

**6** Show the actual population numbers on the face of the chart.

In: *Lesson 5-18: Add data labels to a chart,* you added data labels above each bar in a bar chart showing the values being charted.

A filled map chart enables you to add three types of data: *Series Name, Category Name* and *Value* (individually or in any combination).

1. Click just inside the border of the chart.

   The *Chart Elements* and *Chart Style* icons appear next to the top-right corner of the chart.

2. Click the *Chart Elements* icon.

3. Click the *Data Labels* flyout menu arrow and then *More Data Label Options…* from the flyout menu.

The *Format Data Labels* task pane appears.

Notice that you are able to add *Series Name, Category Name* or *Value* data labels (or any combination of the three).

4. Check the *Value* check box.

5. Population numbers appear on the face of the chart.

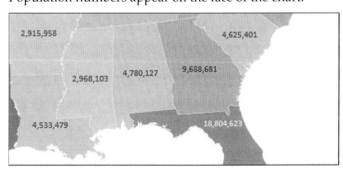

Note that these numbers will not appear if the area available on the chart is too small to show them. If you re-size the chart more population numbers will appear.

6. Experiment with the *Category Name* and *Series Name* check boxes.

**7** Save your work as *USA Population by State-1.*

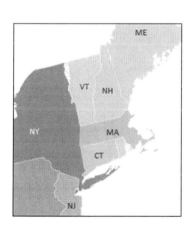

## Session 5: Exercise

**1**      Open *Exercise 5* from your sample files folder.

**2**      Click any cell in the range A3:F8.

**3**      Click: Insert→Charts→Insert Column or Bar Chart→2-D Column→Clustered Column.

        The chart will look strange at first as there are many errors to correct.

**4**      Switch rows and columns so that the European country names are shown in the *Legend*.

**5**      Use the *Select Data Source* dialog to remove the *Year* series and place the years along the *Horizontal (Category) Axis*.

**6**      Change the scale of the vertical axis so that it has a *Minimum* value of 15 and a *Maximum* value of 50.

**7**      Format the *Legend* so that a solid line black border appears around it.

**8**      Apply a *Chart Filter* so that sales are only shown for the UK, Spain and Italy.

**9**      Increase the font size of the legend to 12 points.

**10**      Change the *Chart Title* text to: *European Sales*.

**11**      Add a gradient fill to the *Chart Area* element using the *Light Gradient – Accent 5* preset.

**12**      Save your work as *Exercise 5-1*.

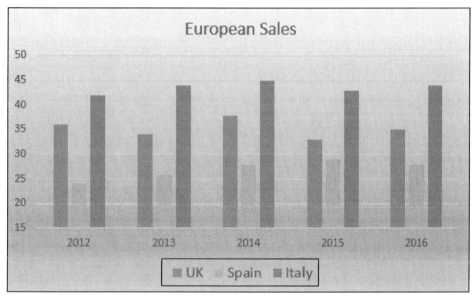

Exercise 5

If you need help slide the page to the left

## Session 5: Exercise answers

These are the questions that students find the most difficult to answer:

| Q 11 | Q 8 | Q 6 | Q 5 |
|------|-----|-----|-----|
| 1. Right-click just inside the border of the chart and click *Format Chart Area…* from the shortcut menu.<br><br>2. Choose the *Fill & Line* icon ⬦ in the *Format Chart Area* task pane.<br><br>3. Click the *Fill* menu item.<br><br>4. Click the *Gradient Fill* option button.<br><br>5. Select the *Light Gradient – Accent 5* preset gradient.<br><br>This was covered in: *Lesson 5-27: Add a gradient fill to a chart background.* | 1. Click just inside the border of the chart to select it.<br><br>2. Click the *Chart Filters* icon ▽ at the top right of the chart.<br><br>3. Uncheck the *France* and *Germany* check boxes.<br><br>4. Click the *Apply* button.<br><br>This was covered in: *Lesson 5-10: Apply a chart filter.* | 1. Click the vertical axis to select it.<br><br>2. Right-click the vertical axis and click *Format Axis…* from the shortcut menu.<br><br>3. Click the *Axis Options* icon 📊 in the *Format Axis* task pane.<br><br>4. Type the value **15** in the *Minimum* text box and press the **<Enter>** key.<br><br>Make sure that **50** is shown in the *Maximum* value text box.<br><br>This was covered in: *Lesson 5-21: Add gridlines and scale axes.* | 1. Right-click just inside the border of the chart and click *Select Data…* from the shortcut menu.<br><br>2. Click the *Year* item in the *Legend Entries (Series)* list and then click the *Remove* button.<br><br>3. Click the *Edit* button on top of the *Horizontal (Category) Axis Labels* list.<br><br>4. Select cells A4:A8.<br><br>5. Click the OK button on each dialog.<br><br>This was covered in: *Lesson 5-16: Create a chart with numerical axes.* |

If you have difficulty with the other questions, here are the lessons that cover the relevant skills:

**1**    Refer to: *Lesson 1-5: Download the sample files and open/navigate a workbook.*

**2**    Refer to: *Lesson 1-5: Download the sample files and open/navigate a workbook.*

**3**    Refer to: *Lesson 5-2: Create a simple chart with two clicks.*

**4**    Refer to: *Lesson 5-13: Understand Data Series and Categories.*

**7**    Refer to: *Lesson 5-7: Manually format a chart element.*

**9**    Refer to: *Lesson 5-7: Manually format a chart element.*

**10**   Refer to: *Lesson 5-5: Add and remove chart elements using Quick Layout.*

**12**   Refer to: *Lesson 1-6: Save a workbook.*

# Session Six: Working with Multiple Worksheets and Workbooks

> *There are no big problems; there are just a lot of little problems.*
>
> *Henry Ford (1863-1947)*
> *American industrialist and pioneer of assembly-line production*

Henry Ford knew that big problems are really just a lot of little problems bundled together.

Often you will find that a worksheet is getting over-complicated and difficult to work with. This session will give you the skills needed to quickly break one very complex worksheet into many smaller and easier to manage worksheets.

This session will also show you how to view different parts of large worksheets at the same time and how to create cross-worksheet formulas that summarize data from several different worksheets.

## Session Objectives

By the end of this session you will be able to:

- View the same workbook in different windows
- View two windows side by side and perform synchronous scrolling
- Duplicate worksheets within a workbook
- Move and copy worksheets from one workbook to another
- Hide and unhide a worksheet
- Create cross worksheet formulas
- Understand worksheet groups
- Use find and replace

# Lesson 6-1: View the same workbook in different windows

Excel allows you to view the same worksheet in two separate worksheet windows. This is useful when you need to compare different areas of the same worksheet.

1   Close any Excel workbooks that are currently open.

2   Open *Sales First Quarter 2016* from your sample files folder.

> This workbook has only one worksheet containing 242 rows of data.

3   Open a new window to see February 2016 and January 2016 sales at the same time.

> Click: View→Window→New Window.

> Nothing seems to have happened, except that the Title bar now reads: *Sales First Quarter 2016:2*

> Two views of the same workbook are now open at the same time but, because they are both maximized, you can only view one at a time which isn't very useful.

4   View both windows at the same time.

> Click: View→Window→Arrange All.

> The *Arrange Windows* dialog appears.

5   Select the *Horizontal* option and then click the OK button.

> Both worksheets are displayed on your monitor, one below the other. You are able to freely scroll to any position in either window.

**Sales First Quarter 2016**

You will now appreciate the importance of closing any open workbooks in step 1. If you had several workbooks open, you would now be viewing all of them in multiple windows.

In the screen grab below I've scrolled the bottom window down to see February sales:

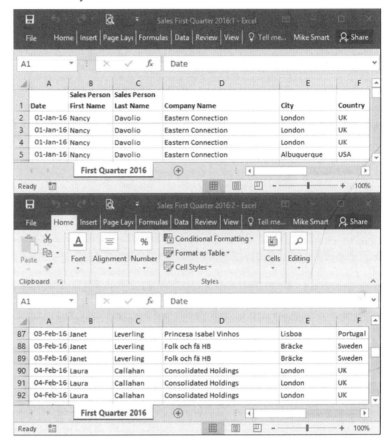

It's important to realize that you are not looking at two different worksheets, but two different views of the same worksheet.

If you change a value in one of the views, you'll immediately see the changed value in the other.

Click in the *Sales First Quarter 2016:2* window. Notice how the title text changes color to indicate that this is now the active window.

6    Close the *Sales First Quarter 2016:2* window and maximize the *Sales First Quarter 2016:1* worksheet.

1.   Click the *Close* button in the top right-hand corner of the worksheet.

2.   Click the *Maximize* button in the top right-hand corner of the *Sales First Quarter 2016* worksheet.

# Lesson 6-2: View two windows side by side and perform synchronous scrolling

When only two workbooks are open, the *Arrange All* method covered in the previous lesson will work just fine.

It is more likely that you will have many workbooks (or views of the same workbook) open and will want to see two specific workbooks on screen at the same time.

You may sometimes be given a workbook that somebody else has changed and need to identify what has been altered. You'll use Excel's synchronous scrolling feature to make this task easier.

1     Close any Excel workbooks that are currently open.

2     Open *Exercise 6* from your sample files folder.

3     Open *Sales First Quarter 2016 Revised* from your sample files folder.

4     Open *Sales First Quarter 2016* from your sample files folder.

     Three workbooks are now open but only the last workbook opened: *Sales First Quarter 2016* is visible on screen.

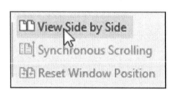

5     Click: View→Window→View Side By Side.

     The *Compare Side By Side* dialog is displayed.

6     Select *Sales First Quarter 2016 Revised* as the workbook that you want to view with the current workbook and then click the **<OK>** button.

     The workbooks should display one above the other.

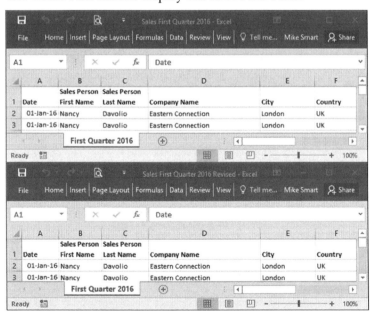

If you don't see this, click:

View→Window→Reset Window Position.

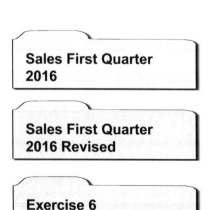

Sales First Quarter 2016

Sales First Quarter 2016 Revised

Exercise 6

This is often needed when the workbooks have been moved or re-sized.

Notice that when you use the scroll bars to move up and down the list (scroll) in one window, the other window scrolls at the same time. This is called *synchronous scrolling*.

**7**    **Unlock the windows so that they no longer scroll together.**

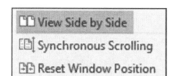

1. Click: View→Window→Synchronous Scrolling to switch synchronous scrolling off. You are now able to freely scroll each window independently.

2. Scroll each window to the top (so that row 1 is at the top of each window).

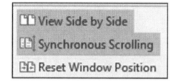

3. Click: View→Window→Synchronous Scrolling to switch synchronous scrolling back on so that both windows automatically scroll together.

**8**    **Identify differences between the two workbooks.**

Scroll down so that you can see row 77. Notice that row 78 has gone out of synchronization because one of the 29-Jan-16 sales to Hungry Owl has been deleted from the *Revised* workbook.

**9**    **Re-synchronize the windows.**

1. Click: View→Window→Synchronous Scrolling to switch Synchronous Scrolling off.

2. Scroll so that the first transaction on 30th Jan 2016 is on the first row in both windows.

3. Click: View→Window→Synchronous Scrolling to switch Synchronous Scrolling back on.

**10**    **Close all open workbooks without saving.**

---

# Lesson 6-3: Duplicate worksheets within a workbook

In this lesson you're going to disassemble a large worksheet and make it into three smaller worksheets.

You'll often find that data is easier to work with if you divide it into logically separated sections.

1    Open *Sales First Quarter 2016* from your sample files folder.

This workbook shows all sales completed in January, February and March 2016. Your task will be to split them into separate months.

2    Create a new worksheet and name it *January*.

This skill was covered in *Lesson 1-9: View, move, add, rename, delete and navigate worksheet tabs.*

3    Select every cell in the *First Quarter 2016* worksheet.

1.   Click the *First Quarter 2016* worksheet tab.

There's a special button at the top left corner of every worksheet called the *Select All* button.

| | A | B | C |
|---|---|---|---|
| 1 | Date | Sales Person First Name | Sales Person Last Name |
| 2 | 01-Jan-16 | Nancy | Davolio |

2.   Click the *Select All* button to select every cell in the worksheet.

4    Copy all selected cells.

The easiest way to do this is to right-click within the selected range and then click *Copy* from the shortcut menu.

5    Paste the copied cells into the *January* worksheet beginning at cell A1.

Click the *January* tab, right-click in cell A1 and select *Paste* from the shortcut menu.

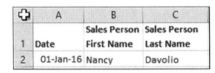

6    Create another copy of the worksheet using *Move or Copy*.

Excel provides a simpler way to duplicate a worksheet.

1.   Right-click the *First Quarter 2016* worksheet tab and choose *Move or Copy…* from the shortcut menu.

The *Move or Copy* dialog appears.

2.   Select *(move to end)* in the *Before sheet* list.

3.   Check the *Create a copy* check box.

4.   Click the *OK* button.

**Sales First Quarter 2016**

Notice that Excel has named the new worksheet: *First Quarter 2016 (2)*.

7    Change the name of the new worksheet to *February*.

This skill was covered in *Lesson 1-9: View, move, add, rename, delete and navigate worksheet tabs*.

8    Create another copy of the worksheet using *drag and drop*.

There's an even quicker way to create a duplicate worksheet.

1.   Click once on the *First Quarter 2016* tab to select it.

2.   Hold down the **<Ctrl>** key.

3.   Click and hold the mouse button on the *First Quarter 2016* tab.

The cursor changes shape to a page with a plus sign:

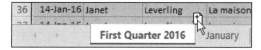

4.   Drag to the right until you see a black insertion arrow to the right of the *February* tab.

When you release the mouse button another copy of the worksheet is created.

9    Change the name of the new worksheet to *March*.

10   Remove rows from the January, February and March workbooks so that only the named month's transactions remain.

This was covered in: *Lesson 3-1: Insert and delete rows and columns*.

11   Save your work as *Sales First Quarter 2016-1*.

# Lesson 6-4: Move and copy worksheets from one workbook to another

In *Lesson 6-3: Duplicate worksheets within a workbook,* you worked with a single workbook.

It is also possible to move and copy worksheets between different workbooks using a similar technique.

1   Close any workbooks that are currently open.

2   Open *Sales First Quarter 2016-1* from your sample files folder (if it isn't already open).

3   Open *First Quarter Sales and Bonus* from your sample files folder.

4   Arrange the windows *Horizontally* in the Excel window.

Click: View→Window→Arrange All→Horizontal.

The two workbooks are now shown together.

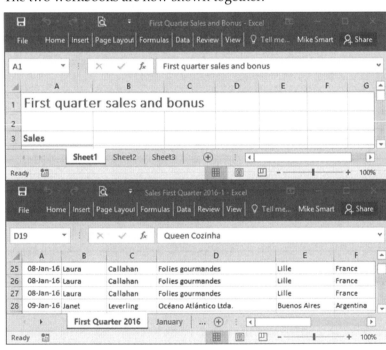

5   Rename *Sheet1* in the *First Quarter Sales and Bonus* workbook to *Bonus*.

This was covered in: *Lesson 1-9: View, move, add, rename, delete and navigate worksheet tabs.*

6   Hold down the **<Ctrl>** key and drag and drop the *Bonus* sheet from the *First Quarter Sales and Bonus* workbook to the *Sales First Quarter 2016-1* workbook.

A copy of the *Bonus* worksheet is created in the *Sales First Quarter 2016-1* workbook.

**First Quarter Sales and Bonus**

**Sales First Quarter 2016-1**

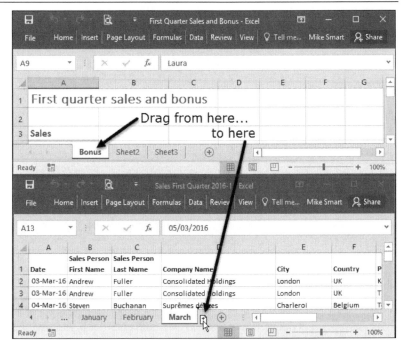

7    Drag and drop the *Sheet3* worksheet from the *First Quarter Sales and Bonus* workbook to the *Sales First Quarter 2016-1* workbook.

You will have to click the *First Quarter Sales and Bonus* workbook once to activate it before you can drag and drop the sheet tab.

This time, because you didn't hold the **<Ctrl>** key down, the worksheet is moved rather than copied.

8    Change the name of the moved worksheet from *Sheet3* to *Summary*.

This skill was covered in: *Lesson 1-9: View, move, add, rename, delete and navigate worksheet tabs.*

9    If necessary, move the worksheet tabs in the *Sales First Quarter 2016-1* workbook so that they appear in the following order:

This was covered in: *Lesson 1-9: View, move, add, rename, delete and navigate worksheet tabs.*

10   Maximize the *Sales First Quarter 2016-1* workbook window.

This was covered in: *Lesson 1-4: Maximize, minimize, re-size, move and close the Excel window.*

11   Save your work as *Sales First Quarter 2016-2*.

# Lesson 6-5: Hide and unhide a worksheet

## note

### Hiding and unhiding a worksheet using the Ribbon

The right-click method is far faster than using the Ribbon but here's how it can be done:

**To *Hide* a worksheet**

Click:

Home→Cells→Format→
Hide & Unhide→Hide Sheet

**To *Unhide* a worksheet**

Click:

Home→Cells→Format→
Hide & Unhide→Unhide Sheet

Then select the sheet that you want to hide/unhide from the dialog and click the OK button.

**Sales First Quarter 2016-2**

Sometimes you'll want to prevent users from viewing and changing one or more worksheets.

In this case you will want to *Hide* the worksheet.

A hidden worksheet becomes invisible to the user but is still there. You can bring back hidden worksheets by *Unhiding* them.

1    Open *Sales First Quarter 2016-2* from your sample files folder (if it isn't already open).

In this workbook you may not want viewers to see the *First Quarter 2016* worksheet as the information is already contained in the *January/February/March* worksheets.

You might also want to hide the *Bonus* worksheet as it contains confidential information.  Note that you should not rely upon hidden worksheets to secure confidential information (see sidebar).

2    Select the *First Quarter 2016* and *Bonus* worksheets.

1.   Click on the *First Quarter 2016* worksheet tab.

2.   Hold down the **<Ctrl>** key.

3.   Click on the *Bonus* worksheet tab.

Both worksheet tabs should now be highlighted:

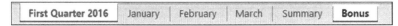

3    Hide the *First Quarter 2016* and *Bonus* worksheets.

The easiest way to do this is to right click either of the selected tabs and then click *Hide* from the shortcut menu.

The worksheets vanish.

It's also possible to do this less efficiently from the Ribbon (see sidebar).

4    Unhide the *Bonus* worksheet.

Excel will never allow you to hide all of the worksheets, so this method of unhiding sheets will always work.

1.   Right-click on any of the visible worksheet tabs.

2.   Click *Unhide* from the shortcut menu.

The *Unhide* dialog is displayed:

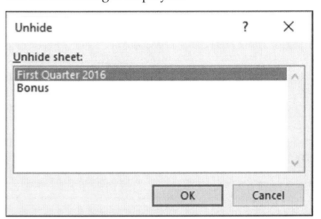

3.   Click *Bonus* and then click the OK button.

You can also unhide the worksheets less efficiently by using the Ribbon (see facing page sidebar).

5    Save your work as *Sales First Quarter 2016-3*.

# Lesson 6-6: Create cross worksheet formulas

You'll often want to summarize information from multiple worksheets within a workbook.

This can be done by simply prefixing the cell reference with the worksheet name followed by an exclamation mark.

1   Open *Sales First Quarter 2016-3* from your sample files folder (if it isn't already open).

2   Select the *January* tab and scroll to the bottom of the range.

3   Type the word **Total:** into the first empty cell in column G (cell G87).

4   Right-align cell G87.

> This was covered in: *Lesson 4-5: Horizontally align the contents of cells.*

5   Bold-face all of row 87.

> This was covered in: *Lesson 1-15: Use the Mini Toolbar, Key Tips and keyboard shortcuts.*

6   Use AutoSum to add totals to columns H and J.

> This was covered in: *Lesson 2-3: Use AutoSum to quickly calculate totals.*

| | G | H | I | J |
|---|---|---|---|---|
| 85 | Gumbär Gummibärchen | 10 | 24.90 | 249.00 |
| 86 | Tourtière | 40 | 5.90 | 236.00 |
| 87 | Total: | 2,401 | | 66,692.80 |

7   Add similar totals to the *February* and *March* worksheets.

8   Select the *Summary* tab.

9   Type the text: **First Quarter Summary** into cell A1 and apply the *Title* cell style.

> This was covered in: *Lesson 4-10: Use cell styles and change themes.*

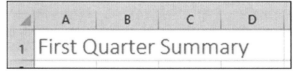

10  Type **Month**, **Units** and **Price** into cells A3, B3 and C3.

11  Type **Jan** into cell A4 and then AutoFill down two cells to add Feb and Mar.

> This was covered in: *Lesson 2-14: Use AutoFill for text and numeric series.*

12  Apply the *Heading 2* style to cells A3:C3.

**Sales First Quarter 2016-3**

13 Apply the *Heading 4* style to cells A4:A6.

14 Add a formula to cell B4 to display the total units sold in January.

1. Click cell B4.

2. Press the equals key on your keyboard (**=**) to begin a formula.

3. Click on the *January* tab.

4. Scroll to the bottom of the screen using the scroll bars or arrow keys, being careful not to click on any cell.

5. Click on cell H87 (the cell with the total units in it).

6. Press the **<Enter>** key on the keyboard.

The total is shown on the *Summary* sheet.

| | A | B | C |
|---|---|---|---|
| 3 | Month | Units | Price |
| 4 | Jan | 2401 | |

15 Use the same technique to add summary totals to **Units** and **Price** for all three months.

| | A | B | C |
|---|---|---|---|
| 3 | Month | Units | Price |
| 4 | Jan | 2401 | 66,692.80 |
| 5 | Feb | 2132 | 41,207.20 |
| 6 | Mar | 1770 | 39,979.90 |

16 Examine the formulas that Excel has created.

Click in cell B4 and then look at the formula bar at the top of the screen. Note that the formula is:

The formula is simply the worksheet name, followed by an exclamation mark, followed by the cell reference.

Note the important sidebar information regarding worksheet names that contain spaces.

17 Save your work as *Sales First Quarter 2016-4*.

## important

## You must use quotation marks if a worksheet name contains spaces

The example worksheet names used in this session do not contain any spaces.

If you had a worksheet called *January Sales* you would have to construct your formula like this:

='January Sales'!K22

Because worksheet names with spaces are more difficult to work with, many Excel users prefer to name their sheets without spaces by capitalizing the first letter of every word.

## Example:

JanuarySales
EuropeIncludingSouthAfrica

# Lesson 6-7: Understand worksheet groups

A very interesting (and little known) feature of Excel is its ability to group worksheets into a three-dimensional array of worksheet cells.

When worksheets are grouped, it is possible to perform a single operation upon all of the worksheets in the group. This can be very useful when you need to:

- Print out all of the worksheets in the group.

- Enter data into the same cell for all worksheets in the group.

- Apply formatting to the same cell or range for all worksheets in the group.

1 Open *Widget Supplies Price List* from your sample files folder.

The formatting of this workbook leaves a lot to be desired. It consists of three worksheets all showing similar information but lacking any style.

| | A | B | C | D | E | F | G |
|---|---|---|---|---|---|---|---|
| 1 | Price List | | | | | | |
| 2 | Prices Effe | 20th March 2016 | | | | | |
| 3 | When calculating prices the following exchange rates will be used | | | | | | |
| 4 | | | | | | | |
| 5 | | USD | GBP | EUR | JPY | | |
| 6 | USD | 1 | 1.49367 | 1.08498 | 0.00816 | | |
| 7 | | | | | | | |
| 8 | Descriptic | Dollars | Pounds | Euros | Yen | | |
| 9 | Standard \ | 3.75 | 2.510595 | 3.456285 | 459.5588 | | |
| 10 | Premium | 5.5 | 3.682206 | 5.069218 | 674.0196 | | |
| 11 | De-luxe g | 7.95 | 5.322461 | 7.327324 | 974.2647 | | |

You're going to use the magic of grouping to format all three worksheets at the same time.

2 Select all three worksheets to create a worksheet group.

1. Click the *Widgets* worksheet tab.

2. Hold down the **<Shift>** key and click the *Sprockets* worksheet tab.

All three tabs now have a white background to show that they are selected.

Something else has also happened. The title bar at the top of the screen now indicates that the worksheets form a worksheet group.

Widget Supplies Price List [Group] - Excel

3 Apply formatting to the *Sprockets* worksheet to make it look attractive.

**Widget Supplies Price List**

When you have grouped every worksheet in a workbook, you have a little problem. You can't switch between worksheets and still keep the group selected. As soon as you click a selected sheet the other two are de-selected.

To work-around this you'll have to insert a new blank worksheet. The sheet's only purpose is to allow you to switch between sheets in the selected group.

1. Add a worksheet called *Dummy*.

2. Select the *Widgets, Grommets* and *Sprockets* group as before.

3. Click on the *Sprockets* tab. The group remains selected and the *Sprockets* worksheet is now active.

4. Apply the comma style to the range B9:E11. This was covered in: *Lesson 4-3: Format numbers using built-in number formats.*

5. Adjust the widths of all columns so that they fully display their contents. This was covered in: *Lesson 2-9: Re-size rows and columns.*

6. Apply the *Title* style to cell A1, the *Heading 4* style to cells A2, A6 and A9:A11 and the *Heading 3* style to cells B5:E5 and A8:E8. This was covered in: *Lesson 4-10: Use cell styles and change themes.*

7. Adjust the height of rows 2, 3 and 4 to tidy the top part of the price list.

8. Click on each of the other two tabs to ensure that columns are also wide enough for their contents. Adjust if needed.

4    With the group still selected, change some exchange rates and the *Prices Effective* date.

I saved the best bit for last. You can now update the exchange rates for all three price lists at the same time. This would be regularly needed as exchange rates fluctuate. When a group of worksheets are selected, any change made to one worksheet is also made to all of the others.

5    Save your work as *Widget Supplies Price List-1*.

# Lesson 6-8: Use find and replace

## note

### Other ways to display the Find and Replace dialog

### Find

Use the <Ctrl>+<F> keyboard shortcut.

### Replace

Use the <Ctrl>+<H> keyboard shortcut.

## note

### Searching only part of a worksheet

If you only select a single cell, *Find and Replace* will search the entire worksheet.

If you select a range of cells, *Find and Replace* will only search within that range.

Excel's find and replace tool is amazingly powerful. There are several special features that can massively shorten many common tasks.

This lesson will explore all of the special features and suggest useful ways in which they can be used to solve real-world problems.

1    Open *Sales First Quarter 2016-4* from your sample files folder (if it isn't already open).

2    Use *Find and Replace* to change the text *Davolio* to *O'Reilly* throughout the workbook.

Nancy Davolio has married Sean O'Reilly and she is very proud of her new name. She's made a special request for you to change her name throughout the workbook too!

1.    Click: Home→Editing→Find & Select→Replace. The *Find and Replace* dialog is displayed.

2.    Click the *Replace* tab.

3.    Type **Davolio** in the *Find what:* text box and **O'Reilly** in the *Replace with:* text box.

4.    Click the *Options>>* button. Options >>

You don't want to only look in the current worksheet, but in all of the worksheets in this workbook so select the *Within: Workbook* option.

5.    Click the *Find Next* button. The first instance of *Davolio* is found on the worksheet.

6.    Click the *Replace* button to replace just this one instance. The cursor moves to the next instance found.

7.    Click *Replace All* to replace all remaining instances of *Davolio* with *O'Reilly*. Excel prompts that it has made 28 replacements.

8.    Click the *OK* and *Close* buttons to close both dialogs.

9.    Examine the worksheets. Notice that Nancy's surname has now changed in every worksheet.

3    Apply the *Good* style to cell G21 on the *January* worksheet.

## note

### Wildcard searches

Sometimes you will only have a partial idea of what you need to find.

In this case you can use the wildcard characters – the asterisk (*) and the question mark (?).

The asterisk means that any number of wildcard letters can occur between the letters.

The question mark means that one wildcard letter can occur for each question mark.

It is easiest to show how wildcards work with a few examples:

C*g  Finds **Containing**
      Finds **Citing**
      Finds **Changing**

S??d Finds **Said**
      Finds **Sand**
      Finds **Seed**
      Doesn't Find **Sound**
      Doesn't Find **Surround**
      Doesn't Find **Sad**

## important

### The Look in: option

Searches are normally done on the contents of the formula bar.

This works well for text entries but can cause problems when searching for values.

Imagine that you want to search for all cells containing the value 25. If you search the formula you will also find cells with values such as =25*A1 while missing cells with formulas such as =5*5.

In this case you'd select **Look in: Values** to find all cells displaying the value 25.

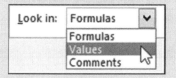

---

Click cell G21 to select it and then click:

Home→Styles→Cell Styles→Good

The *Good* cell style has a light green background and dark green text.

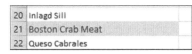

4    Apply the same style to every other mention of *Boston Crab Meat* in the workbook.

1.    With cell G21 still visible on the workbook click:

       Home→Editing→Find & Select→Replace…

2.    Click the *Replace* tab.

3.    Type **Boston Crab Meat** in the *Find what:* text box.

4.    Delete the current contents of the *Replace with* box.

5.    Click the *Format* button drop-down arrow alongside *Replace with:* and select *Choose format from Cell…* from the drop-down menu.

It is really important that you click the lower of the two *Format* buttons. If you get it wrong click: Format→Clear Find Format, to start again.

The cursor shape changes to an eye-dropper. Click on cell G21.

The same format now appears in the *Replace with:* format text box on the *Find and Replace* dialog

6.    Click *Replace All* to re-format all instances of *Boston Crab Meat* to the *Good* cell style. Excel advises that it has changed the format of seven cells.

7.    Click the *OK* and *Close* buttons to close both dialogs.

8.    Examine all of the worksheets and notice that every cell containing the text *Boston Crab Meat* has now turned green.

5    Save your work as *Sales First Quarter 2016-5.*

---

## Session 6: Exercise

**1**    Close any workbooks that are open.

**2**    Open *Exercise 6* from your sample files folder.

**3**    View two copies of the worksheet in different windows stacked horizontally.

**4**    Scroll one of the windows so that the first USA sale is visible in the first row.

**5**    Close the *Exercise 6:2* window and maximize the *Exercise 6:1* window.

**6**    Make two duplicate copies of the *First Quarter 2016* worksheet and name them *USA* and *UK*.

**7**    Delete all of the non USA rows from the USA worksheet and all of the non UK rows from the UK worksheet.

**8**    Hide the *First Quarter 2016* worksheet tab.

**9**    Use AutoSum to create totals at the bottom of Columns H and J (*Quantity* and *Total*) for both the *USA* and *UK* worksheets.

**10**    Add a new worksheet and name it *Summary*.

**11**    Complete the summary sheet as illustrated below using cross-worksheet formulas to calculate the totals.

| Country | Units | Sales |
|---------|-------|-------|
| USA | 913 | 26,572.20 |
| UK | 379 | 7,299.40 |
| Total | 1292 | 33,871.60 |

(USA and UK Sales Summary)

**12**    Save your work as *Exercise 6-End*.

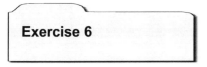

Exercise 6

If you need help slide the page to the left

## Session 6: Exercise answers

These are the questions that students find the most difficult to answer:

| Q 11 | Q 8 | Q 6 | Q 3 and 4 |
|------|-----|-----|-----------|
| In the example the following styles were used:<br><br>A1      Title<br>A3:C3   Heading 2<br>A4:A5   Heading 4<br>A6:C6   Total<br><br>1. Click cell B4 and type an equals sign into it (=).<br><br>2. Click the *USA* tab.<br><br>3. Use the scroll bars to make the total cell (cell H27) visible, being careful not to click on any of the cells within the worksheet.<br><br>4. Click cell H27 and then press the **<Enter>** key.<br><br>This was covered in: *Lesson 6-6: Create cross worksheet formulas.* | 1. Right-click the *First Quarter 2016* worksheet tab.<br><br>2. Click *Hide* on the shortcut menu.<br><br>This was covered in: *Lesson 6-5: Hide and unhide a worksheet.* | 1. Click on the *First Quarter 2016* worksheet tab to select it.<br><br>2. Hold down the **<Ctrl>** key.<br><br>3. Click and drag the *First Quarter 2016* worksheet tab to the right.<br><br>4. Double-click the duplicated worksheet's tab and type the tab's new name.<br><br>This was covered in: *Lesson 6-3: Duplicate worksheets within a workbook.* | 1. Click:<br><br>View→Window→ New Window<br><br>2. Click:<br><br>View→Window→ Arrange All<br><br>3. Click the *Horizontal* option in the *Arrange Windows* dialog.<br><br>4. Click the OK button.<br><br>5. Scroll one of the windows to the first USA sale (Row 21).<br><br>This was covered in: *Lesson 6-1: View the same workbook in different windows.* |

If you have difficulty with the other questions, here are the lessons that cover the relevant skills:

**1**    Refer to: **Lesson 1-4: Maximize, minimize, re-size, move and close the Excel window.**

**2**    Refer to: **Lesson 1-5: Download the sample files and open/navigate a workbook.**

**5**    Refer to: **Lesson 6-1: View the same workbook in different windows.**

**7**    Refer to: **Lesson 3-1: Insert and delete rows and columns.**

**9**    Refer to: **Lesson 2-3: Use AutoSum to quickly calculate totals.**

**10**    Refer to: **Lesson 1-9: View, move, add, rename, delete and navigate worksheet tabs.**

**12**    Refer to: **Lesson 1-6: Save a workbook.**

# Session Seven: Printing Your Work

> The greatest misfortune that ever befell man was the invention of printing.
>
> *Benjamin Disraeli, British Prime Minister and Novelist (1804-1881).*

As the world of commerce moves nearer to the paperless office, printing will become less important.

In the last few years, screen and rendering technology have improved to the extent that I now prefer to read on-screen rather than from paper.

Apple now claim that their "retina" display has such a high pixel density that the human eye is unable to notice pixelation at a typical viewing distance. This suggests that there is no longer any quality advantage in printing on paper.

Perhaps the world is not far away from a time when all communication will be done electronically, but in today's world, paper printed documents are still used in many areas of business.

Excel has a range of tools that will allow you to present your work as polished and professional printed reports. This session will give you all of the skills you need to control every aspect of printing your work on paper.

## Session Objectives

By the end of this session you will be able to:

- Print Preview and change paper orientation

- Use Page Layout view to adjust margins

- Use Page Setup to set margins more precisely and center the worksheet

- Set paper size and scale

- Insert, delete and preview page breaks

- Adjust page breaks using Page Break Preview

- Add auto-headers and auto-footers and set the starting page number

- Add custom headers and footers

- Specify different headers and footers for the first, odd and even pages

- Print only part of a worksheet

- Add row and column data labels and grid lines to printed output

- Print several selected worksheets and change the page order

- Suppress error messages in printouts

# Lesson 7-1: Print Preview and change paper orientation

1    Open *Sales Report* from your sample files folder.

Make sure that you open the Session 7 *Sales Report* file as there's also a sample file of the same name in an earlier session.

2    *Print Preview* the worksheet to see how it will look on paper.

1. Click: File→Print.

   The *Backstage View* appears, showing a preview of the printed page in the right-hand pane.

2. Click the *Next Page* and *Previous Page* buttons to page through the document.

## tip

### Add a print preview button to the Quick Access toolbar

I use the *Backstage Print View* so often that I like to display it with a single click (instead of two). To do this I always add the *Print Preview and Print* button to the Quick Access Toolbar.

I recommend that this button is a "must have" for the Quick Access Toolbar.

You learned how to add buttons to the Quick Access Toolbar in:
*Lesson 1-14: Customize the Quick Access Toolbar and preview the printout.*

The above lesson also includes a screen grab of my own heavily modified Quick Access Toolbar and may give you more ideas for buttons you'd like to add.

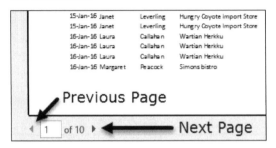

Notice that the paper isn't wide enough to show all of the columns. Excel tries to help out by printing the left-most columns across the first five or six pages followed by the right-most columns on the next five or six pages.

**Sales Report for First Quarter 2016**

| Date | Sales Person First Name | Sales Person Last Name | Company Name | City | Country |
|---|---|---|---|---|---|
| 01-Jan-16 | Nancy | Davolio | Eastern Connection | London | UK |
| 01-Jan-16 | Nancy | Davolio | Eastern Connection | London | UK |
| 01-Jan-16 | Nancy | Davolio | Eastern Connection | London | UK |

| Product Name | Qty | Unit Price | Total |
|---|---|---|---|
| Thüringer Rostbratwurst | 21 | 99.00 | 2,079.00 |
| Steeleye Stout | 35 | 14.40 | 504.00 |
| Maxilaku | 30 | 16.00 | 480.00 |

You would have to take the two pages, cut them with scissors, and tape them together in order to see all of the rows and columns.

3    Change the paper orientation to *Landscape* in order to print more columns on each sheet of paper.

Click the drop-down arrow next to *Portrait Orientation* in the center pane of the *Backstage View* and then click on *Landscape Orientation*.

Sales Report

In *Landscape* orientation the paper is printed as if it had been put into the printer sideways.

The printout is very nearly there now, but there is still a problem with the last column which prints out all on its own.

### Sales Report for First Quarter 2016

| Date | Sales Person First Name | Sales Person Last Name | Company Name | City | Country | Product Name | Qty | Unit Price |
|---|---|---|---|---|---|---|---|---|
| 01-Jan-16 | Nancy | Davolio | Eastern Connection | London | UK | Thüringer Rostbratwurst | 21 | 99.00 |
| 01-Jan-16 | Nancy | Davolio | Eastern Connection | London | UK | Steeleye Stout | 35 | 14.40 |
| 01-Jan-16 | Nancy | Davolio | Eastern Connection | London | UK | Maxilaku | 30 | 16.00 |

| Total |
|---|
| 2,079.00 |
| 504.00 |
| 480.00 |

You'll discover a solution to this problem later in: *Lesson 7-2: Use Page Layout view to adjust margins.*

4 **Print a copy of the worksheet.**

If you'd like to save the forests (and save the cost of sixteen sheets of paper), you may wish to skip this step.

Click the *Print* button.

Print

Even if you didn't actually print the worksheet, I'm sure you will believe that the printout would not have been very good. You'd be back to the scissors and tape if you wanted the pages to show that missing last column.

The printout would have been in *Landscape* orientation because you've told Excel to do that.

5 **Save your work as *Sales Report-1.***

# Lesson 7-2: Use Page Layout view to adjust margins

You discovered how to change between Excel's three "views" in: *Lesson 1-16: Understand views.*

*Page Layout View* is a bit like *Print Preview* as you can see just how your page prints. The big difference is that, unlike *Print Preview,* you can edit a worksheet in this view. You can also set up many page layout features including margins, headers, footers and page numbering.

You'll be exploring all of this view's features in coming lessons. This lesson will focus upon changing the page margins (the blank areas at the top, bottom, left and right of the printout).

1    Open *Sales Report-1* from your sample files folder (if it isn't already open).

2    Display *Page Layout* view.

The fastest way to do this is to click the *Page Layout* button on the status bar at the bottom right of the screen.

You can also do this from the Ribbon by clicking:

View→Workbook Views→Page Layout

Page layout shows almost exactly how the worksheet will print.

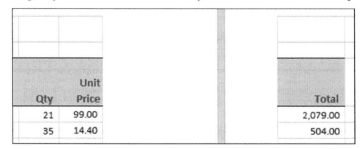

The missing *Total* problem is immediately obvious.

3    Make sure that the rulers are visible.

Unless you've turned them off, you'll see a ruler at the top and left of the page that contains the active cell.

Click cell A1, to make it the active cell, and look for the rulers.

Rulers

Sales Report for Fi

Sales Report-1

**note**

**Changing ruler units to inches, centimeters or millimeters**

1.  Click:

    File→Options→
    Advanced→
    Display→Ruler units

2.  Select *Inches, Centimeters* or *Millimeters* from the *Ruler Units* drop-down list.


**note**

**Can I change the default margin settings?**

You can set the default margins, and any other Excel default setting, by incorporating the margin settings into a replacement *Blank Workbook* template.

The technique of using a replacement *Blank Workbook* template to change default settings is discussed in: *Lesson 4-9: Understand themes (sidebar).*

If you don't see the rulers, switch them on by clicking:

View→Show→Ruler

4    Adjust the left margin using the rulers.

1.  Select column A.

    Notice how a portion of the ruler above column A is shaded green. This gives you a visual indication of where the margin begins.

2.  Hover the mouse cursor over the left-hand side of the ruler's green shaded section.

    The cursor shape changes to a double headed arrow and the current left-hand margin size is displayed. (See sidebar if the margin doesn't display in centimeters)

3.  When you see the double-headed arrow, click and drag to the left to reduce the margin to about one centimeter. You'll probably find it impossible to set exactly 1.0 centimeters with this method and will have to settle for 1.01.

    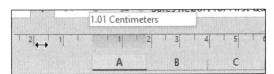

    All of the columns now fit onto one page.

| Sales Report for First Quarter 2016 | | | | | | | | | |
|---|---|---|---|---|---|---|---|---|---|
| Date | Sales Person First Name | Sales Person Last Name | Company Name | City | Country | Product Name | Qty | Unit Price | Total |
| 01-Jan-16 | Nancy | Davolio | Eastern Connection | London | UK | Thüringer Rostbratwurst | 21 | 99.00 | 2,079.00 |
| 01-Jan-16 | Nancy | Davolio | Eastern Connection | London | UK | Steeleye Stout | 35 | 14.40 | 504.00 |

5    Save your work as *Sales Report-2*.

# Lesson 7-3: Use Page Setup to set margins more precisely and center the worksheet

In the last lesson you adjusted the left margin using the horizontal ruler, and that's often the best way. It is quick and easy and you can immediately see the results of the change on the printed output.

Sometimes you will want the pages in your report to have precise margins. This would be the case when you were going to insert the report into another report (perhaps prepared in Word) and you need the margins to be consistent throughout the publication.

Another common requirement is the need to center the report on the printed page.

1 Open *Sales Report-2* from your sample files folder (if it isn't already open).

2 Display *Page Layout* view (if you aren't already in it).

This was covered in: *Lesson 7-2: Use Page Layout view to adjust margins.*

3 Set margins to the *Narrow* preset.

1. Click: Page Layout→Page Setup→Margins.

A rich menu appears, showing three preset margin setups along with the last custom margins applied.

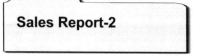
Sales Report-2

2. Click the *Narrow* option to apply left and right margins of 0.64cm.

Notice that all of the margins have now changed to the *Narrow* specification.

4   Set a custom left and right margin of exactly one centimeter.

Imagine that this report will be bound within another that uses margins of one centimeter.

Since there's no suitable preset you'll have to apply the margins manually using the *Custom Margins* options.

1.  Click:

    Page Layout→Page Setup→Margins→Custom Margins…

    The *Page Setup* dialog appears with the *Margins* tab selected.

2.  Type directly into the text boxes, or use the spin buttons, to set the left and right margins to exactly one centimeter.

3.  Click the OK button.

5   Horizontally center the printout on the page.

The page would look better centered.

1.  Bring up the *Page Setup* dialog again by clicking:

    Page Layout→Page Setup→Margins→Custom Margins…

2.  Check the *Center on page Horizontally* check box.

3.  Click the OK button.

    The page is now perfectly centered, both on the screen and on any hard copy printed.

6   Save your work as *Sales Report-3.*

# Lesson 7-4: Set paper size and scale

Imagine that *Landscape* orientation isn't an option for you.

You need *Portrait* orientation and you simply must get all of the columns on each page.

There's only two ways you can achieve this.

1. Buy some bigger paper. As long as your printer can accept it, you will have a larger area upon which to print.

2. Print everything in a smaller font.

The second option often works well (as long as you have good eyesight).

You'll be relieved to know that you don't have to manually re-format every font on the page. You can automatically scale the existing fonts to fit.

1    Open *Sales Report-3* from your sample files folder (if it isn't already open).

2    Display *Page Layout* view (if you aren't already in it).

This was covered in: *Lesson 7-2: Use Page Layout view to adjust margins*.

3    Change the paper orientation back to *Portrait*.

Click: Page Layout→Page Setup→Orientation→Portrait.

Notice that the columns no longer fit upon one sheet of paper.

| City | Country | | Product Name |
|------|---------|--|--------------|
| London | UK | | Thüringer Rostbratwurst |
| London | UK | | Steeleye Stout |

4    Change the paper size to A3.

You will not see an A3 paper option if there are no printer drivers installed on your machine that support A3 (see sidebar).

Click: Page Layout→Page Setup→Size→A3.

In the USA and Canada, the nearest equivalent of A3 is ANSI B 17X11 (see sidebar on the facing page for more on this). For the purposes of this lesson you should still set the size to A3 if you are able to.

That works fine. All columns now fit across one sheet of A3 paper.

But what if you don't have an A3 printer, or if the report has to fit on a sheet of A4 (or Letter sized) paper?

5    Change the paper size to A4 (or Letter) sized.

In every country in the world except the USA and Canada the normal business paper size is A4.

Sales Report-3

## trivia

### A4 and Letter paper size

A long time ago everybody used different sizes of paper until the Germans produced a DIN standard (Din 476) in 1922.

So good was their DIN standard (that defined the familiar A0, A1, A2, A3, A4... A8 sizes) that it was gradually adopted by every country in the world except the United States and Canada. It is also the official United Nations document format.

As Din 476 was now a world standard, it was ratified in 1975 as ISO 216.

The genius behind the guiding principle of ISO 216 was the German scientist George Lichtenburg (1742-1799). George noticed that if a sheet of paper with an aspect ratio of the square root of two was folded in half, each half would also have the same aspect ratio.

The wonderful thing about this system is that paper merchants only need to stock one size of paper (A0) to be able to cut A1, A2, A3, A4...A8 without any waste. It also means that a document designed in any A size will perfectly scale to all other sizes in the series.

A0 has an area of 1 square meter. Fold it in half and you have A1. Fold that in half for A2, then in half again for A3 and so on.

The USA and Canada are the only major countries that use a different system.

In 1995 the American National Standards institute defined a series of paper sizes based upon 8.5"X11" *Letter sized* paper. Unlike the ISO standard, the arbitrary size means that the series has alternating aspect ratios for other derivative sizes.

The ANSI A size (8.5X11) is the nearest to ISO A4 and the ANSI B size (17X11) is nearest to A3.

In the USA and Canada, the slightly narrower and longer Letter size (or ANSI A) is the most common.

Click: Page Layout→Page Setup→Size→A4.

6   Make the report fit on a sheet of A4 (or Letter size) paper by scaling the print.

Click the Page Layout→Scale to Fit→Scale spin button. Each time you reduce the percentage, the worksheet shrinks until it fits the page at about 70%.

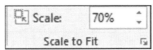

Bear in mind that, even though it fits the page, the information on the page may not be very easy to read at such a small type size.

Another method of achieving the same result would have been to set the *Width* to one page.

The advantage of this approach is that the content will perfectly fit between the page margins. This will look better and will avoid the need to center the printout on the page.

7   Save your work as *Sales Report-4.*

# Lesson 7-5: Insert, delete and preview page breaks

## note

### If you don't see the dotted line page breaks, somebody has switched them off

By default, automatic page breaks are shown as dotted lines in *Normal* view. Manually inserted page breaks are shown as solid lines.

Like so many features in Excel, Microsoft has given users the ability to switch this feature off, though I can't imagine why anybody would want to.

If you don't see the dotted lines, somebody has done just that on your machine.

To bring the dotted lines back click:

File→Options→
Advanced→
Display Options for This Worksheet→Show Page Breaks

This check box needs to be checked in order to display page breaks in *Normal* view.

After you've either printed a worksheet (or entered *Page Layout* view or *Page Break Preview* and then returned to *Normal* view), you will see thin dotted lines indicating where the page will break.

Sometimes you need to take control of page breaks. This lesson will show you how.

1 Open *Sales Analysis Chart* from your sample file folder.

Note that no page breaks are shown. This is because the worksheet has never been printed or previewed.

2 Use the *Backstage Print* view to Print Preview the worksheet.

Click: File→Print.

The *Print Preview* reveals that the printout will cut the pie chart in half:

| | | | |
|---|---|---|---|
| 09-Oct-15 Germany | Dairy Products | 1,112.00 | USA |
| 10-Oct-15 Spain | Condiments | 422.40 | Venezuela |
| 10-Oct-15 Spain | Grains/Cereals | 249.60 | **Grand Total** |
| 10-Oct-15 Spain | Beverages | 310.00 | |
| 11-Oct-15 Sweden | Beverages | 304.00 | |
| 11-Oct-15 Sweden | Dairy Products | 672.00 | |
| 11-Oct-15 Sweden | Seafood | 579.60 | |

You need to solve this problem by inserting a vertical page break.

3 Return to *Normal* view and notice that page breaks are shown as dotted lines.

Click the *Back Button* at the top left of *Backstage View* to return to *Normal* view and notice the dotted lines showing the vertical and horizontal page breaks.

If you don't see any dotted lines, somebody may have disabled them. See the sidebar for instructions on how to switch them back on.

It is immediately clear where the problem lies. The vertical break needs to occur at the left of column E to solve the problem.

4 Insert a page break to the left of column E.

1. Click cell E1. It is important to choose row 1, otherwise both a horizontal and vertical page break would be inserted.

2. Click: Page Layout→Page Setup→Breaks→Insert Page Break.

**Sales Analysis Chart**

A solid line appears to the left of the active cell to show the new position of the vertical page break. When you see a solid line (rather than a dotted line) you know that the break was manually inserted (rather than automatically added by Excel).

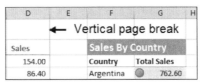

5 Confirm that the worksheet will now print correctly.

1. Click: File→Print to Print Preview the worksheet (or view the page in *Page Layout* view) and move to the last page in the printout to confirm that the worksheet will now print correctly.

2. Click the *Back Button* at the top left of *Backstage View* to return to *Normal* view.

6 Insert a horizontal page break above row 78.

Row 78 displays the first sale for November 2015.

| 75 | 31-Oct-15 Germany | Beverages | 216.00 |
|----|-------------------|-----------|--------|
| 76 | | | 37,515.73 |
| 77 | | | |
| 78 | 01-Nov-15 USA | Condiments | 616.00 |

For presentational reasons you want November's sales to begin on a new page, so you need to insert a page break above row 78.

1. Click in cell A78. It's important to click in column A otherwise both a horizontal and vertical page break would be inserted to the left of, and above the active cell.

2. Click: Page Layout→Page Setup→Breaks→Insert Page Break.

A solid line appears above the active cell (row 78) to show the position of the new (manually inserted) horizontal page break.

7 Confirm that the worksheet will now print correctly.

Print Preview the worksheet or view the page in *Page Layout* view.

The page now breaks at row 77 and a new page begins for row 78.

8 Remove the horizontal page break above row 78.

1. Click anywhere in row 78 except cell E78. If you were to select cell E78 you would remove both the horizontal and vertical page breaks.

2. Click: Page Layout→Page Setup→Breaks→Remove Page Break.

The solid line disappears, indicating that the page will no longer break before row 78.

9 Save your work as *Sales Analysis Chart-1*.

# Lesson 7-6: Adjust page breaks using Page Break Preview

In the last lesson you learned how to adjust page breaks in *Normal* view. Many users also like to adjust page breaks in *Page Layout* view.

Microsoft recommends that you don't use either. There's a purpose-built view just to handle page breaks called *Page Break Preview* view.

I tie my tongue in knots during my classes just trying to say *Page Break Preview view*!

This view allows you to click and drag page breaks (something that you can't do with the other views).

1   Open *Sales Analysis Chart-1* from your sample file folder (if it isn't already open).

2   Display *Page Break Preview* view.

Click the *Page Break Preview* button at the bottom right of the screen.

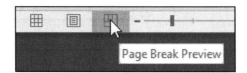

You can also select this view from the Ribbon by clicking:

View→Workbook Views→Page Break Preview

Just like *Normal View*, *Page Break Preview* allows you to see which breaks are manual and which are automatic. Breaks shown as solid lines were manually inserted. Breaks shown as dotted lines were automatically inserted by Excel.

| | A | B | C | D | E |
|---|---|---|---|---|---|
| 48 | 21-Oct-15 | France | Confections | 100.00 | |
| 49 | 22-Oct-15 | Ireland | Beverages | 85.12 | |
| 50 | 22-Oct-15 | Ireland | Dairy Products | 200.00 | |
| 51 | 22-Oct-15 | Ireland | Dairy Products | 122.88 | |

Notice that your manually inserted vertical break (to the left of column E) is shown as a solid line while Excel's automatic page break (after row 49) is shown as a dotted line.

3   Move the automatic break from between rows 99 and 100 to between rows 77 and 78.

1.   Move the mouse cursor over the dotted blue line between rows 99 and 100 until you see the double-headed arrow cursor shape.

| 99 | 12-Nov-15 | Portugal | Meat/Poultry |
|---|---|---|---|
| 100 | 13-Nov-15 | Austria | Dairy Products |

**Sales Analysis Charts-1**

2. When you see the double-headed arrow, click and drag to move the page break up the page so that the line is between rows 77 and 78.

| 77 | | | | | |
|---|---|---|---|---|---|
| 78 | 01-Nov-15 | USA | Condiments | 616.00 | |

When you release the mouse button, the page break is shown as a solid blue line.

| 77 | | | | | |
|---|---|---|---|---|---|
| 78 | 01-Nov-15 | USA | Condiments | 616.00 | |

4    Automatically scale the sheet so that all of November's sales fit on one sheet.

An interesting feature of *Page Break Preview* is its ability to scale a page to fit the paper. You did this manually in: *Lesson 7-4: Set paper size and scale*. The process is far more intuitive in this view.

1. Scroll to row 127. Notice that there is an automatic page break between rows 127 and 128.

2. Drag this page break to a new position between rows 145 and 146.

   Excel hasn't inserted another automatic break anywhere in Page 3 even though Page 3 is now a lot longer than it was before. The only way that Excel can possibly print Page 3 is by automatically scaling it down to fit the page.

3. Click: File→Print to Print Preview the worksheet and notice that the fonts for the entire report have been reduced. Excel cannot scale a single page in isolation; it scales all pages to keep the font size of all report pages consistent.

4. Click the *Back Button*  at the top left of *Backstage View* to return to *Page Break Preview* view.

5    Remove all manually applied page breaks.

Excel's automatic scaling system means that it is easy to lose track of what is happening. Sometimes you want to set everything back to the way it used to be and start again.

Click: Page Layout→Page Setup→Breaks→Reset All Page Breaks.

All solid lines disappear and Excel's automatic page breaks (shown as dotted lines) reappear.

6    Save your work as *Sales Analysis Chart-2*.

---

---

# Lesson 7-7: Add auto-headers and auto-footers and set the starting page number

Headers and footers are displayed at the top and bottom of each printed page.

If you are printing a long report it is very useful to add page numbers. Other items commonly added to page headers and footers include:

- A title.
- The date and time that the report was printed.
- The report author's name.
- The name of the Excel file that was used to generate the report.
- The full path to the Excel file.
- A company logo.
- Copyright notices.
- A distribution list or the security level of the document (for example you may want to include the word: *Confidential*).

1 Open *Sales Report-4* from your sample files folder.

2 Display *Page Layout* view (if you aren't already in it).

This was covered in: *Lesson 7-2: Use Page Layout view to adjust margins.*

3 Click in the page header area at the top of the screen.

The page header area contains the text: *Add header.*

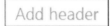

When you click in this area a new tab appears on the Ribbon.

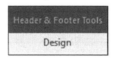

You will use this tab to access Excel's *Auto Header and Footer* feature.

4 Add an Auto Header that will display page numbers at the top of each page in the format: *Page 1.*

When you click in the header area you are able to access the *Header & Footer Tools Design* tab.

1. Click:

   Header & Footer Tools→Design→Header & Footer→Header

2. Choose the option *Page 1* (see sidebar). Page numbers are now shown at the top of each page (you may need to scroll up and down the page to see the page number update).

Sales Report-4

5    Add an Auto-footer to show the filename at the bottom of the page.

   1.    Click in the *Add footer* area at the bottom of the page.

      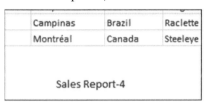

   2.    Click:

      Header & Footer Tools→Design→Header & Footer→Footer

   3.    Choose the *Sales Report-4* item from the drop-down list (see sidebar).

      The filename is now shown at the bottom of every page in the report (you may need to scroll up and down the page to see the footer update).

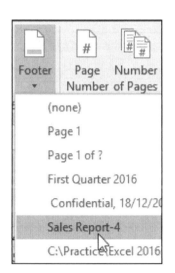

6    Change the page numbering so that numbering begins at page ten.

   It is very common to print an Excel report and then collate it into another report (perhaps produced using Word). If the pages were to be inserted after page nine you would want Excel to begin numbering at page ten.

   1.    Click: Page Layout→Page Setup→Dialog Launcher.

   2.    Click the *Page* tab and type the number 10 into the *First page number* text box.

      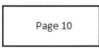

      Click the OK button. Page numbering now begins at Page 10.

      Page 10

7    Save your work as *Sales Report-5.*

# Lesson 7-8: Add custom headers and footers

Auto-headers and footers provide a quick and convenient method when your needs are simple. Custom headers allow you to combine your own text with report fields (such as page numbers). You are also able to add text to three different sections in the header and footer areas (Left, Right and Center).

1 Open *Sales Report-5* from your sample files folder (if it isn't already open).

2 Display *Page Layout* view (if you aren't already in it).

This was covered in: *Lesson 7-2: Use Page Layout view to adjust margins.*

3 Click in the *Page Header* area.

Notice that when you click the *Page Header* area the contents change from **Page 10** to **Page &[Page].**

The Ampersand (&) is called an *escape character*. It tells Excel that whatever text follows is a field rather than literal text. The field &[Page] tells Excel to insert the current page number.

4 Change the page header to: *The Gourmet Food Company*.

Click in the center of the header area (where you currently see the page number) and type **The Gourmet Food Company**

5 Place the date and time on the left-hand part of the page header.

There's no Auto-header for date and time. In this case you'll have to create your own custom header field.

1. Click in the **left-hand** section of the header area.

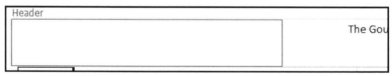

2. Type the text **Printed on:** followed by a space.

3. Click: Header & Footer Tools→Design→ Header & Footer Elements→Current Date.

4. Type a space followed by **at:** and then another space.

5. Click: Header & Footer Tools→Design→ Header & Footer Elements→Current Time.

The left-hand section of the header bar now contains the following text:

> Header
> Printed on: &[Date] at: &[Time]

## note

### Adding a graphical header

Sometimes you will need a page header that requires more sophisticated formatting than Excel is capable of. The solution is to create the header as a graphic using a program such as Adobe Photoshop.

When the graphic has been prepared click:

Header & Footer→Design→ Header & Footer Elements→ Picture

Picture

You are then able to insert the graphic into the header.

When a graphic appears in the header a new *Format Picture* button appears in *the Header & Footer Elements* group.

When you click away from the header section the date and time are displayed. The date is displayed in a format dictated by the locale of your operating system. In this example it is the date: Aug 22, 2018 displayed in UK format (day/month/year):

> Printed on 22/08/2018 at: 14:34

6    Place the page number on the right-hand side of the page header.

There is an *Auto Header* for this purpose, but you can't use it. Auto headers may only be used in the center section of the header. You'll have to make your own using the *Header & Footer Elements* just as you did for the date and time.

1. Click in the right-hand part of the page header and type **Page:** followed by a space (the last space won't appear on screen but don't worry, it is there).

2. Click: Header & Footer Tools→Design→ Header & Footer Elements→Page Number.

3. The right-hand section of the header bar now contains the following text:

> Page: &[Page]

When you click away from the header section, the current page number is displayed:

> Page: 10

---

Printed on: 26/09/2017 at: 12:58                    The Gourmet Food Company                    Page: 10

---

7    Apply an attractive format to the page header section.

1. Click the left-hand section of the header. The text is automatically selected.

> Header
> Printed on: &[Date] at &[Time]

## note

### Good design practice

It is always a good idea to restrict your font choice to one of the two provided by the current theme.

The reasons for this are discussed in *Lesson 4-11: Add color and gradient effects to cells* (sidebar).

2. Click: Home→Font→Font and set the font face to *Calibri Light 10 Point Bold*. Note that, following good design practice, this is one of the two theme fonts (see sidebar).

3. Click: Home→Font→Font Color and set the color to the *Blue-Gray, Text 2* theme color.

4. Apply the same format to the right-hand section of the header.

5. Format the center section of the header as *Calibri Light, 28 point, Blue-Gray, Text 2*.

---

Printed on: 26/09/2017 at: 13:00          The Gourmet Food Company          Page: 10

---

8    Save your work as *Sales Report-6*.

# Lesson 7-9: Specify different headers and footers for the first, odd and even pages

If you look at the pages in this book, you'll notice that there's a different header and footer for odd and even pages. The first page of each session is also different.

If the sample worksheet needed to be inserted into a publication similar to this one, you'd need to specify three different headers and footers, one for odd pages, one for even pages, and one for the first page.

1    *Open Sales Report-6 from your sample files folder (if it isn't already open.*

2    Display *Normal* view (if you aren't already in it).

    Click the *Normal* view button at the bottom right of the screen.

3    Insert five blank rows above row 1.

    This was covered in: *Lesson 3-1: Insert and delete rows and columns.*

4    Insert a manual page break above row 6.

    This was covered in: *Lesson 7-5: Insert, delete and preview page breaks.*

    A solid line appears above row 6.

    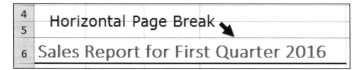

5    Merge and center cells A2:J2 and enter the text: **Sales Report Jan-Mar 2016** into the merged cell.

    This was covered in: *Lesson 4-6: Merge cells, wrap text and expand/collapse the formula bar.*

6    Apply the *Title* style to the newly added text.

    This was covered in: *Lesson 4-10: Use cell styles and change themes.*

7    Merge and center cells A3:J3 and enter the text: **Private & Confidential.**

8    Apply the *Heading 4* style to the newly added text.

9    Apply a fill color of *Blue, Accent1, Lighter 80%* to cells A2:A3.

10   Resize Row 1 so that it is about 200 pixels deep.

11   *Print Preview* the worksheet.

    Click: File→Print.

Sales Report-6

You can see that you've created a cover sheet for the report. It doesn't look bad but the header and footer are spoiling things. You need to suppress the header and footer from the cover sheet.

12    Remove the header and footer from the first (cover) page.

1.    Click the *Back Button* 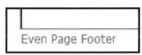 at the top left of *Backstage View* to return to *Normal* View.

2.    Change the view to *Page Layout* View.

3.    Click in the *Header* area of the first page.

4.    Click: Header & Footer Tools→Design→ Options→Different First Page.

The header and footer information vanishes from the cover page.

13    Set a different odd and even page header and footer.

1.    Click in the *Header* area.

2.    Click Header & Footer Tools→Design→ Options→Different Odd & Even Pages.

The header and footer information vanishes from odd pages but remains on even pages.

14    Remove all header and footer information.

You're going to replace the existing page header and footer, so delete the contents of all header and footer sections.

15    Add odd and even page footers so that the page number appears on the right of all odd pages and on the left of all even pages.

If you look at the footer of this book, you will see that the page numbers are arranged in this manner.

1.    Click in the footer area of any of the pages except the first page.

Notice that when you click in the footer area, Excel indicates which footer you are editing (odd or even).

```
|
|
| Even Page Footer
```

2.    Insert a page number into the odd and even page footer area.

If you're wondering why Excel thinks that even pages are odd, and odd pages are even, see the sidebar for an explanation.

While a cover page is useful in all reports, the different odd and even page headers will only improve the presentation of reports that will be printed on both sides of the paper and then bound.

16    Save your work as *Sales Report-7.*

## Important

### Page numbering confusion

You have set this workbook to begin its page numbering at page 10 (an even page).

As far as Excel is concerned the "real" starting page number is page one (an odd page).

This can cause a little confusion as you will find:

```
Even Page Header
|
```

... at the top of the second page in this report even though it has a page number of eleven and is thus an odd page.

Excel uses the "real" page numbers when it labels the page header and footer areas.

## note

### Print areas do not have to be contiguous

You may want to print several different sections from your worksheet.

Simply select the non-contiguous (non-adjacent) ranges (covered in: *Lesson 2-7: Select non-contiguous cell ranges and view summary information*) and then use either of the techniques discussed in this lesson to print the selected cells.

**Sales Report-7**

# Lesson 7-10: Print only part of a worksheet

Sometimes you will want to print a selection of cells from a worksheet.

Excel provides two ways to do this. The first method is applicable when the requirement is a one-off. In other words, the next time you print, the entire worksheet will be printed in the usual way.

The second method involves setting a print area. If you then save the worksheet, the defined print area will remain until you clear the print area.

In this lesson you'll explore both methods.

1 Open *Sales Report-7* from your sample files folder (if it isn't already open.

2 Display *Normal* view (if you aren't already in it).

Click the *Normal* view button at the bottom right of the screen.

Imagine that you need to print a listing for all of January's sales.

3 Select all of the transactions for January 2016 (cells A8:J93).

4 Print only the selected cells.

1. Click: File→Print.

    The *Backstage Print* view is displayed showing many print settings along with a print preview.

    Notice the first option in the *Settings* list currently shows:

    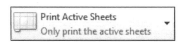

2. Click the drop-down arrow and select *Print Selection* from the drop-down list:

    Notice that only January transactions (cells A8:J93) are now displayed in the right-hand *Print Preview* window.

    If you were to click the *Print* button at this stage only January sales would be printed.

5 Save, close and re-open the workbook and then enter *Backstage Print* view.

1.  Save and close *Sales Report-7*.

2.  Re-open *Sales Report-7*.

3.  Click: File→Print to return to *Backstage Print* view.

    Notice that the print settings have reverted to *Print Active Sheets*.

    In other words, the instruction to only print the selected cells is lost when the workbook is closed.

    But consider the case of a worksheet where you will only ever want to print a selected range. In this case you'd like the print settings to be saved with the workbook.

6   Set the print area to Jan 2016 transactions (A8:J93).

    1.  Click the *Back Button* ⬅ at the top left of *Backstage View* to return to *Normal* View.

    2.  Select cells A8:J93.

    3.  Click: Page Layout→Page Setup→Print Area→Set Print Area.

        When you set the print area it remains set even if you close and re-open a workbook.

    4.  Click: File→Print to return to *Backstage Print* view.

        Notice that only January sales are shown in the preview in the right pane of the window.

7   Save, close and re-open the workbook and then enter *Backstage Print* view.

    1.  Save and close *Sales Report-7*.

    2.  Re-open *Sales Report-7*.

    3.  Click: File→Print to return to *Backstage Print* view.

        Notice that only January sales are still shown in the preview in the right pane of the window, proving that the print area was saved with the workbook

8   Clear the print area.

    1.  Click the *Back Button* ⬅ at the top left of *Backstage View* to return to *Normal* View.

    2.  Click: Page Layout→Page Setup→Print Area→ Clear Print Area.

9   Print preview to prove that the full worksheet will be printed in future.

    Click: File→Print to enter *Backstage Print* view.

    Notice that the cover sheet, along with all sales, are now shown in the preview in the right pane of the window.

10  Save *Sales-Report 7*.

## note

### The print area is implemented using a named range

Excel has a feature called "named ranges". The definition and use of named ranges is an expert-level skill covered in the next book in this series: *Learn Excel 2016 Expert Skills with The Smart Method*.

When you set a print area, Excel simply creates a sheet-level named range called *Print Area* for the currently active worksheet. Each worksheet can have its own print area.

If you do progress to become an Excel Expert, it is possible to define this named range manually and to use it in formulas.

# Lesson 7-11: Add row and column data labels and grid lines to printed output

1 Open *Sales Report-7* from your sample files folder (if it isn't already open).

2 View the worksheet in *Page Layout* view.

There's a slight problem with this worksheet. The first page is easy to understand as it has a column header row to indicate which data is in each column (such as Date, City and Company Name):

| Sales Report for First Quarter 2016 | | | | |
|---|---|---|---|---|
| Date | Sales Person First Name | Sales Person Last Name | Company Name | City |
| 01-Jan-16 | Nancy | Davolio | Eastern Connection | London |
| 01-Jan-16 | Nancy | Davolio | Eastern Connection | London |

The second page isn't so easy to understand because the column header row is missing:

| | | | |
|---|---|---|---|
| 23-Jan-16 | Robert | King | Mère Paillarde |
| 23-Jan-16 | Robert | King | Mère Paillarde |
| 24-Jan-16 | Michael | Suyama | La maison d'Asie |
| 24-Jan-16 | Michael | Suyama | La maison d'Asie |

3 Add column headings to each printed page.

1. Click: Page Layout→Page Setup→Print Titles.

The *Page Setup* dialog is displayed with the *Sheet* tab selected.

2. Click inside the *Rows to repeat at top* text box.

3. Select all of row 8 by clicking anywhere in row 8.

The row reference appears in the dialog.

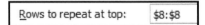

| Rows to repeat at top: | $8:$8 |
|---|---|

The dollar signs denote an absolute reference. You learned about absolute references in: *Lesson 3-12: Understand absolute and relative cell references.*

4. Click the OK button

Notice that the column headings now appear for every page in the printout.

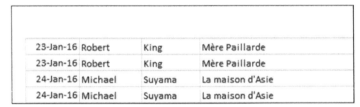

| | | Sales Person First Name | Sales Person Last Name | Company Name |
|---|---|---|---|---|
| 75 | | 23-Jan-16 Robert | King | Mère Paillarde |
| 76 | | 23-Jan-16 Robert | King | Mère Paillarde |

Sales Report-7

4    Add gridlines to the printout.

Sometimes it is difficult for the eye to track across printed lines. For this type of report, it is useful to print gridlines onto the printed page in a similar way to the ones displayed on the worksheet.

Click: Page Layout→Sheet Options→Gridlines→Print.

5    Print Preview the worksheet.

Click: File→Print to enter *Backstage Print* view.

The *Print Preview* in the right-hand pane shows that gridlines will be printed upon each page:

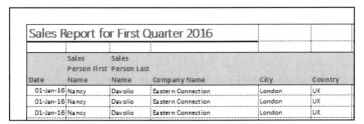

6    Add row and column headings to the printout.

You may want to send a printed worksheet to a colleague and then discuss it on the telephone. It might be useful to be able to ask: "what do you think of the value in cell H11?" This isn't possible because row and column headers are not normally shown on the printed page.

1. Click the *Back Button*  at the top left of *Backstage View* to return to *Normal View.*

2. Click: Page Layout→Sheet Options→Headings→Print.

7    *Print Preview* the worksheet.

Click: File→Print to enter *Backstage Print* view.

The *Print Preview* in the right-hand pane shows that row and column headers will be printed upon each page:

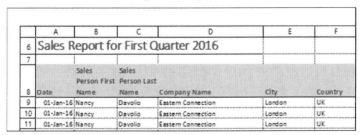

8    Remove the gridlines and column headers from the printout.

1. Click the *Back Button* at the top left of *Backstage View* to return to *Normal* View.

2. Clear the check boxes that were ticked in the previous steps.

9    Save your work as *Sales Report-8*.

# Lesson 7-12: Print several selected worksheets and change the page order

1   Open *Palace Hotel Bar Activity* from your sample files folder.

2   Print Preview the worksheet.

1.   Click: File→Print to enter *Backstage Print* view.

2.   Use the *Next Page* button at the bottom left of the *Print Preview* window  to view each page in the report.

Notice that the worksheet prints first downward (listing all activity between 11:00 AM and 4:00 PM for all days).

When it reaches the bottom of the list it moves across to print all activity between 5:00 PM and 10:00 PM and so on.

3   Change the view to *Page Break Preview*.

1.   Click the *Back Button* at the top left of *Backstage View* to return to *Normal View*.

2.   Click the *Page Break Preview* button at the bottom right of the screen.

In this view it is easy to see the page order by looking at the watermarks on each page (the watermark is the transparent large gray text saying Page 1, Page 2 etc).

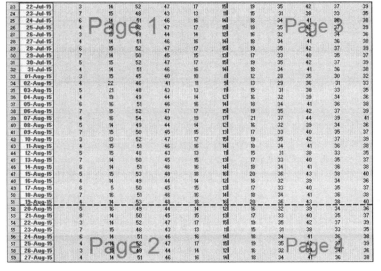

But what if you don't want to print in this order? Perhaps you would like to first print all activity for all times. In other words, you want the above display to make the existing Page 3 into Page 2.

**Palace Hotel Bar Activity**

**4**   Change the print order to *Over, then down*.

1.   Click: Page Layout→Page Setup→Dialog Launcher.

2.   Click the *Sheet* tab.

3.   Click the *Over, then down* option button.

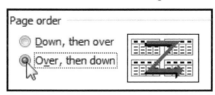

4.   Click the OK button.

It can be seen from the page break preview that the page order has now changed.

**5**   Print the headcount for Jul-Aug and Nov-Dec in one printout.

You can print several worksheets at the same time and they needn't be adjacent.

1.   Click the *Jul-Aug* tab.

2.   Hold down the **<Ctrl>** key and click the *Nov-Dec* tab.

Both tabs are now colored white

3.   Click: File→Print.

The *Backstage Print* view is displayed.

4.   Note that when more than one sheet is selected, the first item in the *Settings* list has the *Print Active Sheets* option selected.

5.   Click the *Next Page* button at the bottom left of the print preview to confirm that the contents of the *Jul-Aug* and *Nov-Dec* worksheets would have been printed.

6.   Click the *Back Button* ⟵ at the top left of *Backstage View* to return to *Page Break Preview.*

**6**   Save your work as *Palace Hotel Bar Activity-1*.

# Lesson 7-13: Suppress error messages in printouts

Excel has several built-in error messages such as the divide by zero error:

#DIV/0!

Sometimes you're quite happy to have these errors appear in a worksheet. For example, divide by zero errors could be quite normal when there is incomplete data.

Even though the errors are fine in the worksheet, you may not want them to appear in your printed output.

1    Open *Average Revenue per Sale* from your sample files folder.

2    View the worksheet in *Normal* view.

| | A | B | C | D | E |
|---|---|---|---|---|---|
| 1 | Average Revenue Per Sale | | | | |
| 2 | | | | | |
| 3 | First Name | Last Name | Sales | Units | Average Revenue per Sale |
| 4 | Andrew | Fuller | 7,639.30 | 15 | 509.29 |
| 5 | Anne | Dodsworth | - | - | #DIV/0! |
| 6 | Janet | Leverling | 29,658.60 | 60 | 494.31 |
| 7 | Laura | Callahan | 19,271.60 | 40 | 481.79 |
| 8 | Margaret | Peacock | 44,795.20 | 90 | 497.72 |
| 9 | Michael | Suyama | 4,109.80 | 8 | 513.73 |
| 10 | Nancy | Davolio | - | - | #DIV/0! |
| 11 | Robert | King | 21,461.60 | 43 | 499.11 |
| 12 | Steven | Buchanan | 2,634.40 | 5 | 526.88 |
| 13 | | Total: | 129,570.50 | 261.00 | |

This is an example of a worksheet with errors. In actual fact, you are simply waiting for Anne Dodsworth and Nancy Davolio to send you their sales figures, so they aren't really errors.

Divide by zero errors occur when you attempt to divide any number by zero.

You want to print out this interim report but replace the ugly #DIV/0 errors with a blank space on the printed page.

3    Replace errors with a blank space in printed output.

    1.    Click: Page Layout→Page Setup→Dialog launcher.

The *Page Setup* dialog appears.

    2.    Click the *Sheet* tab.

**Average Revenue per Sale**

3. Click the *Cell errors as* dropdown list and then click *<blank>*.

| Comments: | (None) | ▾ |
|---|---|---|
| Cell errors as: | displayed | ▾ |
| | displayed | ▲ |
| | <blank> | |
| | -- | |
| | #N/A | ▾ |

4. Click the OK button.

**4** *Print Preview* the worksheet.

1. Click: File→Print to open *Backstage Print* view.

The errors are no longer printed. Blank spaces are substituted for the divide by zero errors.

## Average Revenue Per Sale

| First Name | Last Name | Sales | Units | Average Revenue per Sale |
|---|---|---|---|---|
| Andrew | Fuller | 7,639.30 | 15 | 509.29 |
| Anne | Dodsworth | - | - | |
| Janet | Leverling | 29,658.60 | 60 | 494.31 |
| Laura | Callahan | 19,271.60 | 40 | 481.79 |
| Margaret | Peacock | 44,795.20 | 90 | 497.72 |
| Michael | Suyama | 4,109.80 | 8 | 513.73 |
| Nancy | Davolio | - | - | |
| Robert | King | 21,461.60 | 43 | 499.11 |
| Steven | Buchanan | 2,634.40 | 5 | 526.88 |
| | Total: | 129,570.50 | 261.00 | |

2. Click the *Back Button* 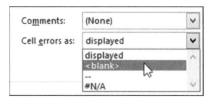 at the top left of *Backstage View* to return to *Normal View*.

**5** Save your work as *Average Revenue per Sale-1*.

## Session 7: Exercise

**1**      Open *Exercise 7* from your sample files folder.

**2**      Change to *Page Layout* view.

**3**      Change the left margin to about 1.0 cm using the click and drag method.

**4**      Click: Page Layout→Page Setup→Margins and use the *Custom Margins...* option to set top and bottom margins to precisely 2.0 cm and the left and right margins to precisely 1.0 cm.

**5**      Horizontally center the printout on the page.

**6**      Change the page orientation to landscape.

**7**      Change the view to *Page Break Preview*.

**8**      Insert a horizontal page break between rows 27 and 28.

**9**      Move the page break so that it now occurs between row 24 and 25.

**10**    Change to *Page Layout* view.

**11**    Add an auto-header to match the following:

> Page 1 of 3

**12**    Make the data labels in row 1 repeat on every page.

**13**    Set the print area to A1:J12 and then *Print Preview* to prove that only these cells would be printed.

**14**    Clear the print area.

**15**    Add gridlines to the printout.

**16**    *Print Preview* to prove that gridlines would be printed.

|  |  |  |  |  | Page 2 of 4 |
|---|---|---|---|---|---|
| Date | Sales Person First Name | Sales Person Last Name | Company Name | City | Country |
| 08-Jan-13 | Laura | Callahan | Folies gourmandes | Lille | France |
| 08-Jan-13 | Laura | Callahan | Folies gourmandes | Lille | France |

**17**    Save your work as *Exercise 7-End*.

Exercise 7

If you need help slide the page to the left

## Session 7: Exercise answers

These are the questions that students find the most difficult to answer:

| Q 13 | Q 12 | Q 8 | Q 5 |
|------|------|-----|-----|
| 1. Select cells A1:J12.<br><br>2. Click:<br><br>Page Layout→<br>Page Setup→<br>Print Area→<br>Set Print Area<br><br><br><br>This was covered in:<br>*Lesson 7-10: Print only part of a worksheet.* | 1. Click:<br><br>Page Layout→<br>Page Setup→Print Titles<br><br>2. Click in the *Rows to repeat at top* text box.<br><br>3. Either click in row 1 with the mouse or type 1:1 into the box.<br><br>This was covered in:<br>*Lesson 7-11: Add row and column data labels and grid lines to printed output.* | 1. Click in cell A28.<br><br>2. Click:<br><br>Page Layout→<br>Page Setup→<br>Breaks→<br>Insert Page Break<br><br>This was covered in:<br>*Lesson 7-5: Insert, delete and preview page breaks.* | 1. Click: Page Layout→<br>Page Setup→<br>Dialog launcher<br><br><br><br>2. Click the *Margins* tab.<br><br>3. Check the *Center on page horizontally* check box.<br><br>This was covered in:<br>*Lesson 7-3: Use Page Setup to set margins more precisely and center the worksheet.* |

If you have difficulty with the other questions, here are the lessons that cover the relevant skills:

**1**     Lesson 1-5: Download the sample files and open/navigate a workbook.

**2,3**   Lesson 7-2: Use Page Layout view to adjust margins.

**4**     Lesson 7-3: Use Page Setup to set margins more precisely and center the worksheet.

**6**     Lesson 7-1: Print Preview and change paper orientation.

**7**     Lesson 7-6: Adjust page breaks using Page Break Preview.

**9**     Lesson 7-6: Adjust page breaks using Page Break Preview.

**10**    Lesson 7-2: Use Page Layout view to adjust margins.

**11**    Lesson 7-7: Add auto-headers and auto-footers and set the starting page number.

**14**    Lesson 7-10: Print only part of a worksheet.

**15**    Lesson 7-11: Add row and column data labels and grid lines to printed output.

**16**    Lesson 7-1: Print Preview and change paper orientation.

**17**    Lesson 1-6: Save a workbook.

# Session Eight: Cloud Computing

> Cloud is about how you do computing, not where you do computing.
>
> *Paul Maritz, Computer Scientist and Software Executive*

In this session you will learn how *Office Online, OneDrive* and *Office Mobile* work together to enable you to access Excel, and all your files, on any modern device, anywhere.

Cloud computing is one of the most rapidly evolving areas of Information Technology today. This session will show you how to make the most of this exciting new way of working.

## Session Objectives

By the end of this session you will be able to:

- Understand Cloud Computing

- Save a workbook to a OneDrive

- Open a workbook from a OneDrive

- Understand operating systems and devices

- Understand Office versions

- Understand Excel Online

- Open a workbook using Excel Online

- Share a link to a workbook

- Edit a workbook simultaneously with other users using Excel Online

## note

### Cloud computing and thin clients

*Office Online* is a true cloud application. It was designed to be used without any software installation, on any device that supports a modern web browser.

The term "cloud computing" (in its modern context) was first used in 2006 (by the Google CEO Eric Schmidt).

There is a much older concept in the IT world called *thin client computing*.

Thin client computing allows traditional applications (written for desktop computers) to be deployed, unmodified, as cloud applications.

In the thin client model, the user doesn't use a web browser but installs a special thin client application.

The user then starts the thin client application and can effectively operate a computer located in the cloud by remote control. The user's computer sends keystrokes to the cloud computer. The cloud computer then returns a copy of the screen display back to the user.

Microsoft's *Remote Desktop Services (RDS)* and products from *Citrix Systems* are the most widely used thin client solutions.

The huge advantage of thin client implementations is that a company can continue to use the old desktop applications that they are used to.

Thin clients are very simple applications compared to sophisticated modern web browsers.

Browsers make better use of Internet bandwidth and usually provides a better user experience than thin client solutions.

# Lesson 8-1: Understand cloud computing

First to mind when asked what 'the cloud' is, a majority respond it's either an actual cloud, the sky, or something related to weather.

*Citrix Cloud Survey Guide (August 2012)*

### Cloud computing simply means the use of Internet-hosted files and applications

When you access Internet hosted applications such as Facebook, Twitter, Google Search, or Amazon using a web browser you are experiencing cloud computing (the Internet is often referred to as "the cloud").

You can access modern cloud applications, without installing any software, by typing a simple URL into any modern web browser. This means that this type of cloud application will run on any device with a modern browser (including the iPad, PC, Apple Mac and nearly all smartphones).

Cloud applications (hosted in a web browser) often have rich functionality that rivals traditional desktop applications. This has only become recently possible with the 2014 release of HTML 5 (the markup language used by modern web browsers).

It is easy to envisage a future where you will never have to install an application onto your computer. You'll simply visit the application's web site and start using it immediately. Instead of saving your files to your local hard drive, you'll save them to the cloud. Microsoft's "hard drive in the cloud" product is called *OneDrive*.

In the case of Microsoft Office, it is already possible to use a special limited-feature cloud version of Office (called *Office Online*). You'll learn about Office Online later, in: *Lesson 8-6: Understand Excel Online*.

# anecdote

## Latency

A long time ago (in the mid 1990's) I was involved in a very early implementation of a cloud project. It was so long ago that the term "cloud computing" wouldn't be invented for another ten years.

The multi-million-dollar project involved connecting a network of computers in Europe and Africa to a common database located in the United Kingdom.

We decided that a thin client solution (see facing page sidebar) was the most appropriate way to cater for the business requirement.

Testing went wonderfully well in European countries but when the software was rolled out to Africa there was a little problem.

The network link was routed via satellite. Satellites are placed 22,236 miles above the Earth's surface to achieve geostationary orbit.

The speed of light is approximately 186,000 miles per second. Unfortunately, this wasn't fast enough to prevent an infuriating lag between African users pressing a key and the corresponding letter appearing upon the keyboard.

This problem is referred to as *latency*.

It would have been very useful to increase the speed of light to solve the problem. Albert Einstein might have advised, however, that that wasn't an option.

Office Online requires no installation and will run in any web browser. When you use Office Online you'll typically also store your files in the cloud (in a Microsoft OneDrive).

## Advantages of cloud computing

Cloud computing promises many advantages over traditional IT implementations:

- Users can work anywhere using any device. They can continue their work while at work, at home or on the road and will always have full access to their files.

- Companies will not need a dedicated IT department as support can be outsourced to technicians working at a remote data center.

- The responsibility for backups can be delegated to the data center. This reduces the possibility of data loss after hardware failure.

- Businesses will not need to concern themselves with keeping software and anti-virus measures up-to-date.

- Access to software will usually be purchased on a subscription basis. When a given piece of software isn't needed any more, the company can simply unsubscribe. This concept is often referred to as: *Software as a Service* (SaaS).

- Computers that only access cloud applications are inexpensive as they do not need powerful processors or large amounts of memory.

## note

### OneDrive subscriptions

Microsoft have offered a range of OneDrive plans over the last couple of years. By the time you read this book they will probably have changed their offerings again.

In August 2018 the following plans were available:

**Free:** This plan is now limited to 5Gb of free (until early 2016 Microsoft offered 15Gb of free storage).

Visit:

https://OneDrive.com

…for all the details that you need to open a free OneDrive account

**Office 365 subscribers:** If you purchased Excel 2016 using a Microsoft Office 365 annual subscription, you will have one Terabyte (1,000 Mb) of storage included (for each user) as part of the Office 365 package.

**Paid Subscription:** If you are not an Office 365 subscriber and need more than 5Gb of storage, you can subscribe to a 50Gb plan for $1.99 per month.

Of course, as with all cloud services, the above plans can change at any time. Visit:

https://OneDrive.com

… for current pricing and availability of all Microsoft OneDrive plans.

# Lesson 8-2: Save a workbook to a OneDrive

In order to complete this lesson, you will need a OneDrive account. At the time of writing (August 2018) a free 5Gb subscription was available. See sidebar for more information about different OneDrive plans.

A OneDrive can be visualized as a "hard drive in the sky". Saving a workbook to a OneDrive means you'll be able to access it from any device, anywhere in the world.

The files are usually stored on one of Microsoft's servers (accessed via the Internet). Some corporate users may prefer to store their OneDrive files on their own servers for security reasons (see sidebar facing page).

1   Open *Smartphone Sales* from your sample files folder.

2   Sign in to your OneDrive account.

    1.   Click the *File* button [File] at the top-left of the screen.

    2.   Click: *Save As* [Save As] in the left-hand list.

    3.   Click *OneDrive* [OneDrive - Personal] in the *Save As* menu.

       You may be prompted to sign in to your OneDrive account if you are not already logged in.

       There may also be a *sign-up* link that will enable you to create a *Microsoft Account* if you don't already have one.

The right-hand side of the screen now gives you the ability to save the file to your OneDrive.

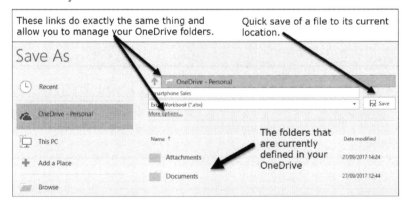

You may see different OneDrive folders as Microsoft change the default OneDrive folders from time to time.

When this book was written (in August 2018) the OneDrive had two folders by default called: *Attachments* and *Documents*.

3   Save the workbook to your OneDrive in a folder called: **Documents\Excel\Practice**

**Smartphone Sales**

1. Click either the *OneDrive – Personal* folder icon or the *More Options* link on the right-hand side of the screen (they both do exactly the same thing).

   A *Save As* dialog appears showing the contents of your OneDrive folder. Notice the file location shown at the top of the screen. You are viewing a OneDrive folder hosted on a remote Microsoft server accessed via the Internet:

   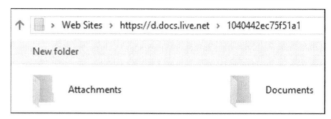

2. Double-click the *Documents* folder.

   The empty *Documents* folder is displayed:

   In *Lesson 1-8: Pin a workbook and understand file organization*, you learned why it is a good idea to place your Excel files into a separate folder within your local *Documents* folder. You will also create an *Excel* folder beneath the *Documents* folder on your OneDrive.

3. Right-click in the empty *Documents* folder and click:

   New Folder

   ...from the shortcut menu.

4. Type **Excel** as the name of the new folder and press the **<Enter>** key.

   If you have any difficulty doing this, right-click on the folder and click *Rename* from the shortcut menu.

   In *Lesson 1-8: Pin a workbook and understand file organization*, you learned why it is a good idea to further organize your Excel files within the *Excel* folder. You will create a *Practice* folder inside the *Excel* folder to do the same thing on your OneDrive.

5. Create a new OneDrive subfolder inside the newly created *Excel* folder and name it: **Practice**

6. Click: *Save* to save the *Smartphone Sales* workbook into the new *OneDrive\Documents\Excel\Practice* folder.

   The workbook is saved, and you are returned to the main Excel screen.

   Even though you are given the impression that the file was saved directly to the cloud it has really been saved to a local OneDrive folder. Windows will now work in the background to upload (synchronize) it to your cloud-hosted OneDrive folder.

4   Close Excel.

## note

### Beware of the "lunchtime lock"

The lunchtime lock happens when you do this:

1. Open a OneDrive file on your home computer.

2. Leave your computer switched on with the file open and go to work.

3. Open the same OneDrive file on your work computer.

When you try to open the file at work you will see a dialog telling you that the file is "locked" and cannot be worked upon.

IT staff call this problem the "lunchtime lock".

A common support problem occurs when a team member goes out to lunch leaving a shared file open. This prevents anybody else on the team from editing the same file.

Later, in: *Lesson 8-8: Share a link to a workbook*

When your workbooks are stored on a OneDrive, it is possible to share them without sending a physical copy of the file to the recipients. This is done by distributing a simple hyperlink via an e-mail, or by pasting the link into a Facebook page, Twitter tweet, blog or other web page.

# Lesson 8-3: Open a workbook from a OneDrive

Once a workbook has been saved to a OneDrive it can be opened from absolutely anywhere, provided you are connected to the Internet.

In: *Lesson 8-7: Open a workbook using Excel Online*, you'll discover that you can also open a workbook from any device that has a web browser (even if Excel 2016 is not installed on the device). This includes smartphones and tablets such as the iPad.

In this lesson you'll consider the scenario where you have a Windows PC at your office, and another Windows PC at home.

You want to be able to view and edit the same workbook on both computers.

1 Open Excel.

The start-up screen is displayed.

2 Open the *Smartphone Sales* sample file from your OneDrive.

1. Click: *Open Other Workbooks* ![Open Other Workbooks] from the left-hand menu bar.

2. Click: *OneDrive* ![OneDrive - Personal] in the *Open* menu.

If you haven't already signed in to your OneDrive account, you will now be prompted for an e-mail address and password.

You will now see your OneDrive's Attachments and *Documents*, folders on the right-hand side of the screen. You may see different folders in your own OneDrive.

3. Click the *Documents* folder.

You will now see the Excel sub-folder.

4. Click the *Excel* folder.

You will now see the *Practice* sub-folder.

5. Click the *Practice* folder.

You should see the previously saved *Smartphone Sales* file in the folder:

**Smartphone Sales**

## note

### OneDrive alternatives

Excel 2016 integrates OneDrive features into the *Save As* dialog.

You can save a file to your OneDrive as easily as saving to your local hard drive.

There are similar rival services to OneDrive offered by Dropbox, Google Drive, Apple iCloud and Amazon Drive, but none integrate with Office as seamlessly as OneDrive.

## note

### The advantages of using a OneDrive instead of a local drive

1. You can access your workbooks from any Internet connected device, anywhere in the world.

This means that you can work with your tablet device, smartphone or laptop when travelling, without having to copy files between devices.

2. You can share files with other users without having to e-mail the files to them.

You do this by sending a hyperlink to the other user rather than the file itself.

You'll discover more about this later, in: *Lesson 8-8: Share a link to a workbook*.

3. You can collaborate more easily with other users by giving certain users the right to edit your files.

4. You can allow users who do not have Excel 2016 installed upon their device to view, or even edit, your workbook.

You'll discover more about this later, in: *Lesson 8-6: Understand Excel Online*.

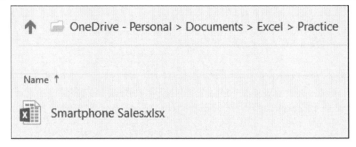

6. Click on the *Smartphone Sales* file to open it.

7. The *Smartphone Sales* workbook opens from the OneDrive:

You can now use this technique to open the same workbook using any computer, anywhere in the world that has Excel 2016 installed.

3    Close Excel.

# Lesson 8-4: Understand operating systems and devices

Excel 2016 can now run on almost all modern devices (such as computers, smartphones and tablet computers). As you'll learn in: *Lesson 8-5: Understand Office versions*, there are several different versions of Office (all with different features).

To completely understand how the different versions of Office fit into the new world of cloud computing, you'll need an overview of the devices and operating systems in common use today (or at least those that were common when this book was written in August 2018)

## What is a smartphone?

A smartphone is a mobile telephone that also includes a computer and a touch screen.

## What is a tablet computer?

Apple's iPad (launched in April 2010) was the first mass-market modern tablet computer. Tablet computers are also sometimes called *pad devices.* A tablet computer is similar to a very large smartphone (though most do not have telephony capability).

Screen sizes are typically 7 to 13 inches. Like a smartphone, they are usually controlled via a touchscreen. Some tablet computers (such as the Microsoft Surface and iPad Pro) have an optional detachable keyboard and mouse available as an add-on.

## What is a microprocessor (or CPU)?

### Desktop and laptop microprocessors

The microprocessor is the computer chip that performs all of the computer's calculations. It can be thought of as the brain of the computer. All microprocessors have an *instruction set* (sometimes called the *architecture*). Operating systems communicate with the microprocessor using this instruction set (you'll learn more about operating systems later in this lesson).

Almost all desktop computers are fitted with a powerful processor that supports the *x64 instruction set* (typically provided by a microprocessor manufactured by Intel or AMD).

### Tablet and smartphone microprocessors.

Tablet computers and smartphones need to have a long battery life and light weight. A different type of (less powerful) microprocessor is typically used in this type of device that combines cool running (meaning

---

## trivia

### The amazing success story of the iPad

As I write this sidebar (in August 2018) it is hard to believe that the iPad has not yet had its ninth birthday. It seems to have been around forever.

When the iPad went on sale in early April 2010 it was an overnight success. Apple sold 450,000 in the first week, 1 million in the first month and 19 million in the first year.

Seeing the success of Apple, many other manufacturers began manufacturing tablet computers that used the rival Android operating system.

In May 2017 it was reported that Apple's all-time worldwide iPad sales had exceeded 360 million units.

---

that no fan is needed) and low power consumption. The market leader is a family of chips that support the ARM instruction set.

## The Intel Atom x5, x7 and 4415Y microprocessors

The Intel Atom x5/x7 (released in March 2015) and 4415Y (released in June 2017) have both the cool-running/low power features needed for tablet computers combined with support for the full x64 instruction set needed to run the full Windows 10 desktop operating system.

Microsoft wasted no time in releasing their Surface 3 tablet computer in May 2015. With an Intel Atom x7 processor, the Surface 3 ran the same full Windows 10 operating system used on desktop computers but still claimed to have a 10 hour battery life.

Microsoft's Surface Go (released in August 2nd, 2018) uses the 4415Y microprocessor to power a new low-cost Windows 10 tablet that weighs in at just 522 grams.

## What is an operating system?

### The desktop operating systems

You are probably using Office 2016 on a desktop, laptop or tablet computer that uses the *Microsoft Windows 10* operating system.

Operating systems are the middleman between applications (such as Microsoft Office) and the computer hardware.

For example, when Excel needs to save a file it doesn't need to know anything about the make, model and type of disk drives fitted to the computer. A request is simply sent to the operating system to save the file. The operating system then handles the request.

Both the *Windows* and *Apple OS X* operating systems (used in almost all desktop and laptop computers) were designed to use the *x64 instruction set* (typically provided by a microprocessor manufactured by Intel or AMD).

### Mobile operating systems

Mobile operating systems are designed for lightweight portable devices such as mobile telephones and some tablet computers that use microprocessors that do not support the x64 instruction set.

There are three common mobile operating systems: *Google Android* and *Apple iOS*. *Apple iOS* is only used on Apple devices such as the iPad and iPhone.

*Google Android* is used on a vast number of devices from many different manufacturers.

# Lesson 8-5: Understand Office versions

## Office 2016 for Windows

This is the full (and most powerful) version of Office that only runs on the Windows 7, Windows 8 and Windows 10 operating systems.

## Office 2016 for Mac

Microsoft produce a version of Office 2016 for Windows that runs on the Apple OS X operating system (used on Apple desktop and laptop computers).

You could be forgiven for thinking that the (confusingly named) *Office 2016 for Mac* was "just the same" as *Office 2016 for Windows*.

Unfortunately, this is not the case.

The *Excel 2016 for Mac* version has a reduced feature set to the *Excel 2016 for Windows* version.

We've produced a different version of this book suitable for Apple Mac users:

**Learn Excel 2016 Essential Skills for Mac with The Smart Method**
**ISBN: 978-1-909253-11-7**

## Office 2016 Mobile

*Excel 2016 Mobile* offers only a (severely) cut-down limited-feature version of the full Excel 2016 desktop application. It is designed to complement Excel 2016 desktop versions, not to replace them.

There are versions of Office 2016 Mobile to support just about every operating system. You can install Office 2016 Mobile on current versions of the *Windows 10 desktop, Android* and *iOS* operating systems.

You can download Office 2016 Mobile free from the Windows Store (for Windows 10 devices), Google Play (for Android devices) and the app store (for iPad and iPhone).

*Microsoft Office 2016 Mobile* is free for personal use but there are some restrictions in the free version:

1.  Commercial use is not allowed.

2.  If the screen size is more than 10.1 inches editing of documents is not possible.

3.  Some Office 2016 Mobile features are not available.

If you are an Office 365 subscriber all the above restrictions are removed (though Office 2016 Mobile remains very limited compared to the full desktop versions of Office 2016).

Here's a screen grab from Office Mobile running on a Windows PC:

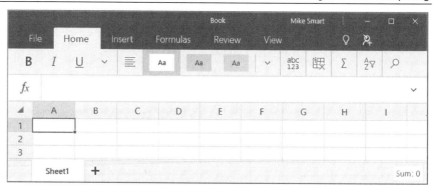

You can see that it is quite primitive when compared to the full version of Excel running on your desktop computer.

## Office 2016 Online

Just like *Office 2016 Mobile*, *Office 2016 Online* has less features than the full Office 2016 desktop applications but it is being continuously improved and upgraded.

Office 2016 Online is a completely free cloud application designed for larger mobile devices (such as tablet computers). It is also useful when sharing documents with users that do not have an Office 2016 license or subscription. This version will be discussed in depth in: *Lesson 8-6: Understand Excel Online.*

Office 2016 Online is very different to the other Office versions as it is a *cloud application*. Cloud applications have many advantages over traditional applications (see sidebar).

Office Online is available to the public free of charge. You can access it from the Office.com website.

## Office 2016 version availability (at Aug 2018)

| Device | Office 2016 for Windows | Office 2016 for Mac | Office Mobile | Office Online |
|---|---|---|---|---|
| Windows 7 or 10 PC or tablet computer | X | | X | X |
| Apple Mac | | X | | X |
| Apple iPad | | | X | X |
| Apple iPhone | | | X | X |
| Android Tablet | | | X | X |
| Android Phone | | | X | X |

*Note that not all Android devices are supported.*

# Lesson 8-6: Understand Excel Online

## Excel 2016 for Windows desktop application

- Application installed on hard drive.
- Workbooks may be saved to hard drive or OneDrive.
- Only runs on Windows computers.

The *Excel 2016 for Windows* desktop application is a conventional locally-installed application. This means:

- You need a license to use the *Excel 2016 for Windows* desktop application.

- You need to install the *Excel 2016 for Windows* desktop application software onto your computer before you can use it.

- The *Excel 2016 for Windows* desktop application will only run on a computer running the Windows 7, 8.0, 8.1 and 10 operating systems.

- The *Excel 2016 for Windows* desktop application is the only Excel version that includes every Excel 2016 feature (see sidebar).

- Workbooks may be saved to (and opened from) either the local hard drive or a OneDrive.

## Excel 2016 for Mac desktop application

The *Excel 2016 for Mac* desktop application runs on the *Apple OS X* operating system found on Apple desktop and laptop computers.

*Excel 2016 for Mac* has a reduced feature set compared to the Excel *2016 for Windows* version.

## Excel Online

Excel Online is a cloud application that runs inside a web browser. This means:

- You don't need a license to use Excel Online.

- You don't need to install any software to use Excel Online.

- Because a cloud app doesn't directly communicate with the operating system, Excel Online will run on any device that has a supported web browser. This includes the Windows PC, Apple Mac, iPad and almost all recent tablet and smartphone devices.

- Excel Online provides only a cut-down limited-feature version of Excel 2016.

### Excel Online makes it possible to share a workbook with just about anybody

If you e-mail a copy of a workbook to another user (as an attachment), you have to assume that the recipient has a Windows computer with a compatible version of Excel installed.

When you send a user a link to a workbook stored on your OneDrive it will open using Excel Online. You can then be confident that the user will almost certainly be able to open the workbook. You'll learn how to share links that open using Excel Online later, in: *Lesson 8-8: Share a link to a workbook.*

The recipient of a link can have any type of device (such as a Windows PC, Windows Surface tablet, Apple Mac, iPad tablet, Android tablet or even a Smartphone) and does not have to have a copy of Excel 2016 installed.

**note**

### Touchscreen gestures

Touchscreen devices (such as tablet computers and smartphones) do not usually have a mouse.

When using a touchscreen, you can use the following gestures to work with Excel Online:

**Left-click:** Tap the touchscreen.

**Right-click:** Touch and hold your finger on the touchscreen.

**Scroll:** Touch a blank area of the workbook and slide your finger in the direction you wish to scroll in.

**Zoom in:** Touch two points on the touchscreen and then move your fingers away from each other. (This is normally done with the thumb and forefinger).

**Zoom out:** Touch two points on the touchscreen and then move your fingers towards each other.

**Select text:** Tap on the text to place the insertion point. If it is in the wrong place, tap again to move it. Drag the circular handles (called *grippers*) to select.

**note**

### Excel Online Automatic Save feature

Excel Online automatically saves changes as you make them.

In: *Lesson 8-9: Edit a workbook simultaneously with other users using Excel Online*, you'll discover how this feature enables multiple users to all edit the same workbook at the same time.

Smartphone Sales

# Lesson 8-7: Open a workbook using Excel Online

Now that you have saved a workbook to your OneDrive, you can use Excel Online to open it from any device that has a supported web browser (see facing page sidebar). This includes most recent smartphones, tablet devices and personal computers. Even if the device does not have Excel 2016 installed, you will be able to view and edit the workbook using the free *Excel Online* cloud application.

If you have a tablet computer (such as an iPad), or recent smartphone, you might find it interesting to use this device (rather than your Windows PC) for this lesson.

1  Open *Smartphone Sales* from a web browser using Excel Online.

1.  Open a web browser on your PC (or ideally using another device).

2.  Enter the url: **https://OneDrive.com**

3.  If necessary, click the *Sign in* link and enter your Windows user name and password to log in.

4.  Click the *Documents* folder. (If you are using a smartphone or tablet computer, see sidebar for the touchscreen gesture that simulates a left-click).

5.  Click the *Excel* folder. You created this folder in: *Lesson 8-1: Understand cloud computing.*

6.  Click the *Practice* folder.

    You will now see the *Smartphone Sales* workbook that you saved in: *Lesson 8-1: Understand cloud computing.*

7.  Right-Click on *Smartphone Sales*

8.  Click *Open in Excel Online* from the shortcut menu (or simply *Open* if you are using a device that does not have Excel installed on it.

In a real-world situation you'd usually select *Open in Excel* (if it is available) because Excel has more features and is faster than Excel Online. For the sake of this lesson, you'll open the file using Excel Online so that you can share the experience of users who do not have Excel installed on their device.

The *Smartphone Sales* workbook opens in Excel Online:

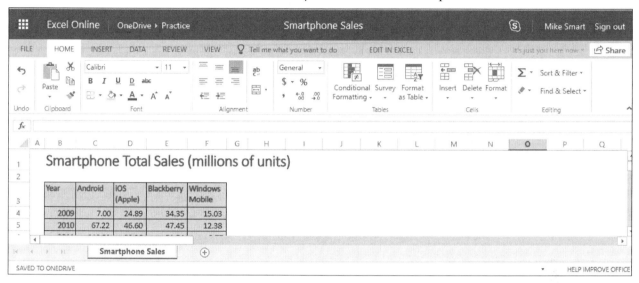

Excel Online looks very much like the desktop Excel application. Many (but not all) of Excel's features are now available from the ribbon.

2   Expand and collapse the Excel Online ribbon.

If you are using a Smartphone or tablet device with a very small screen, Excel Online may open with the Ribbon minimized.

Just like the desktop Excel version, you can double-click (or double-tap) on any of the Ribbon tabs to minimize or maximize the Ribbon.

Try minimizing and maximizing the Ribbon to see this working.

3   Close your web browser.

## note

### If you see a different Share dialog to the one discussed in this lesson

The *Sept 2017 Version 1708 update* introduced a new feature designed to better integrate Excel with users of their *OneDrive for Business* and *SharePoint* products.

This has resulted in a different sharing dialogs for users of *OneDrive for Business* and *SharePoint.*

If you save a file to a *Personal OneDrive* and then try to share the file, you will see the dialogs discussed in this lesson.

If you save a file to *OneDrive for Business* or *SharePoint* and then try to share the file, you will see this dialog:

If you only have access to a *OneDrive for Business* or *SharePoint* account you should still be able to complete this lesson, but you will need to figure out the differences between the dialogs

It is likely that a future Excel version update will use a similar dialog (to the one shown above) for all types of OneDrive.

Smartphone Sales

# Lesson 8-8: Share a link to a workbook

When your workbooks are stored on a OneDrive, it is possible to share them without sending a physical copy of the file to the recipients. This is done by distributing a simple hyperlink via an e-mail, or by pasting the link into a Facebook page, Twitter tweet, blog or other web page.

As discussed in: *Lesson 8-6: Understand Excel Online*, this method ensures that the recipient will be able to open the workbook on almost any device, even if Excel 2016 is not installed. The workbook will automatically open using the free *Excel Online* application.

You can also use the technique taught in this lesson to share Word documents and PowerPoint presentations as there are also *Word Online* and *PowerPoint Online* cloud applications that will open them.

1   Open Excel.

The start-up screen is displayed.

2   Open the *Smartphone Sales* sample file from your OneDrive.

This is the file that you saved in: *Lesson 8-2: Save a workbook to a OneDrive.*

3   Send an e-mail link to yourself to enable the recipient to open (but not change) the workbook.

1.   Click the *Share* button at the top right of the screen.

The *Share* task pane appears (see sidebar if a different dialog appears).

2.   Type your own e-mail address into the *Invite people* text box.

You are able to specify e-mail recipients in two ways:

By typing one or more e-mail addresses into the *Invite people* text box (if there is more than one recipient, separate them with a semicolon).

**OR**

By clicking the icon next to the *Invite people* text box to select one or more recipients directly from your *Outlook Address Book.*

3.   Select: *Can View* from the drop-down list.

The drop-down list has two options.

*Can View* allows recipients to view but not edit the *Smartphone Sales* workbook.

*Can Edit* allows the recipient to make changes to the workbook on your OneDrive. You'll use an *Edit Link* later, in: **Error! Not a valid bookmark self-reference.**.

4. Add a short message.

5. Click the *Share* button. Share

An e-mail with a view link is sent to the recipient(s) you specified (in this case yourself).

4 Examine the e-mail that Excel has sent you.

After a few moments you should find that the e-mail has appeared in your inbox.

5 Log out of your OneDrive.

While you are logged in to your OneDrive you will always have full access to your own files.

This means that even though the link is read-only (a view link) you will still be able to edit the file as if it were an edit link.

To simulate a recipient that is not yourself, you will have to log out of your OneDrive.

1. Open a web browser.

2. Go to: **http://OneDrive.com**

3. Click the icon of a person (or your photograph) in the top right corner.

4. Click: *Sign Out* from the shortcut menu.

6 Test the link.

1. Open the e-mail previously sent to yourself.

2. Click the link in the e-mail.

The workbook opens in Excel Online.

Notice the warning at the top of the window:

This is displayed because you sent a view link that does not allow the recipient to edit the workbook.

Note that the user is still able to save (and then edit) a local copy of your workbook (see sidebar).

7 Close Excel Online.

# Lesson 8-9: Edit a workbook simultaneously with other users using Excel Online

## When working with Excel Online you never have to save

Excel Online has no save button.

While this seems strange at first, it is actually quite logical.

When you open a workbook from your hard drive (using the normal Excel desktop application), the workbook is copied from your hard drive into the computer's memory. When you make changes, they are applied to the copy of the workbook (in the computer's memory) rather than the workbook on the hard drive. If you don't save the workbook, you might lose any changes that you make.

When you open a workbook from a OneDrive (using *Excel Online* or the desktop Excel application), the workbook is not copied into the computer's memory. You work with the actual workbook on the OneDrive and not a copy of it. This means that any changes are instantly applied to the workbook, making a save button unnecessary (as any changes that you make are being instantly made to the actual workbook file).

This new way of working provides an unexpected benefit.

If several users are all working with the same workbook (and the workbook is stored on a OneDrive), any change made (by any user) will magically, and almost instantly, appear on every other user's screen!

This provides a completely new way of collaborating with other users.

> To get the most out of this lesson you will need two devices to simulate two different users. See sidebar if you only have one device.

1 Open Excel 2016 on your Windows PC.

The start-up screen is displayed.

2 Open the *Smartphone Sales* sample file from your OneDrive using Excel (not Excel Online).

This is the file that you saved in: *Lesson 8-1: Understand cloud computing*.

3 Send an *Edit Link* to yourself via e-mail.

This will enable the recipient to both view and edit the workbook via Excel Online.

You learned how to do this in: *Lesson 8-8: Share a link to a workbook*.

4 Close Excel.

### note

### If you only have one device

If you only have one device, you can still work through this lesson.

To do this, you will need to open two web browser windows.

You'll have to imagine that each browser window is a different user with a different device.

**Smartphone Sales**

It is important that you close Excel. If the workbook remained open in Excel, you'd lock the workbook and prevent other users from editing it using Excel Online. File locking was discussed in more depth in: *Lesson 8-3: Open a workbook from a OneDrive.*

5   Use the *Edit Link* to open *Smartphone* Sales on your Windows PC using Excel Online.

1. Open the e-mail previously sent to yourself.

2. Click the link in the e-mail.

The workbook opens using *Excel Online.*

Notice that there is an *Edit Workbook* link on the ribbon (This may say *Edit in Browser* on some devices).

This is because you sent an *Edit* link that allows the recipient to both view and edit the workbook.

6   Use the same *Edit Link* to open *Smartphone Sales* on your other device using Excel Online.

Your other device may be a Windows PC, an iPad, an Apple Mac, an Android device, or any other device that has a supported web browser. If you don't have another device see facing page sidebar.

You now are now viewing the same workbook on both devices. This means that any changes made to the workbook on one device will (almost) instantly appear on the screen of the other device.

7   Put both devices into *Edit* mode and select *Edit in Browser* from the drop-down menu.

It is important that you edit the workbook in your web browser.

If a user opens the file using a local copy of Excel the workbook will be locked and it won't be possible for any other user to edit the workbook using *Excel Online.*

8   Make a change to the workbook on one of your devices.

Notice that the change appears (almost instantly) on the other device.

Note that you won't see the change on the other device unless the device is in *Edit* mode.

9   Sign out of Excel Online on both devices.

Click the *Sign out* button on the top right of the Excel Online window.

There is no need to save the workbook (there isn't even a save button in Excel Online). Your changes were automatically saved to the OneDrive as you made them.

Sign out

## Session 8: Exercise

**1** Open *Broadband Speeds* from your sample files folder.

**2** Create a new sub-folder in your OneDrive documents folder called: Exercise 8

**3** Save the *Broadband Speeds* workbook into the */Documents/Exercise 8* folder of your OneDrive.

**4** Send a *View Link* and an *Edit Link* for the *Broadband Speeds* workbook to yourself via e-mail.

(If you have a slow Internet connection you may have to wait a few seconds until synchronization completes before you are able to do this).

**5** Close Excel 2016.

**6** Use the *Edit Link* to open the *Broadband Speeds* workbook using Excel Online.

**7** Enable editing within Excel Online.

**8** Change the *Average Speed (Mbs)* for *Luxembourg* (cell B4) to: 75.00 and press the <Enter> key.

**9** Click the *Sign Out* button to sign out of Excel Online.

**10** Open the desktop Excel 2016 application.

**11** Open *Broadband Speeds* from your OneDrive.

(If you didn't sign out of Excel Online (users often close the browser window without signing out) you may get a file lock message. Excel will eventually release the lock after several minutes have elapsed).

Note that the average speed for Luxembourg is now 75.00 Mbs.

**12** Change the *Average Speed (Mbs)* for *Luxembourg* to: 100.88

**13** Save the workbook.

**Broadband Speeds**

If you need help slide the page to the left

# Session 8: Exercise answers

These are the questions that students find the most difficult to answer:

| Q 7 | Q 4 | Q 2 |
|---|---|---|
| Click: *Edit Workbook* on the *Excel Online* ribbon (*Edit in Browser* on some devices).<br><br>This was covered in: *Lesson 8-9: Edit a workbook simultaneously with other users using Excel Online.* | 1. Click the *Share* button at the top right of the screen.<br><br>[Share icon: Share ⟲]<br><br>The *Share* task pane appears.<br><br>2. Type your own email address into the *Invite people* text box.<br><br>3. Select *Can view* from the drop-down list.<br><br>4. Click the *Share* button.<br><br>5. Repeat the same operation for the *Edit Link* (this time selecting *Can Edit* from the drop-down list).<br><br>This was covered in: *Lesson 8-8: Share a link to a workbook.* | 1. Click: File→Save As.<br><br>2. Click: *OneDrive* in the *Save As* menu.<br><br>3. Click: *Browse* in the *OneDrive* menu.<br><br>4. Double-click the *Documents* folder.<br><br>5. Right-click in a blank area inside the *Documents* folder and select:<br><br>New→Folder<br><br>6. Type: **Exercise 8** as the name of the new folder.<br><br>If you have difficulty doing this, right-click on the folder and select *Rename* from the shortcut menu.<br><br>This was covered in:<br><br>*Lesson 8-2: Save a workbook to a OneDrive.* |

If you have difficulty with the other questions, here are the lessons that cover the relevant skills:

**1,10**     **Lesson 1-5: Download the sample files and open/navigate a workbook.**

**3**     **Lesson 8-2: Save a workbook to a OneDrive**

**5**     **Lesson 1-1: Start Excel and open a new blank workbook.**

**6**     **Lesson 8-8: Share a link to a workbook.**

**8,9**     **Lesson 8-9: Edit a workbook simultaneously with other users using Excel Online.**

**11**     **Lesson 8-3: Open a workbook from a OneDrive.**

**12**     **Lesson 2-1: Enter text and numbers into a worksheet.**

**13**     **Lesson 1-6: Save a workbook to a local file.**

# Index

## A

A4 size paper, 317
absolute references, 142
accounting number format style, 172
add-ins
    content, explained, 152
    downloading from the office store, 154
    task pane, explained, 152
    uses of, 152
alignment
    horizontal, of cell contents, 176
    vertical, of cell contents, 182
android. *See* operating system
apple
    mac version of Excel 2016, 5, 350
    missing Excel 2016 features in mac version, 5, 350
apple OS X. *See* operating system
arrange all, 68
audio cues, enabling, 26
AutoComplete
    formula entry using, 91
    text entry using, 122
AutoFill
    custom fill series, creating, 98
    date series, examples of, 96
    filling down, right, up and left with, 123
    formulas, using to adjust, 94
    smart tag options, using, 96
    text and numeric series, creating with, 92
AutoFit rows and columns, **83**, 131
AutoSave, 40, *See also* versions
    draft versions, explanation of, 40
    time interval, changing, 40
AutoSum, 70
    AVERAGE functions, creating with, 86
    MAX functions, creating with, 86
    SUM a non contiguous range with, 84
AVERAGE function, 86

## B

backstage view, 48
backup. *See also* AutoSave
    automatic backups, reverting to, 40
    RAID array, use of to improve resilience, 40
    time interval for automatic backups, changing, 40
borders
    adding to cells, 190
    draw border line tool, using to add, 191

## C

cancel button, 66
cells. *See also* styles; comments; formatting
    active cell, 80
    aligning contents of, horizontally, 176
    aligning contents of, vertically, 182
    borders, adding to, 190
    color, adding to, 188
    conditional formatting of, 198
    copying one to another, 124
    copying using drag and drop, 126
    deleting, 86
    deselecting, 78
    entering text into, 66
    entering values into, 66
    gradient fills, adding to, 188
    merging, 178, 180
    selecting a range of, 73
    selecting all in a worksheet, 83
    styles, applying to, 186
    unique values, detecting with conditional formatting, 201
    wrapping text within, 178, 180
channels. *See* update channels
chart source data
    adding series, 249
    assigning non contiguous, 244
    changing, 242
    changing using *select data source* dialog tools, 242
    deleting series, 249
    hidden and empty cells button, 251
    horizontal (category) axis labels, defining, 249
    horizontal (category) axis labels, editing, 253
    legend entries (series), 249
    non-contiguous source data, charting by hiding rows and columns, 250
    numerical axis labels, configuring, 252
    series, deleting, 249
charts. *See also* chart source data; visualizations; sparklines

## G

## H

## I

## J

## K

## X

## Z

# Moving to the next level

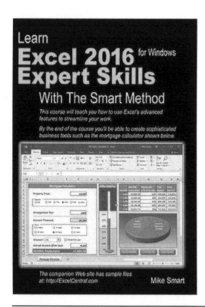

## The next book in the series (Expert skills) covers only the most advanced Excel features.

This book will give you advanced Excel skills that are rarely mastered by the average user. By the end of the book you'll be a true Excel expert, able to use all of the power available from the world's most powerful business tool.

Your Excel skills will be greater and broader than almost all other Excel users in the workplace.

The paper printed book is always in stock at Amazon.

The e-book is published in unlocked, printable PDF format (all of our e-books are published in this way) and is only available from https://thesmartmethod.com (this is the publisher's own web site).

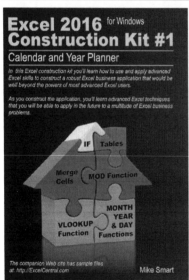

## Learn how to apply your new Excel skills with a Smart Method construction kit

For over 900 years craftsmen have traditionally taught their skills to an apprentice. In this model the apprentice learned his trade by observing how the master craftsman used his skills. This construction kit will teach you advanced Excel skills in the same way. Even if you only have basic Excel skills, the construction kit is designed in such a way that you'll be able to construct a complex, polished professional Excel application that would be well beyond the powers of most advanced Excel users. Available as both a printed paper book and e-book.

Preview the first chapter free at:

**https://thesmartmethod.com**

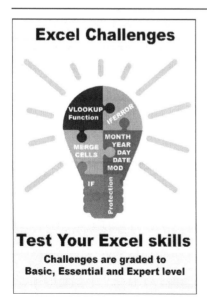

## Excel Challenges

Our Excel online challenges are a little like the exercises at the end of each session in this book. Unlike the exercises, the online challenges will test the application of many skills (covered in different sessions in the book).

We began trialling challenges in July 2018 and (at time of writing in August 2018) we'd published three challenges but by the time you read this book we may have produced more.

Access the challenges online at:

https://thesmartmethod.com/excel-challenges/

# Use your new Excel skills to teach your own classroom courses.

If you've worked through this book carefully you will now have excellent Excel skills and if you progress to the *Expert Skills* book in the series, you'll be a true Excel expert. There is a huge demand, everywhere in the world, for Excel training at all levels. The skills you have learned in this book will enable you to teach an introductory Excel course (providing all of the skills needed by most office workers).

We can directly and rapidly supply books, at educational discount prices, to Excel instructors, corporate clients, schools, colleges and universities from our warehouses in the USA (also serving Canada), UK (also serving Europe) and Australia (also serving New Zealand).

Our books are printed in the USA, UK, Australia, Germany, Italy, Spain, Brazil, Poland, South Korea, China, India, and Russia so are instantly available, in almost every country in the world, by simply quoting the ISBN number (shown below) to any bookseller or wholesaler.

# Use our books to teach all Excel versions.

This book is available for all Excel versions in common use (Excel 2007, 2010, 2013, 2016 for Windows and 2016 for Apple Mac). This means that you'll be able to teach Excel classes even if the client uses an earlier/later version or uses Apple computers. You can use the books as courseware during your classes and then give each student a copy of the book to take home as reference material when the course is over.

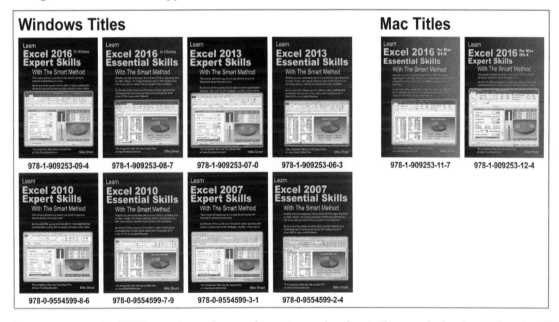

You can quote the ISBN numbers shown above to any book retailer or wholesaler. All major distributors (in every country of the world) have our books in stock for immediate delivery.

# Place a direct order for 5+ books for wholesale prices and free delivery

To place a publisher-direct order you only need to order five books or more (of the same title). To view wholesale prices, go to this web page:

https://thesmartmethod.com/wholesale-printed-books

Printed in Great Britain
by Amazon